Learn Raspberry Pi 2 with Linux and Windows 10

Second Edition

Peter Membrey
David Hows

Apress®

Learn Raspberry Pi 2 with Linux and Windows 10

ISBN-13 (pbk): 978-1-4842-1163-2

ISBN-13 (electronic): 978-1-4842-1162-5

Managing Director: Welmoed Spahr
Lead Editor: Michelle Lowman
Technical Reviewer: Brendan Horan
Editorial Board: Steve Anglin, Louise Corrigan, Jonathan Gennick, Robert Hutchinson, Michelle Lowman, James Markham, Susan McDermott, Matthew Moodie, Jeffrey Pepper, Douglas Pundick, Ben Renow-Clarke, Gwenan Spearing, Steve Weiss
Coordinating Editors: Kevin Walter and Mark Powers
Compositor: SPi Global
Indexer: SPi Global
Artist: SPi Global

Distributed to the book trade worldwide by Springer Science+Business Media New York, 233 Spring Street, 6th Floor, New York, NY 10013. Phone 1-800-SPRINGER, fax (201) 348-4505, e-mail orders-ny@springer-sbm.com, or visit www.springeronline.com. Apress Media, LLC is a California LLC and the sole member (owner) is Springer Science + Business Media Finance Inc (SSBM Finance Inc). SSBM Finance Inc is a Delaware corporation.

For information on translations, please e-mail rights@apress.com, or visit www.apress.com.

Apress and friends of ED books may be purchased in bulk for academic, corporate, or promotional use. eBook versions and licenses are also available for most titles. For more information, reference our Special Bulk Sales–eBook Licensing web page at www.apress.com/bulk-sales.

Any source code or other supplementary material referenced by the author in this text is available to readers at www.apress.com/9781484211632. For additional information about how to locate and download your book's source code, go to www.apress.com/source-code/. Readers can also access source code at SpringerLink in the Supplementary Material section for each chapter.

For Dr. John McDougall, for doing the right thing against all the odds.

—Peter Membrey

To my parents, Peter and Bev, for all their support.

—David Hows

Contents at a Glance

Contents

About the Authors

Peter Membrey is a Chartered IT Fellow with nearly 20 years of experience using Linux and open source solutiuons to solve problems in the real world. An RHCE since the age of 17, he has also had the honor of working for Red Hat and writing several books covering open source solutions. He holds a masters degree in IT (Information Security) from the University of Liverpool and is currently an EngD candidate at the Hong Kong Polytechnic University where his research interests include cloud computing, big data science and security. He lives in Hong Kong with his wonderful wife Sarah and son Kaydyn. His Cantonese continues to regress.

David Hows is an Honors graduate from the University of Woolongong in NSW Australia. He got his start in computing trying to drive more performance out of his family PC without spending a fortune. This lead to a career in IT where David has worked as a Systems Administrator, Performance Engineer, Software Developer, Solutions Architect and Database Engineer. David has tried in vain for many years to play soccer well and his coffee mug reads “Grumble Bum”.

About the Technical Reviewer

Brendan Horan is a hardware fanatic, with a full high rack of all types of machine architectures in his home. He has more than 10 years of experience working with large UNIX systems and tuning the underlying hardware for optimal performance and stability. Brendan's love for all forms of hardware has helped him throughout his IT career, from fixing laptops to tuning servers and their hardware in order to suit the needs of high-availability designs and ultra low-latency applications. Brendan takes pride in the Open Source Movement and is happy to say that every computer in his house is powered by open source technology. He resides in Hong Kong with his wife, Vikki, who continues daily to teach him more Cantonese.

Acknowledgments

Without a doubt, the true heroes of this book are the Raspberry Pi Foundation and the Raspberry Pi community because without either of them, we wouldn't be here. The Raspberry Pi Foundation, the group who bought us the Pi, is a nonprofit charity with the stated goal with the Pi was to reinvigorate the development spirit of the '80s and to provide an affordable platform for generations of youngsters to get into the wonderful world of computing in a truly meaningful way. It has done so much to bridge the digital divide and bring computing to the common man, and for this it deserve our thanks.

If the Raspberry Pi Foundation is the heart, the Raspberry Pi community has to be the soul. These people have sought to provide the tools and support people need to get started with the Pi regardless of skill level. They have invested countless hours (and dollars) in writing, fixing, porting, hacking, and testing things for the Pi. Please feel free to pay a visit to them at `http://www.raspberrypi.org/` and see what we mean.

Introduction

Despite sounding like something grandma would bake on Sunday afternoons or a noise that would make people glare and tut, the Raspberry Pi is in fact a computer. That much you probably knew (although let's be honest the name and logo don't really give much away) but actually, the Raspberry Pi promises more than that. An awful lot more.

The venerable Commodore 64 was released in 1982 and with sales reaching upwards of 17 million, it is often considered the best selling computer of all time. More importantly (at least from my perspective) it was also my first computer. For Christmas, just before my ninth birthday (so when the C64 was nearly a decade old) I received the new model (C64C) which was identical to the classic machine in all but cosmetics. It arrived all set up and attached to a nice new 14" television (it even had a remote control!). I suspect my dad had hatched what he believed to be a most cunning plan; if he could sneak in and set everything up whilst I was asleep, then come Christmas morning, I would be so busy playing with the computer that my parents might get an extra few minutes sleep.

Sadly things did not go quite according to plan. Although everything was set up and even though the television was tuned to the computer's signal, one simple but key thing had been forgotten. It hadn't occurred to anyone to tell me how to actually load a game. Needless to say a lie in was not forthcoming...

Games came on cassette tape (this was before CDs - what do you mean what's a CD?) and at least on the C64 had to be played in a special tape recorder called a datasette. Sadly the datasette spent more time in the shop than being attached to my computer and as it was the only way to load anything into it, I had no choice but to occupy myself with the manual. This I used to great effect and taught myself how to program good old BASIC (Beginners All Purpose Symbolic Instruction Code - can you believe I actually remembered that?).

While I'm sure this story is very gripping, you could be forgiven for wondering why I am boring you with it. Those events happened over two decades ago (boy does time fly) so what possible relevance could they have today? Well tinkering with that machine then and then the Amiga that followed it (still my favorite machine of all time) gave me a real appreciation for what a computer could do. The Amiga was essentially severely under powered compared to PCs of the same era and yet it consistently beat them with better graphics, better reliability and better sound. It was able to do all of this because the hardware was exquisitely designed. Amiga enthusiasts were some of the most resourceful people I've ever seen. Who'd have thought you could turn a real time clock port into a connector for high speed storage?

All of this was only possible because people really understood how all the parts fitted together. They knew how to get the best out of the machine because they really new how the machine worked. These days I spend my working day trying to make fast things go faster. To stand any hope of success, I too need to know how everything works. Companies need people like me to push things forward but they're coming across a bit of a problem. People who really know computers inside out are getting much harder to find - we are a dying breed and this is the situation that the Raspberry Pi Foundation is desperately trying to reverse.

So what happened? Well things changed. Computers went from being the curiosity in the corner to being a basic part of everyone's lives. They evolved to the point where for the most part they just work and everyone knows how to use them. This is similar to the family car. Everyone has a rough idea how a car works, but few people are very interested. The car takes them from place to place and that ability is what is interesting, not how the car achieves it. Computers are generally seen in the same light. People have a rough idea about turning them on, installing software and so forth, but how they actually work at a low level isn't really seen as relevant or interesting. This in turn means that not only are fewer people getting excited by computing itself, but even less people think that there's more to it than double clicking an icon.

This problem has drifted up through schools and into universities. Teaching programming is a relatively challenging task. It requires a certain way of thinking that for many people is tough to get a handle on. Traditionally universities would start a computer science course by teaching about logic gates, how memory works and how to program a CPU. Only once you understood what the bare metal was doing would you try to learn C because although C is a higher level language, it reflects the hardware it runs on. Understanding the hardware makes understanding C that much easier.

But with larger class sizes, more limited teaching time and students arriving with less and less knowledge of computing fundamentals, universities have had to adapt. Rather than teaching all that low level stuff, now they teach Java and scripting languages such as Python. Because these languages handle all of the fiddly bits for you, you can effectively pretend that they don't exist (although this can cause some issues, see "The infinite memory myth"). This is simply fantastic from a productivity point of view, but when you do want to take it to the next level (maybe you're processing data and your script is just too slow) you have no idea where to turn. Worse, when someone tells you the technique for improving that performance, you have no idea what they're talking about.

Of course not all universities have taken this route. I'm studying at the Hong Kong Polytechnic University and their course on Computer Architecture is very detailed and covers a lot of ground. If you want to get the top grade you will need to implement a CPU cache for the CPU simulator program. Needless to say, there is a lot to learn for everyone on this course. That said, we need more than this. It's too late to capture people's interest when they're starting graduate studies. I taught 7 year olds how to program BBC BASIC when I was in my last year of primary school (they even got presented certificates by the school) and they loved it. Computing lets you create a virtual world with your mind (they liked to create little text based adventure games) and ultimate power rested in their hands. They got creative, they added spells, new roads, secret entrances and much more. Okay, they needed a helping hand (they were only 7) but they had the desire to create and to build cool new things.

INFINITE MEMORY MYTH

Over the years I've done a lot of consultancy work with large enterprise customers and that has inevitably meant I've come across Java on many occasions. One of the interesting things I have come across is what I've termed the Infinite Memory Myth. This seems to crop up more in Java applications than in other languages, but that's probably because Java tends to be more widely used in those settings.

The short version of the myth is that developers seem to constantly create new objects, often to the point where the application consumes huge amounts of memory or crashes altogether. They tend to have no idea how much memory each object takes or more worryingly why they should care. As far as they are concerned, they request a new object and one is provided. When an object is no longer used (i.e. nothing points to it any more) Java will at some point get around to cleaning it up (called garbage collection). All of this is automatic; the developer doesn't need to do anything.

The problem is this leads people to forget (or in many cases were never taught at all) that memory is finite and at some point it simply runs out. You can't assume that you can read in every row in a table and that it will always work. You can't assume that just because your test file is 50MB in size that the application will never be given a 5,000MB file to work on.

This lack of understanding stems from not being able to appreciate all the hard work Java is doing on the programmer's behalf. It is running about and managing memory allocation and garbage collection, and the programmer remains blissfully unaware. A good understanding of computing fundamentals would give a developer keen insight into what Java is doing (both the how and the why) and thus appreciate that just because creating new objects is easy, memory itself is not free.

So this is what Eben Upton and the Raspberry Pi Foundation are trying to bring back to the world. They want to rekindle that lost art and make computers cool and interesting again. To do that they have created a computer that even by today's standards is no slouch. Is it as powerful as your laptop? Well no, probably not but can you buy your laptop for $35, slip it into your pocket (possibly not a great idea), generate relatively little heat and drink very little in the way of power? If you answered yes to those questions, I really really want to hear from you - that sounds like a laptop I need to buy!

However you choose to look at it the main selling point (no pun intended) is the price. Anyone can pick up a Raspberry Pi without having to think too much about it. With a modest laptop clocking in at around $500 + and a MacBook pro nearly four times that, it's not the sort of thing you can just splurge on without thinking, especially if it's going to be for experimentation and playing about. However at $35, the Pi is cheaper than some monthly movie subscriptions, you could almost buy a new Pi every month!

Why Eat Raspberry Pi?

Whichever way you look at it, you will come back to the price. Whatever else the Raspberry Pi is and whatever other promises it has in store for us, all of them are interesting because of the price. There are two types of people who will be rushing out to get a Pi. The first group are already clued up on Linux and computing and for them the Pi represents a server in a pocket and a cheap one at that. No longer do they need a full size PC monster guzzling electricity and generating enough heat to rival a bar heater. Oh sure you can get low powered systems in nice shiny boxes, but they're still not all that cheap to buy even if they're cheaper to run. However a device like the Pi is cheap to run and cheap to buy and it has just what you need to build a pretty respectful server.

If you're not one of those people then don't worry, because this book is for you. You like the idea of a cool little computer for $35 and you think you can do some pretty awesome stuff with it; you're just not really sure how. For us the big benefit is that the Pi is at the sort of price where we can afford to buy it just for fun and use it for experimentation. It's not going to replace the family PC and you're not going to need to take out a mortgage to buy one. You can play around with a Pi completely guilt free and try all manner of weird and interesting things without having to worry about cost or destroying your main computer (and thus incurring the wrath of everyone you live with).

Because the Pi is close enough to a normal PC (even though the architecture is a bit different) you can do PC type things with it. In fact, that's the first thing we show you in this book. Thus you don't have to start from scratch, all that you know already you can apply to a Pi (it rhymes if you say that really fast) and so you can hit the ground running. No doubt you will want to do all the things that the first group of people want to do as well. Fear not for we have you covered – by the time you've finished this book you'll be able to do all that and more!

There are lots of reasons why everyone should rush out right now and get some Pi. Actually at the time of writing, there is still a lead time for delivery and when the Pi was initially released, one of the resellers took 100,000 pre-orders in just one day. That's a lot of Pi! Although the lead time will naturally keep changing, the short version is that the sooner you order, the sooner you will get your Pi!

So why all of this interest? What is so special about the Raspberry Pi that it has achieved an almost cult-like following and is still pretty hard to get your hands on?

It only costs $25

Okay, hands up all of you who are only interested in the Pi because it costs significantly less than a night on the town? If you put up your hand, you're not alone. The goals of the Raspberry Pi Foundation are laudable but they all center around getting this powerful machine into our mitts at a price point that won't break the bank.

What really has everyone drooling is not the fact that as far as computer hardware goes, the Pi is effectively free, but more that it is a full computer that can run Linux. That means servers, home automation, video streaming and pretty much anything else you can imagine.

WAIT, IS IT $25 OR $35?

Throughout the book we do bring up the price of the Pi a fair bit, after all it is one of its most distinctive features. However we also mention two prices, $25 and $35, so which is it? Well there are two versions of the Pi, the Model A and the Model B (as uninspiring as those names sound, they're taken from the BBC computers and from a geeky point of view, the names are quite inspired). There isn't a great deal of difference between the two models, with the Model B having 10/100 Ethernet built in and an additional USB port. The Model B also draws a lot more power. The Ethernet adapter is actually connected internally via USB so there is no difference between the built in Ethernet and a USB device that you could plug into the USB port itself.

So which should you buy? Well if you think networking will be useful, the built-in Ethernet port is pretty much required. I love having built-in Ethernet connectivity as it just makes life so much easier. However if you aren't planning on using it all that much, then there really is no need to get the Model B. That said, for $10, it might be worth splashing out just in case you decide you want to play with networking later on…

MOAR PI!

If one Pi is good, then two must be better right? Well, $70 would get you two Pis and while this doubles the cost, it also more than doubles the fun. Now you can experiment with networking and getting the Pis to talk to each other. After all, it's good to talk!

Experiment in safety

I don't know about you but when my computer is out of commission for even a short period of time it is pretty inconvenient. I certainly don't want to fiddle about with something and accidentally erase my hard disk (been there, done that). You'd also be well advised not to try over clocking your CPU on the brand new computer that you were just given as it's not much fun to think you've totaled the machine within an hour of turning it on!

To kill hardware takes a fair bit of effort (such as taping over a pin on the CPU and removing the CPU speed multiplier lock hehe) but it's fairly easy to remove your family photo album and your latest draft of the book you've been working on for the past six months (there is a reason why we dedicated a whole chapter and personal plea in Practical Guide to Performance to backups). If you have a Pi and you nuke it, the worst case is $35 down the drain which is a lot better than what would happen if you toasted your main machine.

Independence

I'm sure some people will point out (quite correctly) that most of the horrors I just described can be avoided if you play in a VM rather than on your main machine. Apart from that not being as fun (real hardware just smells better) it doesn't give you all the benefits of a separate piece of kit. For a start, a virtual machine is only on when your main machine is running. If you happen to have a laptop which follows you everywhere, a virtual machine won't be a great option for a home web server. Also if you ever reboot your main machine, your virtual machine will go down with it. If you were using it to stream movies to your TV, you could end up with some very displeased family members. By having a real piece of hardware you can keep your experimentation completely separate from anything else that you might be doing.

Low Power

The Pi has a very modest power footprint. In fact, the Model A Pi only draws 300ma, which means you can power the whole thing from your USB port. According to Apple, my iMac draws 94 watts at idle and up to 241 watts when the CPU is maxed out. The Model A Pi however draws at most 1.4 watts and the Model B draws at most 3.5. That's an awful lot of power saved. Understandably, these figures only take into account the power requirements of the Pi itself with a bit extra put aside to power modest USB devices. If you add lots of power hungry devices to your Pi, these figures would increase accordingly.

APPLES TO ORANGES

I just know someone is going to cry foul about my power comparison and for good reason. It is true that compared to an iMac, the Pi draws basically no power at all. However, it is also true that an iMac does a lot more. First off it has a big screen, hard disk and a CPU that would blow the ARM on the Pi into the middle of next week. So if I know that I'm comparing two totally different systems and I'm admitting that they're very different(who compares a golf cart to a Formula One car?) why am I wasting ink and paper with this description?

Well, although we are comparing two very different machines, we are comparing the same sort of tasks. If you want to have a little web server or stream video to your TV set, a Pi is more than powerful enough to do that for you. Bear in mind that the Pi is clocked in at 900Mhz and that not too long ago, that was what you'd find on a very powerful desktop. It's not that long ago that you'd find this sort of performance on an enterprise grade server. Ten years ago, it was just a fantasy. In short, the Pi has more than enough juice to do most of the things you'd want from a server and it won't require a small nuclear power station to do it.

The Ingredients for a Raspberry Pi

After extolling all of its benefits you might be wondering why a $35 computer stacks up so well to ones that cost many times that. If you're thinking that, then it won't be long before you wonder why there is such a big difference in price. Surely if you could get something this cheap that does most of the things your main machine can do, then something must be up with the price of the other machines. After all, if a powerful laptop could be made significantly cheaper, it would easily make more money in increased sales than it would lose in reduced profit margin.

Well that's true to a point, but the Pi, powerful as it is, will probably never be a direct replacement for your main computer. It's not any particular one thing that limits the Pi, but a combination of design decisions to balance features with cost that will ultimately prevent it from taking the crown. That said, it is still a fantastic platform and we'll look at some of those highlights right now.

ARM CPU

The major and most obvious difference between the Pi and your desktop is that your desktop will almost certainly have a processor from either Intel or AMD at its core whereas the Pi has an ARM based CPU. The CPU (Central Processing Unit) is the part that actually runs the programs you provide. Before a CPU can run a program it must be translated into a language that the CPU can understand. So all CPUs execute programs, but the program has to be in a language they can understand. An ARM CPU cannot understand instructions written for an Intel or AMD CPU and that effectively means that most off the shelf software (such as Microsoft Windows and games) cannot run on a Raspberry Pi.

Okay so you're not going to be running Windows XP on the Pi, but does the ARM offer any advantages? The first advantage is that ARM CPUs draw much less power. This isn't overly surprising as ARM really came from the embedded hardware industry where power usage and heat generation are a really big deal. In fact you'll find some form of ARM in almost every modern cellphone including the iPhone 6 and Samsung Galaxy S6. In fact they are one of the most widely used processors in the world and can be found in all manner of devices such as DVD players, appliances and even cars.

ARM CPUs also generate very little in the way of heat. If you look at the Pi itself, you will notice the CPU doesn't have a heat sink. If you look at any Intel or AMD CPU you can't fail to miss the huge cooling fan that it requires in order to prevent it burning out. Some people even user water cooling systems to keep their PC processors running at a reasonable temperature.

The last benefit is really a cost to performance ratio. For the vast majority of things, the real bottleneck is not CPU power but how fast data can be fed to it. CPUs have long been much faster than hard disks and even the bus that links all the computers components together can't keep up with even a modest CPU. So what do you get out of this? A low cost processor that almost certainly will do everything you need without the cost penalty.

WINDOWS 10 IOT

In the first edition of this book, we highlighted that although Windows 8 was shipping for ARM devices (most notably for tablets and phones) it would not run on the Pi. It really didn't seem all that likely that things would change in that area either as the Pi is basically a one operating system platform.

However two years on, it seems the tables have turned. Not only will you be able to run Windows 10 on a Raspberry Pi, but it will be officially support by Microsoft and, most importantly it will be free!

So what's the catch? Well, it's still in preview as I write this, and it will be the Internet of Things edition. That is, it will be very cut down and have limited features – you won't be able to run the full version of Windows 10 on your Pi. Still, you will be able to run Windows and gain access to main of the features that people use for building kiosks and data gathering devices and so forth.

As an added bonus, we will be putting together some chapters on Windows 10, just as soon as it comes out of preview. They'll be made available to you as online chapters!

1GB of RAM

The original version of the Pi had only a very modest amount of memory, just 256MB of RAM. Then the second revision of the model B was released and it double to 512MB. Today, the Raspberry Pi 2 clocks in at 1GB of RAM, which is really impressive for such a low cost device. Still, with laptops shipping with 8GB of RAM as standard these days, what can you really do with just 1GB?

Well the answer to that is a lot more than you might think. Remember, Windows 95 was able to operate with a couple of running programs in just 8MB of RAM (which conveniently enough is 128 times less than the Pi) and of course the good old Commodore 64 came with only 64KB (the Pi has something like 16,000 times that) and it was able to run thousands of games to entertain the masses (though admittedly not all at the same time).

So why do we have so much memory in new machines? Memory is cheap these days and although we could do lots of great stuff in very little memory, it's a skill that has gone out of fashion. Why spend so much effort on optimizing memory usage when it will most likely never matter? If 8GB of RAM costs $50, is it worth hours if not days of a programmer's time to save a few megabytes here and there? Probably not.

Remember, the Pi is meant as an experimentation platform, not as a general PC replacement and Linux (especially without a GUI) will run with plenty of memory to spare for all your programs. By keeping the memory to a reasonable minimum, the Pi is able to hit its price point without greatly hindering what you can do with it.

GPU (Graphics Processing Unit)

The GPU is really a specialized form of a CPU. A CPU is generic in what it can do and it tries to be good at everything it does, the classic jack-of-all-trades. A GPU on the other hand does one thing and one thing well. It is specifically designed to handle the intense mathematical calculations needed to render complex displays. This started off predominantly in 3D graphics rendering but has more recently gained traction in day-to-day computing where rather than computing graphics for display, a GPU can be harnessed to execute similar types of instruction for the user. For example, when an application such as Photoshop enhances a photograph, it applies an algorithm to the image and historically the CPU would do this. Today, Photoshop can offload that processing work on to the GPU which due to is very specialized design can do the work much faster - all without needing any assistance from the CPU itself.

The main reason why a GPU is important in a device like the Pi is that even with a modest processor, it can still handle high quality displays and decode high quality video streams. This makes the Pi useful as a media device as well as allowing for a full graphical display that still feels snappy even with a slower processor.

For the most part, the GPU is not something you will directly care about but by knowing that the heavy duty graphics work can be off loaded somewhat from the main CPU, you can be more confident that the ARM that powers the Pi will be able to deliver enough brute force for your needs.

Ethernet Port (Model B only)

You might think that there's not really much to say about an Ethernet port. After all it's pretty straight forward. You plug it in and you can access the network. If you don't have one, then you can't. Simple enough surely?

For me, the ability to connect to a wired network is essential. WIFI can often have issues and sometimes WIFI isn't even available (especially if you decide to turn your Pi into a WIFI access point). Although this feature costs an additional $10, in my experience not having the network card when you really need it will cost you much more than $10 in time, effort and general hassle. It is true you can add a USB network card to the Model A (and technically the card attached to the Model B is actually connected via USB) but then chances are that would cost at least $10 and then you'd have a USB device flapping in the wind. You might say to yourself "If it's USB then I can use it with my other devices too!" but in reality, you probably never will and you're far more likely to lose the damned thing altogether (right when you most need it) than it is to come to your rescue in a time of need.

However, one reason why you might decide on a Model A is that because it doesn't have these extra components, it consumes significantly less power. This probably won't be a major concern for most users, but if you're planning on using the Pi in a battery powered product, then you would be very keen to lower the power requirements as much as possible.

Overall, my recommendation is to get the Model B, just because you get the network card. If you're absolutely 100% positive that you'll never ever need Ethernet (or you want the smallest possible power footprint), then there's probably little point paying the extra cash for this version.

USB

This isn't so much a feature these days as a true requirement. Almost all peripherals connect this way and the Pi is no exception. It will work with all standard USB keyboards and mice and assuming Linux has a driver for it, other USB devices as well (such as the Ethernet card in the Model B).

All models come with USB 2.0 support, although the Model A only has a single port, Model B has two and the Model B+ as Raspberry Pi 2 have 4. As before, unless you have a specific reason not to, you should be looking to get yourself a Raspberry Pi 2.

GPIO Ports

GPIO (General Purpose Input/Output) ports are a very interesting and key addition to the Pi. Most people probably will never use these pins and most people will live a long and happy life having never heard of them. They provide an easy way to connect hardware to your Pi that you can then control through software. If for example you wanted to add a thermometer or light sensor, you could build a device that connects to your PI via the GPIO ports.

If hardware projects don't really interest you then you can probably forget about the GPIO ports. However if you're looking to integrate your Pi with various bits of hardware or make your Pi the brain of some wacky invention, then GPIO ports will give you an easy way to do that.

Baked to perfection

By now you'll have picked up a pretty good appreciation for what the Pi is and what makes it special. It was designed to be low cost so that everyone who wanted one could get their hands on one, but the designers have gone to great lengths to make sure that even though the Pi can't deliver everything a desktop can, it delivers more than enough to make it a fully functional computer laboratory not to mention a very nice server platform.

Whistle-stop Tour

So, what do we have in store for you in the rest of the book? The book is broken down into three core parts. In the first part I'll show you how to get up and running with the GUI. If you've never heard of a GUI then this is definitely where you want to start. The Pi comes with everything you need but out of the box it needs a bit of tweaking. Don't worry, we'll get you up and running quickly and you'll soon be off exploring.

Part two takes you back to the command line and teaches you how to move around. Many people (myself included) spend the vast majority of their time at the command line. It's fast, powerful and always available (even when a GUI is not such as when you want to make a changes via the network) but it is a little bit different from the GUI that most people are used to. Fear not, we all have to start somewhere and in this section we'll make sure you're comfortable and at home on the command line.

In Part three we actually start to do more interesting things. By this stage you're happy on the command line (which puts you ahead of most of the crowd) and now you want to delve a bit deeper and actually make the Pi work for you. We spend this section covering some of the great things you can do and while we're at it we'll give you the solid foundation you'll need to do all of the hardware and software projects in Brendan Horan's "Practical Pi Projects".

Your first bite of Raspberry Pi

In Chapter one we look at what Linux is and why it's on your shiny new Raspberry Pi. We take a brief look at different "distros" and explain why not all "Linuxes" are the same. We take a closer look at the Raspberry Pi and what makes it just that little bit different and then we get your graphical interface up and running.

Surveying the landscape

Following on from where we left off in chapter one is a tour of the desktop and some of the fun things that you can find. We take a look at the surprisingly wide range of software that comes preinstalled on the Pi and show you some of the things that it can do.

Getting comfortable

Now for something just a little bit different. You can use your Pi just like your other computer but now we're going to take it up a notch. In order to get the full benefit from Linux and to get your hands dirty with some very interesting projects (automatic cat detection and prosecution anyone?) you'll need to lift off the crust and start getting closer to the metal.

The first place to start is the command line where you'll be interacting with Linux on a very precise and powerful level. We'll be starting off slow and easing you in to what is likely to be a very alien environment. If nothing else you'll probably find it oh so quaint. We'll discuss the shell, where it came from and why it's important. We'll also look at a bit of the history involved as knowing where it came from (while fascinating in and of itself) will help you get the full benefit from the experience.

The file paths to success

Once you're up to speed on what the command line is, it's time for the most important subject. Most books start by telling you about all the shiny commands you can run and that's all well and good, but first you need some context.

I'll start you off by looking at the Linux file system and explaining the "everything is a file" philosophy that sits at the core of every Unix based operating system. This sounds a bit scary and we won't go into too much depth, but with this under your belt you'll be able to easily pick up new commands and make full use of them.

Essential commands

Now you know about the command line and how Linux lays out all your files, we'll actually showing you how to make Linux do things. I'll show you how to become root (does anyone remember the "power up" scene from He-Man? No?) and how to install new applications and tools. We will also briefly look at some useful command line tricks that will make you a keyboard demon. You will soon find that you can do things far more quickly on the command line than by clicking your mouse...

Editing files on the command line

Next on our tour de force is editing files. I will show you my two editors of choice. One (nano) is simple, easy and great for general use. I use it a lot for making small changes to config files. For more serious heavy lifting, I prefer vim. It has all sorts of magic codes and key presses (really it's like playing dungeons and dragons - not that I ever have) and if you can hold all of the key-combos and commands in your head, well, you will never want to leave! For the rest of us, well, there's always nano...

Managing your Pi: from beginner to admin

Now we're starting to take a look at system services and what makes Linux tick. You'll learn that as smart as Linux is, it's not all that different from all the tools and things you've been running so far. You'll be able to apply your newfound knowledge and be able to start and stop services to your hearts content.

Network services are the bread and butter of any server. Most people have used them from a user's perspective but now it's time to experience them from the pointy end. We'll look at the usual suspects such as OpenSSH and the Apache webserver. After all that we'll have a little sit down and explain the very real dangers of running your own servers on the Internet. There are people out there who would quite like to gain entry to your nice little server and they do not much care who you are. Don't worry, we'll provide a simple list of do's and don'ts that will put you ahead of the game.

A LAMP of your own: a Pi Webserver

We start off our project section with a classic, getting a full LAMP (that is Linux, Apache, MySQL and PHP) stack up and running on your Pi. We will show you why your Pi is an ideal little web server and how it not only provides the perfect environment for development dynamic websites but also makes a great little portable web site demonstration tool!

WiPi: Wireless Computing

What's more fun than a tiny little network server? A tiny little network server that has no wires! We'll show you how to hook up a USB wireless network adapter so your Pi can talk to the world without any wires. If that wasn't enough, we take it one step further and look at ways of cutting the cords altogether and getting your Pi to run off a battery.

The Raspberry sPi: Security cam and messaging service

Want to know who is sneaking into your room and stealing all of your pens? Your sPi has you (or your office) total covered! In this chapter we will show you how to hook up a webcam to your Pi and have it take snapshots of any movement in the room. Not only that but it will promptly email you a copy of the intruder in real time! Even James Bond doesn't have one of these...

Pi Media Centre

Last but by no means least we show you how to turn your Pi into your personal media center. We show you how to stream video to your TV and how to act as an airport device for sharing music around the house. With high resolution streaming video, we really start to push the Pi and show what it is truly capable of!

Summary

We've covered a huge amount in this chapter already. We've looked at how computing has changed over the years and how this has not only had an impact on how we see and use computers in our daily lives but also how this has affected the way computers are perceived in education and the level and depth of knowledge that students are taught. We briefly touched on the Raspberry Pi Foundation and how they hope that the Pi will start to reverse this trend.

Next we looked at some of the more compelling reasons why you might want to get a Pi and why the Pi makes an ideal platform for development and experimentation.

We then looked at what the Raspberry Pi is at the hardware level and discussed the differences between your main computer and the Pi. We examined the trade offs and looked at why some of the decisions were made and what impact they will have on you as a user.

Last but my no means least, we rounded off the introduction with a whirlwind tour of all the things that we're going to cover in the rest of this book. Right then, let's head to the kitchen and make some Pi!

CHAPTER 1

Your First Bite of Raspberry Pi

This chapter is where we finally get our hands dirty. If you decided to skip the introduction in your eagerness to get up and running, that's fine; you won't have missed anything critical for this chapter. However, make a note to pay the introduction a visit in the not too distant future as it gives you a lot of background on the Pi and what makes it so special.

Now, back to dirty hands! We are going to start off by unpacking the Pi and going through the list of things that you need to actually get it up and running. Once we've hooked everything up, we'll then need to sort out something for it to run—in this case, Raspbian Linux (more on this a little later). Once we get Raspbian running, we still need to configure it and some of the options are a little technical and Linux-specific; but don't fret, we have you covered there, too. To round off the chapter, we will bask in the glow of the Raspbian desktop before heading off to Chapter 2 to see what we can actually do with it.

Your Freshly Baked Pi Arrives

Okay, so the postman has just dropped off your long-anticipated package, and after eagerly ripping away the padded envelope you're left with a little box, (*little* being the operative word). You simply can't help but look into the depths of the envelope to see if there is perhaps something lingering at the bottom. Failing to find anything with a visual inspection, you'll no doubt proceed to the old faithful approach of turning the envelope upside down and giving it a bit of a shake. Although you might shake loose the packing sheet (somehow they always seem to super glue themselves to the inside), you won't find anything else.

When you order a Raspberry Pi, this, dear reader, is all that you're going to get (see Figure 1-1).

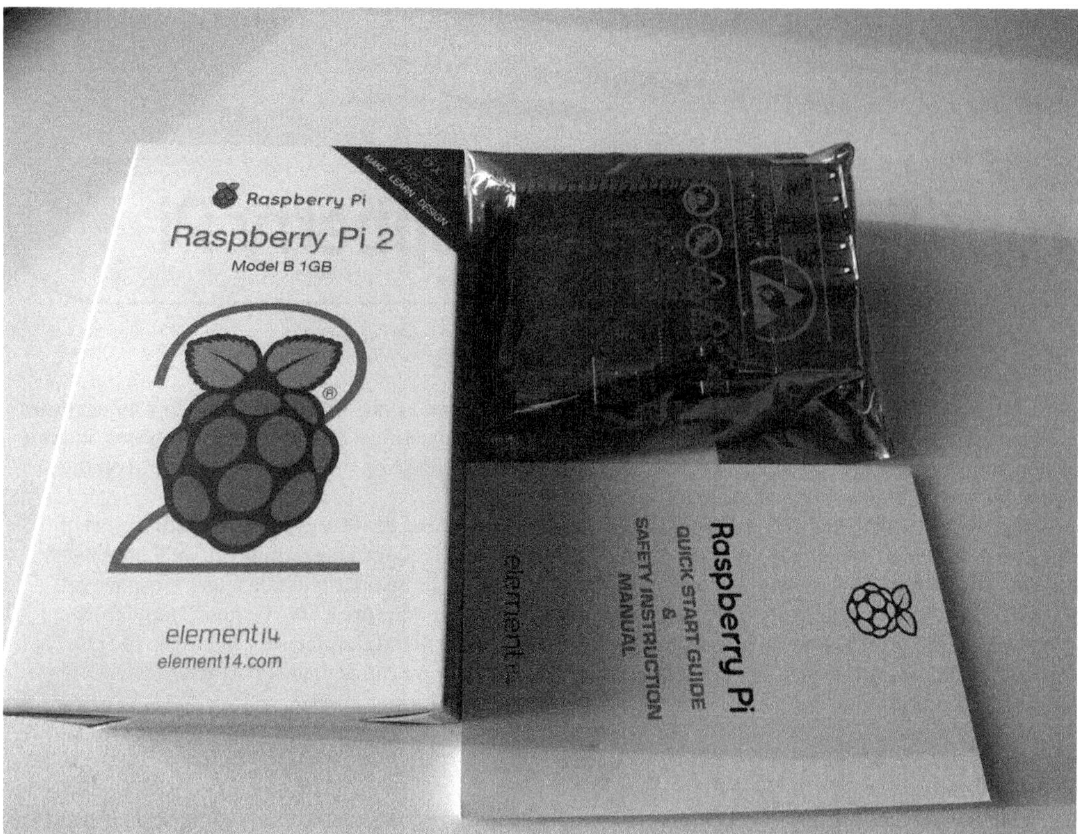

Figure 1-1. *What falls out of the envelope*

WHY A PICTURE OF JUST A BOX AND SOME BITS?

The honest reason is because when this is all that turned up, our first thought was that something must have gone missing. Yes, the site tells you when you order that this is all you are going to get, and it really makes perfect sense.

We want to emphasize that this is all you get, and it's not enough to get your Pi hooked up and in business. You will need other bits and pieces (some or all which you might already have), and it's important to highlight it right at the beginning. In the next section, we will cover the kit you actually need to get started.

If you have yet to order a Pi (or are waiting for it to turn up in the mail), Figure 1-2 shows one sitting next to a blank DVD.

Figure 1-2. *A Raspberry Pi next to a blank DVD*

Even though the size of the Pi is well known and it comes in such a small box, it isn't until you actually hold it in your hands that you realize how small it truly is! After "aw-ing" to ourselves (and anyone else who sadly for them happened to be within earshot), we figured it was time to get the show on the road.

And that's where things came to a somewhat abrupt halt. We had the Pi, but it had only just dawned on us that we didn't have the faintest idea what we actually needed to make it go. Even though we're not exactly new to all this, we had let ourselves get caught up in the moment and for whatever reason hadn't considered that the Pi would need anything special (or at least something that your average geeky type person wouldn't have hanging around the house).

If you're not equipped with a cupboard of odds and ends straight out of Dexter's lab, you might need to pick up a few things. Fortunately, they are all easy to find, and you should be able to pick up everything you need at your local computer shop. If you don't fancy going on a treasure hunt, many companies are offering starter kits that come with everything you need. Because these kits are rapidly changing, the best way to find what's available is to go online and search for "raspberry pi starter kit".

List of Ingredients

To bake your Pi to perfection, you're going to need the following ingredients:

- Raspberry Pi
- Micro USB lead (for power)
- USB power adapter (also for power)
- HDMI lead: Type A to Type A (to connect to your monitor or TV)

- HDMI display
- Micro SD card: 8 GB to 64 GB (for storage - Class 10 required for Windows IoT)
- Micro SD card reader
- USB keyboard and mouse

Micro USB lead

If you happen to have an Android phone or a Kindle sitting about, chances are good that you've got a lead that you can reuse to power the Pi. This lead isn't actually used for transferring data, and although you can draw power from a USB port (you can plug it into your main PC or laptop), you can't use the USB connection for anything else. The different types of USB connectors are hard to describe if you haven't already seen one. Take a look at Figure 1-3 for some examples.

■ **Warning** Although you could run an original Pi from a USB port with a bit of luck, the Raspberry Pi 2 draws nearly four times the power of the original and as non-negotiated USB only provides a tiny amount of current, you cannot run your new Pi from a USB port. Instead you'll need a chunky power supply such as those used to charge tablets. Be warned that even if they claim to provide enough power, they might not play nice with your Pi. If your Pi crashes, has trouble connecting to the network or generally has odd behaviour, check your power supply first.

Figure 1-3. *Different types of USB connectors*

The connector you're interested in is the first one on the left, known as a *micro USB*. Be careful because on quick inspection, a micro USB plug can easily be mistaken for a mini USB plug (second on the left). The last thing you want to do is make a special trip to the store and then come back only to find out that you picked up the wrong one!

USB Power Adapter

As mentioned above, a normal USB port can power a Model A Pi (the one without built-in Ethernet), but for a modern Pi, you're going to need something with a lot more bite.

Fortunately, the sheer number of devices that have adopted USB as a means of charging means that you can get mains adapters really cheaply and easily. As far as which adapter to get, that really comes down to personal choice. However, as the Model B requires 800 ma without anything else plugged into it and you always want to have a bit of room for expansion, you probably should aim to get an adapter that can provide at least 1000 ma (or 1 amp) and preferably 2000ma (2 amp). From our highly scientific tests (wandering around numerous shops and squinting at packaging labels), it seems that 1000 ma is actually the most common rating. We did come across some rated at 500 ma and although that's enough for most USB devices, it isn't enough for your needs.

HDMI Lead

Over the past few years, HDMI has become the *de facto* standard in connecting a myriad of devices to both monitors and TVs. This is really handy because it means that if a device supports HDMI, it can be easily connected to any display that supports it. This might not sound all that impressive, but it wasn't too long ago that TVs and monitors were very separate things and usually there was no direct way to connect, say, a computer to a TV or a VCR to a monitor (although interestingly if you go back 20 years, all home computers connected directly to the TV (for example, the Commodore 64 or Spectrum)). Of course, you could get special hardware, and some higher-end devices did offer a range of different connectors, but as a rule, the two worlds didn't really mix.

Fortunately, the Pi uses HDMI, so we can ignore the irritations of the past. To connect your Pi to a display, you will need a "Type A to Type A" lead. Type A is the size you will find in the back of your TV or monitor; all you have to do is find a lead for connecting some device via HDMI to a TV and where both ends are the same size. Most consumer electronics use Type A, so if you have an Xbox 360 or your laptop has HDMI, chances are you already have a lead of the correct type.

HDMI Capable Display

You probably saw this one coming, but you're going to need some sort of display that supports HDMI. As it has been widely adopted over recent years, practically every new TV comes with one or more HDMI ports and most new monitors do as well. These days, it's fairly common to see three or four ports on a TV because you'll need that many to hook up all your new digital devices.

It's pretty easy to determine whether your TV or monitor supports HDMI. All you have to do is look for a physical HDMI port. You are much more likely to find it on your TV rather than your monitor, but many of even the more basic monitors these days seem to support it.

In our case, it turned out that our aging monitor didn't support HDMI, although the TV in the living room did. Of course, it being the main TV meant that people wanted to watch TV on it and admittedly we were not looking forward to sitting cross-legged on the floor in front of a big TV, trying to convince a Pi to boot. In the end, we decided to get a new monitor that supported it. Although we could have bought a DVI converter, we decided we couldn't pass up on the opportunity to get a new shiny toy.

If you can't reuse your TV or computer monitor, you should be able to get your hands on a basic TV or monitor that supports HDMI quite easily.

Micro SD Card

Most computers use a hard drive of some sort as their primary form of storage. Even laptop-sized disks are larger than the Pi, and although the newer solid state disk (SSD) models draw very little in the way of power, they would certainly drastically increase the amount of power your Pi would need. Fortunately, we have an alternative. Rather than using something heavy duty like a hard disk, we can instead borrow technology that cameras have been using for many years: flash memory. Although the cards can't match a hard disk for space or for performance, they are exceptionally good for power usage and despite being smaller than their erstwhile cousins; 64 GB (the maximum for your Pi) is still a reasonably impressive amount and probably more than you will need for your Pi.

Micro SD cards are standardized so there isn't too much more to say about them. You do want to get a high-performance card if you can (often referred to as *Class 10*) but they ultimately all do the same job. That said, we have heard of some micro SD cards that haven't worked with the Pi, but if you stick to a well-known brand you get a class 10 card, you should be fine. Linux is pretty tolerant on the performance of the card, but it seems that Windows 10 IoT is very picky. We could only get it to work on Class 10 SD, and this seems supported by Microsoft's latest documentation. If you want to try out Windows, you will definitely need a Class 10 SD card.

As there are lots of different types of memory cards floating about these days, Figure 1-4 shows what an micro SD card actually looks like.

Figure 1-4. *SD card with micro SD and adapter*

The card on the far left is your typical SD card; on the far right is a micro SD card. They have become pretty popular for use in smartphones (particularly Android-based phones), and because most phones come with small cards (in terms of storage space), it's not unusual to either buy a larger card or have one thrown in as part of your phone package. If you happen to have one of these floating about, you can use it with your Pi.

Micro SD Card Reader

Now that you have your micro SD card, you need some way to actually use it. The Pi has you covered and has a micro SD card slot built right in. However it doesn't actually have any other storage on the device, so it's effectively a blank slate until you insert an SD card with something useful (like Linux) installed on it. The thing is, to put Linux on the card, you need a device that's already up and running that can also read and write to the card. This is a classic Catch-22 situation. Even if you could borrow someone else's card with Linux already installed, you couldn't simply swap out the cards because as soon as you do that, you won't have Linux anymore!

Again, thanks to the proliferation of digital cameras, many computers come with card readers built in. Many (often dubbed as *media PCs*) come with a whole range of slots for various different card types. So chances are you already have a way to read the card. If you don't have a reader already, you can pick up any cheap multicard reader from your local computer store. They're generally inexpensive and will support lots of different types of cards. Just make sure that it has a micro SD card slot (often hidden on a different side for some reason) before you hand over your hard-earned cash! For reference, the adapter we are using looks like the one in Figure 1-5.

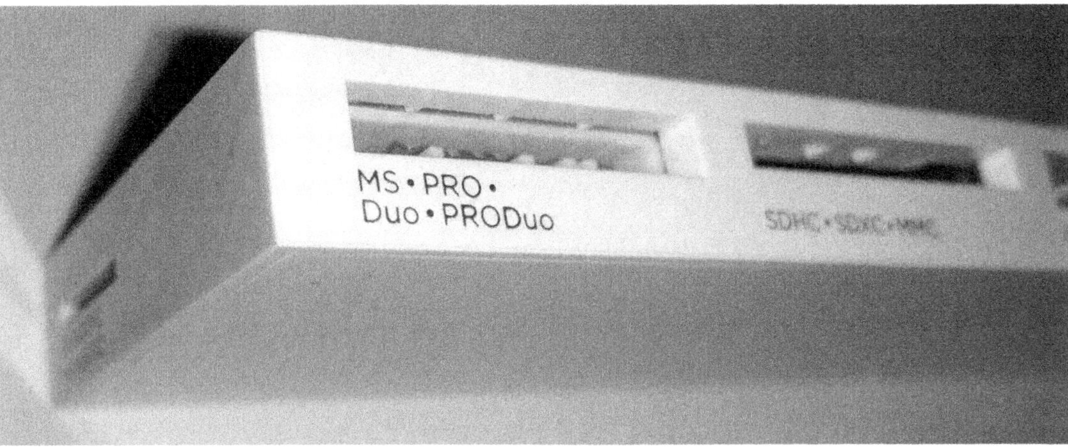

Figure 1-5. *Multicard reader (micro SD reader is on the left edge near the bottom)*

USB Keyboard and Mouse

Last but not least is the good old keyboard and mouse. Advanced as the Pi is, it doesn't yet have telepathy so you're going to need some way to control it. This is common sense, but with modern computers often coming with a wireless keyboard and mouse and a fair few of those using Bluetooth with no USB adapter (even some with an adapter have been known to cause problems), you might find that your current keyboard and mouse just won't work with your new toy (no Bluetooth on the Pi, I'm afraid). There's really no need to go into any detail here as any standard keyboard and mouse will do, and this is mostly a reminder to check what you actually have before you go out to buy your Pi-making ingredients to avoid untold frustration when you get home and find you're completely stuck.

Whew, We're Done!

Finally we have everything we need! Hooking all this stuff up to your Pi is very easy, especially as each item has a unique shape so it will fit into only one slot (see Figure 1-6 for the finished Pi).

Figure 1-6. *A fully loaded Pi*

If you put everything together, plug in the power, and turn on your TV you should see... a completely black screen.

Don't Panic!

When your PC or laptop boots, there is a piece of software called the BIOS that kicks everything off for you. It tests the memory, sets up a basic display, and allows all your devices to initialize. On some machines (notably those from Apple) the machine will have an EFI instead of a BIOS. For all intents and purposes (at least from our point of view), they're basically equivalent. Regardless of the technology used, it is this system that finally hands control over to your bootloader, the piece of software responsible for starting your operating system.BIOSs are by nature very noisy, and if you get something wrong it will either bleep a lot (with some magic number code that you can only find in the BIOS manual that you threw in the bin 3 years ago) or display some helpful yet cryptic message on the screen. In short, it may not do what you want, but at least you know that your computer is still alive. Although it has a little red LED "on light", the Pi won't do a thing unless it has a bootable operating system on its SD card. If you were expecting some sort of splash screen or other sign of life (hands up; we know we were), you're out of luck (and probably thinking you have a dead Pi).

Now that you know what you need to restore the Pi to life (a bootable operating system) it's time to move on to Phase 2 of our master plan and get us some Linux!

Linux

As this is a book for beginners, we're going to take the time to talk a little about Linux, where it came from, what's special about it and some of the little gotchas that trip people up from time to time. If you already know this stuff (or simply don't care), feel free to skip to the next section "Downloading NOOBS." For those who want a quick refresher, just keep on reading.

What Is Linux?

Ah, this simple question opens a big can of worms that many people go out of their way to avoid. The reason is that in technical terms, Linux means one thing but in general speech, it tends to mean something else. When talking about operating systems in general, we see Microsoft Windows and Apple OSX to be discrete, whole things. If you say "I run Windows," everyone knows what you're talking about. With Linux, it's a bit different.

Linux is just an operating system kernel, which means that it handles all the low-level bits and pieces such as handling device drivers, and providing easy access to networks and hard disks. What actually makes Linux usable is all the software that is wrapped around it. Not much trouble there, but it starts to get complicated when you realize that people have differing opinions about what software should be wrapped around it. There are no simple or minor opinions when it comes to computing!

As this software is open source, and anyone can put it together in pretty much any way they like, people have been able to build their own Linux distributions. This is an operating system with Linux at its core, but with the surrounding ecosystem set up to match the goals of the people who built it. For example, Red Hat Enterprise Linux (RHEL) is built to be robust, supportable, and stable over long periods of time. Fedora, on the other hand, is released every 6 months or so and has the latest and greatest of everything in each build. Gentoo requires that you build your software from source (so it can be completely optimized for your machine), and Debian goes to great lengths to remain stable and secure at the cost of introducing new features.

OPEN SOURCE

In the olden days, when computers cost millions of dollars, it was the machine itself that sold, not the applications that ran on it. It was common practice for a company to write software for you, in order to get you to buy their machine. It wasn't until computers became commodity items that suddenly the value was in the software, and companies moved to start protecting the software they'd written. One way to do this is to provide the software ready to use without the source code (which is effectively the blueprint on how to make the software). This meant that you couldn't change the software or make improvements to suit your changing needs.

Many people believe that software should always come with the source code so that people can make changes. Open source revolves around the idea of people being able to freely exchange, modify, and improve software collectively. This can only be done when the source code is provided freely and permission is given (through an open source license) to make those changes.

Entire books can and have been written on this topic, but you can find a presentation on this topic that Peter gave at his university a few years ago: `http://www.youtube.com/watch?v=c-1LQIGh6cI`

So which one is best? Well, that depends on your needs! There's no perfect distribution; just the best fit for a particular job. For the Pi, the official and supported platform is Raspbian, which is based on the Debian distribution. Because it is supported and because it's the easiest to use (and quite likely the fastest to get updated and fixed when things go wrong), we're going to stick to using Raspbian in this book. If you do fancy something a little different, Brendan Horan's book (also from Apress), *Practical Raspberry Pi* will show you in great depth how to install Fedora and (if you're feeling particularly brave) how to make a custom build of Gentoo!

When the Linux kernel first debuted in the early 1990s, no one really appreciated the huge impact it would have on the world of computing. Open-source software had already been around for a long time before this, and countless tools for the UNIX platform had already been released (such as the awesome GCC compiler). However, they were just tools and software packages. They still needed a proprietary operating system to run (the only kind available at the time). To be fully compatible with the open-source ethos, what was needed was an open-source kernel to power these systems and this is what Linux delivered. While many will talk about how this brought freedom and hope to the world of computing, we will save you from that particular lecture (although admittedly there is quite a bit of truth to it) and simply say that it was the Linux kernel that really brought open source to the eyes of the general public.

Now that the world has Linux, what exactly can we do with it? Almost anything we like—such as installing it for free on our Pi.

Introducing NOOBS

At this point in the first edition of the book, we were off to download a Raspbian image file. Back then all of the different Pi distributions were distributed as image files. All you had to do was download the image of interest and write it out to your SD card.

Well, it's not just the Pi's hardware that has improved over the last couple of years. Today you can download a Pi installer that is even easier to set up and provides a whole list of operating systems to choose from (although we will still be using Raspian, check out the "Why Raspbian" sidebar).

NOOBS was developed as an easy way for Pi users to be able to pick an operating system and install it with the least amount of hassle and headache. For seasoned users, writing out an SD card wasn't much hassle, but it is a pretty alien thing to do for most users. It also meant understanding how imaging works and the difference between copying a file and writing it out as an image.

With NOOBS this is a thing of the past. First, instead of downloading an image file, you download a zip file, something almost everyone is familiar with these days. You then extract the contents of that zip file directly onto an SD card. And, well, that's it, you're done! Simply pop out the SD card, boot your Pi and you're off.

So how does this work? Well, on your average PC, you need to have things set up just so, so that the BIOS can find the operating system and boot it. The Pi is different in that it doesn't come with firmware in the traditional sense and instead loads everything from the SD card. This makes it a bit slower to start up, but makes it very easy for the Pi foundation to update things that otherwise would need special tools to update. So instead, the Pi looks for a specific file on the SD card and simply executes that. In the case of NOOBS, you're running an installer, and from there, you can pick which operating systems you'd like to install – all through a nice graphical interface!

The two NOOBS

There are two versions of NOOBS that you can download. The first is the full installer, simply called NOOBS and the second is NOOBS lite. The only material difference between them is that NOOBS comes with Raspbian and NOOBS lite doesn't come with anything. Remember, NOOBS is an installer not an operating system itself and so it needs to have a means of retrieving whichever operating system you're interested in. In all cases, if you don't want Raspbian, NOOBS will go online and download the release from the Internet. If you do want Raspbian (and honestly, you probably do) then you might as well get the full version of NOOBS. If on the other hand you're only interested in the other operating systems, there is absolutely no benefit in downloading the full version and you should instead stick to NOOBS lite.

Downloading NOOBS

Whatever version of NOOBS takes your fancy, you can get it by going to the Raspberry Pi download site shown in Figure 1-7.

`https://www.raspberrypi.org/downloads/`

Figure 1-7. *Pick your NOOBS*

As we mentioned previously, there are two versions available for download. If you're following along with this book, then we highly suggest you choose the full version of NOOBS as you're going to want to install Raspbian. You could admittedly still do this with NOOBS lite, but if you want to install a number of Pi's for example you'd have to effectively download Raspbian each time you do the install.

WHY RASPBIAN?

As you can see from the download page, there are numerous distributions to choose from, and especially if you've used Linux elsewhere you might be tempted to pick something other than Raspbian. However, before you download that exotic distribution, you should know that the majority of people using a Pi run Raspbian—and as such most of the support, blog posts, and tutorials (not to mention this book) are all based on it. This means if you pick something else, you might find it much harder to get help if something doesn't go quite according to plan.

The other more subtle issue is that the Raspberry Pi is an ARM-based device. It doesn't quite work the same way as your PC does. For example, the Pi doesn't have a PCI bus, so any tools that expect there to be one (and there are more than a few) just won't work. There are also quite a few gotchas for these other distributions, and they might not be as well maintained as Raspbian. In short, you will be taking on much more work if you don't pick Raspbian to start out.

Getting NOOBS onto Your SD Card

"Getting Raspbian onto your SD card isn't as easy as simply copying across the file." - That's how we started off this section in the first edition. Today however, it is exactly as easy as copying across the files to an SD card. First though we need to make sure your SD card is ready for use. For this example we're going to use Windows as that's what most people will be using. However if you're using a Mac, the process is basically the same and you'll probably have no trouble following along.

First let's insert the SD card. Under "This PC" we can see the card has been detected (Figure 1-8):

***Figure 1-8.** Freshly inserted SD card*

Now this is a card that was literally taken straight from its packaging (seriously, I'm still oozing blood from trying to rip it out of its "easy open" packaging). As you can see it has no files on it, an important perquisite for installing with NOOBS (Figure 1-9):

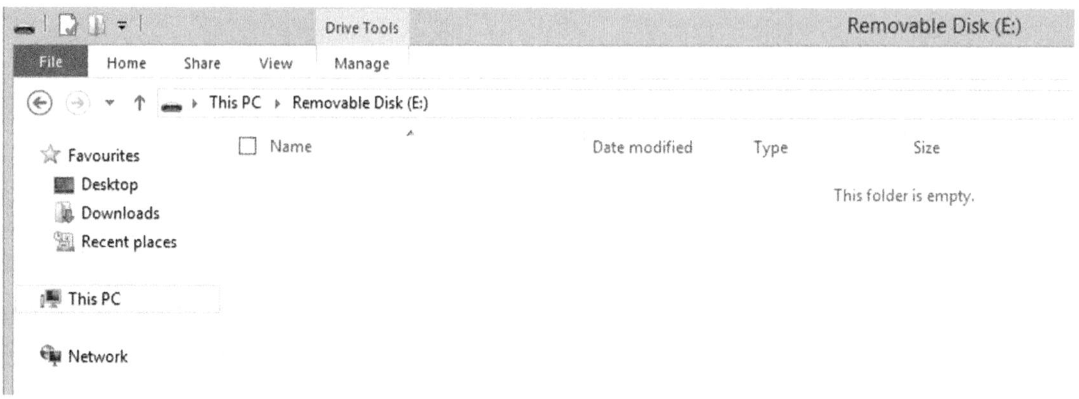

***Figure 1-9.** The card is empty*

So far so good, now all we need to do is open the NOOBS zip file and extract the content directly into this disk. If you haven't done anything special, your browser will download NOOBS into your "Downloads" folder. You're looking for an icon that looks like this (Figure 1-10):

***Figure 1-10.** What you'll see in Explorer*

When you double click to open it, (assuming you haven't installed a different application to handle zip files such as WinZip) you'll see what looks like a normal folder with files in it (Figure 1-11):

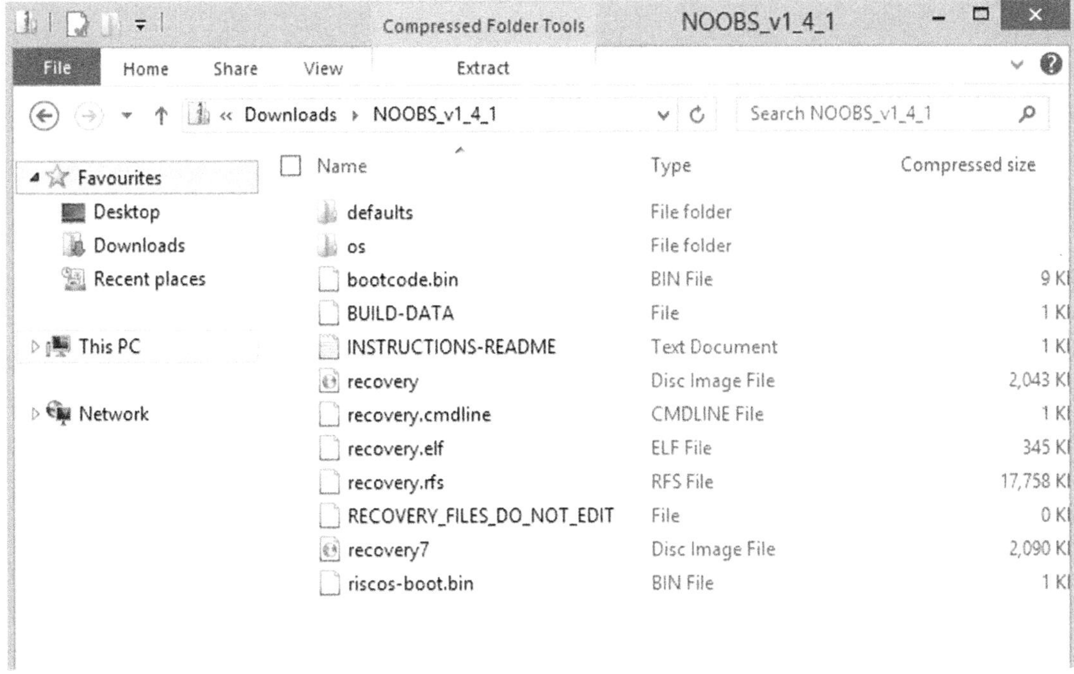

Figure 1-11. *The contents of the NOOBS zip file*

Now we just need to extract it. If you click on "Extract" you will get a pop up menu. You can ignore the stuff on the left, you want the "Extract All" icon that's on the right Figure 1-12):

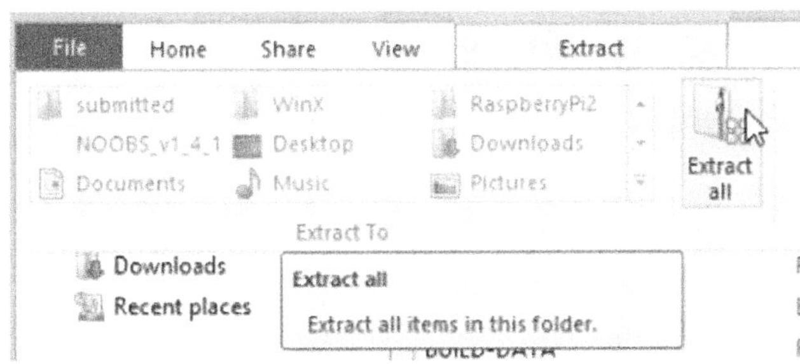

Figure 1-12. *Extract all*

If you've followed the steps so far, you'll be ahead of the game at this stage because you'll have a nice clean SD card plugged into your computer already. In the earlier example, we showed you that our SD card had been picked up as "E:". We hit browse and selected our SD card and you should do the same. When it goes back to the main screen it will only show the device name, which in our case is of course "E:" (Figure 1-13):

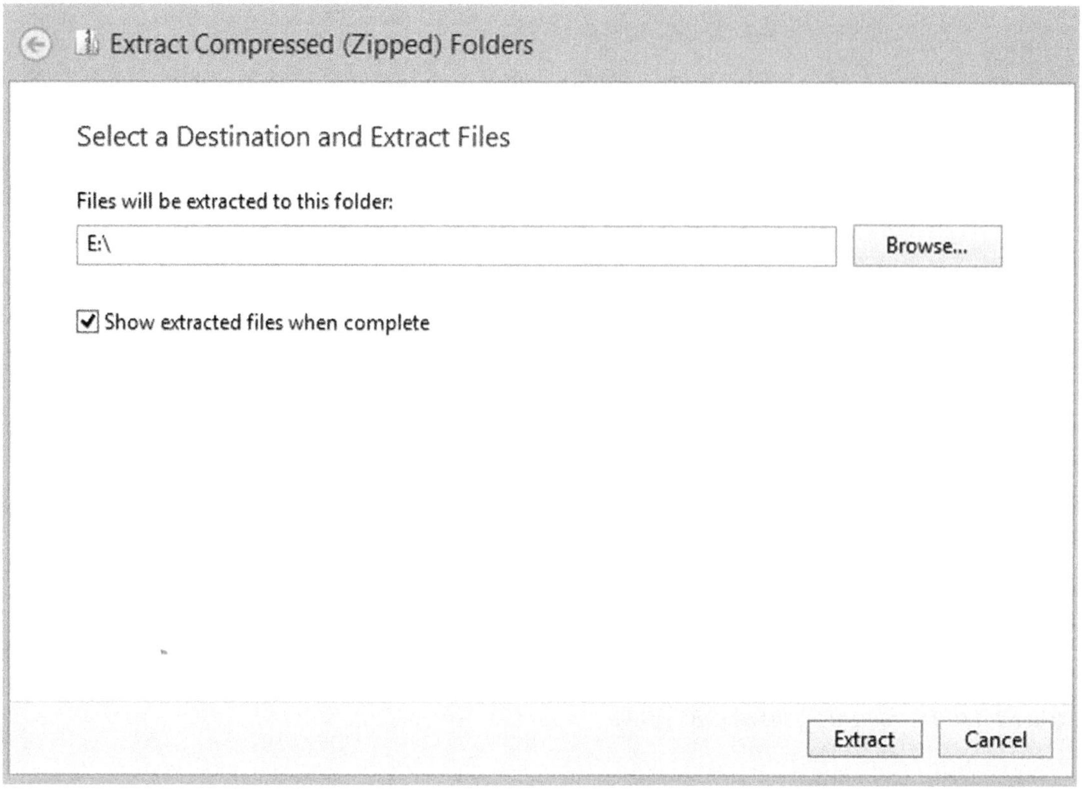

Figure 1-13. *Extract everything to the SD card*

Once you've chosen your SD card you can press the Extract button. Windows will give you a nice pretty progress bar. If your computer is anything like ours, this will take a bit of time so now might be a good time to get and grab that coffee. In total it took about five minutes for Windows to extract all the files to the SD card. We are using a class 10 card for this, so if you're using a slightly older card (say a class 4) then you might find that it will take quite a bit longer (Figure 1-14):

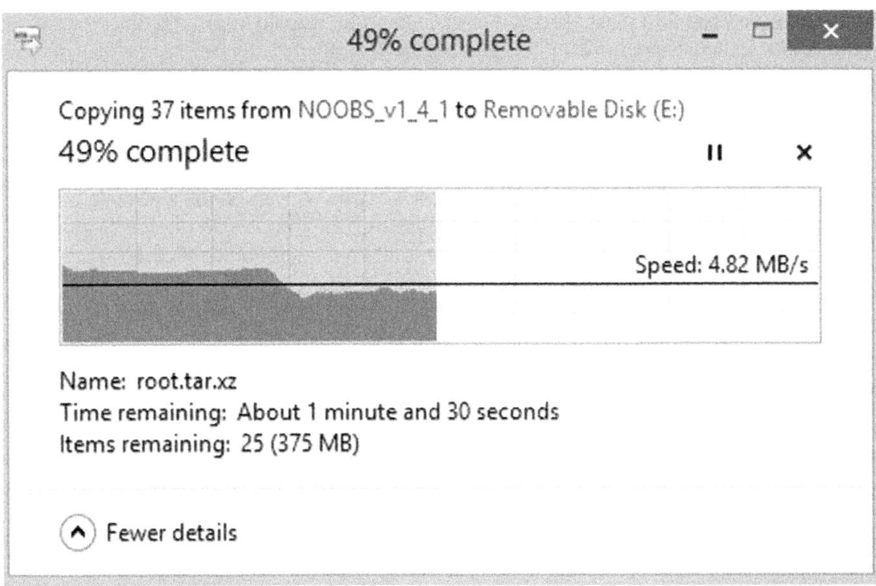

Figure 1-14. *This can take a while to copy, but at least it's pretty!*

When finished it will open your SD card and show you the files. All being well it should be exactly the same as what we saw in the zip file earlier. If you see something similar to the following screen grab then you're in business. All that's left now is to actually try and boot your Pi with it (Figure 1-15):

Name	Date modified	Type
defaults	17/02/2015 12:45	File folder
os	17/02/2015 14:14	File folder
bootcode.bin	18/02/2015 16:26	BIN File
BUILD-DATA	11/05/2015 15:53	File
INSTRUCTIONS-README	18/02/2015 16:23	Text Document
recovery.cmdline	18/02/2015 16:26	CMDLINE File
recovery.elf	18/02/2015 16:26	ELF File
recovery	18/02/2015 16:26	Disc Image File
recovery.rfs	18/02/2015 16:26	RFS File
RECOVERY_FILES_DO_NOT_EDIT	18/02/2015 16:26	File
recovery7	18/02/2015 16:24	Disc Image File
riscos-boot.bin	18/02/2015 16:23	BIN File

Figure 1-15. *What your SD card should look like after you're done*

Okay, so that was a little bit tedious, but trust us, this is a lot easier than the old approach that we had to use. So without further ado, let's see if we can book up your Pi (Figure 1-13)!

First Boot

Finally it's time too boot up your Pi! Armed with our freshly imaged SD card, we can finally get started. Plug in your keyboard, mouse, and monitor, and slot your SD card into your Pi. All you have to do now is attach the power lead and you're good to go! All being well, you should initially see a screen like Figure 1-16.

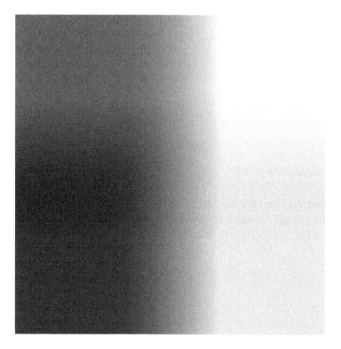

Figure 1-16. *The Pi's first boot—it lives! If you can see something similar, congratulations, your Pi is up and running! You can skip to the next section. If not, there are a few common things that might have gone wrong*

The first thing to check is whether your Pi has a nice red glowing power LED. Now we know this sounds obvious, and we know that it's probably the first thing you checked, but not checking it is also the most common mistake to make. If your desk looks anything like ours, you will have a fair collection of cables draped about. It's not too much of a stretch to see how you might have plugged in the wrong cable or that the cable you're using isn't actually plugged in to a live power source (some laptops, for example, turn off USB power when they go to sleep). Either way, this is what you should check first because if you did make a mistake, only you will know about it. This is much better than having an extended discussion on the forums trying to get help only to then realize that whoops! you forgot to plug it in.

The second thing to check is whether you have selected the right input on your TV or monitor. Most TVs have multiple inputs these days, and monitors often as not don't default to HDMI (ours doesn't), even if that is the only input signal they are receiving. Obviously, we can't tell you exactly how to fix or check this one as it all depends on the equipment you're using. However, it should be fairly easy to flick through the different inputs to see whether or not your Pi turns up. In one interesting case, even though on the TV the port clearly said HDMI2, the Pi was actually visible on HDMI3. We have no idea why, but had we thought to flick through the inputs before fiddling with the Pi, we could have saved ourselves a fair bit of grief.

The third thing to check is that the SD card is fully inserted into its slot. The Pi will quite literally do nothing unless it can find the card and boot from it, so if all you're getting is a black screen, this could well be the reason. If you are sure the card is inserted properly, but you're still not having any luck, it might be that something went wrong when you copied the files to the card. In that case, flip back to the last section and have another go at it. If you still aren't getting anywhere and you've checked that everything is all plugged in nicely, you have the right input on your monitor, and you have a happily glowing power LED, then it's probably something more onerous. Unfortunately, without being there with you to look at your poorly Pi, we can't really give any more specific advice. Fortunately, you're not alone; there are lots of people on the Raspberry Pi discussion forums who are ready to help out. To visit the forum, go to `www.raspberrypi.org` and click the Forum link (just below and to the left of the Raspberry Pi logo). This will get you to the main forum page; the particular board you're looking for is Basic Usage and Setup under Using the Raspberry Pi.

Installing Raspbian with NOOBS

After a short time, you should see NOOBS start up and start initializing itself (Figure 1-17):

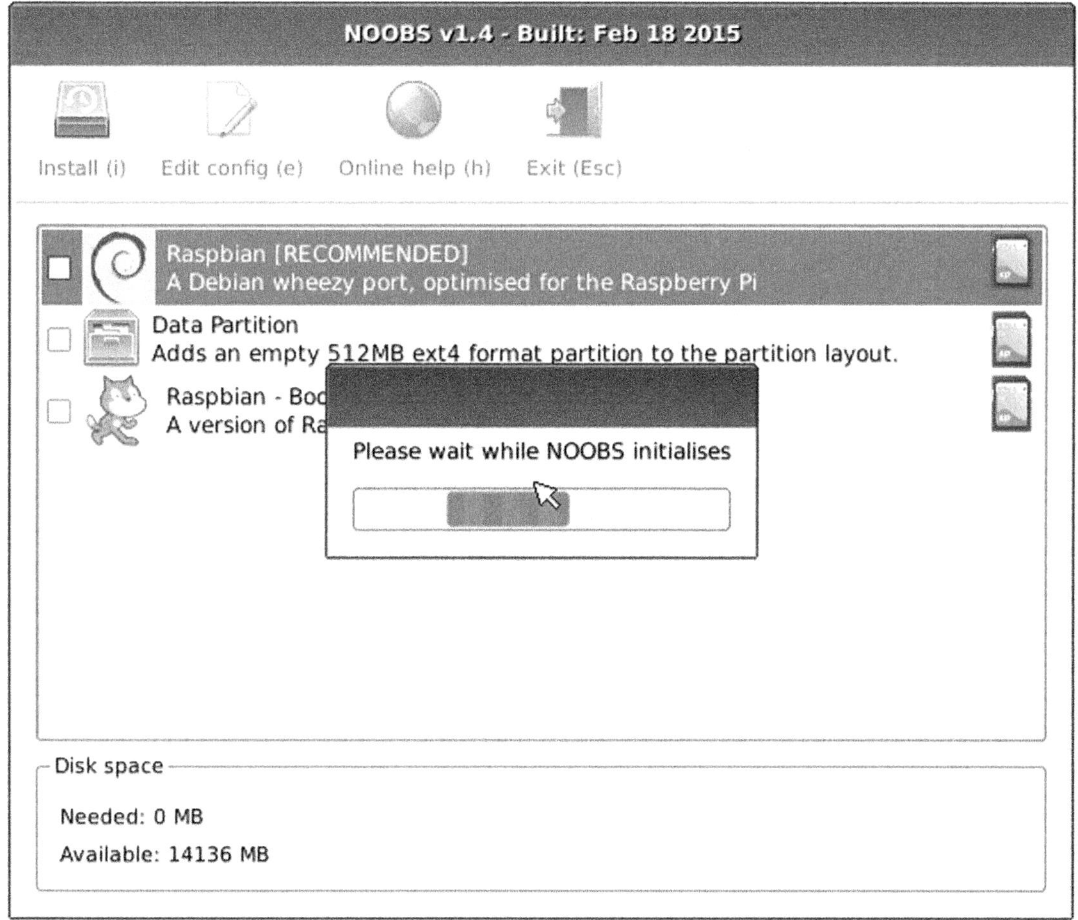

Figure 1-17. *NOOBS setting itself up*

You can see in this screenshot that NOOBS already knows about Raspbian and the icon on the right (an SD card) tells you that the operating system is already on the card and ready to be used. Now in theory what should happen next is that you should see a screen that looks like this (Figure 1-18):

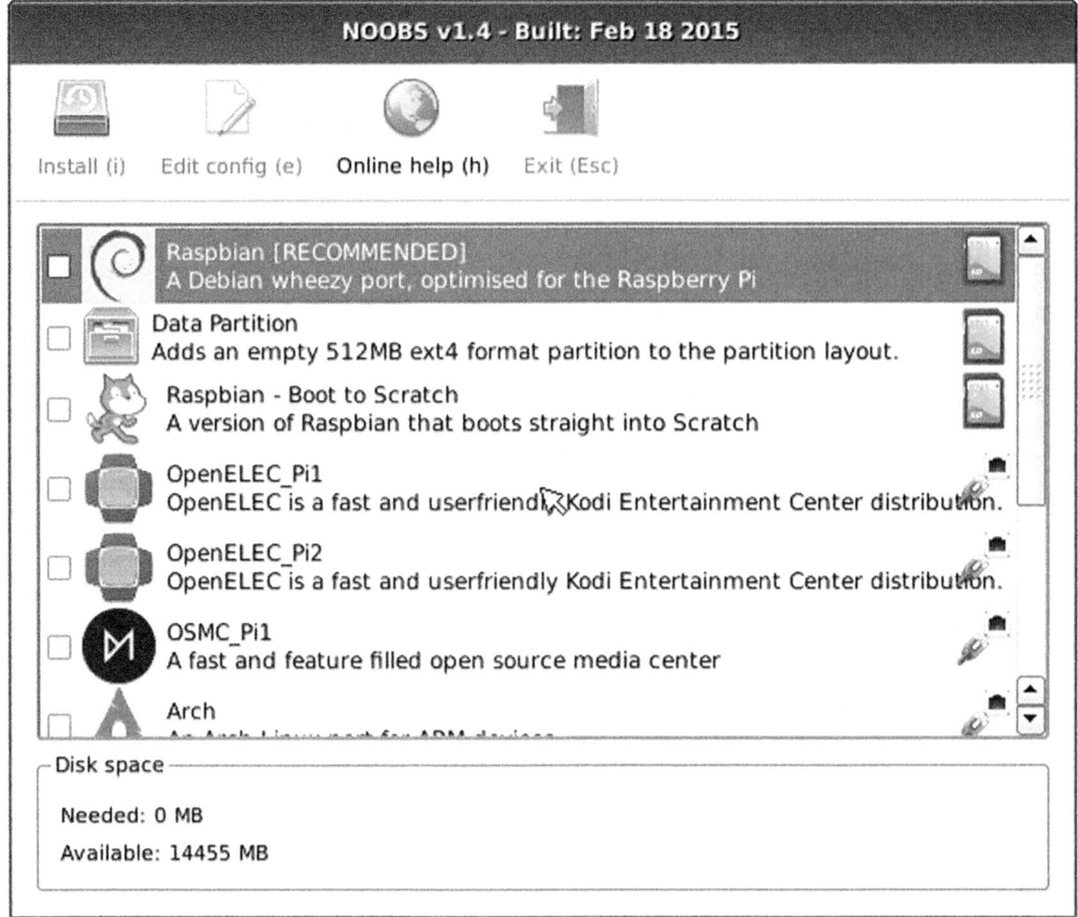

Figure 1-18. *NOOBBS detected lots more operating systems to install*

NOOBS has gone online and found a number of alternative operating systems that you can install. Rather than an SD card icon, these have an Ethernet connector, showing that they are available "on the network" - in other words you need to download them. Now the reason we said "in theory" is because we couldn't get this to work out of the box for us. In fact we had to fiddle around with IP addresses and all sorts in order to get the installer to actually detect the online operating systems. In fact what we got was this (Figure 1-19):

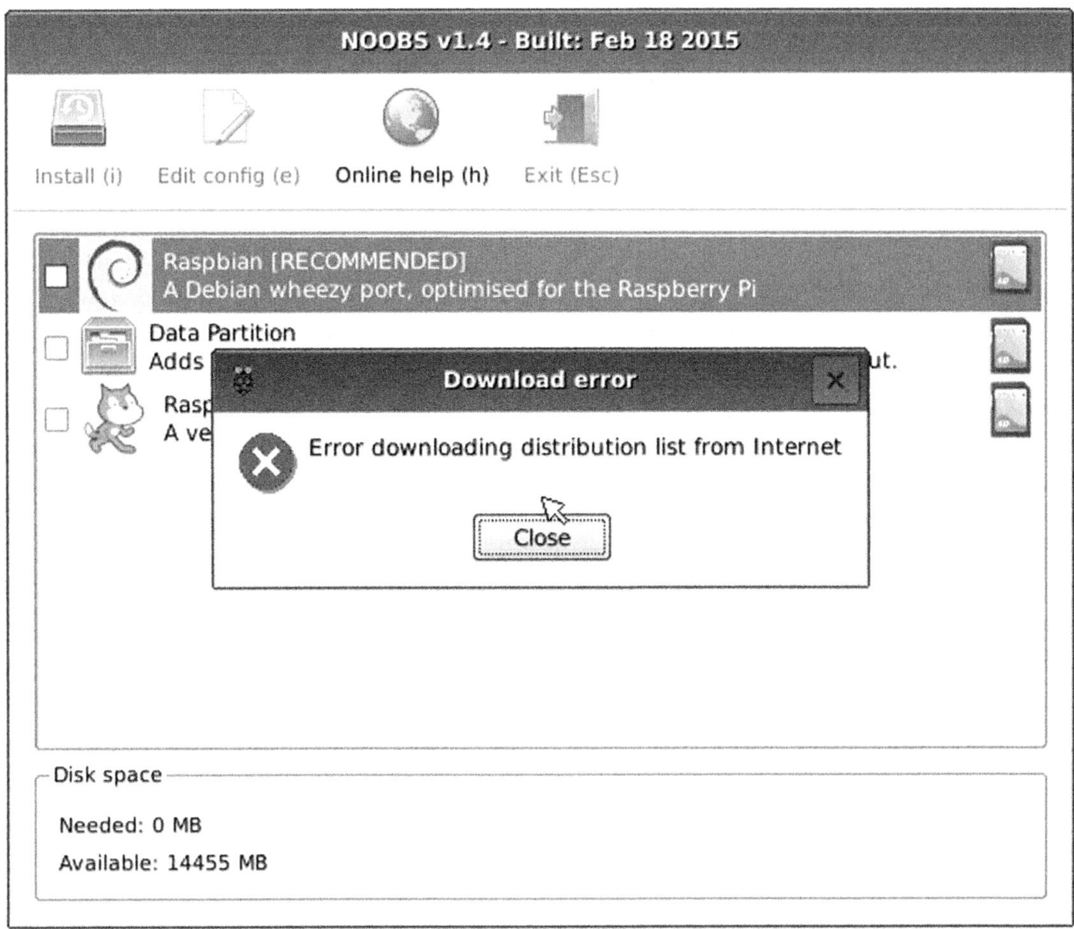

Figure 1-19. *NOOBS network init failed*

Fortunately we're using the full version of NOOBS so it really doesn't matter that we can't get online to download the rest of the operating systems. We expect this is a problem either with our Pi or our set up, and it's probably something you're not going to see yourself. That said we wanted to mention it in case it did crop up and reassure you that you can still get Raspbian installed even with this problem.

Okay, let's actually start the installation process! All you have to do is tick the box to the left of Rasbian and press the "Install" button (Figure 1-20):

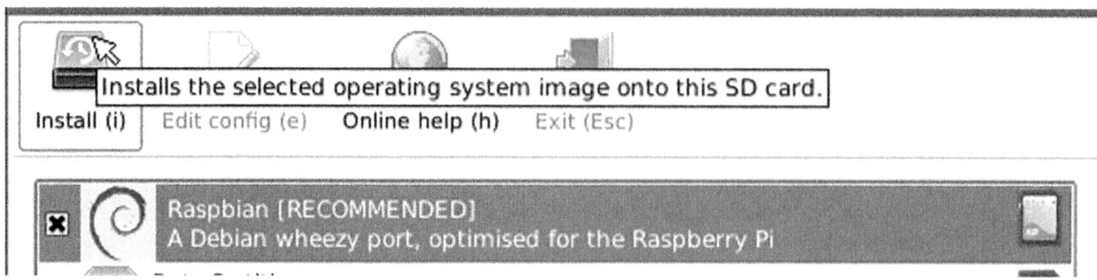

Figure 1-20. *Time to install Raspbian*

You'll get a final warning that this is going to erase the SD card, but that's something of a moot point because you had to erase the card to get NOOBS on there in the first place. Still it's always a good idea to double check, even though you're totally sure everything will be fine (Figure 1-21):

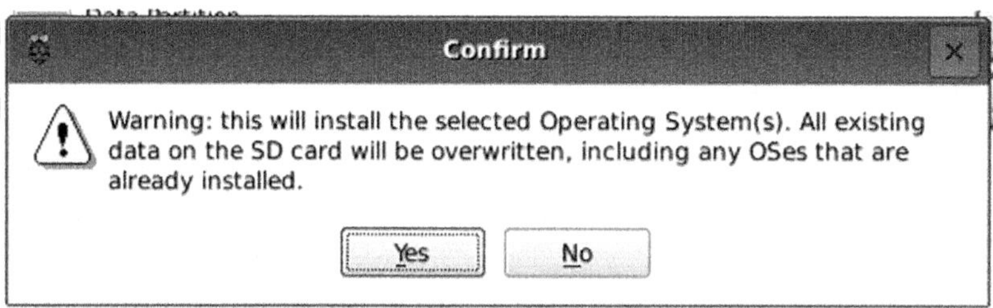

Figure 1-21. *Last chance to back out*

Once you've clicked on Yes, NOOBS will start installing Raspbian and all you have to do is wait. You'll be treated to some useful information screens (which we won't reproduce here for obvious reasons) and again, it might be time to top up that coffee mug as copying large amounts of data to and from the same SD card is a slow process, class 10 SD card or not (Figure 1-22).

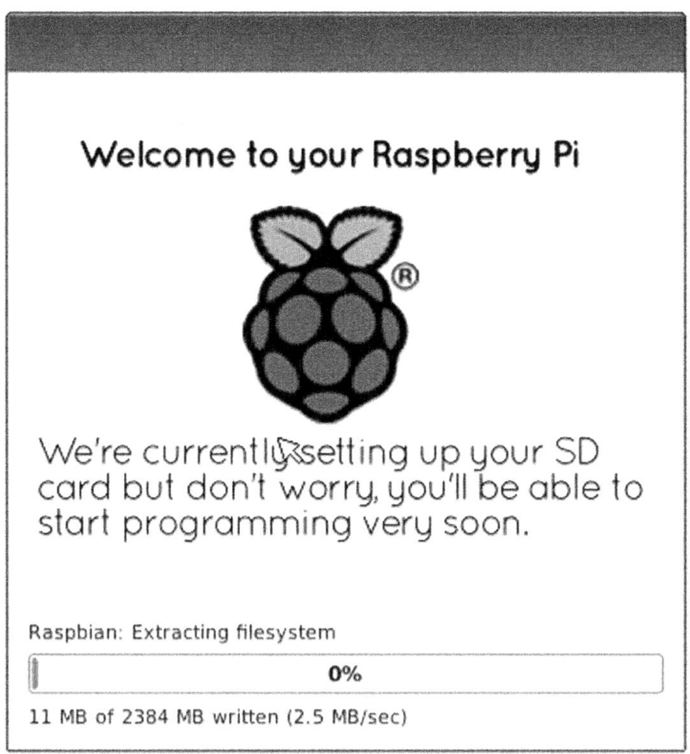

Figure 1-22. *Raspbian is installing*

And finally, everything is installed (Figure 1-23):

Figure 1-23. *Finally everything is installed*

Now it's time to reboot your Pi. This time when it restarts, NOOBS will be gone and it will be replaced with Raspbian. It's taken a fair bit of time to reach this stage, but it's worth it we promise!

When it starts up (for real this time) you should see something like this (Figure 1-24):

```
[    3.978155] usb 1-1.3: new low-speed USB device number 5 using dwc_otg
[....] Synthesizing the initial hotplug events...[    4.082465] usb 1-1.3: New USB device found, idVendor=15d9, idProduct=0a4d
[    4.108016] usb 1-1.3: New USB device strings: Mfr=0, Product=1, SerialNumber=0
[    4.122605] usb 1-1.3: Product:  USB OPTICAL MOUSE
[    4.146090] input:  USB OPTICAL MOUSE as /devices/platform/bcm2708_usb/usb1/1-1/1-1.3/1-1.3:1.0/0003:15D9:0A4D.0003/input/input2
[    4.168797] hid-generic 0003:15D9:0A4D.0003: input,hidraw2: USB HID v1.11 Mouse [ USB OPTICAL MOUSE] on usb-bcm2708_usb-1.3/input0
done.
[....] Waiting for /dev to be fully populated...[    4.483447] random: nonblocking pool is initialized
done.
Starting fake hwclock: loading system time.
Wed May  6 23:29:26 UTC 2015
[ ok ] Setting preliminary keymap...done.
[ ok ] Activating swap...done.
[    6.410957] EXT4-fs (mmcblk0p6): re-mounted. Opts: (null)
[....] Checking root file system...fsck from util-linux 2.20.1
e2fsck 1.42.5 (29-Jul-2012)
root: clean, 86233/922080 files, 699911/3683072 blocks
done.
[    6.685314] EXT4-fs (mmcblk0p6): re-mounted. Opts: (null)
[warn] Creating compatibility symlink from /etc/mtab to /proc/mounts. ... (warning).
[ ok ] Cleaning up temporary files... /tmp.
[info] Loading kernel module snd-bcm2835.
[ ok ] Activating lvm and md swap...done.
[....] Checking file systems...fsck from util-linux 2.20.1
dosfsck 3.0.13, 30 Jun 2012, FAT32, LFN
/dev/mmcblk0p5: 52 files, 9582/30651 clusters
done.
[ ok ] Mounting local filesystems...done.
[ ok ] Activating swapfile swap...done.
[ ok ] Cleaning up temporary files....
[ ok ] Setting kernel variables ...done.
[....] Configuring network interfaces...wpa_supplicant: /sbin/wpa_supplicant daemon failed to start
run-parts: /etc/network/if-pre-up.d/wpasupplicant exited with return code 1
wpa_supplicant: /sbin/wpa_supplicant daemon failed to start
run-parts: /etc/network/if-pre-up.d/wpasupplicant exited with return code 1
done.
[ ok ] Cleaning up temporary files....
[ ok ] Setting up ALSA...done.
[info] Setting console screen modes.
[info] Skipping font and keymap setup (handled by console-setup).
[ ok ] Setting up console font and keymap...done.
[ ok ] Setting up X socket directories... /tmp/.X11-unix /tmp/.ICE-unix.
INIT: Entering runlevel: 2
[info] Using makefile-style concurrent boot in runlevel 2.
[ ok ] Network Interface Plugging Daemon...skip eth0...done.
[ ok ] Regenerating ssh host keys (in background):.
[info] Initializing cgroups.
[warn] Kernel lacks cgroups or memory controller not available, not starting cgroups. ... (warning).
[ ok ] Starting enhanced syslogd: rsyslogd.
Starting dphys-swapfile swapfile setup ...
want /var/swap=100MByte, generating swapfile ... of 100MBytes
done.
[ ok ] Starting NTP server: ntpd.
[ ok ] Starting periodic command scheduler: cron.
[ ok ] Starting system message bus: dbus.
[ ok ] Starting Avahi mDNS/DNS-SD Daemon: avahi-daemon.
[....] Applying config from /boot/os_config.json (if it exists):Setting flavour to Raspbian based on os_config.json from NOOBS. May take a while
Unrecognised flavour. Ignoring
update-rc.d: using dependency based boot sequencing
. ok
dhcpcd[2085]: version 6.7.1 starting
dhcpcd[2085]: all: IPv6 kernel autoconf disabled
dhcpcd[2085]: eth0: adding address fe80::6114:9e0f:9ed8:f064
dhcpcd[2085]: if_addaddress6: Operation not supported
dhcpcd[2085]: DUID 00:01:00:01:1c:dd:60:60:b8:27:eb:2c:ef:82
dhcpcd[2085]: eth0: IAID eb:2c:ef:82
dhcpcd[2085]: eth0: soliciting a DHCP lease
```

Figure 1-24. *Finally Raspbian is booting!*

Configuring Your Pi

After the torrent of incomprehensible text (though we're sure it means something to someone) you should end up at the configuration shown in Figure 1-25. This is where we'll configure your Pi for general use so that next time you turn it on, you will be greeted with a nice desktop rather than some chunky text.

We are only going to cover the basic configuration options here (and you can always go back and change them once you've got your Pi up and running) as we want to get you in front of a working computer as soon as possible.

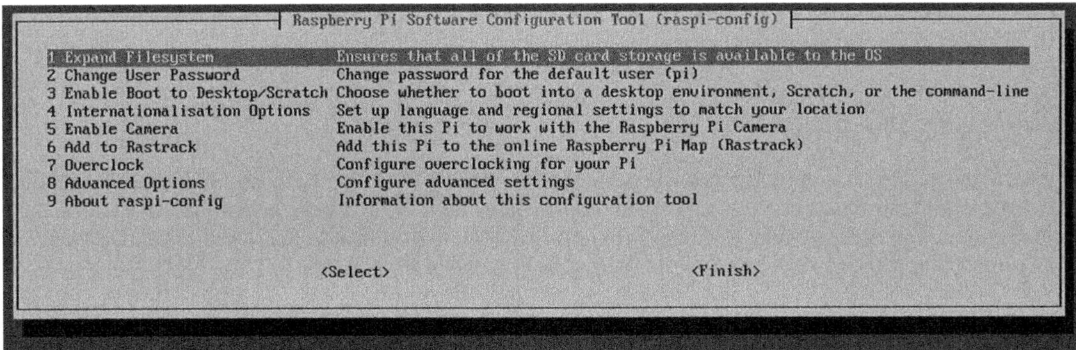

Figure 1-25. *First boot: time to configure your Pi!*

Expanding the Filesystem

The first option of interest is "Expand Filesystem". When you install Raspbian directly from a disk image, it only takes up a small amount of space. The developers don't know how big your SD card is, and no one wants to download a 16GB or larger image just so they can take full advantage of the space on their card. To deal with this, Raspbian supports expanding the disk once it has been installed, allowing the full amount of space to be used. However, this is something NOOBS already takes care of for you, so if you do try this option you're likely to see this message (Figure 1-26):

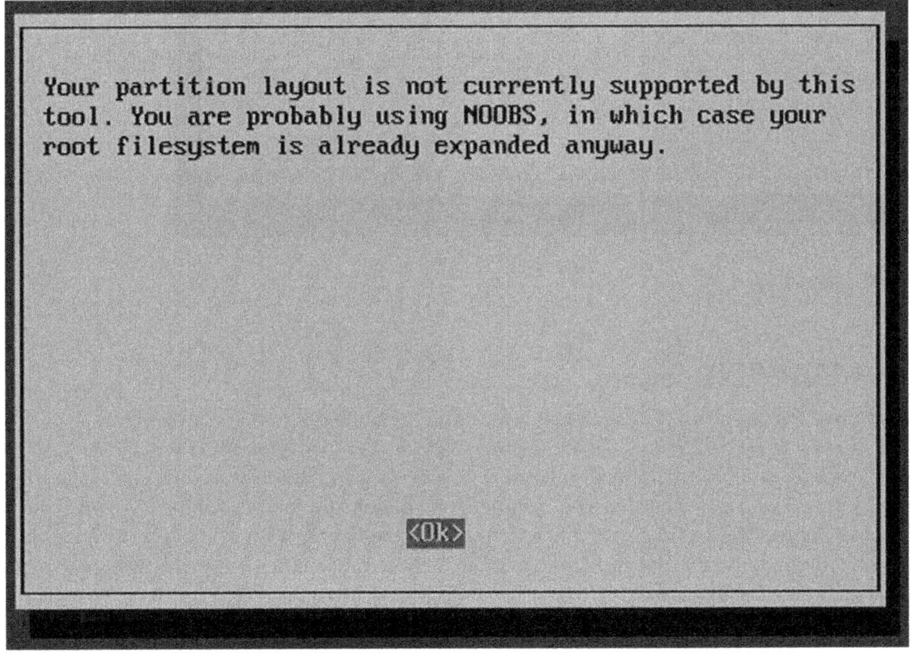

Figure 1-26. *The filesystem is already expanded if you used NOOBS*

The reason we're mentioning it here is that at some point you might decide to install directly from an image, and if you do, you definitely want to use this option!

Booting to Desktop

The next option allows us to configure what mode the Pi will boot in. In the next chapter we'll be taking you on a brief tour of the desktop and for most of the topics in the book we make the assumption that you're actually sat in front of the Pi. With that in mind we want to boot to the desktop. So, select this option and then from the list on the next page select "Desktop Log in as the user 'pi'" (Figure 1-27):

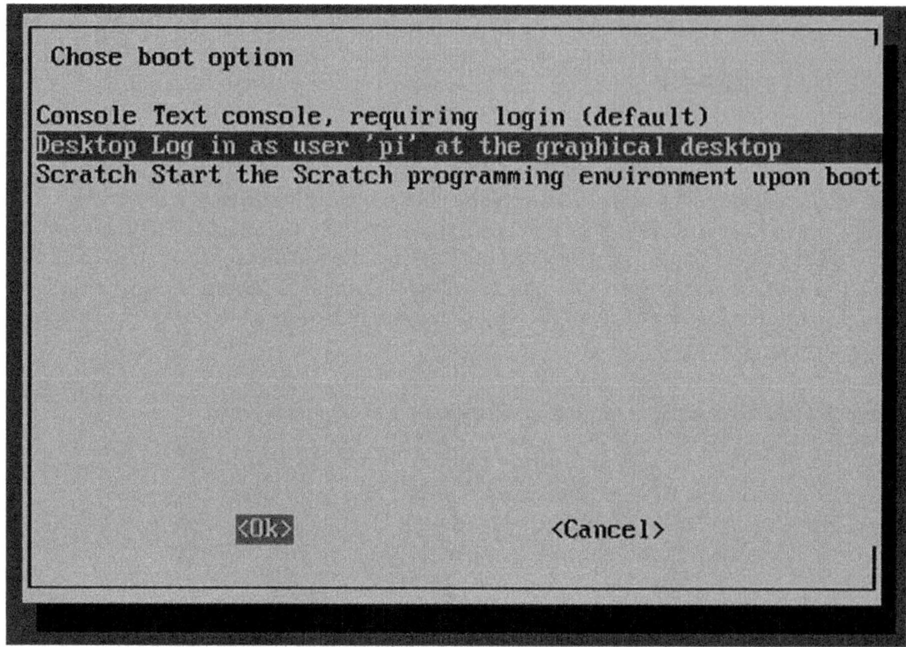

Figure 1-27. *Boot to the desktop*

Changing User Password

Next we're going to change the password for the `pi` user account. This is the account you'll be using throughout the book, and for most people this will be the only account you'll ever need on your Pi. At the moment though the password is set to `raspberry` and as it is the default, it means that anyone can log in to your Pi. While securing your Pi against unauthorized intruders is probably not top of your list of priorities, it is still good practice to change this just in case. Later on, you might make your Pi available via the Internet and in your excitement you might forget that you didn't actually get around to changing the password. Bad things will happen. So let's take the opportunity to make the switch now. Highlight "`Change User Password`" and press Enter, and you'll see something like Figure 1-28.

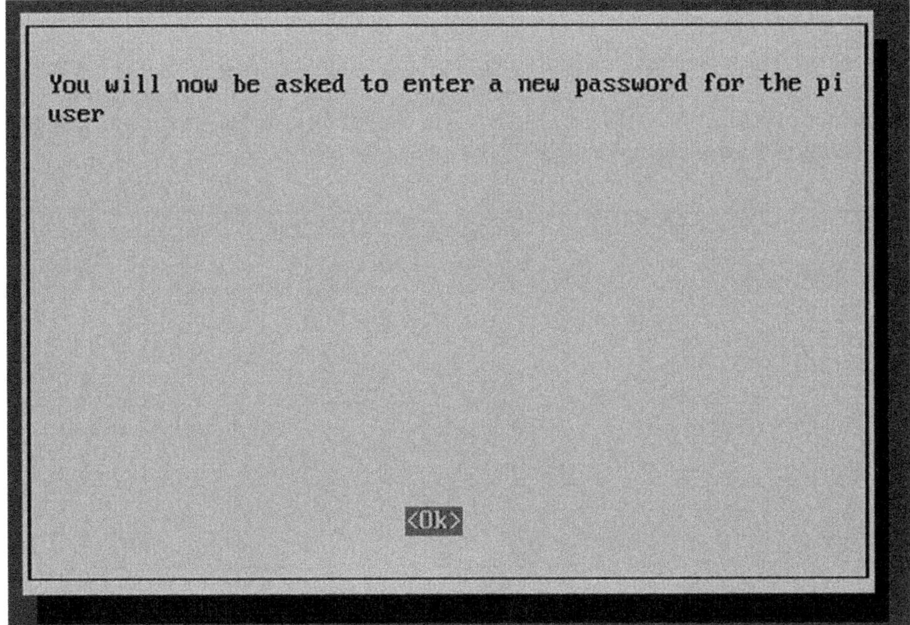

Figure 1-28. *Changing your password*

The configuration tool will execute the standard `passwd` command when you press enter, which is why you're looking at a text prompt rather than a prettier menu. Just enter your new password (remember that it is case-sensitive: *HeLLo* is not the same as *hello* or *Hello*) and press Enter. For security reasons, the password won't be shown on the display and it won't show any stars to let you know you've actually typed something. You will then get prompted to enter your password again (Figure 1-29); after you press Enter, and you will get the acknowledgement shown in Figure 1-30. Press Enter again and you'll be back at the main menu.

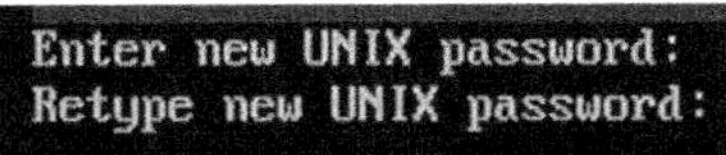

Figure 1-29. *Enter your password*

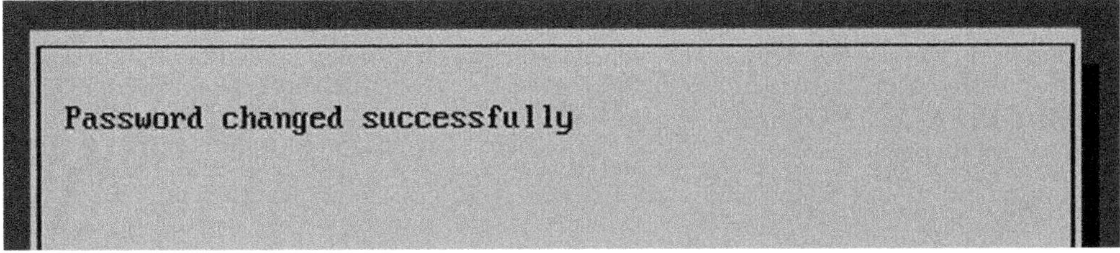

Figure 1-30. *Password changed successfully*

Setting some International Options

One of the nice things about Linux is that it has really good support for internationalization and makes it (relatively) easy to customize your install to match your requirements. There are a number of items that we can configure as you can see in Figure 1-31. As you set each option, you will be taken back to the main menu, so to change the next setting, just select the internationalization menu again:

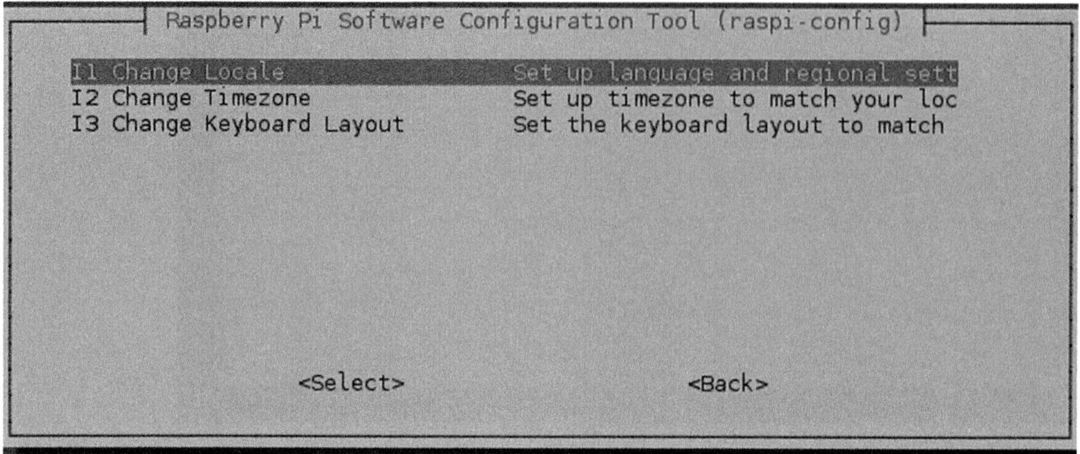

Figure 1-31. *International Settings menu*

First up is configuring your locale. By telling Linux where you are in the world, it can determine useful things such as the separator between numbers and which currency symbol to use. For example, in the United States we might write 1,000.00, but in many places in Europe it would be written as 1.000,00. Either way for maximum comfort and to ensure that everything just looks right, we need to set the locale. Highlight the "Change Locale" option and press Enter.

You'll now be presented with an extensive list of different locales to choose from (see Figure 1-32). The first two letters in the name specify the language while the second pair of letters specifies a regional difference. For example, en_US would be English customized for US users but en_GB would have settings specific to English speakers in the UK. You should select the language and country pairs that most closely match your needs and choose them by pressing the spacebar. You probably want both the ISO-8859 and the UTF-8 versions. If you decide to hedge your bets and select all locales, be warned that you will be in for quite a wait as the Pi generates all the locale settings for you. In fact, we tried this option and after waiting ages for just two locales to be generated, we got fed up and pulled the plug. After you select the locales you want, press the Tab key once to highlight the OK button and then press Enter to move to the next screen (after the locales have been generated see Figure 1-33). Here you'll need to pick the locale you want to use by default (see Figure 1-30). Once you have made your choice, highlight it and press Enter. You'll then see the locale generation process (see Figure 1-34) and after that has completed (it really can take a while) we're once again back at the main configuration page.

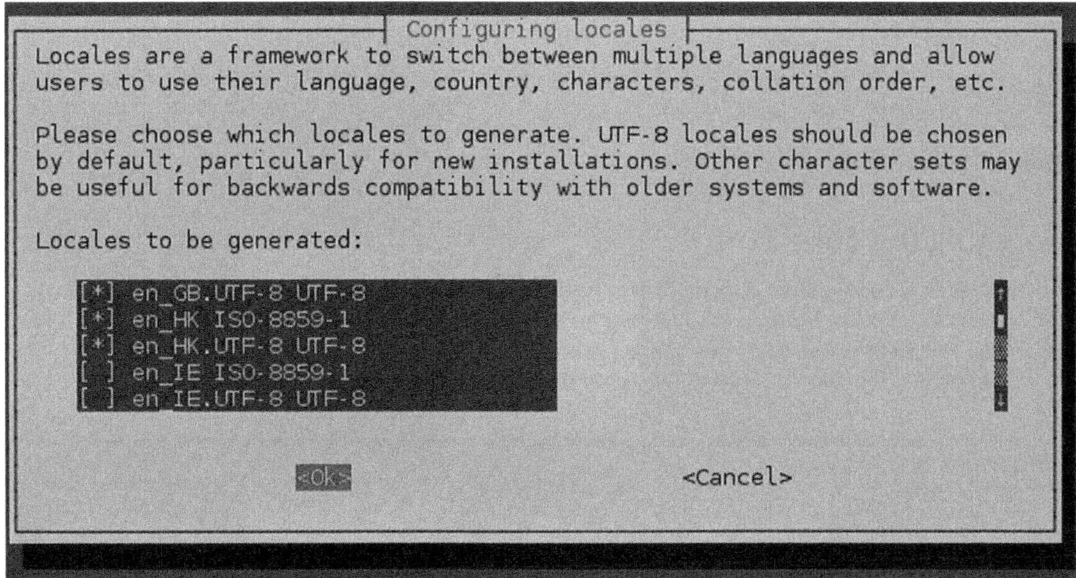

Figure 1-32. *Picking your locale*

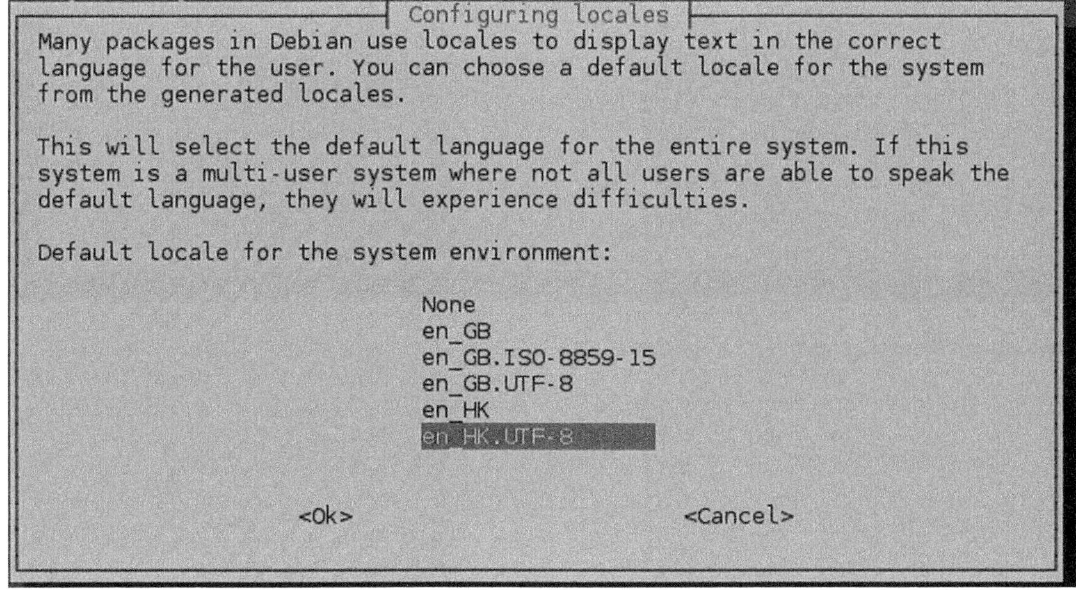

Figure 1-33. *Select the default language*

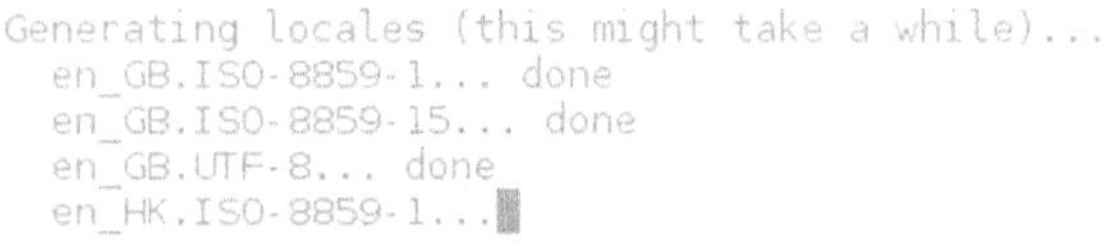

```
Generating locales (this might take a while)...
  en_GB.ISO-8859-1... done
  en_GB.ISO-8859-15... done
  en_GB.UTF-8... done
  en_HK.ISO-8859-1...
```

Figure 1-34. *Generating locales*

Changing the Time Zone

The "Change Timezone" option does pretty much what it says. After selecting this option, you'll be shown a list of regions (shown in Figure 1-35). In this case, we were configuring Pete's Pi, so we selected Asia. The next screen will give you a chance to fine-tune your selection and pick your country or city (see Figure 1-36). Once you've found the closest match to you, select the option and press Enter.

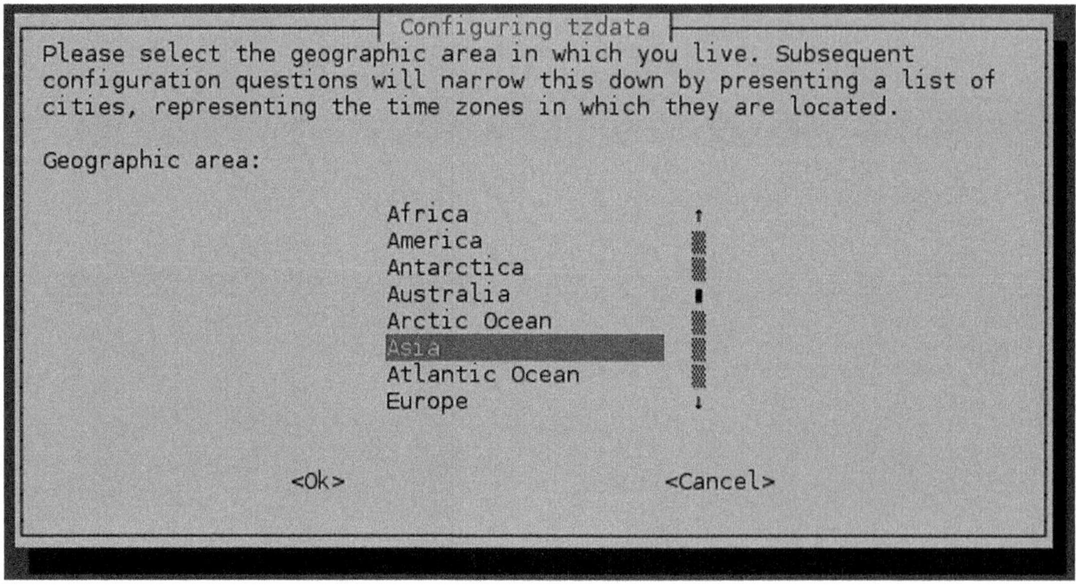

Figure 1-35. *Pick your region*

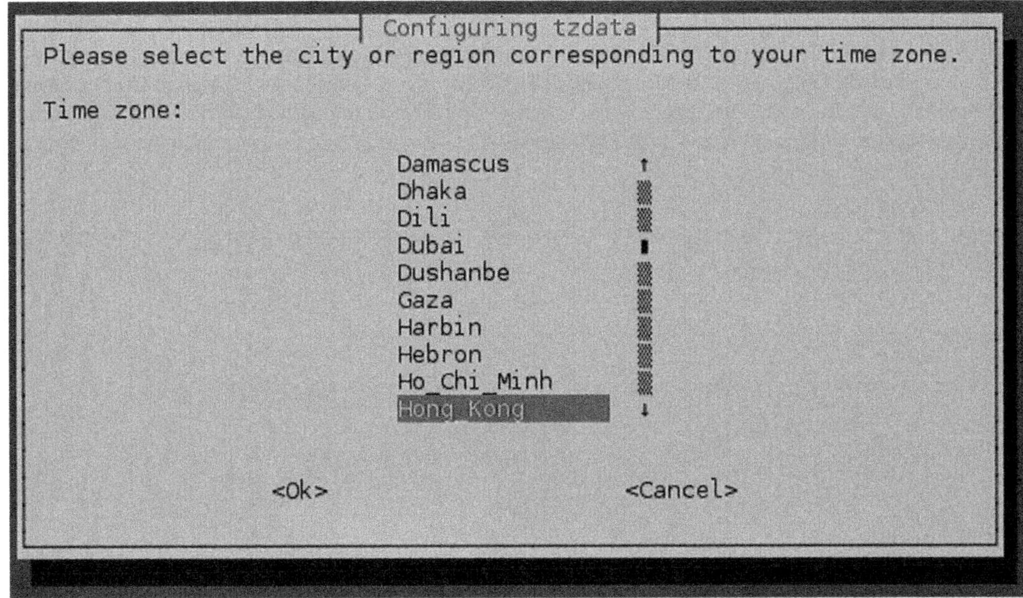

Figure 1-36. *Pick your closest city*

Configuring the Keyboard

The next option of interest is "`Configure Keyboard`". By default, Raspbian assumes a UK keymap, but chances are you will want something else. Be warned, though, that Raspbian knows a huge number of keyboards, and the sheer quantity can be confusing. For instance, do you know if you have a generic 104 key keyboard or is it actually a 105 key version? We weren't sure either, so we stuck with the default: the Generic 104 key PC shown in Figure 1-37.

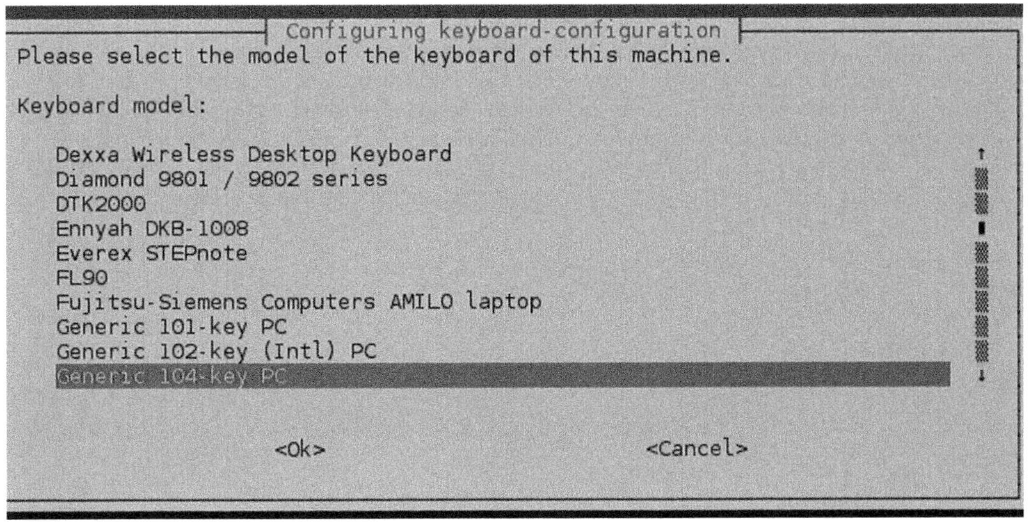

Figure 1-37. *Choosing your keyboard type*

If you can find your exact model, by all means feel free to select it. If you aren't sure, you're probably best off following our lead and sticking to the default. Once you have settled on your keyboard of choice, press Enter to move through to the next screen.Now we get to choose which keymap we want to use. By default, it lists various UK keymaps (as shown in Figure 1-38), but if you aren't lucky enough to own a British keyboard, move the bar down to Other, press Enter, and then scroll through the list to find something more suitable for your needs. Once you've found the right keyboard, again just press Enter to move on to the next screen.

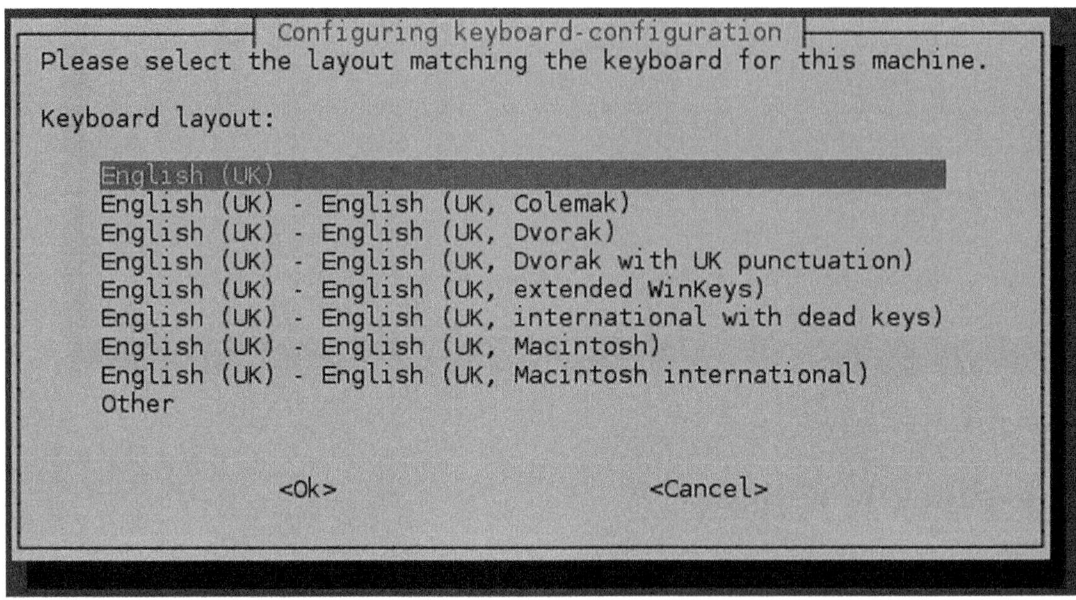

Figure 1-38. *Choose your layoutIf you're not sure what to select from the menu (shown in Figure 1-39), you're not alone*

For most people, the keyboard defaults will be fine because they will include any special key combinations that your particular keymap already offers. This is one of those times when if you need to make a change, you probably already know why and what to choose. If you are in any doubt, just leave the default selected and press Enter. Now you will see another menu that looks suspiciously like its predecessor (shown in Figure 1-40), at least in terms of knowing what to pick. Again you probably already know if you need to change anything here; if you're not sure, you should just select the default by pressing Enter.

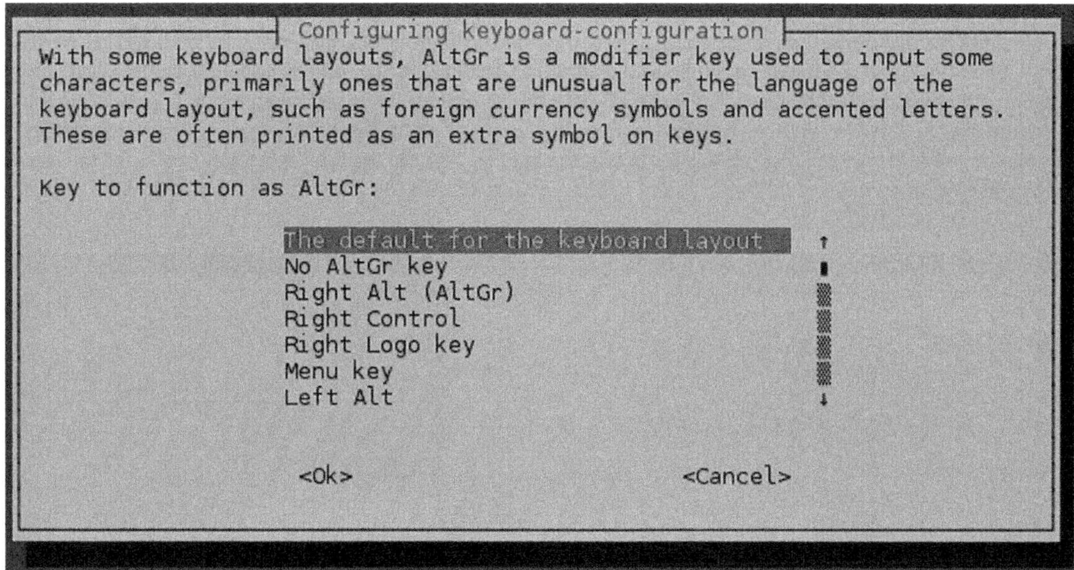

Figure 1-39. *Customize your keyboard configuration*

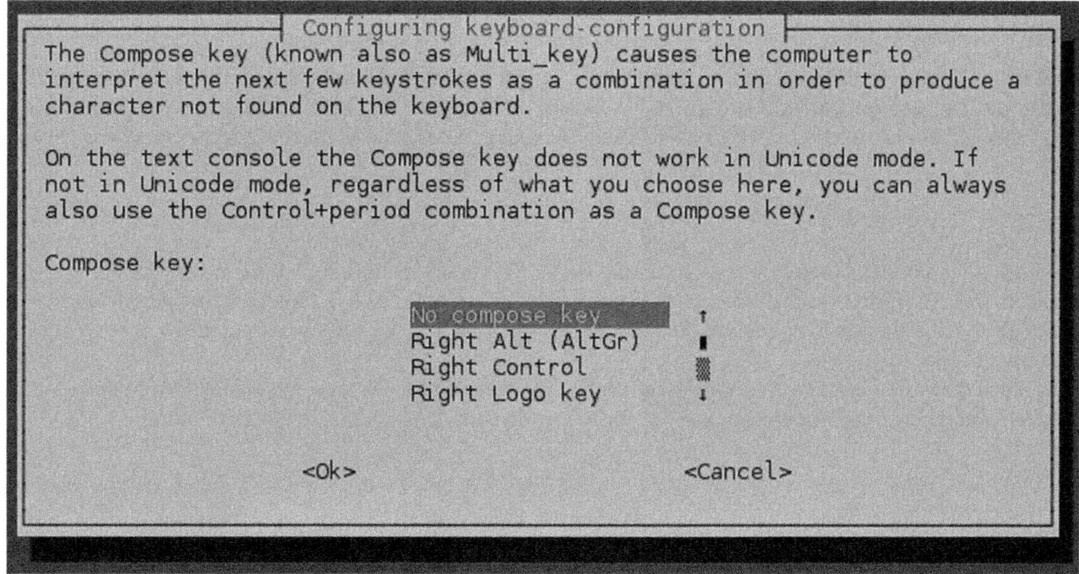

Figure 1-40. *Customize your keyboard some more*

The next menu (shown in Figure 1-41) only really means anything to old-school Linux users. Back in the day, if your GUI decided to crap out on you, you could effectively "reboot" the session by holding down Ctrl + Alt + backspace. As the GUI has become more stable, and Linux has become more mainstream, this feature is more often than not disabled. We haven't had to make use of it for years, although we do happen to think it is quite useful. The default is No, and this is probably what you want. You can always go back and change this later if you find yourself craving this particular feature. To pick the default (and finally return to the main menu), just press Enter.

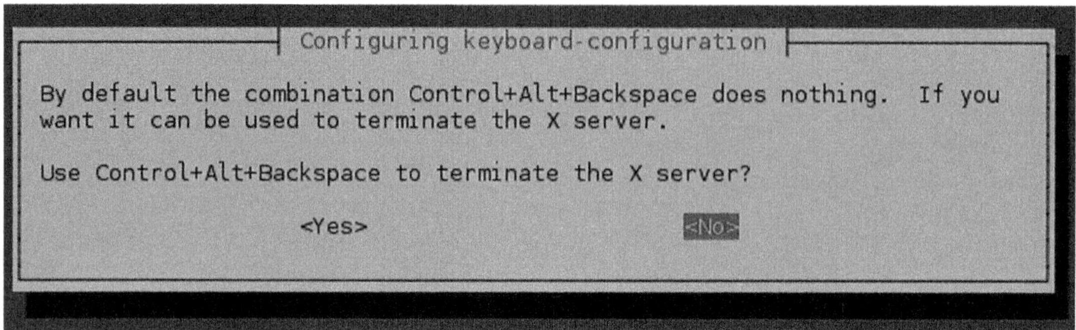

Figure 1-41. *Do you want to enable the X server kill switch?*

Enable Camera

This menu lets you enable the camera. This specifically refers to the camera provided by the Pi Foundation and doesn't affect other cameras such as USB webcams. This is set to Disable by default but you can Enable it here if you happen to have one. We haven't included a screenshot here as there really isn't anything to see.

Add to Rastrack

Rastrack is an unofficial project that asks for voluntary registrations to help see where the Pi's are being used around the world. As the blurb says in Figure 1-42, this is just for a bit of fun, but many people don't particularly want their Pi to be tracked. Fortunately Rastrack is opt-in so you can completely ignore it unless you want to take part.

If you do want to take part, simply follow the simple screens that ask for some details. Once you've entered everything, they will be submitted to Rastrack and you'll be returned to the main menu.

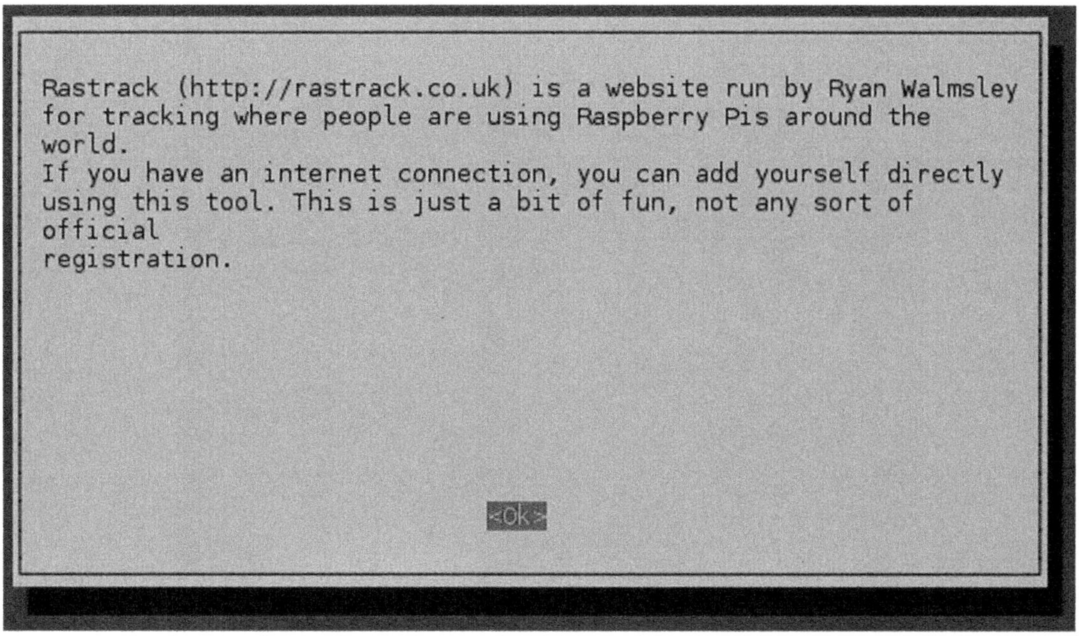

```
Rastrack (http://rastrack.co.uk) is a website run by Ryan Walmsley
for tracking where people are using Raspberry Pis around the
world.
If you have an internet connection, you can add yourself directly
using this tool. This is just a bit of fun, not any sort of
official
registration.

                              <Ok>
```

Figure 1-42. *Register on Rastrack*

Overclock

Enthusiasts have long enjoyed overclocking their CPUs, that is, making them run faster and hotter than they were designed for. The Pi supports this too and many people consider it perfectly safe. However we recommend against it as if the Pi isn't fast enough for what you need out of the box, then you probably shouldn't be using a Pi to do whatever it is that you're doing.

If on the other hand you really really want to make your Pi go faster, you can select one of the speeds from this menu (Figure 1-43):

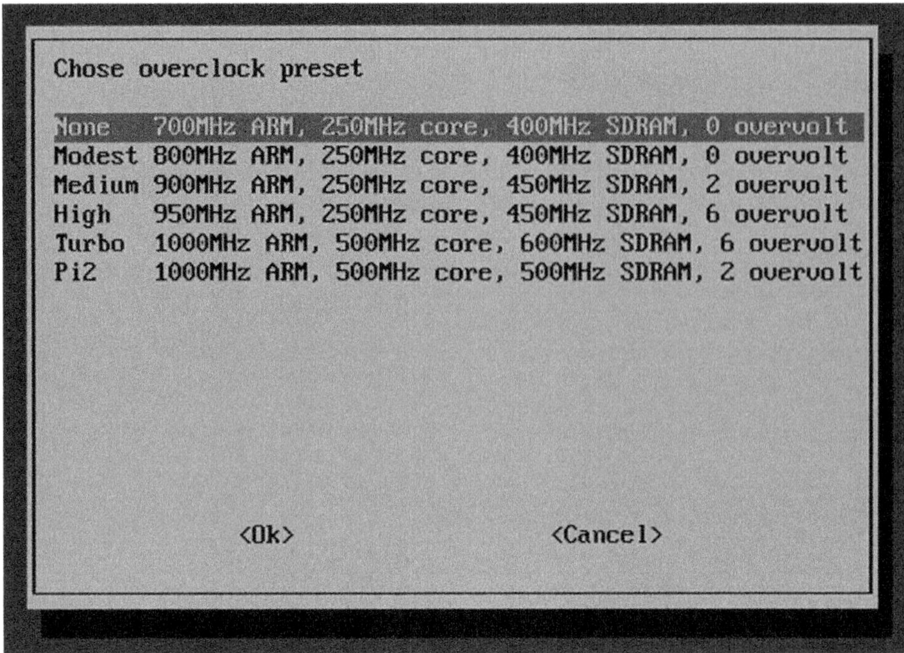

Figure 1-43. *How fast would you like to go?*

Advanced features

We're not going to go through each of these menu items and for many if not most people, the majority of these items will never be used. The only one of interest to us is the memory split. For reference here's what the menu looks like (Figure 1-44):

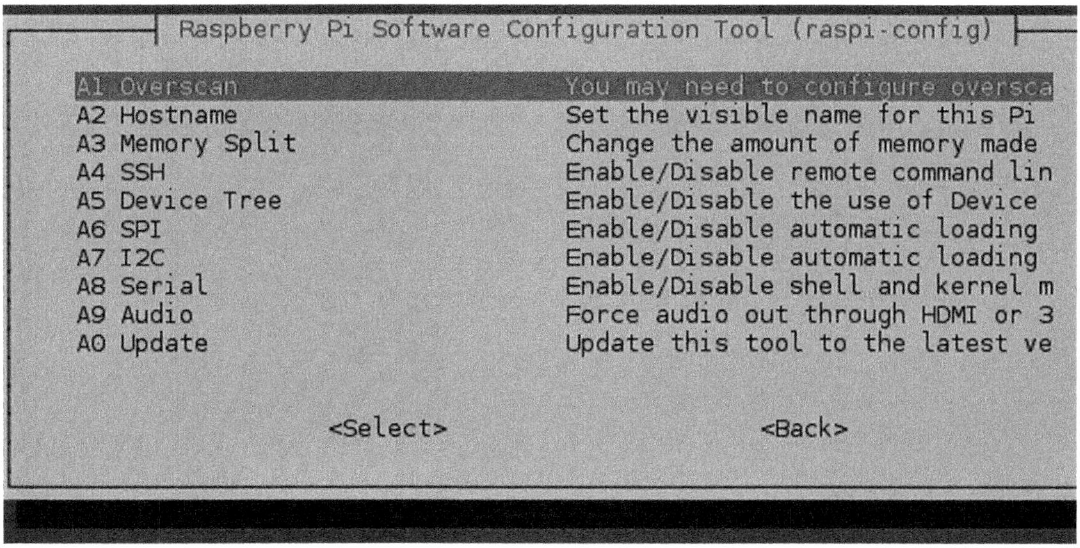

```
Raspberry Pi Software Configuration Tool (raspi-config)

A1 Overscan                          You may need to configure oversca
A2 Hostname                          Set the visible name for this Pi
A3 Memory Split                      Change the amount of memory made
A4 SSH                               Enable/Disable remote command lin
A5 Device Tree                       Enable/Disable the use of Device
A6 SPI                               Enable/Disable automatic loading
A7 I2C                               Enable/Disable automatic loading
A8 Serial                            Enable/Disable shell and kernel m
A9 Audio                             Force audio out through HDMI or 3
A0 Update                            Update this tool to the latest ve

              <Select>                          <Back>
```

Figure 1-44. *Advanced options*

Allocating Memory

The "Memory Split" option needs a bit of explanation. Your Pi has two main processors: the CPU (or central processing unit) and the GPU (or graphics processing unit). The CPU is responsible for the general running of your machine, and the GPU is responsible for handling the display and provides features such as 2D and 3D acceleration as well as hardware support for decoding high-quality video streams. A GPU is dedicated to handling graphics (for the most part) and cannot perform the role of a CPU. However, it does mean that if the CPU can offload all the complex graphics work to the GPU, the CPU doesn't have to be quite so powerful. By having both, the Pi keeps the costs and power requirements nice and low but without sacrificing much in the way of performance.

So far so good; but what does that have to do with splitting memory? The Pi 2 comes with 1GB of RAM in total and it needs to supply both the CPU and GPU. As the GPU is effectively an independent unit, it needs its own allocation of memory. Rather than having dedicated memory for both, it is possible to split the 1GB between the two processors. By default, the Pi allocates only a small amount for the GPU. This is ideal if you want to use the Pi as a server or you never plan to attach a display to your Pi. If you're not using graphics, allocating additional memory to the GPU is somewhat pointless.

On the other hand, if you plan to use your Pi as a mini desktop computer or to display high-quality movies, you're going to want as much memory allocated to the GPU as you can get away with (which in the case of the Pi 2 means allocating 256MB for the GPU). It would be difficult to anticipate how everyone will want to use their Pi, and apart from adding more memory to the Pi itself (and raising the cost) there is no easy solution. Fortunately, we have the ability to choose how we want to allocate the memory ourselves.

For general usage and "getting started"—type tasks, we recommend you allocate 64MB to the GPU. To set this up, select the `memory_split` option from the menu, press Enter, and you'll have something similar to Figure 1-45. Type in the memory split that you want and then press Tab to highlight the OK button and then press Enter.

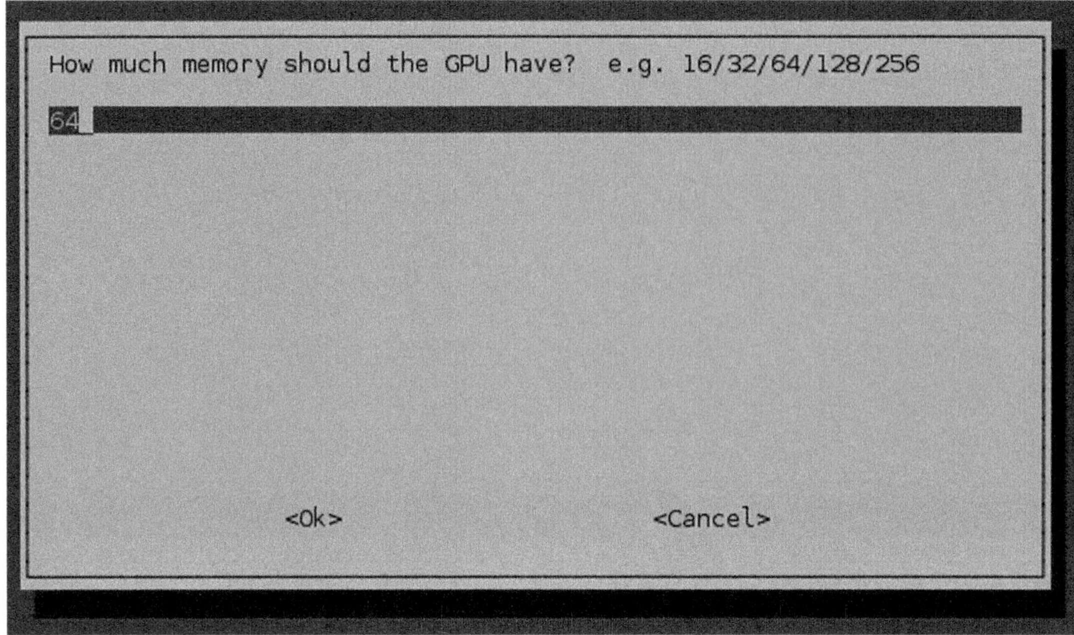

Figure 1-45. *Choose your memory split*

At Last! It's Configured!

Wow, we finally made it to the end! After all that effort, you can now reboot the Pi and (finally) start using it! Press the Tab key twice to highlight the Finish button and press Enter. Your Pi should shut down and then reboot. After all that effort (and a bit more waiting while the Pi boots up), you should finally be at a pretty graphical display that should look something like Figure 1-46.

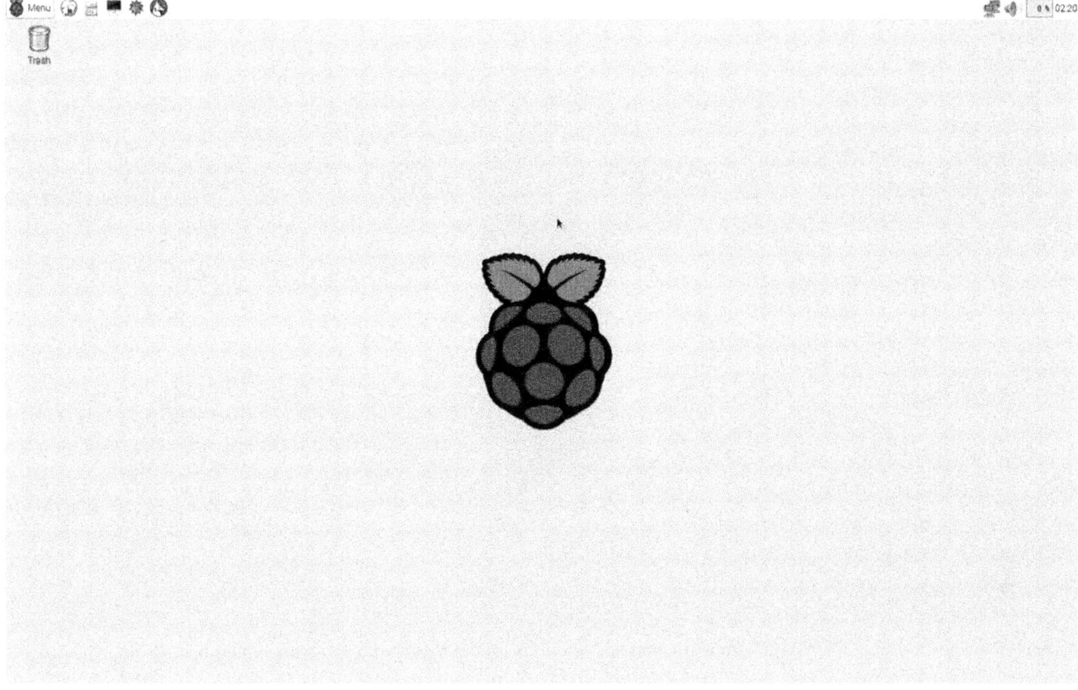

Figure 1-46. *At long last, we have a desktop!Congratulations!*

You now have a fully functional Raspberry Pi! If you don't end up with a pretty desktop, you might need to tweak your configuration a little. At the login prompt, you can log in with the username `pi` and the password you set during the install. If you then run the following you will be able to change the settings ("`Boot behaviour`" is the option you want to change):

```
$ sudo raspi-config
```

You can also try starting the graphical interface manually with this:

```
$ startx
```

Summary

This chapter has taken you from getting your hands on your Pi all the way through getting it up and running. We deliberately took it slow and covered all the basics as it's always the so-called simple things that trip people up (us included!). We looked at what comes in the box (and more importantly what doesn't) and provided a shopping list of all the things you'll need to bake your Pi.

We then touched briefly on Linux—what makes a distribution and why we decided to stick with Raspbian for this book. We then covered how to download NOOBS and get it on your SD card.

Armed with a fully loaded card, we fired up the Pi and walked through the initial setup and configuration process that ultimately ended with us looking at the very pretty Raspberry Pi logo in the middle of an equally impressive desktop.

In the next chapter, we'll start to explore your new desktop. We give you a quick tour of what comes with Raspbian out of the box, and we finish up by showing you how you can tweak and customize it to suit your needs.

CHAPTER 2

Surveying the Landscape

Although the majority of this book focuses on getting you comfortable on the command line and really getting your hands dirty with Linux, we would be completely amiss if we didn't first show you how to use the graphical interface that comes with your Pi. It's not quite as flashy as what you might find on a PC or a Mac, but it's fast, easy to use and will let you do all the things you're used to doing. And of course, it's all on a device that fits in your pocket and draws less power than the monitor or TV it's connected to.

We start off this chapter by looking around the desktop and seeing what interesting things we have to play with. Some are obviously useful applications in their own right and some are probably less useful at this stage (for example the Python development environment won't be of much interest to you unless you're programming in Python). We'll then trundle through the various menus and have a look at what we find.

Welcome to LXDE

Unlike Windows, Linux isn't integrated with a particular GUI and instead uses a separate application (a client and a server in this case) to provide one. This application is known as the X-server and it used to be by far the most complicated fiddly thing in the Linux universe to set up. It has gotten a lot better but not too long ago, great time and effort needed to be spent if you wanted to use the scroll wheel in that new fangled mouse of yours. Needless to say the fun of that wears out pretty quickly. These days the X-server is almost a black box and very rarely do you need to actually touch it. For that reason we're not going to go into any more depth on that subject in this book, but if you are a bit curious to find out more, check out: `http://en.wikipedia.org/wiki/X_Window_System`.

The X-server provides the framework for using a GUI but it doesn't actually provide the pretty desktops that we're used to seeing. These are provided by desktop environments. Again, we're not going to cover how these all work, but suffice it to say, like everything else in the Linux world, you have a choice as to which one you prefer. For most people it comes down to which one comes with their Linux distribution of choice although most distributions offer a selection. The more advanced ones have all sorts of features and special effects and understandably consume a fair amount of resources whilst they're at it. On the latest and greatest desktop or laptop, this is hardly a problem and most people jump at the chance to make their expensive machine actually do some work. However it does become something of a problem when you're running a less than high spec machine such as the Pi.

It's not just the Pi that can struggle - computers of just a few years ago are easily able to run Linux, but could struggle with the new highly graphical interfaces. When you consider even older machines that would often get thrown out, with a suitable display manager they could easily manifest as a perfectly useful PC. There's still more to it though - modern day netbooks are low powered by design with the aim being high efficiency for battery consumption as well as cost. They also benefit from a minimalist design when it comes to the desktop.

When you need to stretch your processing budget the best place to cut corners is in the feature set of the graphical interface. Do you really need all those fancy features? Are transparent windows essential to what you're doing? Do you really need that 3D rendered clock? If not and you want to cut some fat, a desktop environment like LXDE will be right up your street.

LXDE (short for Lightweight X11 Desktop Environment) was designed for machines where energy efficiency and the need to run on hardware at the lower end of the performance spectrum was of critical importance. It aims to be efficient in terms of CPU cycles and memory usage and although some window managers eskew all unnecessary features, LXDE tries to remain featureful at the same time.

Although we now know that the GUI is made up of a lot of moving parts, this is mostly transparent when using it. Really there is no harm in thinking of LXDE as the main environment for your Pi and if you plan to spend most of your time using the GUI, then we feel there's no harm in considering it a core part of the operating system. You can simply just use it and accept it as being available. With that in mind, let's move on to exploring what we actually have when we are using LXDE.

What do we have here?

Once you've installed and setup your Pi and you've powered it up for the first time, you should be left with a screen that looks like Figure 2-1.

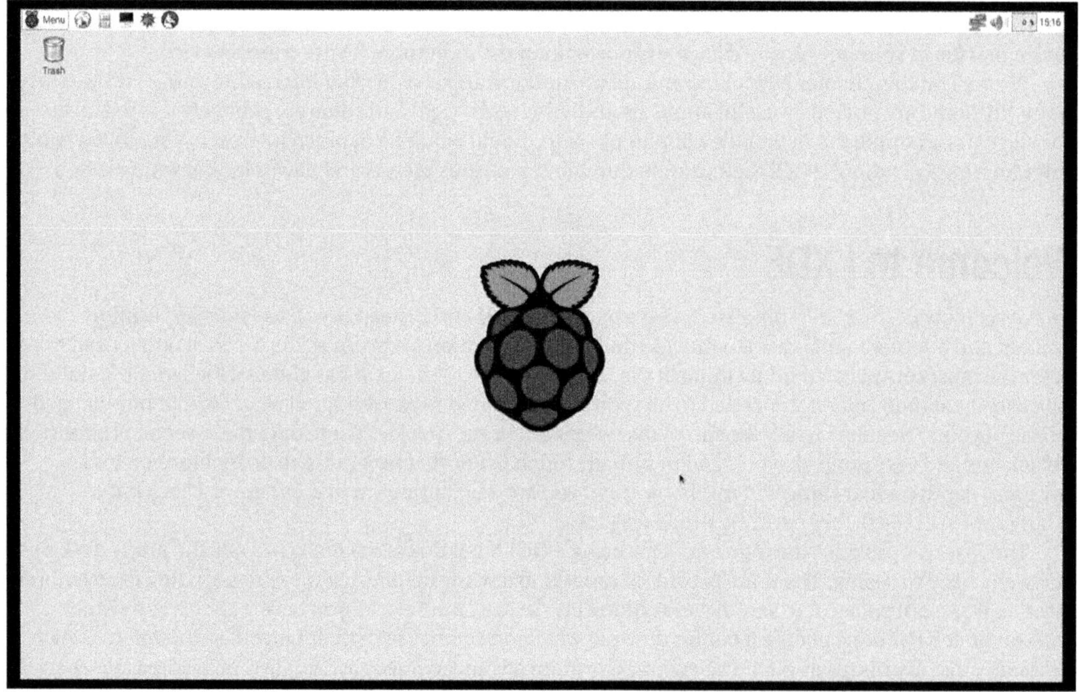

***Figure 2-1.** First boot of your Pi*

How the icons are laid out really depends on the screen you connected to your Pi. It should be pretty similar though with probably the only real difference being how the desktop icons themselves are laid out.

There are some key areas here that are hard to see in one large screenshot so we're going to break each part down individually. For simplicity (not to mention the fact that they have become common idioms) we'll refer to various GUI elements by the name most people are familiar with. Thus we are going to be talking about the start menu and task bar. Let's start with the bottom left of the screen, as shown in Figure 2-2.

Figure 2-2. *Start button and friends*

The Start Menu and Top Left of the Taskbar

The first button on the top left is actually the Pi logo and acts as the start button. The next button starts the default web browser which in the case of the Pi happens to be Epiphany. Like the other apps, you'll find that most of the applications are designed to be lightweight and efficient. The next button will start up PCManFM, the LXDE file manager. This is the tool you reach for when you need to move some files about or do some general tidying.

So far so good. None of these applications are really that different from what you're probably used to doing on your main computer. The next one is a bit different though. This is the button for starting LXTerminal, the best way to get to a command line on your Pi (at least from within the graphical interface).

The next two are especially interesting and are relatively new to the Pi (or at least they weren't around when we wrote the first book). The first is Mathematica, one of the most powerful computational packages around but you do need to know what you're doing. If you're into math and creating models (mathematical ones that is) you'll definitely want to check this out. The icon next to it starts up Wolfram which is the programming language used in Mathematica. This is similar to the command line in Linux in that it lets you get hands on with Mathematica's engine. This is a cool feature, but again, it's probably not something most people are going to be using.

Lastly we have the sole icon on the Desktop - the trash can. This doesn't need much explaining (unless you're coming from Windows 3.11 of course) and it works the way you expect it to.

And on the Right Hand Side...

After the task bar, we have some more icons as seen in Figure 2-3.

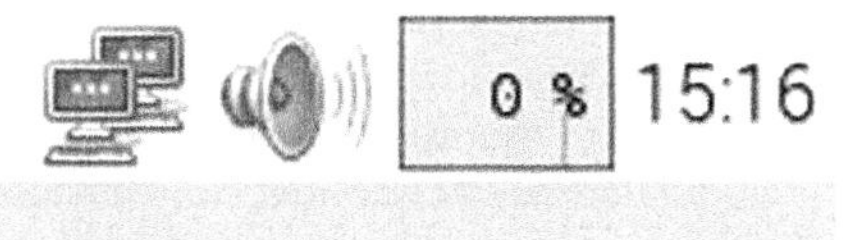

Figure 2-3. *The right hand side of the task bar*

The first one is a picture of two computers that represents your network. In this case we are using wired Ethernet and it's connected so we get this icon, but the icon can change (such as getting a cross on it if the cable is unplugged).

The next icon really needs no introduction. The speaker controls the volume of the sound on your Pi. Like most setups, you can also mute all the sound from here, but there's really nothing else interesting about this one.

The third icon appears to be just an empty box, but it actually acts as a CPU monitor. The more work you give your Pi, the fuller this box will become. It acts like a chart showing you how your CPU is being used over time. You can actually amuse yourself (at least for a few minutes) by rapidly moving your mouse pointer. The faster you move it, the more CPU that is used and the more you will fill the box. Fun and games aside though, this monitor is quite useful because if your Pi starts acting a bit sluggishly, a quick look at the monitor can tell you whether or not you are maxing out your CPU.

Next to the CPU monitor is the clock which doesn't really need much in the way of explanation. In earlier versions of the Pi, there was a shutdown button at the far end of this taskbar. That's a pretty useful feature, and you still get at it but you need to click the "Menu" button and then select "Shutdown" (it has a nice exit logo next to it). This will bring up the familiar shutdown screen (Figure 2-4):

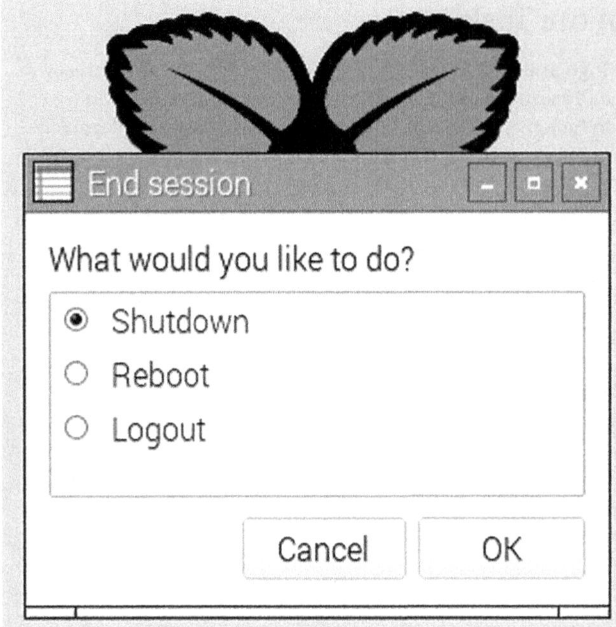

Figure 2-4. *Clicking the shut down button*

Clicking shut down will do pretty much what you expect as will reboot and logout. There is one thing that is worth remembering though, the Pi runs Linux which is a multi-user operating system. That means that things might be happening in the background that you're not aware of. For example someone might be streaming a video from your Pi. If you shut down or reboot, you will understandably disconnect anyone else who is connected to the Pi. Quite possibly this isn't an issue for you right now, but it is something that you probably should be aware of.

And that's pretty much it for what you have on your screen. Now, let's move on to the mysteries of the start menu...

The Start Menu

The start menu concept has become almost ubiquitous across most operating systems (notably not the Mac) since its introduction with Windows 95. Whilst various people might scoff at that and point to places where it might have been seen before or insist that the start menus in Linux are nothing like those found in Windows, we try to move beyond that. The fact is, the start menu concept works very well regardless who thought of it and there is a reason why it's been adopted so far and wide.

Enough of the soap box, let's see what our start menu has to offer us (Figure 2-5):

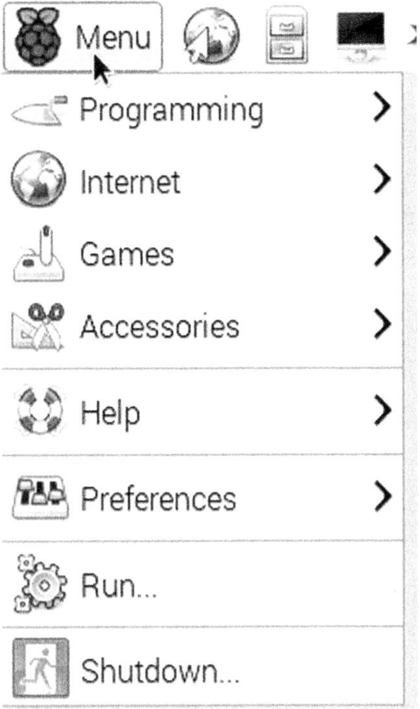

Figure 2-5. The Start Menu

As before, there's nothing really ground breaking here. The first section lists all of the applications that are available to us, all neatly grouped together. In this case, Programming, Internet, Games and Accessories with Help and Preferences bring up the rear. It's hard to decide which of these options we should delve into first. Before we can do that though, we need to wrap up the rest of the items which as there's only two left, shouldn't take us very long.

We've already covered Shutdown and it's fairly straight forward. We'll look at some of the settings (preferences) that you can tweak later on. The final item on our list is the run command. This lets us execute specific commands without the need to pick them from a menu, click an icon or open a terminal. Just like under Windows, this option can be a useful convenience. It also has auto-complete functionality (Figure 2-6):

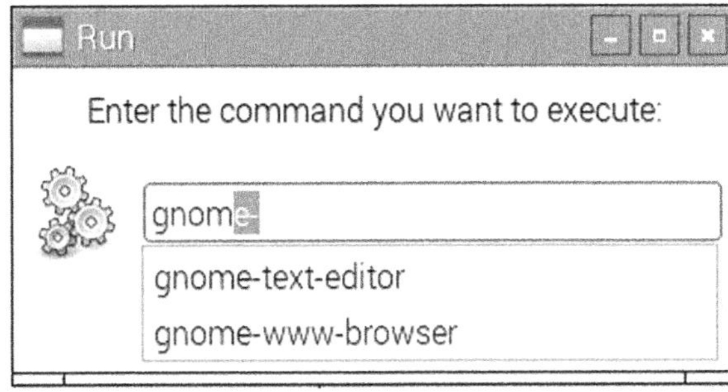

Figure 2-6. The run command and auto complete

Here you can see we typed in "gnom" and it has highlighted all the applications that match this pattern. This can save you a lot of time as over time you will get to know how many characters you need to type before the auto-complete kicks in with the right answer. Quite often command names (especially for GUI apps) can be pretty long and so this can be real time saver!

Accessories

Now let's take a look at what we have under accessories. Like all the other menus, the items here can change as you install more software, and on newer versions of Raspbian it might look a little different. On our Pi, the accessories menu looks like this (Figure 2-7):

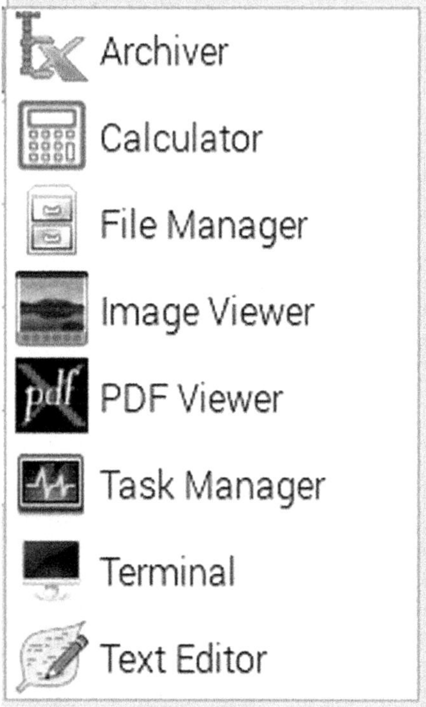

Figure 2-7. *The accessories menu*

XArchiver

XArchiver is less likely to be called directly than Image Viewer but nonetheless is probably an application that will get a fair bit of use on the average system. This tool allows you to create and decompress archives of various formats which is essential when you're downloading content from the Internet. XArchiver looks like this (Figure 2-8):

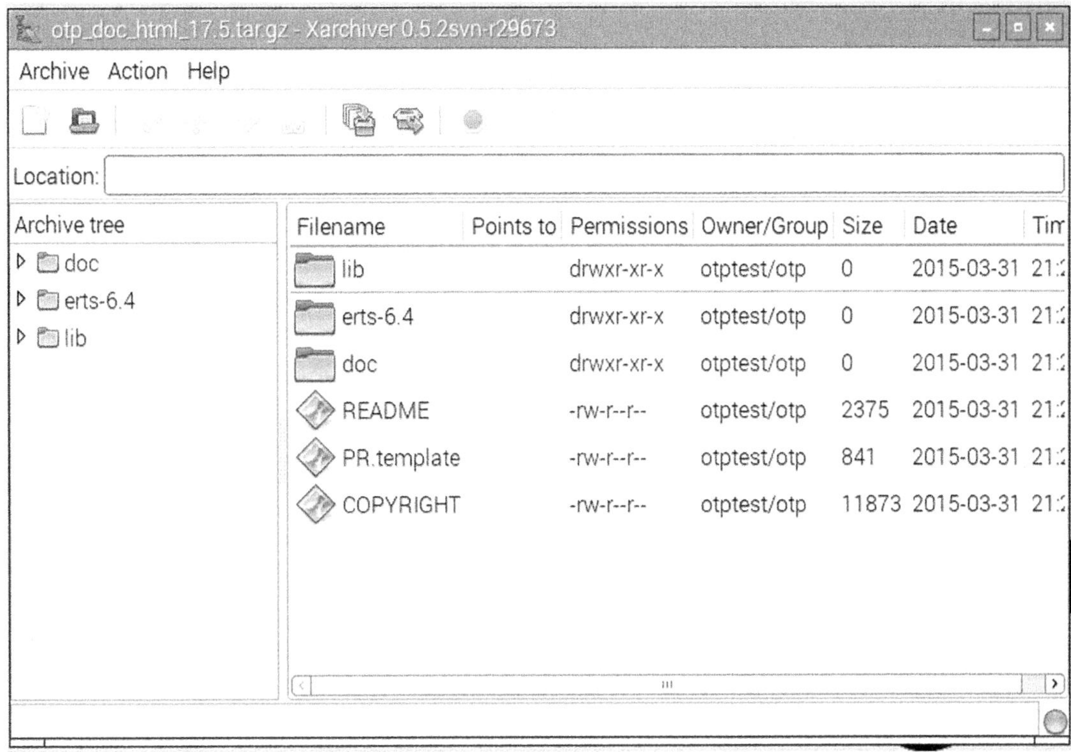

Figure 2-8. *XArchiver when it's opened by hand*

Here we downloaded the documentation to the Erlang platform (it was the first thing that popped into our heads when we needed something to demonstrate XArchiver). After double clicking on the file, XArchiver was opened automatically. The only button we've ever used so far is the extract all button which is the second in from the right. Clicking on this will extract all the contents of the archive which more often than not is what you actually want to do.

Calculator

It just wouldn't feel right if the Pi didn't ship with a calculator – after all it's pretty much the standard application on every computerized device. Does anyone remember calculator watches? We won't put a screenshot in for this one because, well, it looks like a calculator, but it will do the job just fine all the same.

File Manager

As touched on earlier, LXDE ships with the PCManFM file manager. Of course you can access it form the task bar so it's unlikely that you'll ever run it from here. Taking its lead from the minimalist design movement, this file manager is lightweight, simple and easy to use but still has all the features you're going to need. It works in a very similar way to Microsoft's Windows Explorer, so if you're coming from a Windows background you'll feel right at home with PCManFM. If not, you'll be able to pick it up easily with just a few moments of clicking about (Figure 2-9):

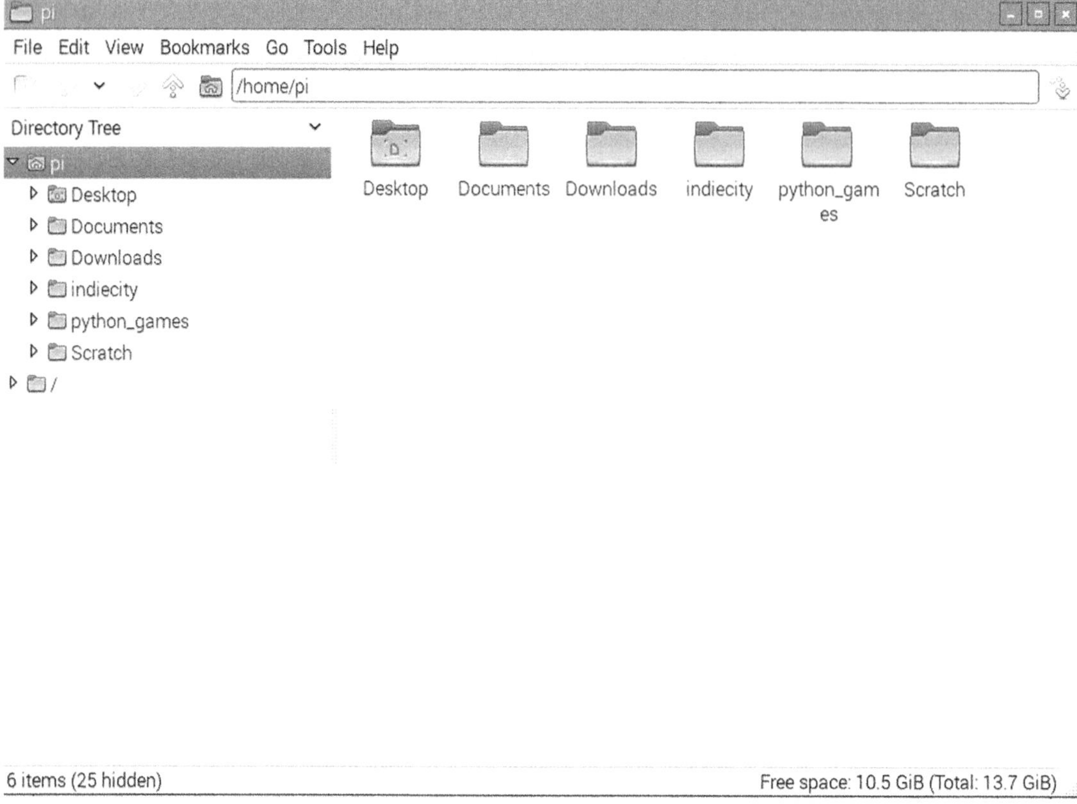

Figure 2-9. *The PCManFM File Manager*

When it initially opens, PCManFM will drop you into your home area. It will show you how much space you available on the bottom right (always useful in devices with relatively limited storage such as the Pi) and lists the most common places on the top left. For browsing you can simply click your way through the folders and you can use the navigation icons on the toolbar to help you move quickly through your files. If you're looking to get a bit more hands on, we cover how to manipulate files in Chapter 5.

Image Viewer

Image Viewer is one of those applications that you'll probably never open directly. You'll almost always open it by double clicking on an image file which by default will then open Image Viewer for you. Simple though it may be, Image Viewer is not lacking in features and has all the basic tools you've come to expect (Figure 2-10):

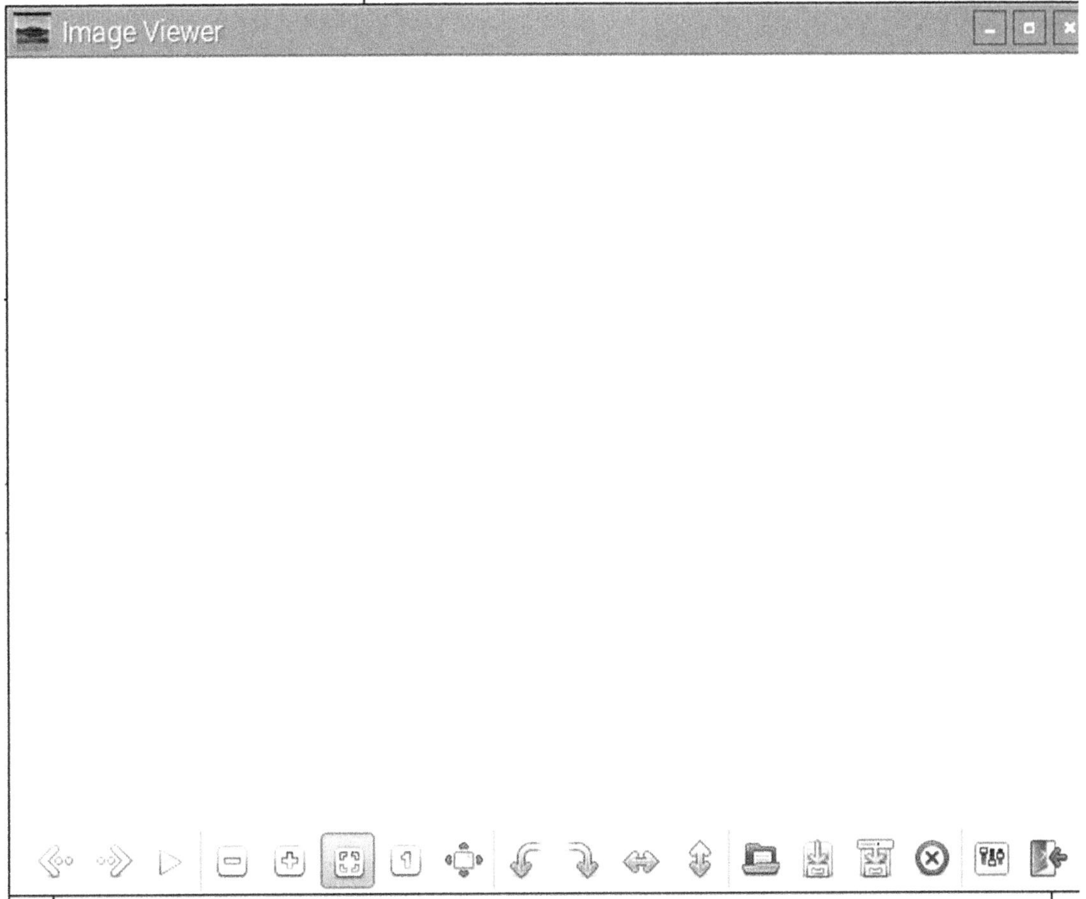

Figure 2-10. *Image Viewer's main interface*

The first two buttons let you move back and forth throughout a collection of images. This is actually surprisingly useful as these days, a lot of the time people are accesing albums rather than specific photos. To help with exactly that, there is also a slideshow feature that you can access by pressing on the play button.

The next section has controls for how you want to actually view the image. The first two are the traditional zoom controls. The third icon is for "fit to screen", the fourth is show at full size (which if it's a photo from a digital camera means you're almost certainly going to have to scroll) and lastly the full screen option to really take advantage of that 60 inch flat screen you just got your hands on.

In the third section are the controls for altering the image itself. The first two are rotate controls (rotate left and right respectively) and the second pair of controls allow you to flip the image horizontally and vertically. This is especially handy when you took the photo at an odd angle and don't fancy tilting your head at 90 degrees in order to see your picture the right way up.

The next set are file controls. They let you open, save, save as and delete the file respectively. The last two icons provide access to the preferences panel (nothing too interesting in there) and allow you to exit the program.

PDF Viewer

You're not likely to fire this application up manually, rather it will get opened when you double click on a PDF or try to view one in a web browser. There's not much to show in a screenshot (apart from a lot of grey where a document might be) so we've left it out, but if you've viewed a PDF before, you're not going to have any trouble here.

Task Manager

As you can see in Figure 2-11, the CPU is practically idle at the moment. Considering that it's running a full operating system (and an advanced one at that) it might be surprising to see that the CPU isn't doing any heavy lifting. Although compared to high-end Intel processors, the ARM chip in the Pi is far from impressive, this truly demonstrates that you can get a perfectly good desktop machine running with surprisingly little resources if you are careful. Our RAM usage tells a similar story. Admittedly we've not got much open at the moment (although you can see from the process list we have a VNC remote desktop session running) but we are still well under 50% usage and with the new Model B's packing 512MB of RAM, this will allow even more applications to run at the same time.

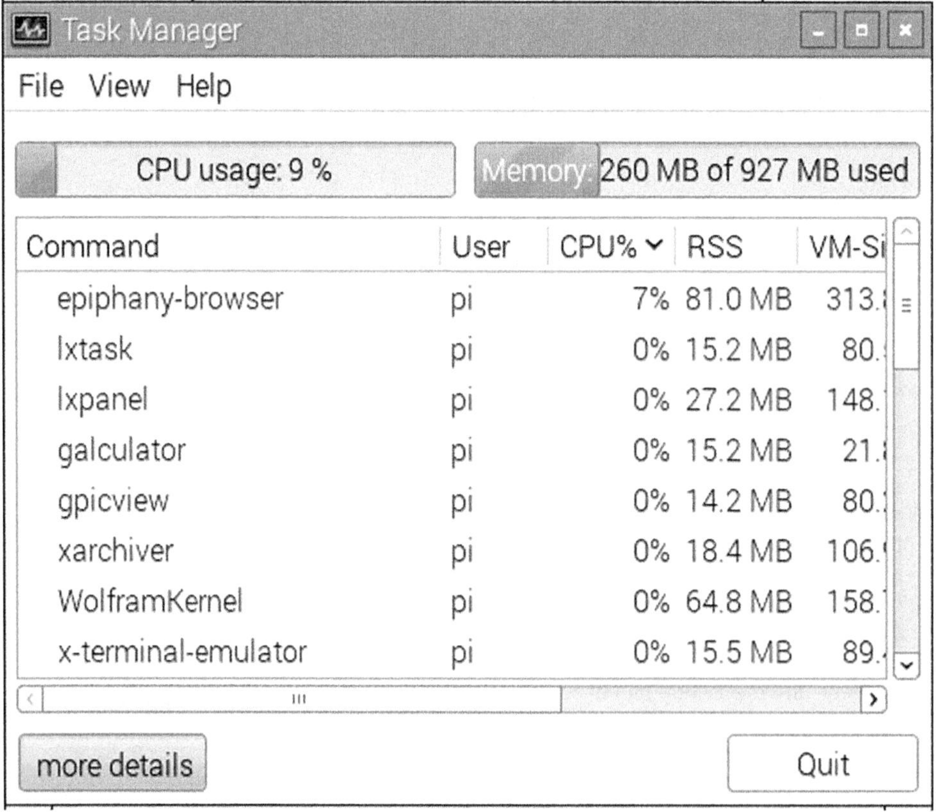

Figure 2-11. *The task manager*

The process list gives you a good indication of what's running on the machine and how much resources are being consumed on an individual basis. This is mostly useful when your Pi is acting a little bit funky and you need to see if an application has suddenly decided to eat all your RAM or set your CPU on fire. If you do find an application that is getting a bit too greedy, you can right click on its name and then select "Kill" which will forceably shut it down and thus hopefully restore our Pi to full health (Figure 2-11).

Terminal

Terminal is a terminal emulator for Linux and gives you access to a virtual console. We're not going to go into any depth on how to actually use this particular application because we go into the details in the next chapter. Suffice to say, this tool is used to give you direct command line access to the operating system. For many people this is a place where angels fear to tread and yet for seasoned administrators, it is somewhere they call home. To find out if the command line is for you though, you'll have to wait until Chapter 4.

Terminal is a simple emulator but gets the job done. It doesn't have all the bells and whistles that some emulators provide but it's perfectly fine for the majority of people and looks like this (Figure 2-12):

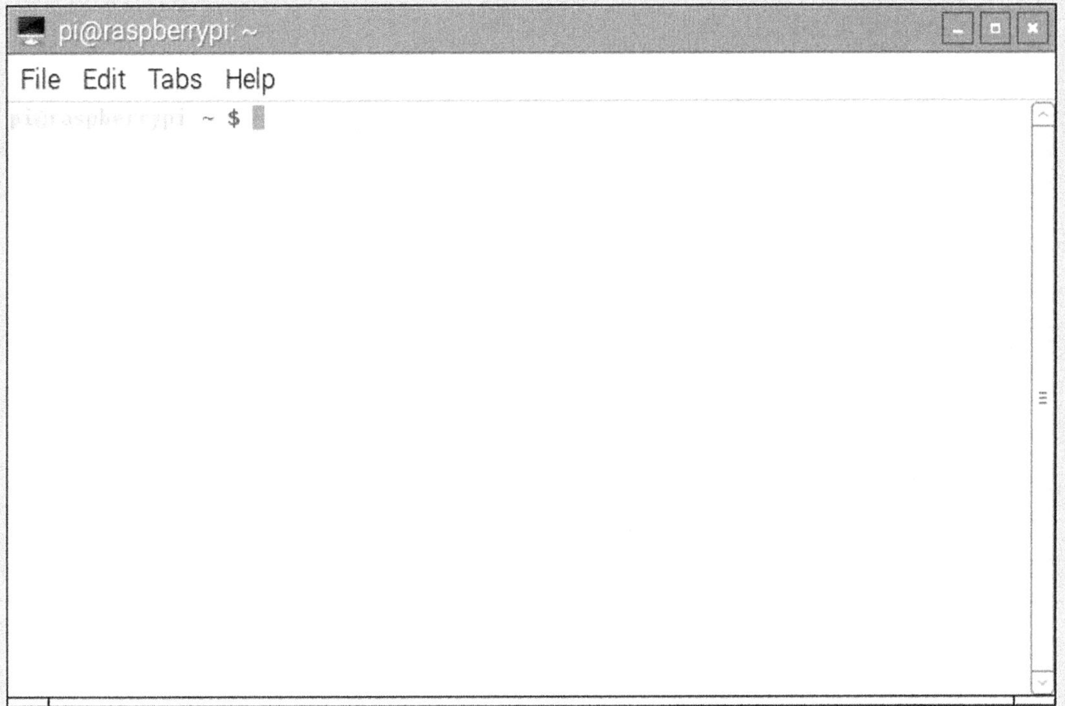

Figure 2-12. *LXTerminal up and running*

One thing we will mention here briefly is the prompt. When the font color is green and the end of the prompt is a dollar symbol, you know you're running as a normal user and that you don't have root privileges i.e. you can't execute any commands that can really hurt the system. Again we'll cover this in more depth in the next chapter but we need to mention this distinction here so that the next program makes sense.

Text Editor

In keeping with the minimalist theme, the Leafpad text editor does the basics and that's about all. It's very similar to later versions of Microsoft's notepad and it's similarly easy to use. It's not much good for writing letters to Aunt Maude or to the council to complain about next door's dog, but it's perfect for when you need to do some light text editing.

Despite its simplicity it still provides some of the most useful tools, namely being able to do a find and replace and enable and disable word wrap. Armed with those tools, you can accomplish pretty much anything.

If you feel that Leafpad is a little under powered for your tastes, then you might want to flip ahead to Chapter 6 where we show you some of the more powerful native text editors that you can get your hands on.

For the most part, Leafpad does exactly what it says on the tin – it edits text and if that's all you need to do, Leafpad is an excellent choice (Figure 2-13).

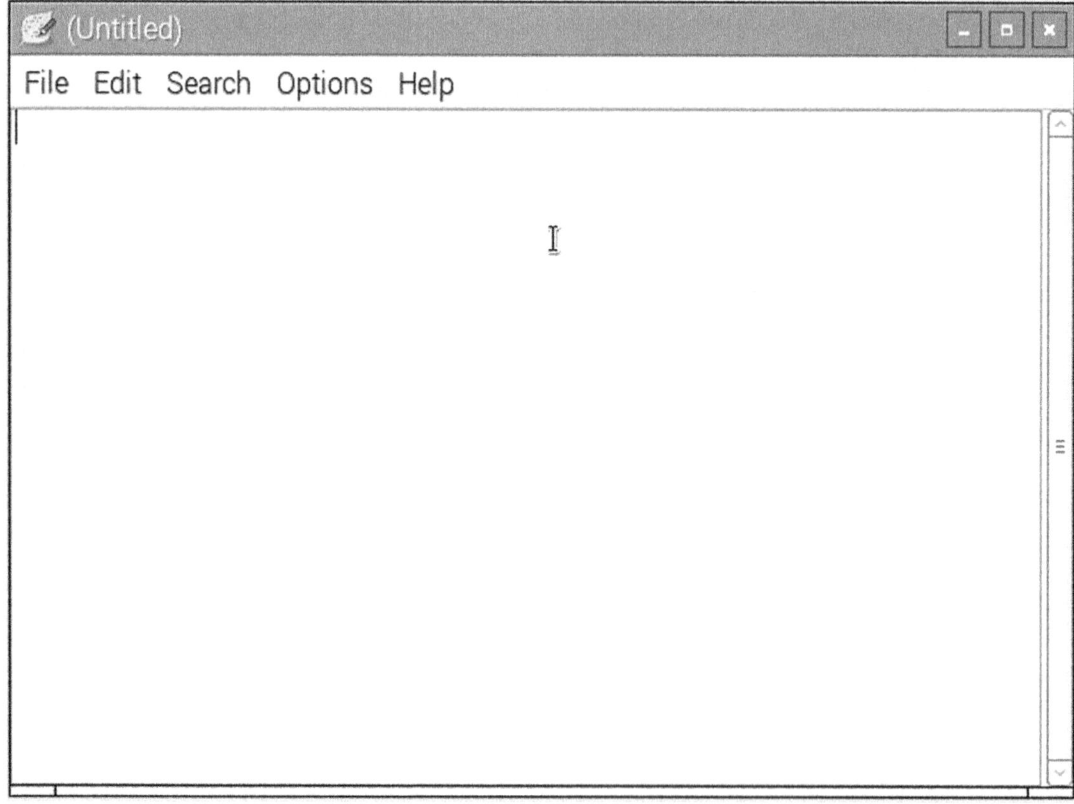

Figure 2-13. *Leafpad has a similar look and feel to Microsoft's Notepad*

Games

The Games menu only has two items but they're still pretty impressive and it's always good to have a way to blow off steam. For some light fun gaming you won't find the Pi wanting.

Minecraft

Unless you've lived on the moon for the past few years, Minecraft won't be new to you (Figure 2-14). In fact for many it's something of a household name. There are even books on how to play it! In any case, there is now a version of it for the Pi but be warned, although it doesn't take much power to run it, it will leech hours of your life at a disturbing rate! We won't cover how to play this game here, but a quick of search for Minecraft on Google will give you all you need and more. Good luck!

Figure 2-14. *Minecraft on your Pi!*

Pi Games

For those of you old enough to remember phones such as the Nokia 3310, you'll remember that they used to come with a selection of time wasting (and highly addictive) games. Classics such as snakes and Space impact could be very entertaining. Pi games is the Raspberry Pi equivalent. All of these games are quick to pick up but very hard to put down. Take some out for a spin and see which ones you prefer (Figure 2-15):

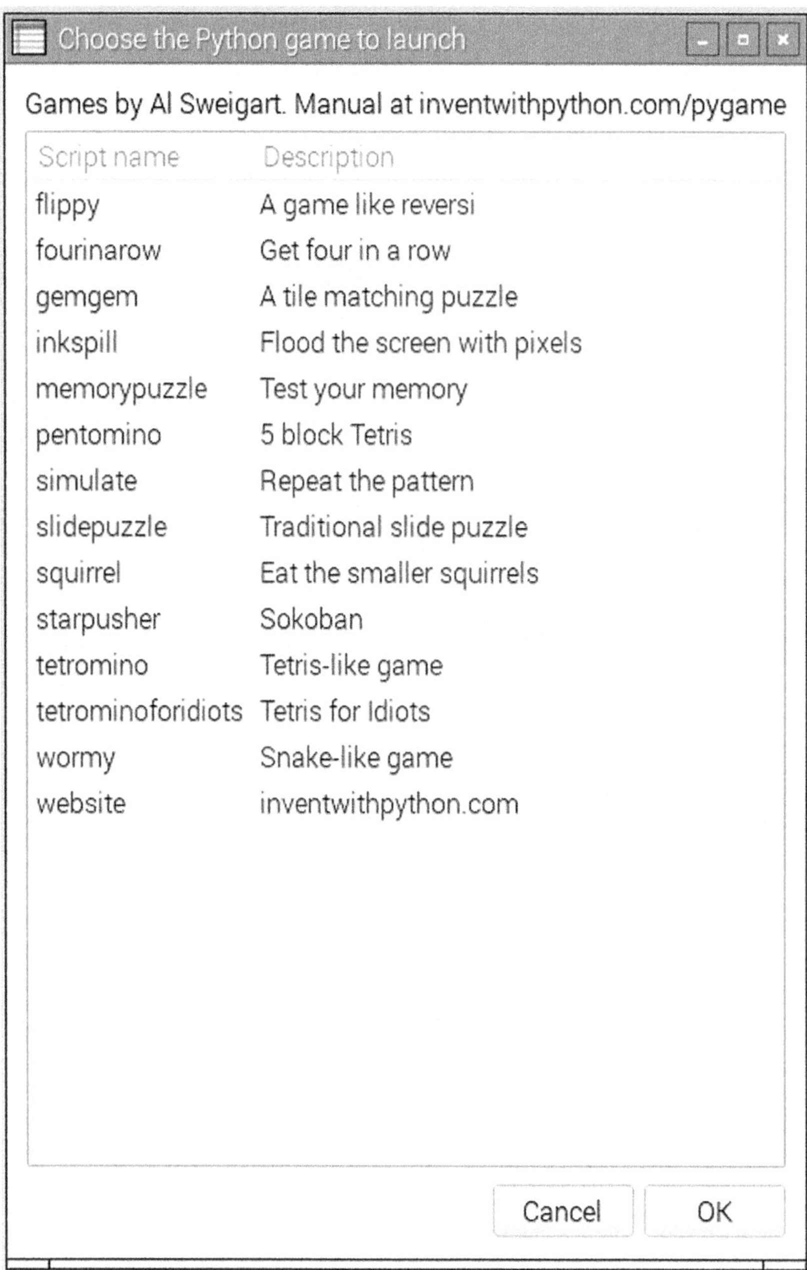

Figure 2-15. *Pi games, say goodbye to your free time*

Internet

The Internet menu unsurprisingly contains applications that are specific for accessing the Internet. On our Pi, the Internet menu looks like this (Figure 2-16):

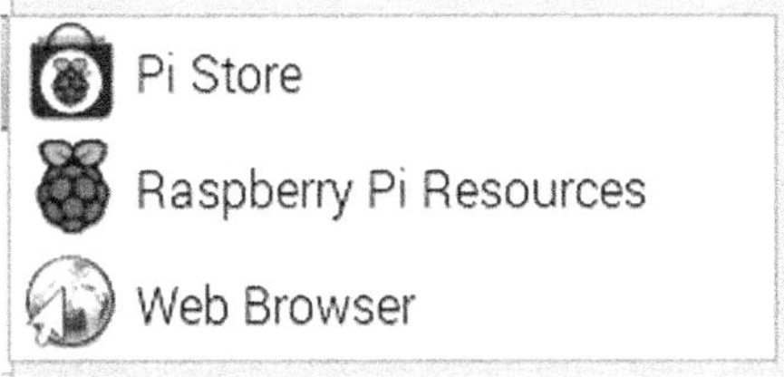

Figure 2-16. *The Internet menu*

Pi Store

The Pi Store aims to be something akin to Android's app store. We've never actually used it for anything as all the things we've wanted have been available through the standard repositories. That said, we're keeping an eye on it because when apps first came out for Android, they weren't all that interesting and yet today they are key to the whole phone experience. So do have a play with this, you might find something you really like (Figure 2-17).

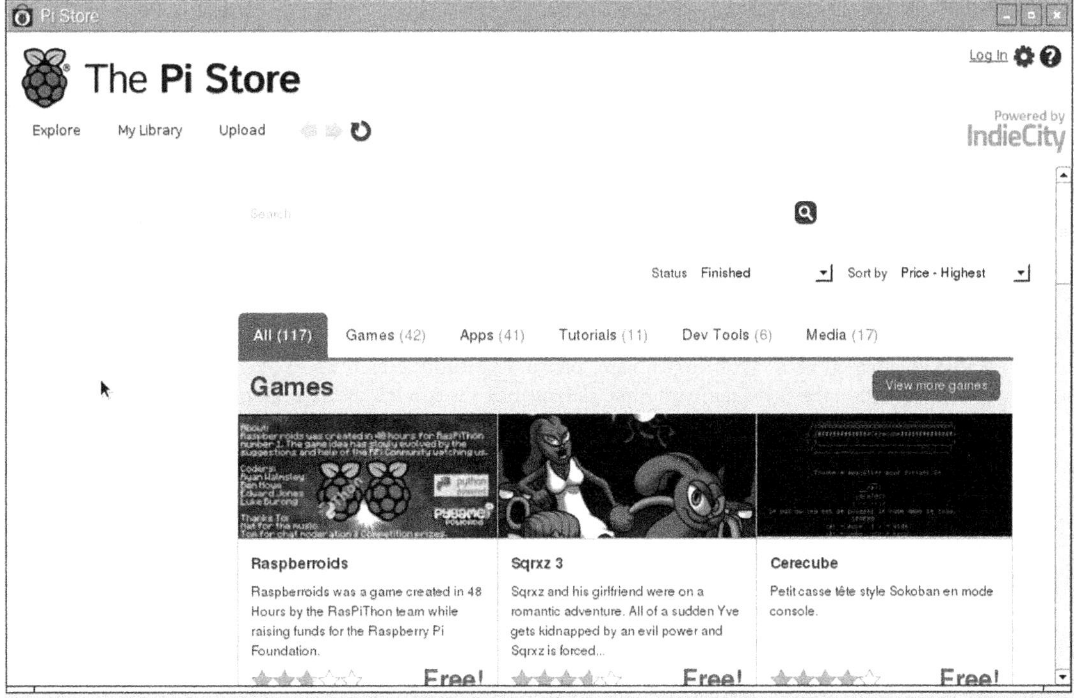

Figure 2-17. *Like the app store but for Pi*

Raspberry Pi Resources

The "Raspberry Pi Resources" is basically a web page that links you to a wealth of information (also known as resources ahem) that will give you information on the Pi as well as a wealth of ideas for learning, teaching and of course making things. There are also articles and other tutorials that are worth a read if you're looking to explore what your Pi can do (Figure 2-18).

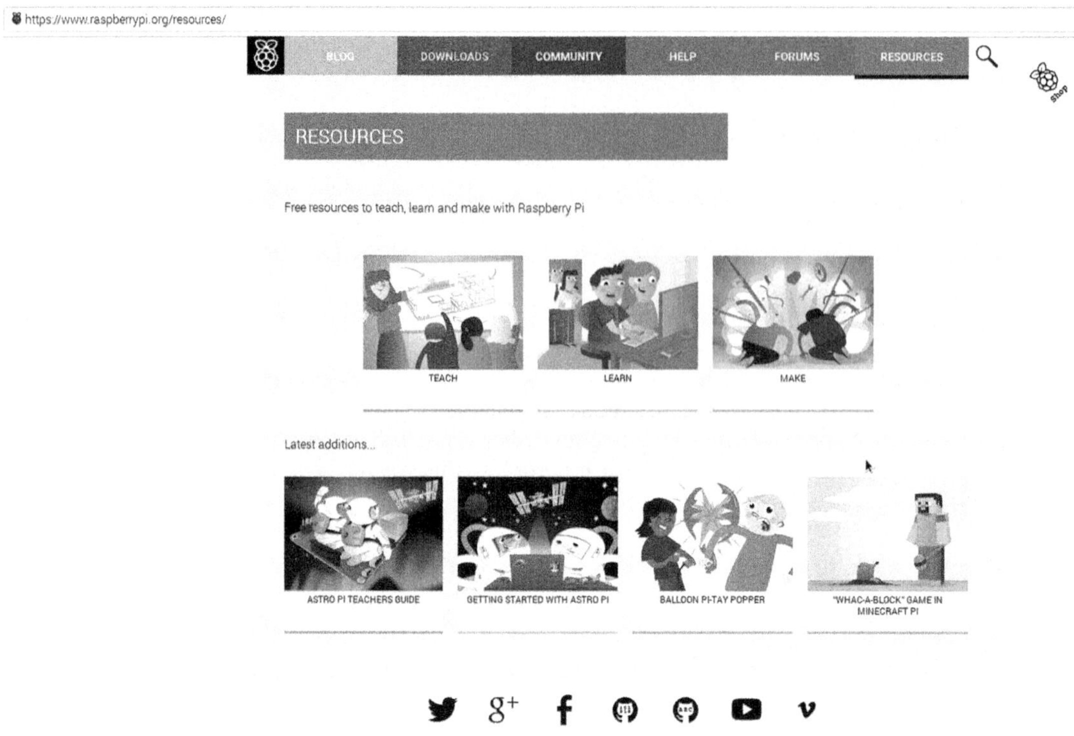

Figure 2-18. *Things to do with your Pi*

Web Browser

Well, this one is pretty standard so we're not going to provide a screenshot. Epiphany is webkit based so you should be able to enjoy all your favourite websites on the Pi without any trouble. Of course as we mentioned earlier you can also open the browser from the task bar on at the top left of the screen.

Programming

The programming menu consists of four items, two of which we covered when we came across them under the Education menu (Figure 2-19):

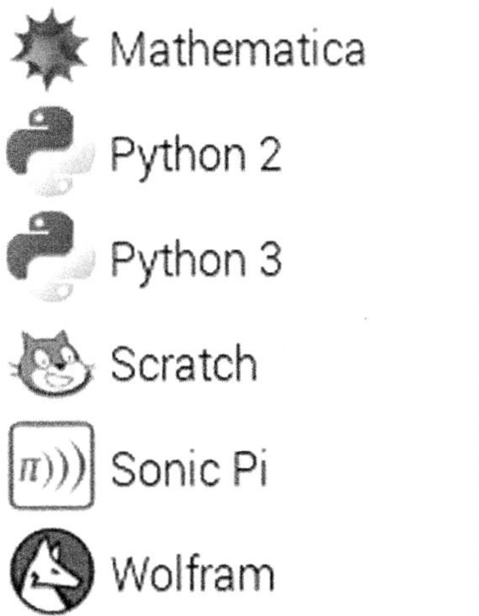

Figure 2-19. *The Programming menu*

We've already briefly touched on Mathematica and Wolfram but it's worth repeating here that although these two tools are pretty epic, you do need to know what you want to do with them. We're excited to see them here, but not being mathematicians or needing to do complex modelling, we don't really know how to properly demo this for you. In any case it has an awesome (and somewhat scary) logo (Figure 2-20):

Figure 2-20. *Firing up Mathematica*

Scratch

Scratch was developed at the MIT media labs by the Lifelong Kindergarten group which was led by Mitchel Resnik. The aim was to create a way to teach people how to program without having to teach all the fiddly bits first. This made the tactile approach in Scratch (where you can drag and drop blocks of logic) much easier to pick up.

We can't claim to be experts in Scratch (in fact we first came across it when we were playing with the Pi) but we are convinced that these sorts of applications will have a huge impact as the Pi spreads out across the waters. Getting people hands on with technology and providing them with a powerful system that lets them get started without having to master all the underpinnings first is definitely a winner in our book.

If you're not convinced, check out this screenshot, it certainly made us take a second look (Figure 2-21):

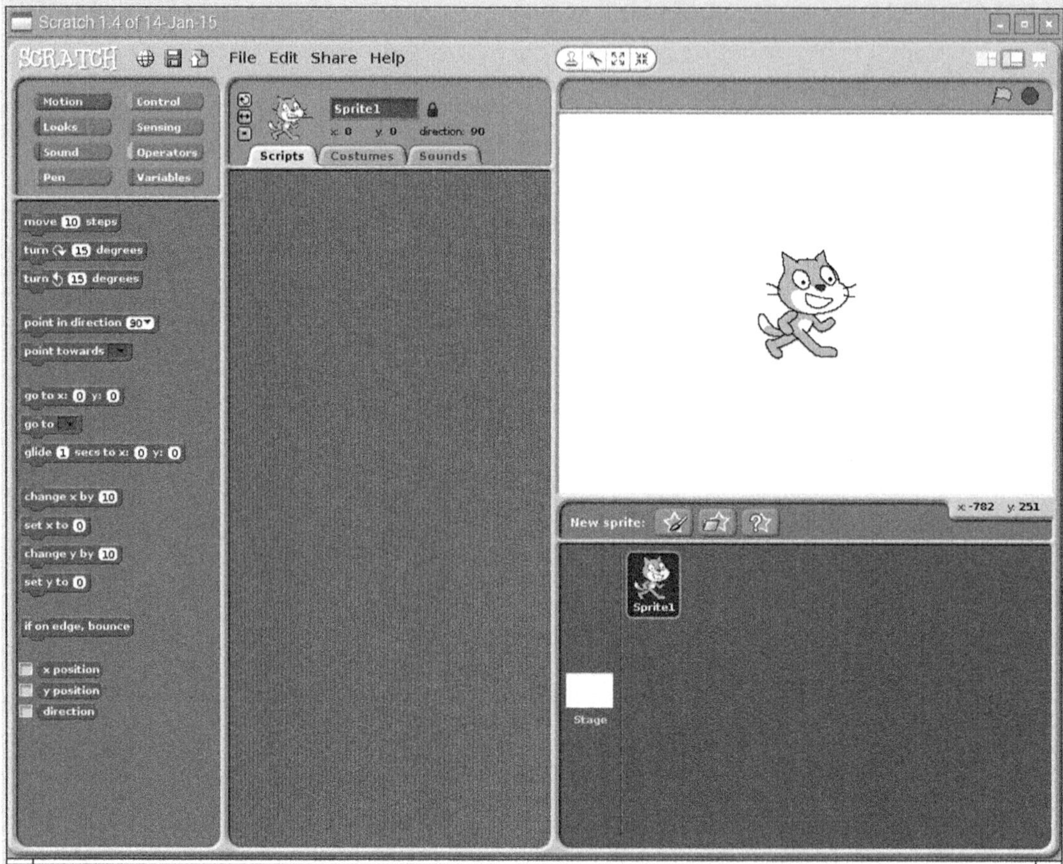

Figure 2-21. *Scratch programming environment*

Python

All we have left is Python 2 and Python 3. Actually, these two are pretty similar in that they are both text based interfaces for the Python programming language. The reason there are two different versions is because there are two current versions of Python which for various reasons aren't mutually compatible. In many ways, scripts that you might write for version 2.x of Python will work just fine in 3.x, but there are quite a few gotchas and changes in the language that make guaranteeing compatibility impossible. This is why you'll often see two versions of Python installed on any given machine.

At the time of writing Python 2.x is still where most people are at and many projects are still actively developed using it. In fact when we write new Python scripts we also use 2.x because it has the most libraries, a history of documentation and blog and forum posts and generally a large community. On the other hand, Python 3.x has had a lot of tweaks and language improvements that will never make it to Python 2.x and of course all the new ideas and development is focused on the new series. Ultimately Python 3.x is the way to go and if you're just starting out in your programming career, we'd recommend you start out on Python 3.x. It certainly won't hurt and you can always look at Python 2.x if for some reason you need to use it and in reality going from one to the other is really not a big problem.

As the two versions of are effectively identical in terms of how they're used, we're going to show you Python 2 (rather than Python 3) (Figure 2-22):

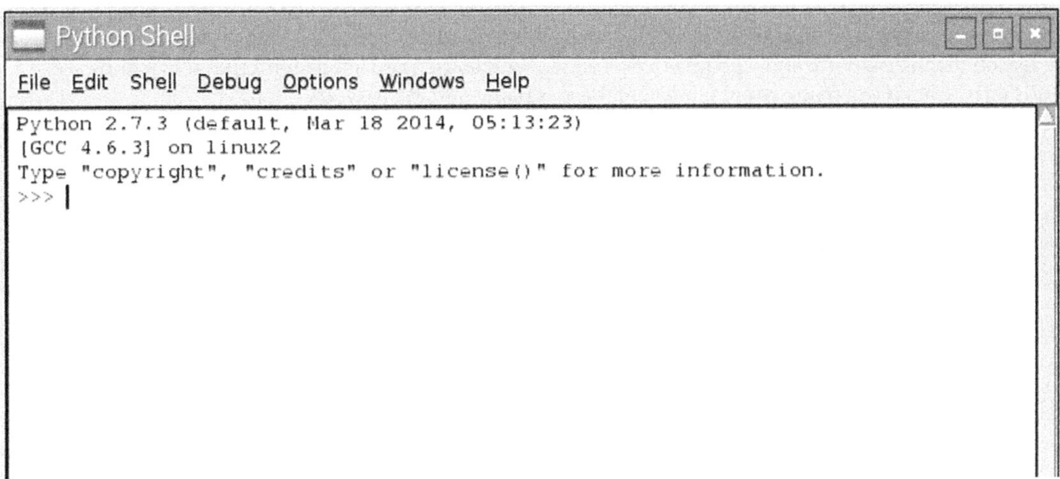

Figure 2-22. *Firing up Python*

Preferences

We're not going to go into any depth in this menu. This is one of those menus that is pretty straight forward and the best way to learn what the things do is to play around with them. We tried previously to give good coverage of the options but the more we covered, the more we seemed to leave out and we couldn't even agree among ourselves which ones to cover. So, this time we suggest that you pull up your sleeves and have a play - after all, you can't break anything!

Help

Last but not least is the Help menu. Here you'll find short cuts for the Debian reference guide and a help guide specifically covering the Raspberry Pi.

The Debian reference guide has been around for a long time and has accumulated a lot of wisdom and knowledge on understanding and using Debian. One of the added benefits here is that this documentation is installed directly on the Pi. This means you can get to it even if you are not able to get the Pi online. This can be very useful for obvious reasons.

The Raspberry Pi help is basically a link to the help page on the Foundation's website. The focus is obviously on the Pi and this makes it a great place to go when you have specific issues that you want to resolve. As it is a website, you will need to be online in order to access this resource (although you can easily access it from another machine if the Pi is playing up). The benefit here is that the resources are updated constantly and you're always going to get up to do date information.

These two resources will provide you with pretty much all you need to use the Pi happily. However there is a wealth of information on the web itself as the Pi has a somewhat massive following. You can find tutorials, FAQs, projects and general help. So if you can't find what you need in the documentation, pay your favourite search engine a visit.

Summary

And that's pretty much it for the whirl wind tour of the desktop! We've really only scratched the surface and the aim is just to get you comfortable enough with what's available to start exploring by yourself. Remember the reason the Pi exists is to allow people to experiment and learn more about computing, so getting your hands dirty (even if you break your Pi now and then) is really nothing to worry about.

In this chapter we covered the applications installed by default and accessible via the start menu and we skimmed over some of the interface features that are somewhat unique to the Linux world.

In the next chapter we start to get really serious (sort of) and take you back in time to the command line where we introduce you to an interface that once you've gotten used to it, you'll wonder how you ever managed to live without it.

CHAPTER 3

Getting Comfortable

Normally we don't start a chapter with a figure (and technically speaking we suppose we haven't this time either) but we're going for some good old-fashioned shock and awe. Take a look at Figure 3-1 (courtesy of Wikipedia).

Figure 3-1. *TeleVideo 925 computer terminal*

You might be wondering why we thought it necessary to show you some technology from the early 80's (late 1982 in this particular case). Well the majority of the second section of this book is all about the command line and getting you comfortable using it. Although things have improved somewhat in the intervening decades, the technology is basically the same.

In this chapter we're going to take a really quick look at the history of computer interfaces and why the terminal has survived as well as it has. We'll then look at the various terminals available to you and how you go about getting to them. We'll then quickly explain the command prompt and let you in on a little known secret about the different shells that are available.

Ye Olde Computer

Although you can now quite literally buy a computer for $25, in the 70's you could expect to pay at least 100,000 times that amount for a computer with any serious amount of processing power. Such machines would take up entire rooms (if not entire floors), require incredible amounts of power and generally look very impressive to passers by. A key problem that owners of these things had to deal with was one of scale.

When your computer is worth more than the building it is sitting in, you want to make sure you that you get the most out of it. One approach to solving the challenge was to use time-sharing. The idea was that compared to a human interacting with the computer, the computer was incredibly fast. In fact even though they were puny by today's standards, they could still run rings around the people who were actually trying to use them. So this begs the question, if the computer is spending most of its time waiting for the operator to enter commands and data, could it be doing other things whilst it is waiting?

It wasn't long before someone figured out that if the computer is sat waiting for input, it could be better utilized if there was more than one person entering data. That way, we could have multiple people entering data at the same time and then we'd no longer be limited to the speed of a single person.

Great idea, but how can we carry it out? To make it work we'd really want to put a screen in front of everyone who needs to talk to the computer and with the available computer technology even a very basic computer would be impractical. Then again, we didn't really need a computer on their desk, we just needed a way for them to communicate with the big computer downstairs. In effect we just want a keyboard and a screen with very long cables.

Say Hello to the Dumb Terminal

That's where the dumb terminal came in. It was called a dumb terminal because it was quite literally just a screen and keyboard. Using instructions relayed from the computer itself, it would draw the text on to the screen. Whenever a key was pressed, this would be sent to the server which would then reply with more updates for the screen. The dumb terminal didn't have any real processing capability, it just worked as an interface and that made them relatively cheap and easy to install and maintain.

The technology did improve over the years and the dumb terminal became well, less dumb. Support for different colors and brightness was added as were fancier features for redrawing and managing the screen. However the basic concept, that of the dumb terminal just being an interface to a remote machine never really changed all that much. In fact although dumb terminals started to be replaced when more modern networks became available (not to mention computing power became much cheaper), the approach itself continued to be used in the newer systems. This wasn't just because there was a lot of legacy systems that people had to keep using (ever see the old green on black screens in some big department stores?) but it actually had some very useful properties that continue to be useful even today.

GUIS AND TUIS

You'll often hear people referring to GUIs (pronounced gooeys) and TUIs (pronounced tooeys) and we'll be referring to them throughout the book as well. Fortunately this pair of acronyms is pretty straight forward and you'll be using them yourself in no time (assuming you'd actually want to of course).

GUI is short for Graphical User Interface. Almost all modern computer systems use one in some shape or another. It used to be really easy to spot a GUI because it was pretty much any device that used a mouse. The lines have blurred somewhat in recent years as thanks to devices such as the iPad and Android smart phones, you can have a GUI that just uses your fingers. It's now much easier to know what a TUI is as generally anything that isn't a TUI is considered a GUI.

TUI is short for Text-based User Interface and is often used interchangeably with CLI or Command Line Interface. A TUI can present basic menu systems but those systems are navigated via keyboard control rather than a mouse.

In short, if you drive it from the keyboard and there's no mouse pointer, it's a TUI. If you can click, point at it with a finger or see pretty pictures, it's a GUI.

Modern Terminals

There's quite a bit of evolutionary history between the dumb terminals we just talked about and what we use on modern Linux systems today. In the interests of preserving your sanity (not to mention crossing the boredom threshold) we're going to leap ahead to the modern day and show what a remote terminal looks like on your Pi (Figure 3-2):

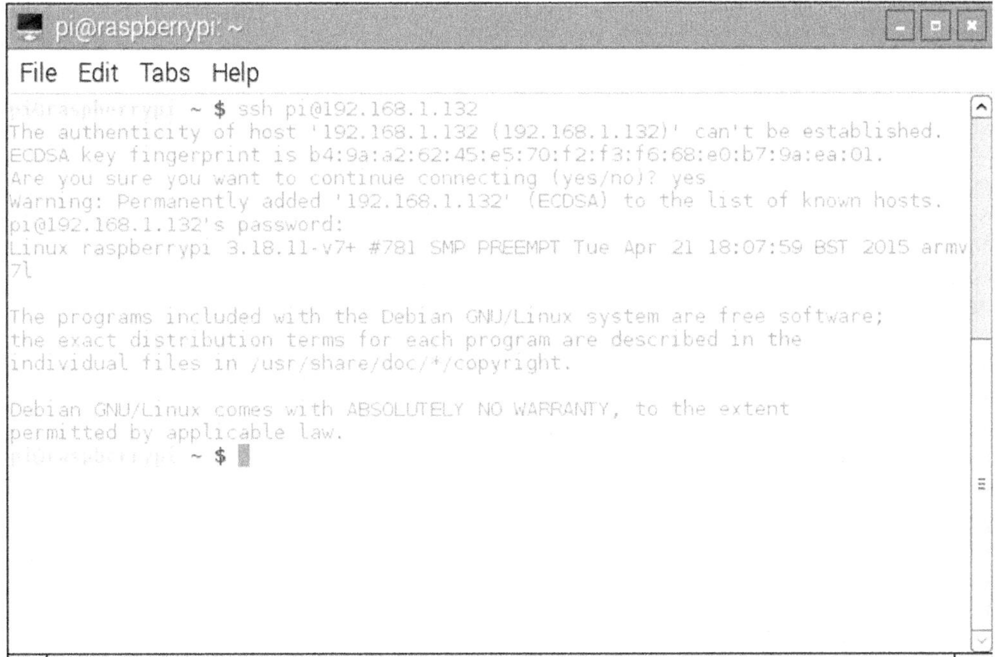

Figure 3-2. *SSH connection to a Raspberry Pi*

As you can see we still have a text based interface and the programs we run are all going to happen on the remote server. We do have some nicer features (we have color for a start) and we can make the terminal as big as our screen can hold (traditional terminals tended to be fixed size). In this particular case we are connected to the Pi via SSH (Secure Shell - more on this later) over TCP/IP.

So Why do We Still Care About these Things?

Good question! In the modern era of iPads, iPhones and Androids, why would we ever want to use a text based interface? For most people, especially if they have never used one before, a text based interface really sounds like something of a backward step and not a skill that they'd be especially interested in acquiring. Needless to say we are most fond of the venerable command line and here are some of the reasons why we think you should invest your time and effort in getting to grips with it.

Simple

One of the key reasons is simplicity. A text based interface is pretty hard to beat when it comes to being simple. Literally all it does is send and receive text. You won't be using a terminal to look at your holiday snaps but it does give you a clean crisp interface to issue commands to your Pi.

Fast

You probably won't believe us right now when we say this but using the command line interface will allow you to complete many of your tasks much faster. The reason for this is that you can be very precise and express a lot of work in a single line of text, the sort of thing that would require multiple clicks or a strange convoluted process to express using a mouse.

Lightweight

Anyone who has had the misfortune of trying to remote control a desktop PC over a slow Internet connection will appreciate exactly what we mean here. Sending screen updates across the Internet (especially for high resolution screens with lots of colors) by its nature simply takes up a lot bandwidth. It can also take a while for the data to arrive at its destination which is what gives remote sessions that unresponsive and blocky feel to them.

Text based sessions don't suffer from this problem because they only send text. They were designed for systems where the maximum speeds were a mere fraction of what is available to us today. So even on a very slow dial-up link a remote terminal session tends to perform extremely well.

It also puts less strain on the server. Maintaining a graphical interface means the computer has to do quite a bit of work. Having a mouse pointer means the computer has to track that pointer and make sure that it reacts properly when it touches an applications window or when the user clicks a button. A surprising amount of work goes on behind the scenes and this is why Linux servers rarely have a graphical interface installed much less running.

Powerful

The command line gives you an awful lot of power. You can express complex thoughts and you can issue commands in a way that just wouldn't be possible via a graphical interface. For example, you can string commands together to make more complex chains. You can take the output of one command and use that as input for another. This technique uses something called pipes and we cover this more thoroughly in the next chapter.

It's Always Available

Although things have gotten better in recent years, one of the most fickle pieces of software on a Linux box tends to be the graphical interface. It always seems to be the first thing to go, and when your server stops booting and you need a rescue environment, it's unlikely that a graphical interface will be available to you.

A terminal however is the native way to talk to Linux (and basically most other Unix like operating systems) and as such, it's the one tool that will always be available to you in some form or another. Knowing how to use the terminal will let you get out of scrapes and deal with situations that would completely stump you if you weren't comfortable with the command line.

Convinced Yet?

Hopefully these highlights have at least convinced you that there might be something to the command line after all. If you're not totally convinced, that's okay, it's hard to really get a feel for the benefits until you've actually spent some time experiencing them for yourself. In the next section we're going to cover how to actually get yourself to a command line, explain what the stuff you're looking at means and cover some basic commands to get you started on your journey.

TERMINAL OR VIRTUAL TERMINAL?

For the most part you won't have to worry about the differences between the two. You will almost always use a virtual terminal that is, either a terminal window inside the Linux GUI itself or connecting via SSH. The only real difference between a terminal and a virtual terminal is that a terminal is a single physical device such as a serial port or sitting at the screen directly connected to the computer (without a GUI). A virtual terminal has a device assigned to it, but there is no corresponding physical device. In fact under Linux, a new device is created and assigned to each new virtual terminal.

We've brought up the distinction here because some documentation (generally speaking old documentation) might refer specifically to one or the other. These days though most of your time will be spent on a virtual terminal and you won't need to worry about the difference.

The Three Terminals

There are three main ways to get to the command line. The first is to sit physically in front of the machine and use what is often referred to as the console, the second is to open a virtual terminal inside the GUI and the third is to connect over the network using SSH.

The Console

Although the console is simply just another terminal, it is a term that has gained a somewhat mythical status over the years. When you're working on the console you are directly working on the machine itself as it is literally a keyboard and monitor plugged directly into it.

It used to be very common for administrators to restrict certain users (such as the root user) to be able to login only when sat directly in front of the machine. As the computer was likely in a locked server room, this provided an additional level of security.

Most distributions do not come with this sort of security enabled and now that remote access over the network is the norm (and sometimes an administrator doesn't even have physical access or the machine is on the other side of the planet), this feature is far less useful.

Still, if you are sitting in front of your Pi you can access the console by holding down the control (ctrl) and alt keys and then pressing F1 through to F6. F7 by default is where the GUI lives so once you have finished with the console you can flip back to your GUI.

When would you need to do this? Well, if you are unable to connect to your Pi via the network and you're having trouble with the GUI, the console will be your new best friend. But generally speaking? You won't be using the console very often if at all. Getting a command line through the other two methods is easier and more flexible as often at least one of those options will be available to you.

Opening a Virtual Terminal in the GUI

Raspbian uses LXDE, the "Lightweight Desktop Environment". As its name suggests it focuses on being lightweight which is just want you want when your computer sits squarely in the feather weight category!

The native terminal for LXDE is called LXTerminal and fortunately for us it not only comes preinstalled but it also features on the taskbar as per the following screenshot (Figure 3-3):

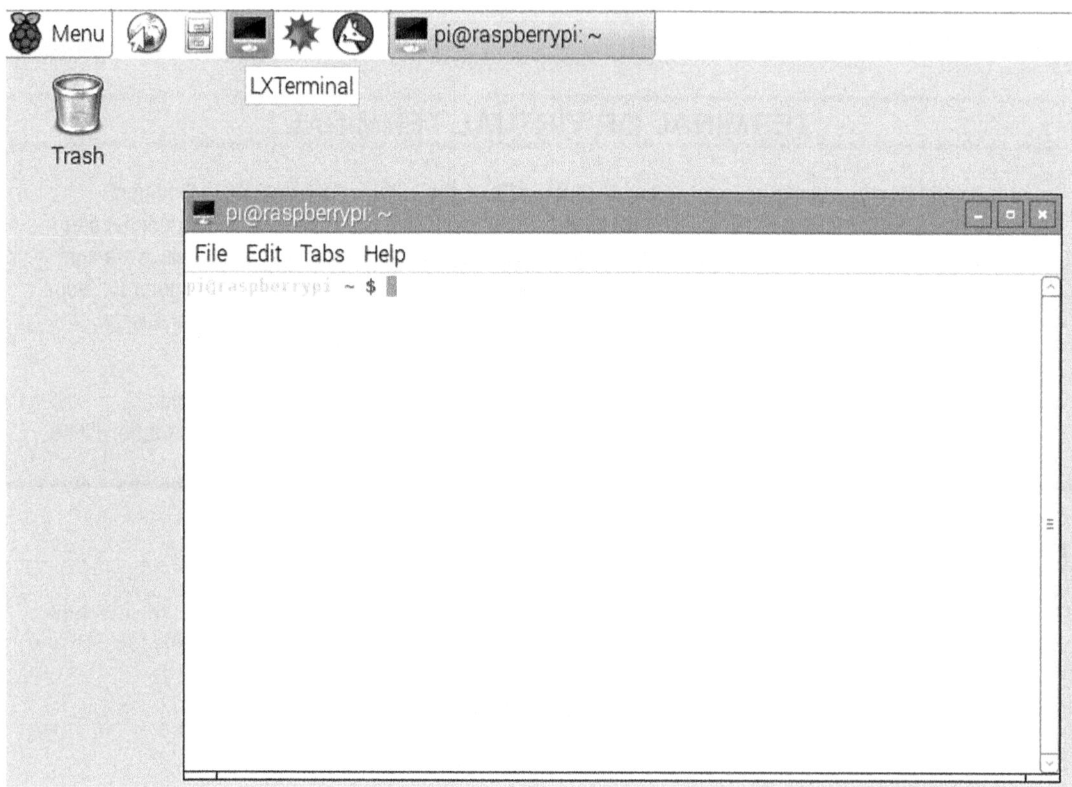

Figure 3-3. *Finding LXTermianl*

We took the liberty of double clicking the icon and you can see that we have what can only be described as a working terminal. Of course there's really not too much to show in this case as a terminal is by definition pretty simple. You will probably find yourself using the terminal a fair bit if you're planning to sit in front of the Pi and use it as a more traditional computer. If you're thinking more about working remotely, then you need the next section which is quite honestly a lot more interesting...

Connecting via SSH

SSH is a great way to connect securely to your Pi over the network (see "What's so special about SSH?"). It gives you all the benefits of a virtual terminal but you can access it from any machine on the network. Potentially this means you could connect to your Pi at home from your work PC and fiddle about with it in complete security. We find that SSH is by far the most common way we interact with servers in general and as most people will use the Pi as a headless device (i.e. no keyboard or mouse attached to it - maybe not even a monitor), we think SSH will be the primary candidate for you as well.

There are two parts to the SSH equation. You need an SSH server and you will need an SSH client. Fortunately both are freely available and easy to set up.

Setting up an SSH Server on the Pi

This one is actually very straight forward because unless you specifically disabled it when you installed Raspbian, the SSH server will already be running (Raspbian enables it by default). In fact all you actually need at this stage is to find out what the IP address of your Pi is.

One of the nice things about covering the Pi's virtual terminal first is that we can now use that to figure out what our IP address is. The Pi takes advantage of DHCP (Dynamic Host Configuration Protocol) which means that on the vast majority of networks it will be able to sort out an IP address for itself. This not only saves us time but also means you don't need to figure out how to choose an appropriate address and then configure it. The marvels of modern technology!

To find out the address we're going to use the 'sudo ifconfig' command. This command (short for "interface configuration") will (perhaps unsurprisingly) show you the configuration of your network interfaces. Here's what it looks like on our Pi (Figure 3-4):

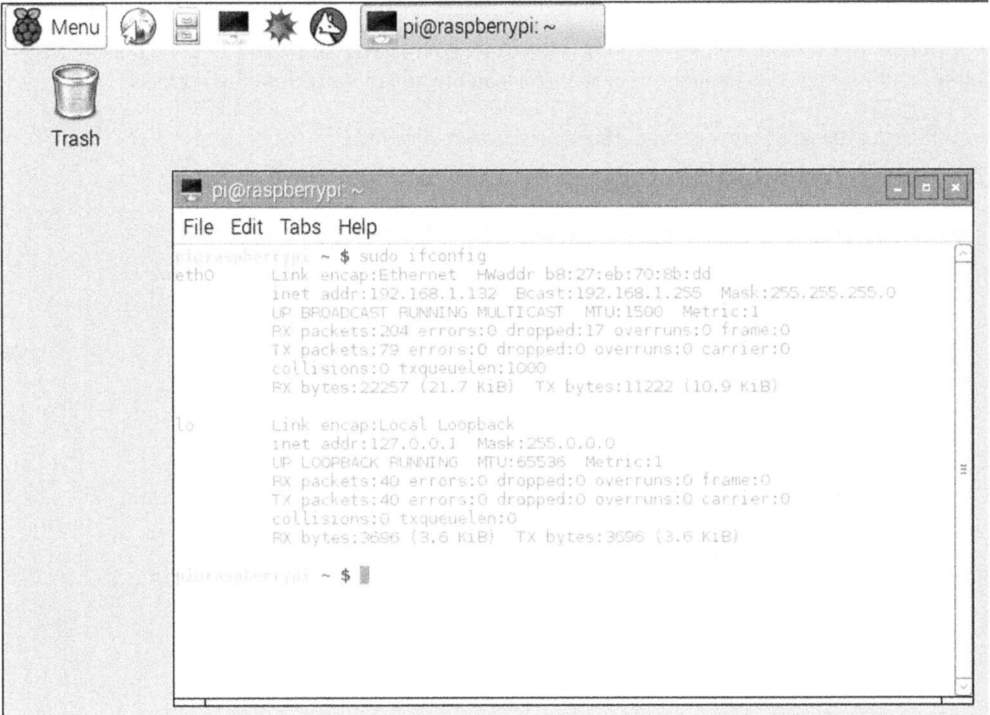

Figure 3-4. *Running ifconfig on our pi*

Here you can see that we have two network interfaces. The local loopback device (or 'lo' to its friends) is a virtual interface that network applications can use to talk to each other on the same machine. As no hardware is involved, it's more efficient to use the lo interface as well as it being always available and configured in the same way. Under Linux most system services (such as printing and even the GUI) operate as client/server applications and make extensive use of this interface.

Right now though we're not all that interested in the lo device, we're far more interested in the network interface that connects the Pi to our physical network. eth0 (short for Ethernet device number 0 - remember computers tend to start counting at zero) represents our link to the real world. At this stage we won't bore you with what all the information means and it's not really something you would look at on a regular basis. The most common reason for running ifconfig is to find out the IP address and that is of course why we are here. From the screenshot above you can see the line:

```
inet addr: 192.168.1.132 Bcast: 192.168.1.255 Mask: 255.255.255.0
```

We're really only interested in the IP or inet address which in this case is 192.168.1.132. Armed with this piece of information, we should be able to connect to the Pi from anywhere on your network.

Sorting out an SSH Client

We are making the assumption that you're either connecting from a Windows PC or from a Mac. If you are using a different operating system, then don't panic, there is probably a suitable client for you to download. You can still follow along with the other two tutorials as regardless of which client you use (or on which platform) the general process is the same.

Putty for Windows

Putty is pretty much the standard that all other SSH clients are compared against and for good reason. Not only is it full of features but it also happens to be free. You can download Putty from this address:

```
http://www.chiark.greenend.org.uk/~sgtatham/putty/download.html
```

As it is a little long for typing, you can get a similar result by searching Google for "Download Putty". Once you get to the download page, you will want to get the first link on the page, putty.exe (Figure 3-5):

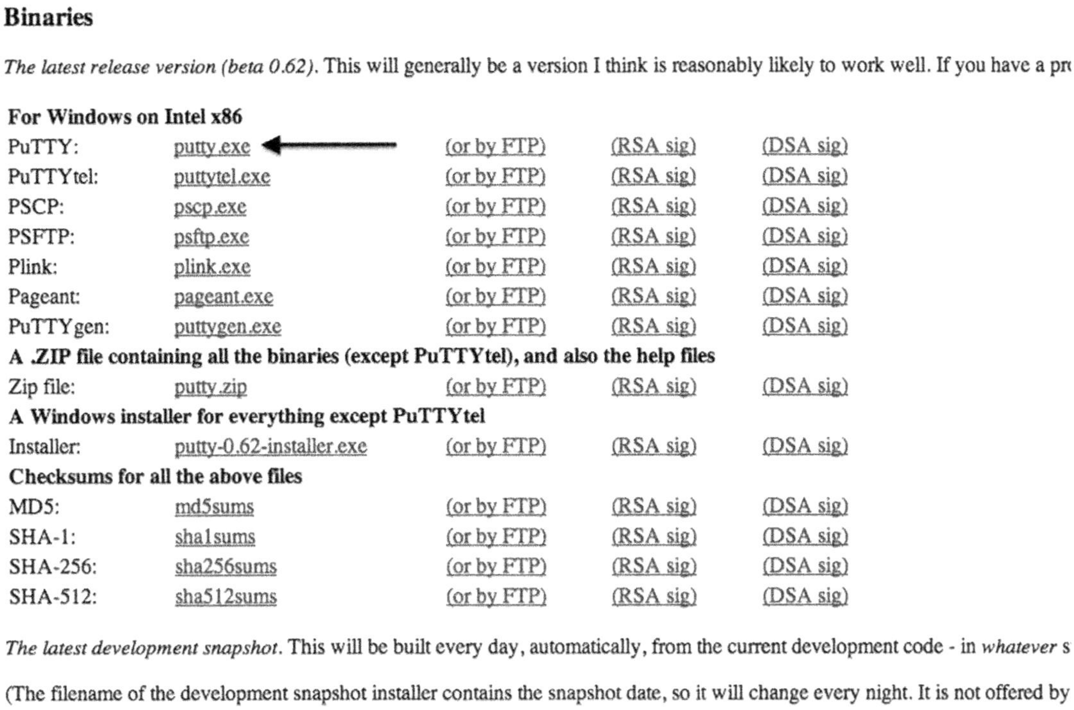

Binaries

The latest release version (beta 0.62). This will generally be a version I think is reasonably likely to work well. If you have a pr

For Windows on Intel x86				
PuTTY:	putty.exe ←	(or by FTP)	(RSA sig)	(DSA sig)
PuTTYtel:	puttytel.exe	(or by FTP)	(RSA sig)	(DSA sig)
PSCP:	pscp.exe	(or by FTP)	(RSA sig)	(DSA sig)
PSFTP:	psftp.exe	(or by FTP)	(RSA sig)	(DSA sig)
Plink:	plink.exe	(or by FTP)	(RSA sig)	(DSA sig)
Pageant:	pageant.exe	(or by FTP)	(RSA sig)	(DSA sig)
PuTTYgen:	puttygen.exe	(or by FTP)	(RSA sig)	(DSA sig)
A .ZIP file containing all the binaries (except PuTTYtel), and also the help files				
Zip file:	putty.zip	(or by FTP)	(RSA sig)	(DSA sig)
A Windows installer for everything except PuTTYtel				
Installer:	putty-0.62-installer.exe	(or by FTP)	(RSA sig)	(DSA sig)
Checksums for all the above files				
MD5:	md5sums	(or by FTP)	(RSA sig)	(DSA sig)
SHA-1:	sha1sums	(or by FTP)	(RSA sig)	(DSA sig)
SHA-256:	sha256sums	(or by FTP)	(RSA sig)	(DSA sig)
SHA-512:	sha512sums	(or by FTP)	(RSA sig)	(DSA sig)

The latest development snapshot. This will be built every day, automatically, from the current development code - in *whatever* s

(The filename of the development snapshot installer contains the snapshot date, so it will change every night. It is not offered by

Figure 3-5. *Downloading Putty*

Putty is a standalone tool, so you can run it as soon as you've downloaded it, you don't have to install anything on your machine. This is generally pretty useful because it means you can stick it on a USB stick and carry it around with you and you can generally run it on other machines without needing Administrator privileges (i.e. there's nothing to install). However if you keep losing track of Putty (it's amazing how easy it is to do) you might want to download the "Installer" version which will install it on your machine and set up the Start Menu and Desktop shortcut icons for you.

Now that we have Putty, it's time to fire it up. Double click on the icon and you will probably see something that looks a lot like this (Figure 3-6):

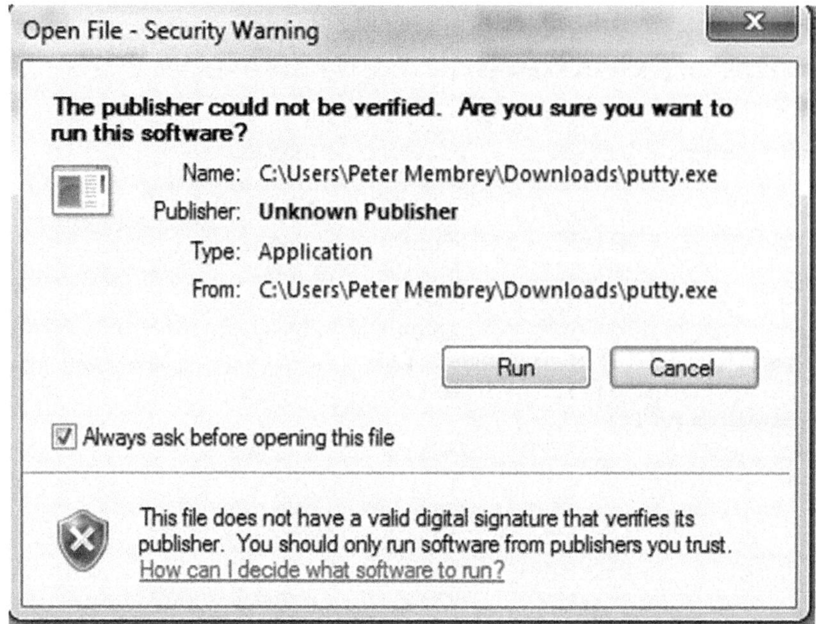

Figure 3-6. *Windows getting excited*

Windows is just warning you that the program hasn't been digitally signed. You've probably come across this one before but when you're installing some supposedly security enhancing software, the last thing you want to do is install something unpleasant instead. In this case, the official version of Putty isn't signed and you can ignore this error. If you plan to use Putty a lot, you should probably untick the "Always ask before opening this file". Trust us, if you don't do it now, you will after ten or eleventh time you run it.

After you've convinced Windows to stand down, you'll get a connection box that looks like this (Figure 3-7):

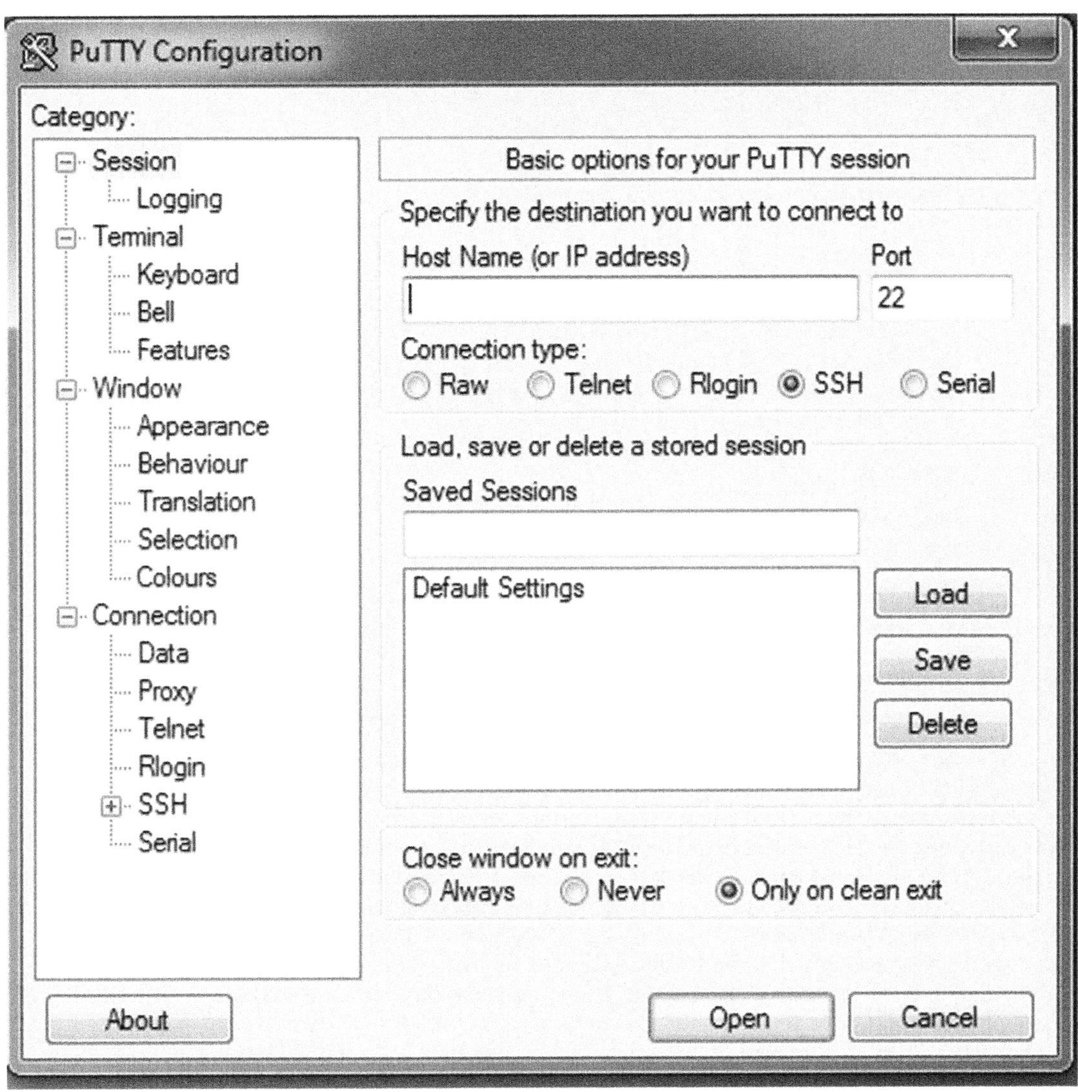

Figure 3-7. *Starting up Putty*

The default settings are fine for connecting to your Pi, you just need to supply the IP address we discovered earlier. Punch this into the "Host Name (or IP address) box and then click on Open. As this will be the first time this particular machine has connected to your Pi you will get a warning similar to the one below (Figure 3-8):

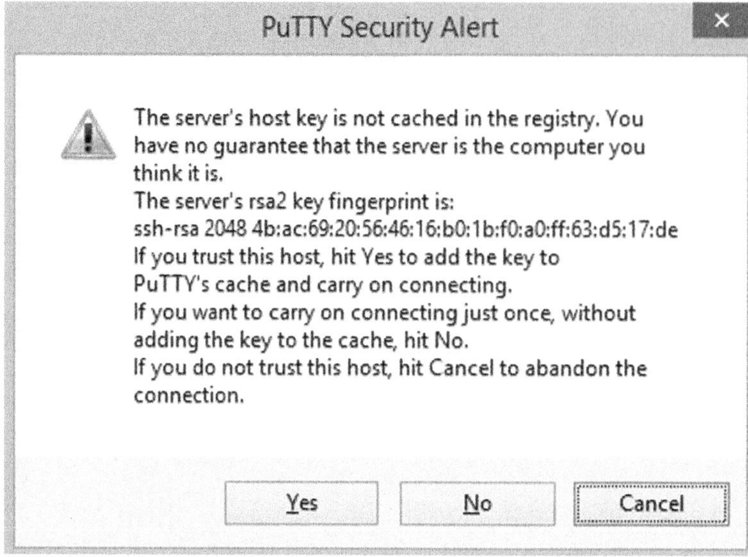

Figure 3-8. *Security warning when connecting for the first time*

Don't worry, this is part of SSH's security system. It is letting you know that it hasn't seen this particular server before (well it wouldn't have would it?) and is showing you the key for confirmation. We don't know anyone who has memorized their SSH fingerprint (although remembering the first four and last four digits goes a long way to making sure you have the right one) and in any case we were expecting to see this warning. Once Putty has remembered the key, it will check it against the IP address and hostname each time you connect in future. If the remote server ever sends back a different fingerprint, Putty will warn you that there could be a problem. More often than not, this occurs when you rebuild or buy a new server and so you know why the key has changed. If you see a warning and you can't think of a good reason for it, then think very carefully before logging into that machine. In our particular case, we know the key will be new so we can simply select "Yes, Save Key".

Now you will be back to a somewhat familiar black screen with some text. So far it will only be:

Username:

As we haven't gotten around to setting up different user accounts we're going to login as the 'pi' user so just enter pi and press Enter. So far so good. Now we just need to provide it with the password you set when you did the initial install. Now we know that you changed the password like we suggested (you did right?) but just in case you didn't, the default password is raspberry. Punch the password in, press Enter and at long last we should have what we're looking for, the command prompt:

```
pi@raspberrypi ~ $
```

If you don't have a Mac (or aren't particularly interested in using SSH from one), jump ahead to the next section – the command prompt.

LOOK BEFORE YOU LEAP

This falls under the "obvious until proven otherwise" category but when you're working with remote terminals, it is disturbingly easy to get disorientated and start running commands on the wrong machine. If you are trying to reboot the Pi on your desk you don't want to accidentally reboot something else such as a corporate server (you never know where you new Linux skills will take you!).

SSH on the Mac

If you're using a Mac rather than a PC, you won't be able to use Putty. That's not a problem because thanks to its Unix roots, the Mac comes with a good SSH client built in. All we need to do is open a Terminal window and run the SSH command.

First, let's get Terminal up and running. You can find it in the "Utilities" directory inside "Applications". You can also find it by using Spotlight (the magnifying glass at the top right of the menu bar and typing in "Terminal".

You'll find that it's not too different from the terminal you were using on the Pi and there's a good reason for that. As we mentioned earlier, the Mac is actually based on Unix just as Linux (and hence Raspbian) is. Although the Mac does a good job of keeping its Unix side well hidden (you can use a Mac for years and never come across it) you might want to dig into it a bit more if you find Linux and the command line to your liking.

Now that we have Terminal open, let's connect it to your Pi. We're going to use the ssh command and because there is no GUI, we're going to have to specify the relevant options on the command line itself. Based on our previous example, your Terminal should look something like this (Figure 3-9):

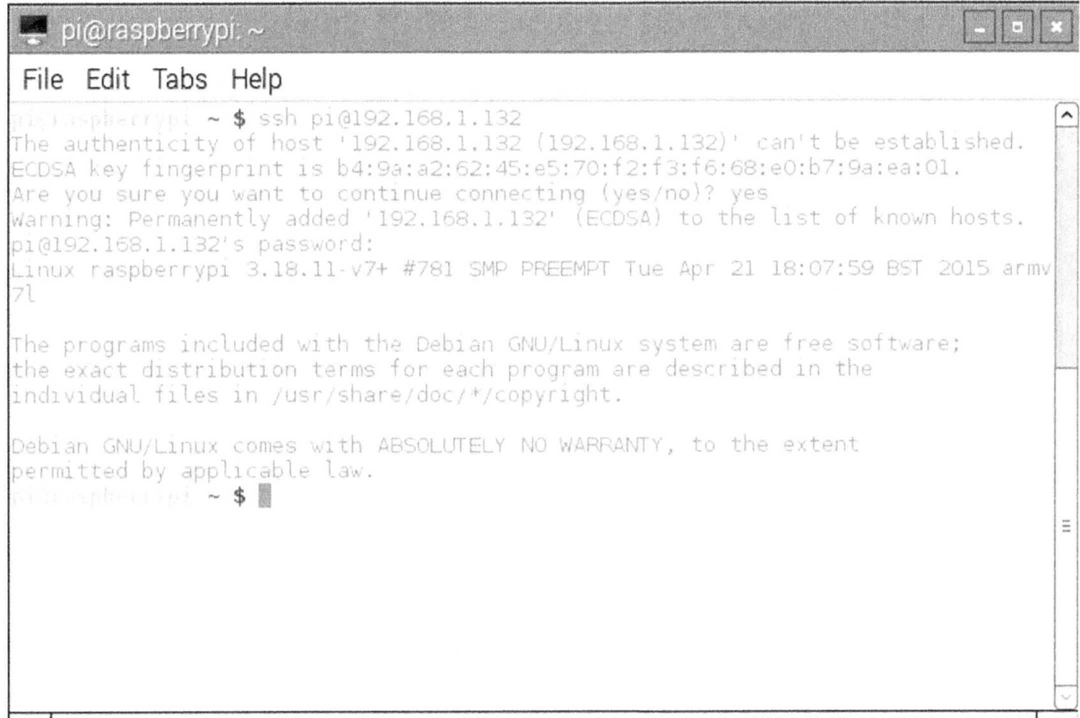

Figure 3-9. *Connecting to your Pi over ssh*

To save space, the screenshot above shows the whole process rather than just an empty terminal window. The bit we're interested in right now is at the very top:

```
$ ssh pi@192.168.1.132
```

The command itself is ssh but we have provided some additional information; the user and IP address that we want to connect to. You can read the options as "user pi on server 192.168.1.132". A bit like an email address, it is a nice succinct way to show who we want to connect as and where we want to connect to. You should of course replace our IP address with the one of your Pi.

The first block of text is something you'll see whenever you connect to a new machine:

The authenticity of host '192.168.1.132' can't be established.

ECDSA key fingerprint is b4:9a:a2:62:45:e5:70:f2:f3:f6:68:e0:b7:9a:ea:01.

Are you sure you want to continue connecting (yes/no)? yes

Warning: Permanently added '192.168.1.132' to the list of known hosts

pi@192.168.1.132's password

This is just ssh's way of warning that you it can't determine whether you're connecting to the server you think you're connecting to and shows you the key that the server used to identify itself. In this case you can ignore the warning and say yes. If you want to know a bit more about what it all means, we covered it briefly in the SSH on Windows section. After you enter your password (raspberry is the default) you should end up at the following prompt:

```
pi@raspberrypi ~ $
```

Now that you have your command prompt, we're going to look at what it actually means.

WHAT'S SO SPECIAL ABOUT SSH?

SSH or Secure Shell is the defacto standard for accessing any Unix like machine remotely. It is even supported by many network enabled devices such as printers and high-end switches. The reason why it is so popular is because it encrypts all the data between your computer and your server. If someone is listening to your connection, all they will get is garbage. It also allows you to authenticate the server is the server you think it is.

Before we had SSH, everyone used telnet. This is a very simple protocol and doesn't have any sort of encryption. This meant that if anyone could see your traffic (think public machines or WIFI access points), it would be possible to simply read your password off the network in clear text. Telnet also had no way to confirm the identity of the machine you were connecting to which meant you could never be sure that you weren't accidentally providing your username and password to somebody else.

It is still possible to install a telnet server on Linux but this is highly discouraged. There really is no good reason to prefer telnet over SSH and so you should always use SSH when working on your server remotely.

Welcome to the Command Line

Whichever route you take to get to a terminal, the end result will ultimately always be the same, that is, you'll end up sitting at a command prompt (or simply prompt) that will look something like this:

```
pi@raspberrypi ~ $
```

There is actually quite a bit of information here but what does it all mean? You can probably figure most of it out from what we've been doing so far in the book, but for completeness, here is how it breaks down.

The first part (pi in the example) is the username. This isn't especially useful (or awe inspiring) when you only have a single Pi and a single user. It is however quite useful when you end up having to manage many users or when you have a variety of accounts of different machines. This is where the second part comes in (raspberrypi in the example) as it tells us the hostname of the machine we're connected to. Together, this let's us know who we are and where we are. Again, not terribly useful with one Pi, but this information will come in handy some day.

■ **Caution** We've highlighted this elsewhere, but it's so important we're going to say it again. When you have more than one terminal open, it is all too easy to run a command on the wrong server. Sometimes you end up running more than one command before you realize your mistake. Often no harm is done, but if you accidentally reboot a critical server at work when you actually meant to reboot your Pi, you're going right to the top of your IT department's revenge pending list.

The next item on the prompt (the ~ or tilde) actually tells us which directory we're currently in. The tilde is a special case as it refers to the home area of the current user. You can think of it as short hand because really that's all it is. Any time you refer to your home directory (which in this case is /home/pi) we can simply replace it with the tilde. Time for a quick example:

```
pi@raspberrypi ~ $ pwd
/home/pi
pi@raspberrypi ~ $ cd ~
pi@raspberrypi ~ $ pwd
/home/pi
pi@raspberrypi ~ $
```

Here we used the 'pwd'(short for "print working directory") which prints out the full path of the directory we're currently in. In our example, it printed out /home/pi as that's the pi user's home directory. We then used the 'cd' command (short for "change directory") to go to the ~ directory. We used 'pwd' again and were able to verify that after changing directory we were back where we started. We'll be explaining these commands more thoroughly in the next chapter, but isn't this command line stuff at least a little bit interesting?

When referring to the '~' in general speech, you refer to it as "home directory". So if you were sat at the prompt in our example and someone asked you what directory you were in, you would say you were in your home directory or if you wanted to be explicit you would say that you were in the pi user's home directory. If you wanted to get really specific you could even mention the hostname as well. You wouldn't say that you are in the tilde or "wiggly line" directory.

However when you are giving someone a path to enter you would say tilde. For example if you wanted the user to go to "~/test/" you would say "type cd space tilde slash test slash and then press Enter". This is because tilde in this case refers to something specific which you are using as a convenience to get to a location, rather than actually telling someone what that location is. It also helps prevent confusion with relative paths, but again, that's something for the next chapter.

■ **Note** We've heard tilde pronounced as both "tilled" and as "till-duh" so you should expect to hear both of these in the wild. Interestingly though, you might find that whichever one you use, people might have trouble understanding you and this applies even to experienced administrators. It's not because you're pronouncing it wrong, it's just they don't know that the "wiggly line to the left of the 1 key" is actually called tilde. If you find yourself in that situation, referring to it as "the wiggly line one" seems to be a fairly safe bet.

The last part of the command prompt shows you what your access level is. Linux systems are pretty basic when it comes to system privileges. It can generally be summed up as you are either the root user or you're not. If you are root, then you can do pretty much anything you please without let or hindrance. If you are any other user, expect to find your abilities drastically curtailed. This isn't as true today as it once was because there are tools such as `sudo'which allow an administrator to grant the ability to run certain commands with root privileges without that user having access to the root account. Of course ultimately, sudo runs as root and it just decides whether or not it will run the command that you asked it to, so really it still obeys the all or nothing rule.

From the prompt's perspective, if you are a normal user, you get a dollar sign as a prompt. We're logged in as the pi user (which obviously isn't the root user) and so we too have the $. If we were logged in as root, we would be a privileged user and so we would get the hash symbol (or pound sign if you're not from the UK). A root prompt looks like this:

```
root@raspberrypi ~ #
```

The hash symbol is a sign (and a warning) that you are running with elevated privileges and that you should therefore be very careful about what you type. The prompt also shows the username as root which provides an added indication. However, these subtle hints are easy to miss (people don't tend to study the prompt before each command) and so again, always check who and where you are before press the Enter key.

That's really all there is to the prompt. Most shells allow you to customize it to show different information and occasionally some administrators do change this. In our experience, most people don't bother and we rarely feel the need to change it ourselves. The reason we're bringing it up here is because if you ever do login to another Linux machine and the prompt is wildly different, it's not a cause for concern. The terminal works in exactly the same way, just the prompt has been customized.

Different Shells

Okay, maybe we over simplified things when we said that all terminals work alike. In truth there are some minor differences, especially in what features they support, but more often than not you won't notice. In fact, what will likely catch you out is when the remote machine is using a different shell. A shell is a program like any other but rather than being a tool for browsing the web or reading email, it provides a command line for you to interact with the operating system. It operates like a wrapper around the kernel and that's how it got its name - by being the shell around the kernel just like a peanut.

So far we've been making use of the BASH or Bourne Again Shell. It is by far the most popular shell in use today and it's available on every Linux distribution. It's also usually the default which is why you'll never have to worry too much about which shell your system is running.

The reason we're bringing this up here is because like everything else in the Open Source world, opinions vary on what makes the best shell. Some take a bare bones approach and only support the most basic features while shells like BASH come with batteries included and have more features than you can shake a stick at. Despite BASH's popularity it is conceivable that at some point in your illustrious Linux career you might come across something else and forewarned is forearmed.

We're not going to spend any more time looking at the different shells because quite honestly you'll probably never need to worry about it. Even if a machine is using a different shell, you can probably start BASH to replace it (most systems have BASH installed even if you get a different shell when you login). As system commands are the same regardless of which shell you use, even if you can't get to BASH you'll probably find you can do everything you would normally do. In fact, most shells are interchangeable for the most part and chances are even if you were using another shell, you probably won't even know it!

Summary

This chapter introduced you to the terminal and its rich (if not exactly fascinating) history. We then discussed how the terminal is still used today and how it has been adapted to suit our modern needs. We then looked at the three main ways that you can get to a terminal on your Pi, mainly the console, a virtual terminal and over the network via SSH. Next we had a quick description of the command prompt and touched on some interesting commands to highlight a point (which we absolutely promise will be explained when you turn the page) and finally we wrapped up the chapter by giving you a heads up about the different shells out there and how they may (but probably won't) trip you up.

Coming up in the next chapter is all you need to know to happily navigate around your Pi, create files, modify files, delete files and much more. This is where we start to get really serious about the command line and where you'll start picking up some real hands on skills.

CHAPTER 4

The File-paths to Success

In this chapter we take a look at what a filesystem is and how different operating systems try to make sense of them. We explain the difference between separate root filesystems and unified root filesystems and why knowing this up front might save you a lot of headache.

We then move on to looking at the filesystem presented to you on your Pi. We explore the standard layout and explain what goes where and what it actually does. We will also show off some simple commands that highlight some benefits of the Unix "everything is file" approach to system design.

Next we will show you how to move around your system and you'll learn about fully qualified and relative paths. We'll show you how to create directories and files (and then copy, move and delete them) and we'll show you how to create the Linux equivalent of short cuts.

We'll then round off the chapter with an exploration of Linux file permissions and show you how Linux decides who can do what to your files. We'll also touch on users and groups and show you how to set ownership and file permissions on your own files.

What is a Filing System?

We had actually planned to start this section off with a dictionary definition of what a filing system is followed by our interpretation. Unfortunately as most of the definitions we could find basically said "a filing system is a system for filing" we're going to have to skip that part and go straight to our own definition. It does suggest however that although a filing system is easy to talk about, it's a lot harder to define. For us though, we think a filing system is:

A way of sorting and categorizing data that makes finding something easier.

This definition covers everything from having a simple in tray (at least you know where the document is even if you can't put your hand on it right away), to the way you view your contacts on your phone (that's an alphabetical system right there) all the way to some of the more exotic systems such as the Dewey decimal system used to categorize non-fiction content at your local library.

Actually libraries are an interesting use-case for filing systems because most of them have at least two going on at the same time. Generally libraries tend to arrange fictional work by the surname (and then forename) of the author whereas the non-fiction section is sorted based on their Dewey Decimal number. By using two systems at once, they solve a fundamental problem. Storing books by the author's name is great if you have a favorite author and want to find more of their books. When it comes to non-fiction though, you probably want to browse a selection of books on a given topic and more often than not you have no particular author in mind. If those books were sorted by author name you'd probably never be able to find anything.

Some libraries take this a step further by sorting fictional books first by genre (say Sci-Fi or Fantasy) and then within that category they sort by author name. This has some pretty neat benefits. You can still go straight to your favorite author as you'll know the genre, but you can also browse for similar books with the same genre. If you are looking for the next best thing in the fantasy genre, you can simply stand in that section and flick through.

So far so good. Filing systems make finding things easier and we can see that it's important to use the right filing system for the task otherwise you'd probably be better off with no filing system at all. But what does his have to do with computers? Well one of the major tasks for any computer is to process information and that means that it has to be able to store and retrieve information easily. Older computer systems did use the alphabetical system and it worked very well, but as soon as you started to build up a number of files, it started to get very messy and finding what you wanted became a challenge. This was addressed by having the ability to create a directory (often called a folder these days) in which you could put related files. This helped a lot, but the same old problem started to creep up on people. Yes, you could have a directory for accounts and another for tax returns, but what if you were an accounting firm and you had lots of accounts and lots of tax returns? Soon you were back to where you started as you either had a small number of directories with large amounts of files of a large number of directories with only one or two files in them.

The last change to filesystem structure which remains familiar to this day was to allow directories to contain other directories. This would allow you to have a great deal of flexibility to store content in the most appropriate ways. As always, there's more than one way to arrange a given set of files, but by and large the system has served us well and with modern search technology, finding what we're looking for is easier than ever.

More than one Filesystem

Here is where we hit a bit of a snag with this approach. A filesystem sits on top of some form of storage. That can be a hard disk, a USB stick, a DVD or any number of storage mediums. Each device is effectively independent from any other. This makes sense because you can take a USB stick from your laptop and then use it on your desktop machine. Clearly there is no link between the filesystem on the USB stick and your laptop because otherwise your desktop wouldn't have all the information it would need to find the files.

Each filesystem has a 'root directory'. This is the first directory on a device and it holds all of the other files and directories. Like the root of a tree, all the files and directories branch off from this central location. This does pose a bit of a problem though. If each device has its own filesystem and root directory, how do you easily present this structure to the end user? It turns out that they are two approaches to solving this problem. The first is separate roots and the second is a unified filesystem.

Separate Roots

This approach was adopted by Microsoft all the way back to the days of MSDOS and it's still with us today. The approach is very simple. Each device has its own root entry and the user can then use this entry to locate the device of interest and then can simply navigate the filesystem as normal to find the file. Under Windows, each root is assigned its own letter. For historical reasons the system disk on Windows is referred to as 'C:' which you'll often hear people refer to as 'the C drive'. Floppy drives are assigned A: and B: (PCs with hard disks tended to have two floppy drives) and as few people had more than one hard disk, the CDROM drive tended to be assigned to D:.

This system is really easy to use and there is never any confusion about where a particular file is as you can tell simply by looking at the drive letter. However there are a couple of issues with this design. First, as root devices are assigned to letters and there are only 26 letters in the alphabet, you are limited to 26 devices. Hardly an issue to home users even today, but back when businesses were using large mainframes, they could have hundreds of such devices.

The second issue is that the user has to be aware of the physical location of their file. That can actually add complexity because it ties the location of the file to the physical device that the file is on. If a bigger disk is added to the system, and the files were moved to that new location, their root device would change. Any person (or software) that depends on a file's location would need to be updated, and that's never fun.

In short, although the system employed by Windows is simple and effective, it can become an administrative headache on very large and distributed systems. These days there are lots of ways around that and new technologies have emerged to hide this structure beneath the surface, so it really isn't a huge issue for Windows systems today. However back when Unix reigned supreme, these technologies weren't available and they went with the other approach, a unified filesystem.

Unified Filesystem

Linux being based on Unix has a unified filesystem. That means that unlike Windows that has multiple root devices, a Linux system has only one and it is always mounted on '/' which is Unix-speak for the root directory. If there is only one root directory, then how does Linux handle additional devices, all of which we know contain their own filesystems?

The solution is to take the root directory of the new device and then attach it on an existing directory in the tree. This is known as mounting a filesystem. This allows Linux to have an almost unlimited number of devices as it can attach them anywhere in the existing tree. This means that you could mount one device and then mount another device on a directory inside the first device. From the user's point of view, they can move through all these different directories as though they were all on one big device. The physical structure (that is all the disks and the raw data on them) is completely hidden from the end users. They have no way to tell they've crossed from one device to another.

This solves the issues highlighted with the separate root approach in that the unified filesystem is consistent regardless of what the underlying mechanism is. In fact you can mount network file shares and even virtual file systems in to the tree. Of course the benefits of the separate root approach have now become the downside for the unified approach. It's no longer easy to see where things are going and this again can make things more confusing. Like Windows, Linux systems have evolved over time so that these problems aren't quite as pronounced as they would otherwise be. However these benefits are mostly seen in the GUI and tend to be far less pronounced when using the command line.

The Mac has to be Different

As an interesting comparison, OSX on the Mac makes use of both approaches. Under the covers, OSX is a Unix based system and so it does have a unified file system. However unless you go to the command line (and most Mac users don't), you will never see evidence of this. When you attach a USB stick to the Mac, it will mount it in a similar way as Linux, but it will show it to the user as though it were it's own root device in a similar approach to Windows. However the Mac doesn't assign a drive letter, it just sets up a unique name.

Bring it all Together

Admittedly that's a fair bit of theory and you're probably wondering where all the fun commands are that we promised to show you. You might also be wondering why we just bored you with all that and when (if ever) such information might be useful. The reason we've put emphasis on this theory up front is because when we started out with Linux a lot of the things that caught us out where preconceptions from using other operating systems. When one of us first installed Linux some 15 years ago, it took several hours of swearing before he figured out what "You need a root '/' device meant". This isn't just a Linux thing, a dabbling with the BSD family of operating systems and its alternative way of handling disks caused us to wipe the wrong disk because we were thinking Linux and not BSD.

So hopefully this last section will save you from some of the pain that we went through when we first started out. You don't need to memorize all the theory, but if you come away from this section with an appreciation that despite many similarities, Linux is not Windows or a Mac, then you will be ahead of the game.

Everything as a File

Now normally when we discuss this topic, we start by talking about hard disk partitions, because most people are familiar with those and there's a nice easy mapping between the way Linux presents them and the physical device itself. As the Pi doesn't technically have a hard disk (it pulls some strings to make the SD Card look and feel like one), this easy example isn't actually available on the Pi. The thing is, it's too good an example to pass up and so we're going to stick with the classic. So without further ado, here are the files that describe the disk set up on one of our servers:

```
/dev/sda
/dev/sda1
/dev/sda2
/dev/sdb
/dev/sdb1
```

As you can see, these files all live in the /dev directory which is where Linux keeps all the device files. There's quite a bit more to say on this, but we'll come back to it a little later as trust us, it will make much more sense if we cover it last. So for now, let's ignore the directory and focus on our collection of files. You'll notice that in this example, all of the files start with the 'sd' prefix. This is because they are all 'SCSI Disks' and share the same driver. Out of interest, for machines that have IDE based disks, the prefix is 'hd' for 'Hard Disk'.

So now we know that we have some SCSI based disks (SATA disks also show up as SCSI) but what else can we tell from those files? Well, you'll notice that we have sda and we have sdb. The first SCSI disk on the system is assigned to sda and the second is assigned to sdb. It will probably come as no surprise to learn that the third disk will end up being assigned to sdc. As we don't see an sdc in our example, we can assume that there are only two disks on this system.

Now we're really getting somewhere. We can see that we have two SCSI disks on our system and now we just have one more thing to discuss - the numbers stuck on the end of the names. In this case, the number refers to the partition number on the drive. The first partition is 1 and the second partition is 2. Nice and simple with no real surprises we're sure. With this additional information we cannot only specify which disk but also which partition on that disk.

This does of course beg the question of why you should care. Surely there must be an easier way to find out what disks are attached to the system? Well you'd be right, but we're not looking at this to discover what's connected to the system, rather we're looking at how we can specify a particular device that we want to access. Remember, everything in Linux is a file and so even physical devices are represented in that way. When we want to access a hard disk or we want to access a particular parition we do so be accessing the relevant file.

Some real world examples would be useful here. When you want to make changes to the partition table on a hard disk, you use the 'fdisk' tool. The fdisk tool will of course need to know which disk you want to work. Assuming you want to partition your second disk, the command would look like this:

```
fdisk /dev/sdb
```

Because we're partitioning the drive itself, we want to refer to the whole device and /dev/sdb lets us do that. But let's say we have done our partitioning and we have one big partition that we want to format for Linux to use. The command for that is mkfs.ext4 (on modern Linux distributions) and as before, you're going to need to tell the command what you want to format. In this case we want the first partition on our second disk so the command would look like this:

```
mkfs.ext4 /dev/sdb1
```

Again, this makes sense as we're referring to a specific partition on a specific device. No big leaps of faith here, but we can now share a little secret with you. The mkfs.ext4 command, doesn't really care what filename you give it. If you had forgotten to put the '1' on the end, it would have happily formatted the entire device. This is a case of "everything as a file" at work - because everything is a file and files are all accessed in the same way, our tools simply read and write to files - they neither know or care what it is they're writing to!

This concept takes a bit more effort to really understand. Under the covers Linux manages all of these different devices for us, each with its own specific requirements and drivers. To keep things simple for application developers (not to mention the users), Linux hides all of this complexity and instead presents each device to us as a specific file. This brings us nicely back to the /dev directory (we told you it would come up). The files in that directory are special in that they don't really exist, at least not as physical files that are stored anywhere. Linux creates a virtual filesystem that it then populates with files for the devices that are available on a given computer. As our Pi doesn't have any SATA or SCSI disks, you won't find any /dev/sd files on your Pi.

Filesystem Layout

Okay, now let's take a look at how the filesystem is laid out on your Pi. You'll find that the structure is very similar to what you'd find on any Linux system so not only will this help you master your Pi but you'll also be able to navigate servers as well. So let's get stuck in...

/ (Root Directory)

This is the root directory (not to be confused with the root user's home directory) and represents the top of the file hierarchy. Everything goes somewhere in or under this directory, no exceptions. As we discussed earlier in the chapter, Linux has a unified hierarchy and this is where it all starts.

/root

This is the home directory for the root user and spends a large amount of its time being confused with the root directory (that is '/'). It can get more confusing because if you are in the root directory and someone asks you to "go into the root directory", which one do they actually mean? Often you can easily tell from context, but if not, don't be afraid to ask for clarification; you'd be surprised how often this one comes up.

/etc

/etc is arguably one of the most important directories on your system. It contains all of the configuration files for not only your system but also the applications that you might have installed (such as the Apache web server). Many users new to Linux take care to back up their applications but often forget about the configurations stored in /etc. At the end of the day the application can usually be replaced quite easily, but getting that config right from scratch can be a real headache. This is a directory you want to take great care of.

/proc

/proc is a virtual filesystem that the kernel uses to provide easy access from userland tools. Everything you ever needed to know about the system state or running processes can be found in /proc. Two common examples are the CPU configuration (stored in /proc/cpuinfo) and memory usage (stored in /proc/meminfo). Most of this information is read only which makes sense as it is just a virtual representation. However some files do allow communication to go both ways and you can potentially use it to tweak kernel and system settings whilst the machine is running.

/var

/var is generally where you'll find files created by your applications and the system itself. For example most applications will store their logs in /var/log/ and many will store the lock files in /var/run/. The apache web server used to use /var/www/ for storing a website's files. In fact we highlighted this feature in a previous book. In modern distributions this is no longer the case with such files tending to be located in the /srv/ directory.

/boot

Traditionally the /boot directory actually lived on its own small partition on the first hard disk. At the time, the majority of computers were unable to boot from a single big partition, so it was very common to see these split out. On modern machines, this is no longer a problem and so this directory is often included in the root directory directly. As its name suggests, it holds the key files needed to boot a system, including the bootloader and the Linux kernel itself.

/bin and /sbin

These locations store user and administrative programs respectively. Usually a normal user only has /bin in their path and so they effectively can't see applications in /sbin. There are some applications that the user can access even though they're generally used only by administrators, but the user needs to know where they are. Generally this doesn't pose a problem and you won't ever need to go looking for anything.

/dev

We've already touched on this directory in the "Everything as a file" section. It contains a file for each device or sub-device on the current system and provides a way for system tools (and of course users) to easily access the hardware on a particular machine. Apart from the disk devices that we touched on earlier, there are also devices for graphics cards, sound cards, virtual terminals and more.

■ **Note** You won't find network cards in the /dev directory as they're considered a special case. To find information on network interfaces, you need to use the 'sudo ifconfig -a' command. This will list all the network devices that Linux knows about.

/home

Traditionally all user home directories would be stored under /home and this was often its own partition, disk or network share. The idea was to keep user data separate from system data and applications. Most Unix based systems still follow this rule but there are occasions where you will some home directories living elsewhere i.e. the root user's home directory. The Mac for example stores home directories in /Users and some businesses will put different users in different locations based upon their needs. While /home generally only contains home directories, there's no requirement that home directories actually reside here.

/lib

This directory contains library files that are needed by various applications. Libraries allow functionality to be packaged up and then shared by other applications. A good example might be a database driver. So that these applications can find those libraries, they need to be installed in a known location and with a known file name. It's rare that you'd need to poke around in this directory, but if you do you should be careful because breaking things in here could affect the stability of your system.

/lost+found

We mention this one for completeness but it's not really part of the filesystem structure per se. Rather it's where files get placed when the filesystem loses track of them. For example if a disk were to be damaged, you would need to run a disk repair. Some files may be recovered but for various reasons, it may be impossible to determine where that file came from. If that happens, Linux will place those lost souls in this directory. We've never had cause to look into this directory and most likely you'll never need to look in there either. Lastly, this directory can turn up in the root directory of any mounted filesystem, not just in / because each filesystem has to track its lost souls independently.

/media

This directory is relatively new to Linux and was added to make a clear distinction between mounted external devices (such as those in /mnt) and removable media such as USB sticks, cameras and media players. These are usually handled automatically under Linux and so usually you won't manually add or remove anything in this directory.

/mnt

Short for mount, the /mnt directory was traditionally where you would mount additional filesystems. If you wanted to attach a network share or an external hard disk, you would create a directory in /mnt and mount in there. Floppy disks and CDROMS were also generally found here as /mnt/floppy and /mnt/cdrom respectively. However in recent years this directory has mostly fallen by the wayside.

/usr

This is where most of the software on the machine ends up and so it is often the largest directory on a server (at least if you don't count user home areas). Although it's useful to know where the software lives on your machine, because everything is handled automatically for you, everything in here should "just work".

/opt

This directory is a jack of all trades. On some systems it is packed full of applications and on others it remains completely empty. It's usually used for third party software and applications. For example the Oracle database server installs in /opt/ by default. You probably won't find much cause to use this directory, but be careful if you do because it's easy to forget things that are sitting in /opt/ when it comes to taking backups and so forth.

/srv

Another relative newcomer, the /srv/ directory is the designated location for storing data for services that serve files. This is the new home for the Apache web server for example. Although this directory seems to be present, some applications still don't make use of it either out of custom or simply because everyone is used to the contents being somewhere else. If you're looking for things that used to be in /var/ this is probably a good place to look next.

/sys

This directory contains system information and like /proc it is stored only in memory, as it's a virtual system. It doesn't seem to get an awful lot of use and we ourselves have never even had to look inside this directory. However, we have it on good authority that /sys is very useful and something we should be very happy to have.

/tmp

This directory is the computers scratch pad and all sorts of applications create files in this directory. It is used whenever temporary file storage is used (such as during processing). Historically this directory was supposed to be emptied on a reboot, but in practice it rarely was. With newer distributions moving to systemd, /tmp will almost certainly be vaporized on a reboot. Be very careful if you're putting anything in here, as it is unlikely to survive you rebooting your Pi.

Wrapping it up

That pretty much sums up the key areas on the Linux filesystem. No doubt there are other little nooks and crannies that you might come across as you look around your system but they will probably be a sub set of these. Remember, although this structure is followed by most systems, most doesn't necessarily mean all and you might come across some differences or where directories are used in other ways.

Putting it to Work

We've covered a huge amount so far in this chapter. We've looked at how filesystems work and how Unix systems (and Linux in particular) have adopted a unified approach. We looked at "Everything as a file" and we showed how these special files and filesystems fit into the grand scheme of things. We wrapped all of that up with an overview of what goes where on the filesystem and what they do. What we haven't done yet is actually used the filesystem ourselves.

So far we have been pretty much "hands free" but that's all going to change in this section. We're going to start off by showing you how to create directories and move about on the file system. Once we've given you the power to create, we'll then give you the power to destroy and you'll be able to remove files and directories at will (not always a good idea mind). We'll wrap this section up with a quick overview on Linux file permissions and how to read and set them. Let us begin!

Where are we? Using pwd

The first thing we need to show you is how to figure out where you are on the system. The easiest way to get your bearings is to look at the command prompt. We talked about this in the last chapter. As a quick refresher here is what the command prompt looks like while we're sitting in our home directory:

```
[pi@raspberrypi ~]$
```

The tilde (aka the squiggly line) is short hand for the current user's home directory. We've highlighted this feature already when we first introduced it so we won't go through it again, but let's see what it looks like when we're in the /usr/lib directory:

```
[pi@raspberrypi lib]$
```

Well this could pose a problem. We know we're in /usr/lib but the prompt only shows us the last part of the path. This is actually a good idea because although you can set your prompt to show the whole path (and it seems like a good idea at the time) you will soon get irritated when the path takes up most of the screen. That doesn't solve the problem though. For all we know we could be in /usr/lib or /danger/lib. Needless to say this could have unpleasant consequences. So what we need is the 'pwd' command. We touched on this useful tool in the last chapter as well, but in case you missed it, here it is again:

```
[pi@raspberrypi lib]$ pwd
/usr/lib/
[pi@raspberrypi lib]$
```

This tool is very useful for telling us where we are but it doesn't tell us anything about what's in the same location with us. It's like being blindfolded and told you're standing in the kitchen; it's a great start, but you're still effectively blind. You'd certainly like to know who and what is in the room with you and for that we need the 'ls' command. This command does have a large number of options though and so we will only cover the most common ones, those that we use every day. Actually you can just remember them as recipes because you'll often just pass the same options time after time (or at least we do).

First, let's get back to our home directories with:

```
[pi@raspberrypi lib]$ cd ~
```

What's in here with us? Using ls

Now let's see what's in here with us:

```
[pi@raspberrypi ~]$ ls
Desktop    python_games
[pi@raspberrypi ~]$
```

Although we can't easily show it in the book, Desktop and python_games are both colored deep blue. This tells us they are directories. At present we don't have any files in this directory, or do we? Actually we do but by they are considered hidden files. Under Linux any file that begins with a period (or full stop) is considered hidden. There's nothing special about the files themselves and more often than not they are various config or temporary files that various applications have created. We generally don't want these files cluttering up our display, so ls and friends don't show them. We can however force ls to show us those files with the '-a' flag like so:

```
[pi@raspberrypi ~]$ ls
.  ..  .bash_history  .bash_logout  .bashrc  .profile  python_games
[pi@raspberrypi ~]$
```

Creating Files to Play with, Using Touch

For now we'll leave the -a flag alone and create our own files to play with. As we haven't covered how to create and edit text files yet (we will show you how to do that in Chapter 7) we'll introduce you to another little tool called 'touch.' Under Linux, files have two timestamps - the creation timestamp and the last modified timestamp. These allow you to see when a file was created and when it was last updated. This is useful from an administration point of view because you can see which files are actively being used, but various tools (such as backup scripts) use this timestamp to figure out if a file has changed since they last looked at them. Sometimes it is useful to be able to update that timestamp without changing the contents of the file and this is where touch comes in. It touches the file which updates the timestamp but if the file doesn't currently exist, then touch will create it for you. In other words it's a great tool for creating empty files. So, let's start off by creating a couple of originally named files:

```
[pi@raspberrypi ~]$ touch raspberry
[pi@raspberrypi ~]$ touch pi
[pi@raspberrypi ~]$ ls
Desktop pi python_games raspberry
[pi@raspberrypi ~]$
```

And that's all there is to it. As you can see from the ls that followed it, we now have two additional files. This time they are gray in color which tells us that they're normal files. By coloring the entries for us, ls makes it much easier to see what we're doing. For example, any file that is executable, will be colored in green, but we'll come back to file permissions later in this chapter.

So far we only have two files, but if we had ten or twenty, it would start to get a bit crowded in here. The way to handle that is of course to create directories to store our files (and potentially other directories) in and that's what we'll look at next.

■ **Note** Directories and folders are basically the same thing. Originally called directories, Microsoft started referring to them as folders which they felt was a better description. Although Linux used to use the term directories, as it has become more of a desktop operating system with people moving over from Windows, the folder terminology has become increasingly common.

Somewhere to Store our Files, Using Mkdir

To create a directory, we use the 'mkdir' or 'make directory' command. Unsurprisingly this will create a new directory. However if there is a file with the same name or the directory already exists, you will get an error message. Let's create a directory called 'pifun' to store our files:

```
[pi@raspberrypi ~]$ mkdir pifun
[pi@raspberrypi ~]$ mkdir pifun
mkdir: cannot create directory 'pifun': File exists
[pi@raspberrypi ~]$
```

As you can see, trying to create the directory twice will cause an error. Don't be distracted by 'File exists', this could actually refer to either a directory or a file. Another quick ls and we'll see that things are moving along quite nicely:

```
[pi@raspberrypi ~]$ ls
Desktop pi pifun python_games raspberry
[pi@raspberrypi ~]$
```

Making Use of Our New Directory, Using the mv Command

So now that we have our directory, let's tidy up the mess we've been making. As we want to move the files into our new directory (rather than just create a copy of them), we'll need to use the 'mv' (or 'move') command. This command is a bit more complicated than the ones we've covered before as it takes two arguments rather than one. This makes sense though because not only do we need to tell mv what we want to move but we also need to tell it where we want it to move the file to. As with most file commands under Linux, the first argument is the source and the second argument is the destination. Let's move those files now:

```
[pi@raspberrypi ~]$ mv pi pifun
[pi@raspberrypi ~]$ mv raspberry pifun
[pi@raspberrypi ~]$ ls
Desktop pifun python_games
[pi@raspberrypi ~]$
```

So far so good. Now we want to make sure that our files arrived in one piece. There are two ways we could do that. We could go into the pifun directory with 'cd' and then run the ls command or alternatively, we could simply give ls the path to the directory that we want to look into. We've already used the first approach, so let's try give the second approach a try:

```
[pi@raspberrypi ~]$ ls pifun
pi raspberry
[pi@raspberrypi ~]$
```

Time for Some Cloning, How to use the cp Command

Admittedly this isn't very exciting, but as a newly minted administrator, you'll be spending a lot of time moving files about and checking where things are. So far you've learned how to move a file but what if you just want to copy a file instead? When taking a back up or getting a selection of files ready to send to a friend, you want to actually keep the originals. For this we use the 'cp' command which you've probably already correctly guessed is short for 'copy'. Let's move into our new directory and copy one of our files:

```
[pi@raspberrypi ~]$ cd pifun
[pi@raspberrypi pifun]$ cp pi pi2
[pi@raspberrypi pifun]$ ls
pi pi2 raspberry
[pi@raspberrypi pifun]$
```

That worked well, we now have pi and pi2 just as we expected. Let's try the same thing again only this time, we'll copy a directory:

```
[pi@raspberrypi pifun]$ mkdir moarpi
[pi@raspberrypi pifun]$ cp moarpi moarpi2
cp: ommiting directory 'moarpi'
[pi@raspberrypi pifun]$
```

That time it didn't quite go according to plan. The reason our copy attempt failed was because by default 'cp' will only copy individual files. It won't copy entire directories. The reasoning behind this is that when you copy a directory, you copy everything within it, including all of its files and directories. This could be a lot of data and could take up a lot of space as well as a lot of time to complete. Forcing us to be explicit about our intentions (which will soon become second nature to you) means that when we mean to copy a single file but accidentally pick a directory, we will get stopped before any copying takes place.

That's all well and good but what if you really did want to copy that directory? When we first looked at the copy command we mentioned tasks like taking backups and let's be honest, you're much more likely to want to back up a directory than a list of specific files. We can get the behavior we're looking for by telling the 'cp' that we want to copy recursively. This will then copy the directory and anything within that directory to the destination. We specify this by using the '-r' flag like so:

```
[pi@raspberrypi pifun]$ cp -r moarpi moarpi2
[pi@raspberrypi pifun]$ ls
moarpi moarpi2 pi pi2 raspberry
[pi@raspberrypi pifun]$
```

Unlike the copy command, when you move a directory there is no need to specify that you want to do so recursively, this is because moving a directory without its contents wouldn't make an awful lot of sense.

The Power to Destroy, Using the rm Command

So far we've shown you how to create files and directories and how to copy and move them about. Now we're going to show you how to destroy those files with the remove or 'rm' command. It goes without saying that the rm command is one of the most dangerous in your arsenal. It can quite easily destroy an entire server if you're not careful and we know people who have accidentally done just that.

For a change of pace, let's look at how we would delete an empty directory. We can use the 'rmdir' command for this which is short for 'remove directory.' Now the catch with this command is that it will only delete directories that are completely empty. If there is even a single file inside, this command will fail. This makes it very safe to use, but not all that practical as generally when you delete a directory, you also want to remove all of its contents. Let's kill two birds with one stone:

```
[pi@raspberrypi pifun]$ rmdir moarpi2
[pi@raspberrypi pifun]$ rm moarpi
rm: cannot remove 'moarpi': Is a directory
[pi@raspberrypi pifun]$
```

We were able to delete moarpi2 with 'rmdir' because the directory itself was empty, but when we tried using the rm command, it refused to cooperate. This is because the rm command was written with similar reasoning to the copy command. As removing a directory is far more dangerous than simply copying it, this is probably a good thing. We can use the same '-r' flag to tell rm to delete recursively:

```
[pi@raspberrypi pifun]$ rm -r moarpi
[pi@raspberrypi pifun]$
```

Success! Now sometimes when you try this, especially on a large directory with lots of files and sub-directories, you can end up with lots of issues that cause rm to give up. For example, some files might be write protected. You can suppress these errors by using the '-f' flag. This means 'force' and is akin to saying "Damn the torpedoes! Full speed ahead!". That sounds like a great idea until you stop to think what would happen if you ran this command (which you should NEVER do):

```
[pi@raspberrypi pifun]$ rm -rf /
```

If you accidentally run that command, rm will proceed to delete absolutely everything on your system. If you happen to have a USB hard disk attached or you've mounted some network shares, then you're in real trouble because rm won't confine itself to your internal disks - it will crawl through the entire tree deleting everything in its wake. This is one of the reasons why you should use a normal user account for day to day tasks. Your own user will not have sufficient privileges to delete anything critical to the system - but even then, chances are high that you can still damage all your attached media. You need to be very very careful whenever you use the rm command and you'd better double and triple check it because Linux will assume you know what you're doing and it won't ask for confirmation!

The 'rm' command can also remove files simply by providing the path to the file. You don't need to use the '-r' flag for this operation so you can simply do:

```
[pi@raspberrypi pifun]$ rm pi2
[pi@raspberrypi pifun]$ ls
pi raspberry
[pi@raspberrypi pifun]$
```

And that in a nutshell is how you move about and manipulate the file system.

Fully Qualified and Relative Paths

In Linux there are two ways to specify a path. You can either give a fully qualified path that starts with a forward slash, or you can give a relative path which starts with either a filename, directory name, a dot or two dots. Strange though these might sound, they are both just ways of providing a specific location to your programs.

A path is considered fully qualified when it starts from a fixed reference point i.e. the root directory. Regardless of where you are on a system, a fully qualified path will always point to the same location. It's like the old bell tower in the middle of town, if you give anyone directions using that as your reference point, you have a common anchor that both you and your friend know how to reach.

On the other hand a relative path depends on your current location to make sense. You can specify paths using `./` to mean the current directory or `../` to mean the next directory up. If you had a path that looks like `../../test.txt`, this would only work from a few specific locations. It's nice and short as well as being easy to type. The same file might be accessible with /home/pi/test.txt. Unlike the relative path, this one can be used from anywhere on the file system without any problem.

So when should you use one or the other? The answer is, you should use whichever option is the most convenient or makes the most sense for the task. Sometimes it's faster or easier to use a fully qualified path. Other times you are buried deep down in the tree and writing fully qualified paths would be tedious at best and totally confusing at worst.

Users and Groups

We're only going to touch on the basics of users and groups here so that you know enough to understand the file permissions section that is coming up next. Users and groups are key to the way Linux secures your files and you'll need to know about them before we move on to the next section.

In the Unix way of thinking every person has their own username. A username identifies a particular person or entity (for example a web server might have its own username) on a particular system. So far we've spent most of our time as the 'pi' user but we've also seen that we can become the 'root' user. Your username is the key that Linux uses to identify you as you.

Groups are similarly straight forward. Each user belongs to one primary group, but may actually be a member of any number of groups on the system. On a university system, a student's username might have its own private group (standard practice on Red Hat and Debian systems these days) but they might also belong to a student group and a research group. They might also belong to a group specific to their department. Groups are useful to us administrators because we can group a selection of users together and treat them as a single entity. This makes things such as file permissions much easier to manage.

When you create a new user on your Pi, you will automatically create a group with the same name. On some systems, users would by default join a user's group - but as you'll see in the next section, this could lead to accidentally giving people access to files which they shouldn't have. Because a private group is by definition private, no one else will be a member and so no one can gain access to your files just because they happen to be in the same group as you. This is why on modern systems you'll usually see that the owner and group of a file happen to be the same.

We cover users and groups in more depth in Chapter 8 on BASH.

File Permissions

File permissions allow you to express who you want to be able to access your files and what exactly they're allowed to do with them. There are three different permissions that you can set. The first is whether or not someone can read your file. The second is whether they can write to your file and third is whether they can execute it (i.e. run it like an application).

Of course just being able to set these permissions on a file isn't particularly flexible. You might want to give access to only a certain group of people and restrict everyone else. This is where users and groups come into play. On Linux there are effectively three roles that a given user might fall into. The first is user and refers to the owner of the file. The second is group which refers to the group that owns the file. The last is technically known as world but it is also often referred to as other.

Each role gets its own combination of permissions, that is you can define whether any of those three roles can read, write or execute your files. We're going to show you how to do just that but before we do that, we need to show you how to see what permissions are actually in effect and so now is a good time to show you how to use the '-lh' option for the 'ls' command. Let's try running it now:

```
[pi@raspberrypi pifun]$ ls -lh
-rw-r--r-- 1 pi pi 0 Oct 7 16:29 pi
-rw-r--r-- 1 pi pi 0 Oct 7 16:58 pi2
-rw-r--r-- 1 pi pi 0 Oct 7 16:29 raspberry
[pi@raspberrypi pifun]$
```

The '-lh' argument specifies that we want ls to show us a list of files (-l) and that we want file sizes to be in human readable format (-h). Without the human readable flag, ls will show us all sizes in bytes which when you're dealing with large files is not very easy to read. It doesn't really matter in this example because our files are empty anyway.

There are two things that we're really interested in as far as file permissions go. The first describes the permissions currently in force and the second shows us which user and group owns the file. Let's break it down for the raspberry file:

```
-rw-r--r-- 1 pi pi 0 Oct 7 16:29 raspberry
```

The file permissions part is:

```
-rw-r--r--
```

There are ten possible slots in that list and for now, we're only interest in the first nine. If a particular permission is missing (or in the case of the first hyphen where it's a normal file), ls will show a hyphen. A normal file always has a hyphen in the first slot. If it was referencing a directory, the first slot would be a 'd' to highlight that it's not a file. This slot can also be an 'l' if the file is a link (or shortcut) and we'll show you how to use these in the next section. For now though we can ignore the first slot and focus on the final nine slots.

The remaining nine slots are grouped in threes to give us three groups. These correspond to user, group and world roles respectively. Each of three slots in each group represents a specific permission, read, write and execute. Where the permission is set, you will see a letter, but when the permission is not set, you will get the hyphen. If our raspberry file had all permissions set, it would look like this:

```
-rwxrwxrwx
```

Let's split that out a bit so it's a little easier to read:

```
-    rwx    rwx   rwx
```

So if we look at the first three, we can see that the owner has read, write and execute permissions. We can also see that group and world also have full permissions. To interpret what these permissions mean though we really need to know who actually owns the file. Let's take a look at the part of the line that shows who owns the file:

```
pi pi
```

Well, that wasn't too painful. Remember on modern Linux machines, users have their own private groups which are named after the user. That's what we're seeing here. The first 'pi' refers to the owner which is of course the pi user. By default when a file is created the group ownership is set to the user's default group. In this case that would be our private group which is also called 'pi'. So if we look at our original file entry:

```
-rw-r--r-- 1 pi pi 0 Oct 7 16:29 raspberry
```

we can read this as "The pi user has read and write privileges. The group has read privileges and world also has read privileges". Linux applies these permissions in a specific order based on who you are. If your username matches the owner of the file, then the user permissions will apply when you try to access it. If you're not the owner but you are in the same group as the file, then Linux will apply the group permissions to you. If you're neither the owner or in the same group, Linux will apply the permissions from the world role. In our example though, the permissions for world and group are identical, so if you're not the owner, regardless you will get the same level of access. However only the owner can actually save changes to the file. There is one exception to this rule however - the root user. The root user is effectively immune to file permissions and can change permissions and file ownership for any file on the system, regardless of who the owner actually is.

The execute permission allows you to execute a file as a program. This is a security feature so you can effectively stop people executing commands that you don't want them to. However you have to be careful because if a user can read your file, there is nothing stopping them from copying it to their own file and making that file executable. The execute bit has another purpose when it comes to directories. Obviously you can't execute a directory so instead this flag means that the user (or group or world) is allowed to browse the directory, that is, they can do an 'ls' on it. They might not be able to access anything in the directory but they can still have a peak and see what's hiding in there. If you give a user permission to read a directory but not to execute, they will be able to read a file inside, but they wouldn't be able to browse for it, they would have to know the file name in advance.

That's really all there is to it. There is a feature called "Extended File Attributes" but we're not going to cover those in this book. They provide a great deal more flexibility than the standard model but are similarly more complicated. If you're used to how Windows handles permissions, then you'll find that extended file attributes are a bit more inline with what you're used to.

Setting File Permissions

First we're going to look at how we can set file permissions and for this, Table 4-1 will be very helpful.

Table 4-1. *Setting Permissions*

Role	How to apply	What to apply
u - user	+ - add	r - read
g - group	- - remove	w - write
o - other /world	= - explicitly set	x - execute
a - all		

We will be using the chmod command which changes file permissions. You can specify permissions as a combination of the above values. These can be combined in three different ways. You can add permissions, take permissions away and explicitly set permissions. The difference is that the first two will leave all the other permissions intact after they've done their thing. If you explicitly set permissions, any unspecified permissions will be revoked.

Let's start out removing all permissions from everyone for our pi file:

```
[pi@raspberrypi pifun]$ chmod a=  pi
[pi@raspberrypi pifun]$ ls -lh
---------- 1 pi pi 0 Oct  8 03:52 pi
[pi@raspberrypi pifun]$
```

We can see that all file permissions have been removed from the file, but how does the command actually work? Well permissions are specified with three parts. Who you want the change to apply to, how you want the change applied and what you want the change to be. In this case we applied the changes to 'a' which is basically short hand for 'ugo' i.e. it applies the changes to everyone. We used the equals sign which means we want to explicitly set the permissions and then we didn't actually supply any permissions. If a permission is absent it is assumed not to be set and so in our example by not supplying any permissions we effectively revoked all of them regardless of what they were previously.

Seeing as it's our file, we want to give ourselves full permissions. Admittedly the execute bit is not much use in this case (but you'll find it invaluable when you start scripting - see Chapter 8) but we're going to give it to ourselves anyway. We can do that with this command:

```
[pi@raspberrypi pifun]$ chmod u+rwx pi
[pi@raspberrypi pifun]$ ls -lh
-rwx------ 1 pi pi 0 Oct  8 03:52 pi
[pi@raspberrypi pifun]$
```

Let's pick this command apart. We specified that we wanted to change only the user's permissions, that we wanted to add them (not that it mattered in this case because we'd removed all permissions before hand so an equals sign would have done the same job) and that we wanted read, write and execute privileges. To wrap up this example let's restore read access to the group and world roles:

```
[pi@raspberrypi pifun]$ chmod go+r pi
[pi@raspberrypi pifun]$ ls -lh
-rwxr--r-- 1 pi pi 0 Oct  8 03:52 pi
[pi@raspberrypi pifun]$
```

Just for completeness let's step through this last example. We want to apply the permissions to the group and other roles, we want to add the permissions to what is already there and we want to grant read privileges. And that is pretty much it for setting file permissions. There is an alternative style that uses numbers rather than letters to specify what permissions you want to set. To get the same effect as what we have already (i.e. it doesn't have any affect) we would use:

```
[pi@raspberrypi pifun]$ chmod 744 pi
[pi@raspberrypi pifun]$ ls -lh
-rwxr--r-- 1 pi pi 0 Oct  8 03:52 pi
[pi@raspberrypi pifun]$
```

In this system, each permission has its own value. Read is 4, write is 2 and execute is 1. To set the permissions, you add up the numbers to get the total. For example to set all permissions you'd add 4 and 2 and 1 to get 7. For read you would simply do 4 plus 0 plus 0 which of course gives you 4. Put them all together we get 744. This syntax is the original syntax used on most Unix systems. Using the letters is a relatively new idea but at the end of the day they both achieve the same results. The main benefit of the new syntax is that it's a lot clearer and easier to pick up. Personally we tend to use the number style but that's only because we've been doing it for so long and it's become second nature to us. You should feel free to use whatever system you feel the most comfortable with.

So now you can manipulate permissions like a guru but we are still missing the second part of the puzzle, we haven't shown you how to change ownership of the file. This is actually a lot less common than you might think, far less common than tweaking the occasional file permission that's for sure. There's also another little wrinkle. A normal user (that is anyone other than root) cannot actually change which user owns the file. The reason for this is that if you accidentally assign the file to another user by accident, you have no way to actually get that file back again. Of course being all knowing and all seeing the root user can change the ownership for any file on the system.

We can simulate "rootness" by using sudo. As discussed earlier this little command acts as a filter of sorts. It always runs as root, regardless of who executes it, and executes commands as root on their behalf. To prevent any shenanigans, sudo will check the user and the command they are trying to run against an approved list. If you're on that list (and the pi user is) you can execute all sorts of magic without every technically becoming root yourself.

To use sudo all we have to do is prefix the command with the 'sudo' command. That's pretty much it. When you first run sudo it will ask you for a password. This is the password for your particular user and not the password for the root user. The aim is that you can prove that you are the pi user and then sudo will check to see what the pi user is allowed to do. This means that if you have lots of users on your computer, and you want to let them do some more powerful commands but don't want to give them root access, you can set up sudo to allow them to execute a specific command without having to hand over the keys to the mansion.

Let's start off by trying to give the file to the root user using the 'chown' (or change ownership) command:

```
[pi@raspberrypi pifun]$ chown root pi
chown: changing ownership of 'pi': Operation not permitted
[pi@raspberrypi pifun]$
```

The operation not permitted is Linux's way of telling us to get stuffed. To pull this off we'll need root privileges so let's put sudo to work for us and run the command again:

```
[pi@raspberrypi pifun]$ sudo chown root pi
[pi@raspberrypi pifun]$ ls -lh
-rwxr--r-- 1 root pi 0 Oct  8 03:52 pi
[pi@raspberrypi pifun]$
```

Success! We were able to change the owner to the root user. This will work with any valid user and any file or directory that you wish to change. There is another command called 'chgrp' which you won't be surprised to know allows you to change which group owns a particular file. Now there is a bit of an issue with this command as well. Although normal users are allowed to change the group, they are only allowed to change it to a group of which they're a member. If your user is only a member of its private group, then you won't be able to do an awful lot with this command either.

Once again it's root and sudo to the rescue. As root can do whatever it pleases, it can change the group accordingly. As it happens, it looks an awful lot like our last command:

```
[pi@raspberrypi pifun]$ sudo chgrp root pi
[pi@raspberrypi pifun]$ ls -lh
-rwxr--r-- 1 root root 0 Oct  8 03:52 pi
[pi@raspberrypi pifun]$
```

And there we go - the file now belongs to the root group and the root user. When you do have to change file ownership though it's much more common to need to change both the user and the group that owns the file. It's relatively rare to change just the group (we can't remember when we last used the chgrp command). The chown command provides a shortcut that allows us to set both a new owner and a new group at the same time. Let's use this shortcut now to return the ownership of the file to our pi user. We'll still need to use sudo of course:

```
[pi@raspberrypi pifun]$ sudo chown pi:pi pi
[pi@raspberrypi pifun]$ ls -lh
-rwxr--r-- 1 pi pi 0 Oct  8 03:52 pi
[pi@raspberrypi pifun]$
```

With the shortcut you just specify the user and the group separated by a colon. One last thing we need to cover with these commands is they only operate specifically on the file you provide. If you provide a directory rather than a file, it will set the permissions on the directory but those changes won't filter down through to all the files. Sometimes that's what you want, but more often you want the changes to propagate.

Unlike the cp and rm commands that use -r, these two commands use -R, (that is they use the capital letter rather than the lowercase letter). Be careful when you use this because often file permissions are precisely set and if you waltz through obliterating them with your new version, there's no way to undo the damage. As always double check what you've typed before you press the enter key.

Shortcuts and Links

Linux allows you to create links (or shortcuts) by using the ln command (short for link). There are two types of link, one is called hard and one is called soft. A soft link is more like what you might see on a Windows system after using the "create shortcut" feature. It creates a file that is just a pointer to the real location of the file elsewhere on disk. The hard link however is more interesting. When you use a hard link you have effectively created two names for the same file. That might sound like semantics, and with most modern applications being able to follow a soft link there's rarely a need to use a hard link. Hard links are also restricted to a single file system and that file system has to support them (most Linux filesystems do). The main benefit of a hard link is that the hard link is completely indistinguishable from the original file, they are simply two names pointing to the same location. To avoid confusion and to allow links to work across filesystems, you should use a soft link.

Let's do a quick example to show this in action:

```
[pi@raspberrypi pifun]$ ln pi pi1
[pi@raspberrypi pifun]$ ln -s pi pi2
[pi@raspberrypi pifun]$ ls -lh
-rw-rw-r-- 2 miggyx miggyx    0 Oct  8 08:14 pi
-rw-rw-r-- 2 miggyx miggyx    0 Oct  8 08:14 pi1
lrwxrwxrwx 1 miggyx miggyx    3 Oct  8 08:33 pi2 -> pi
[pi@raspberrypi pifun]$
```

Let's have a look at what we've got here. pi and pi1 are identical in every way but that's not really a surprise because apart from the name, they are the same file. You will notice that the number after the file permissions block now shows '2' for pi and pi1. This tells us that there are currently two filenames pointing at this particular file. Also not much of a surprise seeing as we're the ones that created the second entry. Much more interesting is pi2 which we created with a soft link. First we can see that the file permissions have all been set. This isn't a problem because when Linux follows the soft link to the real file, it's the real file's permissions that will be used to define who can access the file. The soft link really just points out the location. We can also see that the filename itself is a bit different. It shows the filename that we originally give the soft link but it also shows the file that the soft link points to. In this case the file happens to be in the same directory but it could just as easily have been anywhere on the system.

That's really all there is to it for creating links. They can be useful when you want to make one directory or file appear to be in a new location. For example a program might write to a data directory and you want to move that directory on to a bigger disk. No problem, you can move it to the bigger disk and then create a soft link to it with the same name. The application probably won't even notice. This can really save you a lot of headache, especially when time is something of a premium (and let's be honest when is it not?).

Summary

This chapter has given you the inside scoop on all things filesystem. We've looked at the history and shown why our filesystems look the way they do. We then touched on how they hang together and how the Linux filesystem itself is structured. We then went on to put that to good use and brought you up to speed on all the basics for creating, copying, moving and deleting your files.

We then looked at file permissions and how they are enforced and how we can go about setting them to match our needs. We also looked at the more traditional way of setting file permissions should you ever come across it. We then showed you how Linux applies these permissions and how you can change which user and group owns a specific file. We then rounded everything off by touching on how you can create links and the differences between both soft and hard varieties.

In the next chapter we're going to expose you to all of the most common commands that you'll find on your Pi. These are the commands that will become part of your toolbox that you'll regularly dip into. In fact we use all of these commands in our daily work. So, onwards to Chapter 5!

CHAPTER 5

Essential Commands

You now have this marvelous new Raspberry Pi that you have installed and configured to accept and run a version of Raspbian Linux. You have logged in and can comfortably move around within the system. You can do the basics on your Pi, but now feel that you are ready to take on more.

Well that's what this chapter is dedicated to: teaching you a whole host of commands so that you can empower yourself as a Linux user. These commands will cover a whole host of functionality ranging from becoming the root super user, examining disk space, terminating processes, and configuring your user space and monitoring environment variables. All these tasks are common ones for the systems administrator and can have a big impact on how your system functions. So without further ado, let's get started.

Become the Boss

Root is a word that describes the base of a tree, something from which all the rest grows. In Linux and UNIX, the term is used to denote the start point of a filesystem (as we saw in Chapter 4) and to denote the master administrative user on the system (covered briefly in Chapter 3). To perform any system or administrative function, you need to be identified as root in order to have permission to change core functionality. Because of this, being root is very much a two-edged sword: unlimited power to change your system and unlimited power to break system functionality. Probably one of the truest things I can say about working in a Linux environment is that eventually you will issue a command as root that will break something (if not everything) and this will cause you no end of hassle or may even require you to reinstall your operating system. For this reason (and related security reasons) its advised that a user never actually login to the shell as the root user.

To solve this problem, we use `sudo`, which we've seen a little of in Chapters 3 and 4. As you know, this tool is a wrapper for any shell command you can think of. This means that if you prefix a command with `sudo` (e.g., `sudo ls`), you will no longer be executing this command as your own user but rather as the root super user. This does make working as the super user slightly more complex, but also far less risky. In fact, many distributions of Linux no longer set a root password, but rather assign a new user the power of `sudo` on creation. This means that all administration must be done via an empowered user with the `sudo` command to issue all the requisite admin functions.

So that you can execute as root, `sudo` requests your user password in order to validate that you are who you say you are, not just someone with access who left their keyboard unattended. In addition to asking all users for their passwords, `sudo` also has a steering file that governs which users and groups have access to the `sudo` command and even the capability to limit which programs they can execute via `sudo`. There is a special command, `visudo`, to edit this steering file (called the sudoers file) that must be run as root (so prefix with `sudo`):

```
$ sudo visudo
```

This code fires up a special instance of one of the system's text editors (normally vi or nano) with the sudoers file already loaded to be edited. For a quick runthrough of how to use vi and nano, please check out Chapter 6.

Inside the sudoers file are a number of things that control how the sudo environment works, including a PATH variable (which we will cover later). The important thing, however, is the line down in the userauth section that looks like this:

```
root    ALL=(ALL:ALL) ALL
```

This line states that the root user on all hosts can access all commands on all other hosts (a *host* is a server on the network). This is a bit confusing, but it basically grants full access to any user that can identify itself as root. There is also another line:

```
%sudo   ALL=(ALL:ALL) ALL
```

This line says that members of the sudo group can also do the same things as the root user: accessing from all hosts on the network all commands that can be executed on all hosts on the network. You will notice the leading % that is used to signify that this is a group name. The basic format of one of these lines is this:

```
<user>  <From which hosts>=(<On which hosts>:<which commands>) < command options and
commands >
```

This syntax is a bit confusing at first so let's have a look at creating a particular set of permissions for your pi user as an example. First we will need to create a new basic set of user permissions that will look just like the root users, but will instead refer to our pi user. This line will look like:

```
pi    ALL=ALL   ALL
```

I have removed the <on which hosts: which commands> section and replaced it with one generic ALL to make things a bit easier to understand. Now let's say that we want the pi user not to be asked for a password. To do this, we add a NOPASSWD: before the final ALL that represents commands. This gives us a new line:

```
pi    ALL=ALL   NOPASSWD: ALL
```

If you add this now, you can run all commands as the pi user without needing to even provide a password. This is a very dangerous command, so let's modify it slightly to make it only the visudo command that can be executed. To do this, we replace the final ALL for commands with the command we wish to use, which in this case is visudo. But we can't just write visudo, we need to provide the whole path to the application, which is /usr/sbin/visudo. So we get the following:

```
pi    ALL=ALL   NOPASSWD: /usr/sbin/visudo
```

Now you should be getting the idea of what you can do within the sudoers file to control how the sudo command is accessed. You can have multiple entries that govern how these commands can be run, by whom and under which conditions. There is also a large amount of functionality for adding aliases, which can be large combinations of commands, hosts, or users. Much of the syntax for these commands is available from the manual for sudoers.

Finally, one last command for you to be aware of is the su command, which is short for switch user. This command does exactly what it implies and switches which user you are, and if you aren't root it will prompt you to enter the password of the user you wish to switch to. One of the niftiest cheats for gaining root access is to combine sudo and su to switch into the root user, with only the current user's password instead of the root user's. This command is the way that many people get round the "no known root password" limitation placed by many Linux distributions:

```
$ sudo su -
```

The minus sign denotes that you wish to gain a login to the environment, and because no other arguments are provided, it will attempt to log in as the super user. You can also use this to switch users by adding the username for a given user prior to the minus. You can also use the sudo command with the -i option to gain an interactive shell that will achieve the same thing:

```
$ sudo -i
```

RTFM

One of my favorite refrains from the tech world is *RTFM*, which is short for *Read The Flaming Manual*. While I have found that asking people for assistance is good, it's always comforting to know that there is a manual you can read, and Linux is no exception. Most applications come with a manual document that can be accessed by using the man command! This command takes whatever you wish to get the manual page for as its first argument. So, if you wanted to look at the manual page for the sudoers command in order to get a better idea of how to write your sudoers file, you would type this:

```
$ man sudoers
```

And then the manual page would appear. Navigating a man page is done in the same way one would navigate a document opened with less (which is a command we will cover further on in this chapter), so navigation is done with the arrows and with page up and page down keys. You can also search for a string by pressing / and then typing what you wish to search for. The n key will help you navigate your way through the file. So, if you ever find yourself in need of some more information on a command, remember to Read The Flaming Man Page!

System Resource Monitoring

One of the key things that a systems administrator will need to do is monitor the usage of resources on his system. While some of these commands may be of less use to your average Pi user, there are some times when being able to see what your system is doing will come in handy.

The first system command to be aware of is top, which is a command for displaying the current usage of resources within your system and displaying which processes are consuming what level of resources. The top command is incredibly powerful and displays a whole host of information about your systems resource usage. The output of top normally looks like Figure 5-1.

```
top - 22:22:11 up 6 days, 20 min,  1 user,  load average: 0.11, 0.08, 0.06
Tasks:  66 total,   1 running,  64 sleeping,   1 stopped,   0 zombie
%Cpu(s):  0.0 us,  0.0 sy,  0.0 ni, 99.9 id,  0.0 wa,  0.0 hi,  0.1 si,  0.0 st
KiB Mem:    123156 total,   109784 used,    13372 free,    30340 buffers
KiB Swap:        0 total,        0 used,        0 free,    41608 cached

  PID USER      PR  NI  VIRT  RES  SHR S  %CPU %MEM    TIME+  COMMAND
 7445 raspbian  20   0  4608 1312  960 R  16.0  1.1   0:00.08 top
    1 root      20   0  1832  680  592 S   0.0  0.6   0:22.11 init
    2 root      20   0     0    0    0 S   0.0  0.0   0:00.45 kthreadd
    3 root      20   0     0    0    0 S   0.0  0.0   0:00.00 ksoftirqd/0
    5 root      20   0     0    0    0 S   0.0  0.0   0:59.85 kworker/u:0
    6 root      -2   0     0    0    0 S   0.0  0.0   0:03.20 rcu_kthread
    7 root       0 -20     0    0    0 S   0.0  0.0   0:00.00 khelper
    8 root      20   0     0    0    0 S   0.0  0.0   0:00.01 kdevtmpfs
    9 root       0 -20     0    0    0 S   0.0  0.0   0:00.00 netns
   10 root      20   0     0    0    0 S   0.0  0.0   0:04.19 sync_supers
   11 root      20   0     0    0    0 S   0.0  0.0   0:00.18 bdi-default
   12 root       0 -20     0    0    0 S   0.0  0.0   0:00.00 kblockd
   13 root      20   0     0    0    0 S   0.0  0.0   0:00.28 khubd
   14 root       0 -20     0    0    0 S   0.0  0.0   0:00.00 rpciod
   16 root      20   0     0    0    0 S   0.0  0.0   0:00.42 khungtaskd
   17 root      20   0     0    0    0 S   0.0  0.0   0:00.51 kswapd0
   18 root      20   0     0    0    0 S   0.0  0.0   0:00.00 fsnotify_mark
   19 root       0 -20     0    0    0 S   0.0  0.0   0:00.00 nfsiod
   20 root       0 -20     0    0    0 S   0.0  0.0   0:00.00 crypto
   27 root       0 -20     0    0    0 S   0.0  0.0   0:00.00 kthrotld
   28 root       0 -20     0    0    0 S   0.0  0.0   0:00.00 VCHIQ-0
   29 root       0 -20     0    0    0 S   0.0  0.0   0:00.00 VCHIQr-0
   30 root       0 -20     0    0    0 S   0.0  0.0   0:00.00 dwc_otg
   31 root       0 -20     0    0    0 S   0.0  0.0   0:00.00 DWC Notificatio
   32 root      20   0     0    0    0 S   0.0  0.0   0:00.00 kworker/u:1
   33 root      20   0     0    0    0 S   0.0  0.0   2:11.51 mmcqd/0
   34 root       0 -20     0    0    0 S   0.0  0.0   0:00.00 ext4-dio-unwrit
  125 root      20   0  2904 1324  728 S   0.0  1.1   0:00.65 udevd
  190 root       0 -20     0    0    0 S   0.0  0.0   0:00.00 bcm2708_spi.0
  951 root      20   0     0    0    0 S   0.0  0.0   1:53.66 RTKTHREAD
  956 root      20   0  5588 1204  848 S   0.0  1.0   0:19.18 wpa_supplicant
  983 root      20   0  6332 2148  396 S   0.0  1.7   0:00.01 dhclient
 1102 root      20   0  2304  796  584 S   0.0  0.6   0:02.77 rpcbind
 1133 statd     20   0  4112 1728 1148 S   0.0  1.4   0:00.06 rpc.statd
 1145 root      20   0  2736  444  264 S   0.0  0.4   0:00.00 rpc.idmapd
 1452 root      20   0 27928 1452 1008 S   0.0  1.2   0:03.53 rsyslogd
 1482 daemon    20   0  2084  324  200 S   0.0  0.3   0:00.02 atd
 1524 root      20   0  3744  784  628 S   0.0  0.6   0:02.29 cron
```

Figure 5-1. *Top in action!*

The output from the top command is huge and if you watch, all the values there are updated regularly. Let's go over the top output line by line so you can understand what you are looking at.

Uptime and Load Average

The first line gives information about the current time and then uptime of the system. It then shows the number of users on the system and finally the load average. *Load average* is one of the most complex things to understand; it is a "meta" variable because it refers to what is going on within your system relative to your system's capability to perform. It contains 3 values that give the average of the current minute, the last 5 minutes and the last 15 minutes. Load average represents the average of actual computation usage and demand for your system's computation resources.

Probably the best way to think of load average I have heard is as a freeway. Normally the percentage value of CPU usage represents how much of the current available computation resources are being used. This is akin to measuring how much traffic is currently on the freeway. The load average compares both how much computation is being used and how much demand there is for CPU usage. This is like examining both the freeway and its onramps. The difference between the two comes when looking at it from the perspective of a "busy lunchtime," meaning that there are lots of cars on the freeway, but just because "it's a busy lunchtime," everyone can get onto the freeway and use it, nobody is stuck waiting on the ramp, and traffic is flowing nicely.

This is why load average is such a powerful metric; it allows you to see demand for your system's computing power in real time so that you can see when your demand begins to spike and can thus take action to lower demand.

Wow, that's a lot on just one line!

Tasks

The second line of the `top` output lists the tasks that the system is currently performing:

- The total number of processes
- The number of actively running processes
- The number of processes that are sleeping in the background
- The number of stopped processes
- The number of zombie processes

Most of these processes are general purpose for being aware of what is going on within your system. But zombie processes can be a real problem. These processes are processes that have finished executing, but are still resident in system memory—often because they need to send a return value to the process that spawned them, but are yet to do so and thus must wait there as the living dead before they can send their final message and depart to the afterlife.

Having a long running zombie process can indicate a problem with the application that is used to spawn it, which is called its parent. If you see zombie processes on your system have a look to see which process spawned them and check over its running state and log files (log files are output from applications that are written to disk, so you as the systems administrator can see what they are doing), as this may be indicative of a larger issue.

CPU Utilization Percentage

The third line of the `top` command is the CPU utilization percentage value. This shows in terms of percentage how much of your current computation resource is allocated to which domain of your system. The values are the following:

- `us` (for user applications)
- `sy` (for system applications)
- `ni` (for processes that have been "niced" in order to give them more or less CPU priority)
- `id` (representing idle)
- `wa` (for processes that are waiting for I/O completion)

- `hi` (for processes waiting for hardware interrupts)
- `si` (for processes waiting for software interrupts)
- `st` (which indicates time stolen by a hypervisor—a *hypervisor* is software that runs a virtualization platform like Xen or VMWare ESX)

Of these values, the one that will normally have the most computation resource allocated to it is `id`, which represents free available computation that can be used elsewhere. Seeing high values of `wa`, `hi`, `si`, or `st` are never good signs as they suggest that your system is waiting on a particular piece of hardware or another function to finish processing. If these numbers stay high, you should look at investigating which processes cause them and see if you have any hardware issues.

Memory Usage

Lines 4 and 5 represent the memory usage of your system. Line 4 is for the actual memory usage, and line 5 is for the swap space usage. Both of these lines will show the total, used, and free memory in their given space. This final value represents the buffers and cached value. These two are interrelated and are the cause of much concern for users new to Linux. This hass to do with the way that RAM is allocated. Linux can sometimes take up all available RAM and place it into a buffers, which means that it is taken by the buffers but can still be used later for your applications. Linux will treat this RAM as being used, but it is just sitting there in the buffers waiting. The buffers value can be a little hard to understand; this leads to another command showing how these resources are used (I will cover it next).

Process Table

After the fifth line there is a large section that contains a process table, which lists all running processes and, in near-real-time updates, which processes are consuming how much of which resource. The following shows a number of different columns and the pieces of information they represent:

- *PID*: The processes' ID number
- *USER*: The user who owns the process
- *PR*: The priority of the process
- *NI*: The nice value for the process
- *VIRT*: The amount of virtual memory consumed by the process
- *RES*: The size of actual resident virtual memory
- *SHR*: The amount of shared memory the process is using
- *S*: The process status (e.g., sleeping, running, zombie)
- *%CPU*: The percentage of CPU consumed
- *%MEM*: The percentage of RAM consumed
- *TIME+*: The total CPU time the task has used since it started
- *COMMAND*: The actual name of the command

`top` also has a host of keypress actions that can manipulate the order in which these processes are displayed; you can check them out in the man page for `top`.

So `top` is a fantastic command for showing all the ins and outs of your system's resource usage and one of the best tools for diving into the exact nature of what your system is doing within itself.

Using free to View Memory Allocation

As mentioned earlier, there is an easier way than using `top` to see what your memory allocation is like. The command to do this is the `free` command, which you can invoke with the unit you wish to have it display in (`-k` for kilobytes, `-m` for megabytes, `-g` for gigabytes, and so on). For our purposes. megabytes is best, so invoke it as follows:

```
$ free -m
```

Your output should look like Figure 5-2.

```
             total       used       free     shared    buffers     cached
Mem:           231        157         74          0         18         79
-/+ buffers/cache:         59        172
Swap:           99          0         99
```

Figure 5-2. *Free as in free*

From this, you can see the `+/- buffers and cache` line that change the `used` and `free` values. This is a great way to question any time your system shows spikes of memory up to 100%, as it just may be lots of buffers and cache in action. From these two utilities you should be able to gain great insight into exactly what is going on within your system and how its resources are being used.

Disk Usage

Now that we have looked at CPU and RAM usage, which are fairly dynamic, it's time to have a look at something of a more static nature, disk utilization. In most operating systems you can quickly and readily view how much of the available storage space is in use, and Linux is no exception. The command to show the current usage of the whole system's disks is `df`, which is short for *disk free* and can be used on the command line with no arguments to show everything you need. If you do, your output will resemble Figure 5-3.

```
df: `/root/.gvfs': Permission denied
Filesystem     1K-blocks    Used Available Use% Mounted on
rootfs           1828696 1757188         0 100% /
/dev/root        1828696 1757188         0 100% /
tmpfs              23688     504     23184   3% /run
tmpfs               5120       0      5120   0% /run/lock
tmpfs              47376       4     47372   1% /tmp
tmpfs              10240       0     10240   0% /dev
tmpfs              47376       0     47376   0% /run/shm
/dev/mmcblk0p1     57288   34784     22504  61% /boot
```

Figure 5-3. *Disk free, ouch!*

Figure 5-3 shows disk free in action and shows that the main `rootfs` mounted on / is basically 100% full—ouch. You can see the number of 1 k blocks being used by the system, but the values don't stand out very easily. You will also note that there is a permission denied error at the top.

Fortunately, there are solutions for both these issues. First is to run this command with sudo so that it has root access to the whole system. The second is to add the -h argument. This argument is fairly universal in being one of two things: either -h for *help* or -h for *human*, which is to say human readable units. So we run this command:

```
$ sudo df -h
```

The output should be much more understandable to the average human being (see Figure 5-4).

```
Filesystem        Size  Used Avail Use% Mounted on
rootfs            1.8G  1.7G     0 100% /
/dev/root         1.8G  1.7G     0 100% /
tmpfs              24M  504K   23M   3% /run
tmpfs             5.0M     0  5.0M   0% /run/lock
tmpfs              47M  4.0K   47M   1% /tmp
tmpfs              10M     0   10M   0% /dev
tmpfs              47M     0   47M   0% /run/shm
/dev/mmcblk0p1     56M   34M   22M  61% /boot
```

Figure 5-4. *df for humans*

As you can see, the human readable flag has changed those Size and Used values over to a human readable number with a nice little flag on the end denoting unit. Experimenting with display flags is a great way to help you make sense of some of the complex data coming out of Linux commands. Normally you will find a huge section detailing (in way too much depth) all the flags for a command in its man page.

So, we have seen the full disk utilization of the system, but let's say we want to find the detailed utilization of all the files in a folder. There is another command we can use to do just this: du, which is short for *disk usage* and is used to summarize the disk usage of each file, recursively for directories. If you run du, it will tell you what the estimated usage of each file within this folder is and that of each subfolder and each item within it and its subfolders, and so on. du will also take advantage of the -h for human flag that was in df. So if we run it, we get an output like this:

```
$ du -h
4.0K    ./.cache/dconf
12K     ./.cache/menus
576K    ./.cache/midori/web
4.0K    ./.cache/midori/thumbnails
24K     ./.cache/midori/icons
608K    ./.cache/midori
4.0K    ./.cache/openbox/sessions
12K     ./.cache/openbox
640K    ./.cache
12K     ./.dbus/session-bus
16K     ./.dbus
5.0M    ./.tor
12K     ./.ssh
1.8M    ./python_games
8.0K    ./.dillo
```

```
20K     ./.vnc
4.0K    ./.gvfs
124K    ./.gnupg
8.0K    ./.fltk/fltk.org
12K     ./.fltk
48K     ./Desktop
8.0K    ./.config/lxpanel/LXDE/panels
16K     ./.config/lxpanel/LXDE
20K     ./.config/lxpanel
8.0K    ./.config/pcmanfm/LXDE
12K     ./.config/pcmanfm
8.0K    ./.config/lxterminal
28K     ./.config/midori
4.0K    ./.config/enchant
28K     ./.config/openbox
104K    ./.config
76K     ./.fontconfig
16K     ./.netsurf
40K     ./.local/share/gvfs-metadata
36K     ./.local/share/webkit/icondatabase
40K     ./.local/share/webkit
88K     ./.local/share
92K     ./.local
9.0M    .
```

Wow, that's a big output for such a simple command. It shows the utilization of every folder within the current folder, and right down the bottom it shows the total usage. This is where we can take advantage of another flag in order to shorten the output: the `-s` flag that stands for *summary*. Doing this will only print the total allocation for this directory and all within it, rather than everything as we have just seen. So go ahead and execute the command; your output should look much neater:

```
$ du -sh
9.0M    .
```

That's much better. You will notice that the output is using the `.` value to denote the current directory because `du` will work on the current working directory if not told where else to look. You can specify a directory to use by simply adding one to the end. The next example will look at `/var/log`, which is where all system logs are kept, so we will need to run this command as root using `sudo` as some of these logfiles are protected:

```
$ sudo du -sh /var/log
9.8M    /var/log
```

And there you have it! With these two utilities, you can find out the current disk usage of your system and even work out which parts of your system are consuming the most space.

Managing Processes

Probably one of the most important tasks when working within a Linux environment is knowing how to manage running processes. After all, a computer is just a processing system, and if you can't manage what it is processing, how can you make truly good use of your machine? The first command you should become aware of is the ps command. The ps command is short for *processes snapshot* and can be used to list all the current processes being run by your user; when invoked, you should get an output like the one shown in Figure 5-5.

```
  PID TTY          TIME CMD
 1951 pts/0    00:00:01 bash
 2162 pts/0    00:00:00 ps
```

Figure 5-5. *Current processes*

Yes, it's a little lackluster right now as I am only running two processes: the bash application that is running my user shell and the copy of ps. Since this is a snapshot, the application will always capture itself. This is useful if I want to control those processes run by my current user, but if I am to do more, I will need to add some arguments to my ps command. The argument to show every process on the system in the standard syntax is -ef, so go ahead and run that and see how your output changes (see Figure 5-6).

```
root      1756     1  0 17:05 ?        00:00:05 Xtightvnc :1 -desktop X -auth /root/.Xauthority -geometry 1280x800 -depth 24 -rfbwait 120000
root      1760     1  0 17:05 ?        00:00:00 /bin/sh /root/.vnc/xstartup
root      1771  1760  0 17:05 ?        00:00:00 /usr/bin/ck-launch-session /usr/bin/dbus-launch --exit-with-session x-session-manager
root      1805     1  0 17:05 tty1     00:00:00 /sbin/getty --noclear 38400 tty1
root      1806     1  0 17:05 tty2     00:00:00 /sbin/getty 38400 tty2
root      1807     1  0 17:05 tty3     00:00:00 /sbin/getty 38400 tty3
root      1808     1  0 17:05 tty4     00:00:00 /sbin/getty 38400 tty4
root      1809     1  0 17:05 tty5     00:00:00 /sbin/getty 38400 tty5
root      1810     1  0 17:05 tty6     00:00:00 /sbin/getty 38400 tty6
root      1811     1  0 17:05 ?        00:00:00 /sbin/getty -L ttyAMA0 115200 vt100
root      1815  1771  0 17:05 ?        00:00:00 /usr/bin/ssh-agent /usr/bin/ck-launch-session /usr/bin/dbus-launch --exit-with-session x-ses
root      1817     1  0 17:05 ?        00:00:00 /usr/sbin/console-kit-daemon --no-daemon
root      1887  1771  0 17:05 ?        00:00:00 /usr/bin/lxsession -s LXDE -e LXDE
root      1890     1  0 17:05 ?        00:00:00 /usr/bin/dbus-launch --exit-with-session x-session-manager
root      1891     1  0 17:05 ?        00:00:00 /usr/bin/dbus-daemon --fork --print-pid 5 --print-address 7 --session
root      1897  1887  0 17:05 ?        00:00:00 openbox --config-file /root/.config/openbox/lxde-rc.xml
root      1899  1887  0 17:05 ?        00:00:12 lxpanel --profile LXDE
root      1900  1887  0 17:05 ?        00:00:01 pcmanfm --desktop --profile LXDE
root      1906     1  0 17:05 ?        00:00:04 /usr/lib/notification-daemon/notification-daemon
root      1908     1  0 17:05 ?        00:00:01 nm-applet
root      1910     1  0 17:05 ?        00:00:00 /usr/lib/arm-linux-gnueabihf/lxpolkit
root      1914     1  0 17:05 ?        00:00:00 /usr/lib/arm-linux-gnueabihf/libmenu-cache1/libexec/menu-cached
root      1916     1  0 17:05 ?        00:00:00 /usr/lib/gvfs/gvfsd
root      1918     1  0 17:05 ?        00:00:00 /usr/lib/gvfs//gvfs-fuse-daemon -f /root/.gvfs
root      1919  1724  0 17:05 ?        00:00:01 sshd: pi [priv]
root      1933     1  0 17:05 ?        00:00:00 /usr/lib/arm-linux-gnueabihf/gconf/gconfd-2
root      1937     1  0 17:05 ?        00:00:00 /usr/lib/gvfs/gvfs-gdu-volume-monitor
root      1939     1  0 17:05 ?        00:00:00 /usr/lib/udisks/udisks-daemon
root      1940  1939  0 17:05 ?        00:00:00 udisks-daemon: not polling any devices
root      1943     1  0 17:05 ?        00:00:00 /usr/lib/gvfs/gvfs-gphoto2-volume-monitor
root      1945     1  0 17:05 ?        00:00:00 /usr/lib/gvfs/gvfs-afc-volume-monitor
pi        1950  1919  0 17:05 ?        00:00:03 sshd: pi@pts/0
pi        1951  1950  0 17:05 pts/0    00:00:01 -bash
root      1980  1724  0 17:09 ?        00:00:00 sshd: pi [priv]
pi        1987  1980  0 17:09 ?        00:00:00 sshd: pi@pts/1
pi        1988  1987  0 17:09 pts/1    00:00:00 -bash
root      2094  1724  0 17:48 ?        00:00:00 sshd: pi [priv]
pi        2102  2094  0 17:48 ?        00:00:00 sshd: pi@pts/2
pi        2103  2102  0 17:48 pts/2    00:00:00 -bash
root      2137     2  0 18:02 ?        00:00:00 [flush-179:0]
root      2138     2  0 18:08 ?        00:00:00 [kworker/0:1]
root      2189     2  0 18:18 ?        00:00:00 [kworker/0:0]
root      2208     2  0 18:25 ?        00:00:00 [kworker/0:2]
pi        2209  1951  0 18:26 pts/0    00:00:00 ps -ef
```

Figure 5-6. *ps -ef*

Wow, that's a lot of output, so much that it went off the top of the screen! There are always a large number of processes running on your system when you run `ps -ef` as this lists all the systems background processes along with all user processes. If you want to see them in a list, you can simply add a `| less` to the end of your command, which will let you go up and down and manipulate the list (I will explain what the `less` command actually does a little later in this chapter):

```
$ ps -ef | less
```

`ps` is a lot like `top`, but does require fewer resources and has a few other advantages that we will cover later in this chapter. For now, you should just be aware of what each of the columns in `ps` means:

- *UID*: Represents the user who owns this process
- *PID*: Represents the process's PID number
- *PPID*: Represents the PID number of the process that created this one
- *C*: Represents CPU utilization of this process
- *STIME*: Represents the start time of this process
- *TTY*: Represents the terminal controlling this process
- *TIME*: The cumulative CPU time consumed by this process
- *CMD*: The command-line argument of this process

So you might be saying, "Well fine. You have shown all the processes in the system, but what can I do with them now?" This is where the magic of `ps` comes in; it makes it very easy for us to pick out the PID of a particular process. The PID number is very important as it is a unique number for each process and is the way that the system references processes. This will come of use in our next command: `kill`.

Killing a Process

`kill` is used to do exactly what its name implies: kill processes. But it also provides a number of other useful functions via the mechanism through which it kills processes. In Linux and UNIX, a *signal* is a low-level system message that is passed into an application from the operating system. Signals have no actual function beyond being a signal, and it is up to the application to respond to it in the correct manner. This is not true for all signals, as some cannot be handled within the application, but it is true for most. The function of the `kill` command is to send signals to applications. There are 64 signals that the version of `kill` on Raspbian can send to an application. To list them all, issue this command:

```
$ kill -l
```

I won't list all the functions of the signals now, but you will need to be aware of these, the most common signals:

- *Signal 1 (SIGHUP)*: Short for *hang-up*. Tells the application to hang up its current connection. Normally used to make an application reinitialize itself.
- *Signal 3 (SIGQUIT)*: Signals that this application should gracefully close itself down and quit.
- *Signal 6 (SIGABRT)*: Signals that the program is aborting; it is to close immediately.
- *Signal 9 (SIGKILL)*: Signals to forcibly "pull the plug" on an application.

These signals are the most common as they are used to perform application shutdowns, with nine being the most prevalent. The format of the `kill` command is this:

```
kill -<signal> <PID>
```

So to kill a process with the highest force, execute this:

```
$ kill -9 <PID>
```

This is the point where those PIDs out of the `ps` command come into play. Those PID numbers are the ones that you will feed into `kill` in order to direct the signals from `kill`.

Reading Information in /proc

Since we are playing with PIDs, it's probably good to revisit the `/proc` filesystem, first discussed in Chapter 4. This is part of the OS in which all the process information lives. If you use `ls /proc`, you will see a number of files and a set of numbered directories. These directories correspond to each of the process PIDs. If you look within one of these directories, you should see a whole host of files that relate to a given process. While you should never edit any of these willy-nilly, there are some files within these directories that are very useful.

Probably the most commonly used is a system-wide file that contains information on all the system's processors. This is the `/proc/cpuinfo` file. You can output the contents of a file to the screen using the `cat` command, which is short for *concatenate* and is normally used to get the contents of a file into a buffer (in our case, it is the console screen). Go ahead and issue this:

```
$ cat /proc/cpuinfo
```

Your output should look like this:

```
Processor       : ARMv6-compatible processor rev 7 (v6l)
BogoMIPS        : 697.95
Features        : swp half thumb fastmult vfp edsp java tls
CPU implementer : 0x41
CPU architecture: 7
CPU variant     : 0x0
CPU part        : 0xb76
CPU revision    : 7

Hardware        : BCM2708
Revision        : 0003
Serial          : 000000007a8a46ba
```

This is the Linux internal information on the Raspberry Pi's processor. If you are ever in doubt on some of the particulars of your processor, this is the place to look.

In addition to `cpuinfo`, there is another file within `/proc` that you can take advantage of when diagnosing system configuration information. It is the `/proc/<pid>/cmdline` file. This file lists the full command-line argument used to invoke a process. If you need to get your hands on the commands used here, executing `cat` against this file is the best way to do it.

File Commands

As mentioned earlier, you can use the `cat` command to output the contents of a file. There are a number of other tools you can use to work with the contents of files within your system. The first is one that was mentioned earlier: the `less` command. It is a command to display the contents of a file to the screen in a way that can be moved around and searched as if it were a text editor. This is a great command for working with logfiles or the output of long commands such as `ps. less` allows you to move up and down the file with the arrow keys or with the page up and page down keys. You can also search using simple word searches by typing / and then entering your search string. `less` will then highlight the found instances of your expressions, and you can tab between them with the `n` key to go down and the `N` key to go up.

In addition to being able to search within a file for things, `less` has the ability to watch the file and constantly display any new content on the `last` line. This is great for watching growing logfiles as you can pick up new lines without needing to reopen the file, to get `less` to perform this function, simply press the `F` key. Along with this, you can also automatically navigate to the end of a file by pressing the `G` key. This process will also grab any new lines that have been added to the file and display them. You can also use the lowercase *g* to navigate to a specific line number, so if you wish to go to the first line, would press `1g`. Finally, `less` is able to respond to all of its command-line arguments within itself. This is useful for enabling line numbers as you can simply give `less` the command `-N<enter>` and it will display numbers next to each line.

After `less`, one of the commands that provide a startling amount of flexibility is the `find` command, which is used to find files. It does this by examining every file within the given directory and all of its subdirectories. `find` is useful on its own, but extraordinary when paired with other commands as you will see later. It also has a healthy cache of options that are interchangeable and can also be combined. I will cover a few that I have found incredibly useful here:

- The first is `-L`, which says to follow symlinks, which `find` does not do by default.
- Second is `-maxdepth <number>`, which represents how many directories deep this command will search through. Just the one? Just this and all its subdirectories?
- Third is `-newer <file>`, which shows anything that was changed more recently than a given file.
- Fourth is `-empty` and it, as its name implies, finds empty files.
- Fifth is `-atime <number>`, where the number represents the number of days that have passed since a file was accessed.
- Sixth is `-name <filename>`, which searches for files named exactly like the name passed in.
- Last is `exec <command>`, which tells `find` to execute a given command on each of the files and is where the real power of `find` comes out. You can use this command to find specified files and then execute commands on them. In this way, using `find` is a fantastic way of executing a cleanup of older unwanted files for instance. I'd also advise that when using `find` in this manner you should test first and test thoroughly because one incorrect key stroke could spell doom for your system or your data.

Combining these commands, you can achieve something that looks like this:

```
$ find /mnt/Volume1 -empty -name fooBar -exec rm
```

This command will find all empty files within `/mnt/Volume1` that are empty and named `fooBar` and then remove them! There is so much power in the `find` command that you can harness when administering your Pi.

Another command that has a significant if limited use is the file command. The file command is used to go through the contents of a given file and determine what "kind" of file it is. *Kind* is a bit of a loose term here because file knows only a moderate number of different file types. However, it is fantastically useful when you want to know an answer to this question: "Can I safely open that file in a text editor, or is it a binary application?" This particular command can save you much heartache. You can also use file to determine which archival format an application is written in, which is a great help when you need to extract from an archive but don't know what kind! As an example, if you run file against a binary executable such as /bin/bash, you should see the following:

```
$ file /bin/bash
/bin/bash: ELF 32-bit LSB executable, ARM, version 1 (SYSV), dynamically linked (uses shared libs),
for GNU/Linux 2.6.26, BuildID[sha1]=0xe370a0be978f49569f115c9f41bc54688be9fe32, stripped
```

The code shows that the file is an ELF 32-bit LSB executable compiled for an ARM system, so the file should be compatible with your Pi. This is a good way to diagnose any issues you may have with applications downloaded from the Internet because they may be compiled for x86!

The last file command I have for you in this section is one of those commands that many people hate and many more love: grep. grep is short for *Generalized Regular Expression Parser* and is best known as being a pattern matcher. Like less and find, grep is both useful on its own and useful when combined with other commands. You can use grep to search a given file for any lines that contain a given text string. The basic format of grep is this:

```
grep <pattern> <file>
```

Both these values will take the wildcard format, so you can use grep to search through every file in an entire directory for a string. As an example, let's look for the word *find* in the /etc/init.d folder:

```
$ grep find /etc/init.d/*
```

The output would be this:

```
/etc/init.d/checkfs.sh:# Include /usr/bin in path to find on_ac_power if /usr/ is on the root
/etc/init.d/checkroot.sh:# Include /usr/bin in path to find on_ac_power if /usr/ is on the root
/etc/init.d/kbd:             LIST_CONSOLES='cd /etc/init; find -name 'tty*.conf' -printf '%f
' | sed -e 's/[^0-9 ]//g''
/etc/init.d/kbd:             # eventually find an associated SFM
/etc/init.d/nfs-common:# particularily heavy daemon, so we auto-enable it if we find an /etc/exports
/etc/init.d/rc:# Now find out what the current and what the previous runlevel are.
/etc/init.d/sudo:                 find /var/lib/sudo -exec touch -t 198501010000 '{}' \;
```

grep also has some wonderful command-line options, including -i, which makes the search case insensitive. grep also has the -v option. which turns a search on its head and returns everything *not* matching the given search string! This should give you an idea of how powerful a tool grep can be when you wish to find a given piece of information and thus why it is an awesome part for a systems administrator's arsenal of commands.

Combining Commands

Now we get to the fun part! The ability to combine commands so that you can use the output of one command and give it to a second command to work with. There are also a number of commands that I will detail here as they are fantastic when combined with others. But first you need to understand how to combine commands and thankfully it is a rather easy thing to accomplish. To combine commands, we use the pipe symbol (|).

Yep, it's that simple. Let's say we wanted to grep some things, but wanted the output in a more manageable way. We would simply write the grep, add a pipe, and then add a less. By doing this you will find yourself inside less looking at the output for your grep! This is where the fun truly begins. Want to search all the filenames in a given directory? Use ls to list the files and pipe the output to grep to search. In this instance, you don't even need to include a filename with the grep as the pipe will provide grep with what is known as a *buffer* that grep will treat the same as file contents! So the command is this:

```
$ ls <directory> | grep <search string>
```

Combine ps and grep

Now, if you want to play more with things, you can combine grep with ps -ef! In this way, you can search for a specific application; for example, to search for the SSH application sshd,we would run this:

```
$ ps -ef | grep sshd
```

This will generate the following output:

```
root      1722     1  0 19:24 ?        00:00:00 /usr/sbin/sshd
root      1956  1722  0 19:43 ?        00:00:00 sshd: pi [priv]
pi        1963  1956  0 19:43 ?        00:00:01 sshd: pi@pts/0
pi        2030  1964  0 20:33 pts/0    00:00:00 grep --color=auto sshd
```

Add an Inverse grep

Ah! There's a problem! We seemed to have caught our own grep in the command. But that's no problem we can simply pipe again to grep and do a -v for grep, which will return us every line without a grep. This gives us the command:

```
$ ps -ef | grep sshd | grep -v grep
```

This gives an output of this:

```
root      1722     1  0 19:24 ?        00:00:00 /usr/sbin/sshd
root      1956  1722  0 19:43 ?        00:00:00 sshd: pi [priv]
pi        1963  1956  0 19:43 ?        00:00:01 sshd: pi@pts/0
```

Cut Down the Results

Much better! Now you can begin to see what we can accomplish with pipe, but I am far from done with the things you can use this for! Let's introduce the next command: awk . awk is a tool for doing data extraction from a line of text. In this way, you can pull all kinds of information out of whatever commands you're running. By default, awk will pull each element out by splitting on *whitespace*, which is any tab or space between characters. You can set the character to split against using the -F <delimiter> argument. Once you have told awk how to break your text, you will need to output it. awk has an entire syntax for outputting commands, and it is an incredibly complex art form.

However, for most of your needs, simply printing the correct field will do. All awk outputs are wrapped in curly braces { and }, and you will normally need to wrap them in single quotes so the command line will ignore any spaces. This means the basic syntax looks like this:

```
$ awk '{ <command> }'
```

The most useful command for anyone working with awk has to be the print command because it is used to display the delimited variables. Each of these variables is treated as the number it is in the sequence, so $1 for the first, $2 for the second, and so on. Using this we can combine the awk with our ps -ef from earlier to print out the second space delimited field, the PID! This gives us the following command:

```
$ ps -ef | grep ssh | grep -v grep | awk '{print $2}'
```

Wow, these commands are getting *long*! But examine the output of this command:

```
1722
1956
1963
```

Aha! The quick among you will realize what is coming next! We can pipe this to kill! In this fashion, we can use a ps, grep, and awk to grab only the PIDs of processes matching a given pattern and then pass them off to be killed!

xargs to Work with Each Result

This is one of those pieces of magic that never gets old; however we can't pass a list of PIDs directly to kill because we want them passed one at a time. To do this, we need to take advantage of another command, xargs, which works the same way that the -exec does in find. It allows you to treat each line of output from the commands before as an individual argument for another command. To use xargs, we simply have them wrap the command in the same manner sudo does. So if we wanted to pass each of those PIDs to xargs via kill, we would simply run the following and that would be it:

```
$ ps -ef | grep ssh | grep -v grep | awk '{print $2}' | xargs kill -1
```

In this case, I will *not* be killing off my sshd process as I don't want to reboot my Pi. But you should get the idea of how you can begin taking output from one command and passing it through to another command to run further executions on these commands.

There are actually a number of other commands that come in really handy when doing these kinds of "shell-fu." The first is wc, which is short for *word count*. By default, wc will give you the newline, word, and byte counts for a given block of text or file, but it also has some great arguments, such as -l, which will give you the number of lines; -w, which will give you the number of characters; or -m, which will give you the number of words.

Next is sort, which sorts each line of the output into order. You often see sort paired with uniq, which is short for *unique*. With these two, you can pipe an output to sort then to uniq, and you will have only the unique values in your given output!

The final thing to be aware of when working with a number of commands is the output operator >. This operator is from the same family as pipe, but instead of being used to direct your command output to another command, it is used to direct your output to a file. This is a great way to save the output of commands to a file so that you can revisit it later or to have it useable as arguments for another command. By now, you should be getting the impression that the shell is incredibly powerful and you can do all kinds of tricky manipulations by combining commands with pipe!

User Environment

We are going to take a small break from examining commands and have a look at some of the things that make up the environment in which you work. Your environment is launched every time you log in, and each time is the same. This is due to a number of files and commands that provide directives on how your simple shell environment is to be made up and how it is to function. One of the key files involved in performing these tasks is your systems master controlling environment script /etc/profile. This file provides the basis of the shell and environment variables that are the base of each user's session.

The profile file sets a number of variables, including the PATH variable. This variable is one of the key variables in setting up how your shell environment works. So we will have a look at it in depth.

The PATH is one of (if not the most) important variables in your whole environment. It represents the systems search path that basically means where it will look for applications. As an example, I am sure that by now you are aware that all the commands we have run are just words entered into the shell, but in fact they are the names of fully functional applications that are located within the OS. The PATH contains a list of folders that your shell will search through and execute any command from within automatically. This means that you aren't always searching for the exact path of a command; you can just run it as needed by its name. The problem here is that you cannot be certain where the program is being run from, or if you have multiple versions, which one is being run. There is a command that solves this problem: the which command. It outputs the path of the application that your shell would use to execute a given command. For example, let's find the path of the ssh application, we type which ssh and we get this:

```
$ which ssh
/usr/bin/ssh
```

Yep, it's that easy. The PATH is used by a number of programs to find information that they need. Your path variable is initially set within /etc/profile but this can be modified. But before we go out and start playing with the path variable we should find out what it is currently set too. There are two ways you can do this, first is to use the echo command to print the variable. echo will interpret whatever you give it and then print to the command line, so if we execute echo $PATH the echo command will output the contents of the PATH variable like so:

```
$ echo $PATH
/usr/local/sbin:/usr/local/bin:/usr/sbin:/usr/bin:/sbin:/bin:/usr/local/games:/usr/games
```

Okay, that's what the PATH variable is. The *path* is a list of folders separated by colons. This brings us to the second way of viewing the PATH variable: the env command displays all the currently set environment variables. This is a fantastically useful command to check the current state of your whole system environment. Running env should give you an output like this:

```
$ env
TERM=xterm
SHELL=/bin/bash
XDG_SESSION_COOKIE=eb95d80869be1ad62af36ec5502c41a1-1349772229.897557-1575821964
SSH_CLIENT=10.0.0.104 3643 22
SSH_TTY=/dev/pts/0
USER=pi
LS_COLORS=rs=0:di=01;34:ln=01;36:mh=00:pi=40;33:so=01;35:do=01;35:bd=40;33;01:cd=40;
33;01:or=40;31;01:su=37;41:sg=30;43:ca=30;41:tw=30;42:ow=34;42:st=37;44:ex=01;32:*.
tar=01;31:*.tgz=01;31:*.arj=01;31:*.taz=01;31:*.lzh=01;31:*.lzma=01;31:*.tlz=01;31:*.
txz=01;31:*.zip=01;31:*.z=01;31:*.Z=01;31:*.dz=01;31:*.gz=01;31:*.lz=01;31:*.xz=01;31:*.
bz2=01;31:*.bz=01;31:*.tbz=01;31:*.tbz2=01;31:*.tz=01;31:*.deb=01;31:*.rpm=01;31:*.
jar=01;31:*.war=01;31:*.ear=01;31:*.sar=01;31:*.rar=01;31:*.ace=01;31:*.zoo=01;31:*.
cpio=01;31:*.7z=01;31:*.rz=01;31:*.jpg=01;35:*.jpeg=01;35:*.gif=01;35:*.bmp=01;35:*.
pbm=01;35:*.pgm=01;35:*.ppm=01;35:*.tga=01;35:*.xbm=01;35:*.xpm=01;35:*.tif=01;35:*.
tiff=01;35:*.png=01;35:*.svg=01;35:*.svgz=01;35:*.mng=01;35:*.pcx=01;35:*.mov=01;35:*.
mpg=01;35:*.mpeg=01;35:*.m2v=01;35:*.mkv=01;35:*.webm=01;35:*.ogm=01;35:*.mp4=01;35:*.
m4v=01;35:*.mp4v=01;35:*.vob=01;35:*.qt=01;35:*.nuv=01;35:*.wmv=01;35:*.asf=01;35:*.
rm=01;35:*.rmvb=01;35:*.flc=01;35:*.avi=01;35:*.fli=01;35:*.flv=01;35:*.gl=01;35:*.
dl=01;35:*.xcf=01;35:*.xwd=01;35:*.yuv=01;35:*.cgm=01;35:*.emf=01;35:*.axv=01;35:*.
anx=01;35:*.ogv=01;35:*.ogx=01;35:*.aac=00;36:*.au=00;36:*.flac=00;36:*.mid=00;36:*.
midi=00;36:*.mka=00;36:*.mp3=00;36:*.mpc=00;36:*.ogg=00;36:*.ra=00;36:*.wav=00;36:*.
axa=00;36:*.oga=00;36:*.spx=00;36:*.xspf=00;36:
ALL_PROXY=SOCKS://localhost:9050
MAIL=/var/mail/pi
PATH=/usr/local/sbin:/usr/local/bin:/usr/sbin:/usr/bin:/sbin:/bin:/usr/local/games:/usr/games
PWD=/home/pi
LANG=en_US.UTF-8
SHLVL=1
HOME=/home/pi
LOGNAME=pi
SSH_CONNECTION=10.0.0.104 3643 10.0.0.56 22
_=/usr/bin/env
```

There are a lot of variables here that cover a range of things, including the shell we are using (SHELL), the variables governing the colors displayed when we execute ls (LS_COLORS), the path, my current location (PWD), my home directory (HOME), and my username (USER) in addition to the PATH. All these pieces of information can be incredibly useful when trying to diagnose issues with running commands.

Now that we have been able to view the PATH variable, we should look at modifying it. To modify a variable, we need to use the export command in order to assign it into our environment. The syntax for setting a simple variable is this:

```
$ export VARIABLE="SOMETHING"
```

If you run this and run env again, you should see this new variable show up within its output like so:

```
VARIABLE=SOMETHING
```

If we were to do this to our PATH variable, we would reset it to whatever we set it to, which is not what we want. We could also simply rewrite the whole path, but that's quite arduous for a simple change. The easiest way to append something to the PATH variable is to include the PATH variable within the assignment. Let's work with an example: say we want to include the /opt directory into our path. We would start with export PATH= and then we would want to use the current PATH variable (as we would use to display it with echo), so we write "$PATH". To the $PATH we would add a colon as a separator and the new directory /opt, which gives us this command:

```
$ export PATH="$PATH:/opt"
```

When run, this will change your PATH variable to this:

```
/usr/local/sbin:/usr/local/bin:/usr/sbin:/usr/bin:/sbin:/bin:/usr/local/games:/usr/games:/opt
```

Awesome; the /opt was appended to the end. This brings us to a key point; PATH has an order, left to right. Those on the left side of the PATH variable will be used before those on the right. In our example, /opt would be the last place we search for any given file.

Now that you understand your user environment and how PATH works, you should learn about a special file within your home directory. This is your local shell profile override file. In your home directory there are a number of hidden files that end with rc. These files are normally executed by your shell or whichever application upon its execution to load your personal preferences. The file for the standard Linux BASH shell is the .bashrc file. This file is responsible for a number of the environment variables we saw before; it is also the reason that some of your commands have color. For example, the ls command, which is normally located at /bin/ls (you can check with which ls). If you were to execute this instead of the normal ls, you would not see the colors! These colors were added specially by the .bashrc file using the alias command.

alias, as its name implies, is used to alias a command or a group of commands under a single shell command, just like a program. In the case of your .bashrc file, it has aliased the ls command to execute this:

```
$ ls --color=auto
```

This addition means that every time you issue an ls command, you are automatically adding the color argument to ls. The way the .bashrc achieves this is by adding this line:

```
alias ls='ls --color=auto'
```

The great thing about files like .bashrc is they are designed to be user modified—after all, they are your local system variables. In this way, your local environment is made from the base system values given by /etc/profile and the additional values given in .bashrc.

The cron Command

The last command is probably one of the most powerful and useful tools in a systems administrator toolkit: the cron command. cron is a timing application that executes commands at a given time based on rules passed to it by a steering file. cron has a steering file per user called a crontab, which it will check each minute to see if another command needs to be executed. To view your current crontab, you would simply need to execute this:

```
$ crontab -l
```

Unfortunately, you won't have one to begin with, so all you will get from this command is this:

```
no crontab for pi
```

Fear not because we will now go over the basics of creating a crontab timing file. The command to enter the special crontab editor is as follows:

```
$ crontab -e
```

This will open a copy of your system's standard editor and create an initial file with a nice block of comments that outline how a crontab entry is laid out. It provides the following example:

```
0 5 * * 1 tar -zcf /var/backups/home.tgz /home/
```

This command will perform a tar and zip of all users' home directories every Monday at 5 a.m. Recall that tar creates a single archive file of all the documents, and the zip will compress the file—the upshot being a single compressed file containing all the files. The five numbers at the start of the line govern the timing; these numbers represent the following things, in the following order:

- Minute of hour
- Hour of day (in 24 hour format)
- Day of month
- Month of year
- Day of week (Sun, 0 to Sat, 6)

As you can see from the example, this command runs on the zero-th minute of the fifth hour of any day of the month, in any month of the year as long as that day is a Monday. With this combination, you can set up any number of timing jobs in order to perform systems administrative functions. The best part is that you can use all the commands we have discussed earlier to perform these tasks for you! Want to kill a process at a certain time? Write the cron timing out for when you want things killed and then use the ps, grep, awk, xargs, and the kill command we worked up earlier! With the combination of cron and all the commands we covered earlier, there is no limit to the tasks you can do!

Summary

Congratulations, you should now be well on your way to being a fully fledged systems administrator. You have at your disposal more than two dozen individual commands and the ability to combine them in new ways to perform almost any task your heart desires. In addition, you should now have the tools to automate the execution of these commands using cron by editing your crontab file. All these tools form the basis of how a systems administrator will manage a Linux system as they provide the flexibility to write robust commands and have them executed automatically.

CHAPTER 6

Editing Files on the Command Line

Believe it or not, one of the things you'll end up spending most of your time doing on Linux is editing text files. They get absolutely everywhere and you'll find them used for content, source code for applications, configuration files and start up scripts. The reason for this is that despite their somewhat basic and boring nature they are very useful for storing human readable information. When you combine this with ease of use, you know you're on to a winner. Linux doesn't have a registry like Windows and it's extremely rare for applications not to use text files for their configuration. Even Sendmail which has an historically evil config file (so evil in fact you need to write a config file for yet another application which will then create the Sendmail config file for you) stores its config file as plain old text.

In this chapter we're going to give you a brief overview of text files and how they're used today. We'll then introduce the two editors that we're going to cover in this chapter (nano and vim) and then we'll get into the real meat of the chapter and show you how to actually get things done.

What is a Text File?

When a computer stores data on disk, it can store data in one of two formats. It can either store data as a text file or it can store it as a binary file. Naturally as computers store everything as binary data (those good old 1's and 0's), what exactly makes a text file different from a binary file? After all, surely the text file must also be stored in a binary format. If you were thinking along those lines then you're quite correct. It's not so much how the data itself is stored, but more to do with how that data can be read.

The best way to appreciate the difference is to think about the page you're reading right now. The reason you can understand what I'm writing is because we have implicitly agreed to use English to communicate. The content of this page has structure that we both understand. We start sentences with capital letters, we use punctuation to show when sentences end or when to stop for a breath. In short we have quite a complicated protocol here but it works because we are both capable of reading and writing English. We can understand both the structure (how the data is to be read and written) as well as the semantics (what the words actually mean). So, how about this sentence:

Goedemorgen. Hoe gaat het?

Straight away we can tell that it's not English, after all, if it was we would be able to understand it. Unless you happen to speak Dutch (we don't but our good friend does), you probably wouldn't know which language it was written in. Even though the content doesn't make sense, the structure itself does. We can see we have two sentences with one being a statement and the other being a question. In this particular case, we can stab a guess at what the first word means. If we pronounce it as we would English, it sounds very similar to good morning (which is actually what the word translates to). From that we can probably guess that the question is "how are you?".

The reason we can do that is because although we don't understand the content, Dutch and English share a common structure or format. We share an alphabet (although Dutch does have some characters not present in English) and punctuation (full stops, commas and question marks). Now you might not get the pronunciation right (it is after all a foreign language) but because we share a common structure, we can at least handle the content, even if we can't understand it.

Figure 6-1 takes this one step further.

早晨好。你怎么样？

Figure 6-1. *Some Chinese Text*

At least for the average reader of this book, Figure 6-1 will be uninteligable. It's actually the same two sentences that appeared in our Dutch example but this time written in Chinese using Simplified Characters. To the uninitiated, there is no way to tell from this collection of characters how they should be pronounced. In fact depending on the dialect spoken, these characters could be pronounced in many different ways. This is because each character represents an idea rather than a sound, and once you recognize the idea, you know which word to say. This is why in China, it is possible for two people who cannot speak the same language to communicate perfectly well by reading and writing characters.

So why did we side track into foreign languages? Well, text files are like reading and writing English or Dutch. Whether the content makes sense or not depends on whether the reader can speak English or Dutch. This is similar to two applications and their config files. If you give an Apache web server configuration file to the Sendmail email server, it will spit it back in your face (Sendmail doesn't speak Apache) but it can open and read in the file.

Chinese on the other hand is our example of a binary format. It is very alien for most western speakers (although arguably it is far more efficient, elegant and sophisticated than phonetic writing used in West European languages). Unless you know Chinese, you can't understand the content or the implied structure. In computing terms, what you have is a blob of raw data that only makes sense to the application that wrote it.

Now you might be thinking that storing data in an arbitrary format is no big deal. After all, the application that wrote it is the application that will read it and as long as it understands the file, surely that's enough. Well yes and no. What happens if the program breaks? What if you need to read the file on another machine? Perhaps the vendor has provided some special tools to do just that, but therein lies the problem - you need special tools.

Not so for text files. Text files can be opened in any text editor and no special tools are required. As the vast majority of Linux applications all use text files (we can't think of any off the top of our heads that don't), all you need to read or make changes to a configuration file is your favourite text editor and Linux has a stunning variety of editors to choose from. Thus you can become familiar with a single tool and then use that tool to reconfigure all of your applications, write source code when you're doing scripting and even use it for writing books (which is precisely what we're doing right now).

The Contenders

So the text editor is your Linux Swiss army knife and something you never want to leave home without. Of course, just like Swiss army knives there are many different text editors to choose from and also like swiss army knives, some have more features than others. Sometimes you want a basic text editor that just lets your open files, edit some text and then save the results. Other times you might want to do a complex search and replace or delete to the end of the line. Of course you can quite easily use one of the more featureful editors for all of your tasks, after all you don't have to use the features if you don't need them. That said it's been our experience that people are generally familar with at least two text editors, one basic and one fully featured. In this book, that means nano and vim respectively.

The first text editor that we're going to cover is nano. It's a lightweight and easy to use text editor and it tends to be installed on most systems. Some later versions of nano have more features (such as syntax highlighting when writing source code) but all effectively look and work the same way. If you can use nano on your Pi, you'll be able to use it equally well on any platform.

Nano was actually written to be a drop in replacement for the Pico text editor that used to ship with Pine, a text based email client. Pico can still be found on older systems (usually much older) and chances are if you can't find nano you might still be able to find pico. As it's a drop in replacement, the same commands and basic features that you are used to using in nano will also be available in pico. Combined this gives you coverage of most other Unix platforms as well as Linux.

Nano's key selling point is its ease of use, but it does have a number of useful features. However these features are accessed from menus and while it has more than enough features for simply editing a config file, sometimes you need something with a little more power. This is where the vim editor comes in. It can do all the things that nano can do but it can do so much more that's pretty much where the comparison ends. Vim also has syntax highlighting, different color schemes, the ability to cut and paste, delete blocks of text, indent chunks of text, open multiple files an show both at the same time and much more.

Now you might be thinking that if Vim is this great, you might save yourself a lot of headache by simply just learning how to use that text editor instead. Like nano it is available almost everywhere in some form or another and they all have the same basic features and accept the same commands. The reason we're covering nano is that you can be up and running quite literally in just a few seconds. Its features are easy to explain and getting it to do what you want is really easy. Although vim users may disagree, in our experience, vim doesn't exactly hold any ease of use awards. That said, if you really don't want to learn two editors and feel that you'd rather just learn vim, that's fine, you won't really be missing out on anything, it just might take you a bit longer to get productive.

THE HOLY WAR - VI VS EMACS

Believe it or not, the text editor holy war (as it has become known) has gone on for decades and is amazingly even more heated than the Linux vs Windows debate. In fact it has become so heated that Richard Stalman (the creator of Emacs and the founder of the GNU Free Software Foundation) dresses up as St. Ignucius from the "Church of Emacs". He has stated many times that "While vi is the tool of the devil" (vi being 6 in roman numerals) "using vi is not a sin but a penance". Of course the vi crowd weren't going to take that sitting down and formed the "Cult of vi". One of emacs strongest features is that you can write code to make it do practically anything you could imagine. This has caused the vi crowd to say that "Emacs is a great operating system lacking only a decent text editor!".

No one really expects this debate to end and although at times can get quite fiery, it is usually conducted in good humour. At the end of the day, the best text editor for you is the one that makes you most productive and the one that you are happiest using. Still, reading some of the flame wars and reading up on its history can provide good entertainment for those looking for something to do...

Starting Out with Nano

We're starting out with nano for the simple reason that it's really easy to use and doesn't take much explaining. You can quite literally do everything you need to in nano and while you might be able to do it faster in another editor, nano will help you get the job done just fine.

Nano can be run by using the nano command. Okay, no surprises there, but running nano by itself isn't all that useful. After all you've got a text editor now and you want to do some editing. Unless making a few notes, no one ever just writes text without wanting to save it afterwards. Generally then when you open nano you want to open a particular file for editing. That file may or may not exist, but you probably know what it is you want to call it when it comes to pressing the save button. For the sake of our introduction here, we're going to open nano and tell it that we want to edit test.txt. We can do that with:

```
[pi@raspberrypi ~] $ nano test.txt
```

All being well you should get something like this (Figure 6-2):

Figure 6-2. *Freshly opened nano with a new file*

We've connected to our Pi using SSH but because nano is a terminal based application, it will look the same regardless of how you run it. One interesting thing about these sorts of terminal applications is that they are sensitive to how big your terminal is. A fixed terminal (such as the physical console) has a set screen size. When you connect via SSH or use a virtual terminal, you can adjust the size of the screen and this will cause nano to resize along with it. This makes it very flexible and can fit in with your needs regardless of the shape or size of your screen.

So What Does this All Mean?

Nano's screen can be a bit confusing at first (especially the bit at the bottom) but most of the time you won't actually be paying attention to anything other than your text. In fact all the other stuff melts away in the background. For example on the top left of your screen you can see that we're running "GNU nano 2.0.9".

Until we came to write this book we had no idea what version of nano we were running and quite honestly until we had to describe it here, if someone had asked us to draw the nano layout from memory we'd have had a pretty hard time doing it. Actually, we wouldn't have been able to do it at all!

There are two other pieces of information that you can glean from nano's title bar. Smack bang in the middle is the name of the current file that you're editing. In our case, it's "/home/pi/test.txt". Not exactly earth shattering but it's quite common to be working on multiple windows at once and being able to quickly get your bearings can come in handy.

The third piece of useful information is whether or not the file has been modified, that is, are there any unsaved changes. This can come in handy too because although you could just simply write the file again, sometimes if you have edited the file from another location, you're not sure about the changes you've made, and you just want to know whether you have any changes that weren't reflected in the one you've been editing. It's also useful for simply jogging your memory and reminding you to save your work. To see what this looks like, just press the space bar to make a change (Figure 6-3):

Figure 6-3. *Modified file in nano*

That's pretty much it for the title bar. At the bottom of the screen there are actually two sections. The first one is the status line which shows you important information (right now it's telling you that it's a new file) and the second one is the shortcut or menu bar. We're not going to say much more about the status line as it's pretty much self-explanatory. Anything of importance that you need to know, nano will put it there. Of much greater interest (and in fact the key to using nano) is the shortcut bar. Let's take a closer look at it here (Figure 6-4):

Figure 6-4. *The shortcut bar*

When you've been working in Windows or on the Mac, you've probably reached the point where rather than using the mouse to copy and paste things, you instead use the keyboard combinations. On Windows you would use the control and c keys and on the Mac it would be the command key and c. When you use more than one key in concert with another, you end up with a key combination. Well nano works in a very similar way but rather than copy and paste, all of its key functions are driven with key combinations. Because it would be somewhat difficult to remember all the possible options available (although the ones you'll use on a frequent basis will soon be committed to your long term memory), nano displays them in the shortcut bar. Actually it only shows the most common commands but we have never needed to stray away from these.

To make use of any command you need to use the correct key combination. You can find which combo you need by looking at the shortcut bar. A short hand way of writing "control key" is to use the carat or "^" symbol. Looking at the shortcut bar you can see that if you want to get help, you need to use "^G" or in other words, hold down the control key and press the G key.

Saving Your File

Saving a blank text file is pretty boring and it's hard to tell if it saved correctly if all you have is a space character. We're going to go for an old favourite here and punch in "Mary had a little lamb".

Unlike some editors (most notably vim which you'll come across later), nano doesn't have the concept of different modes. That is, when you type into nano that will be interpreted as text to put into the file. Vim on the other hand starts in command mode and if you just start typing, you will get some interesting results. As you might expect, pressing enter after each line will take you to the beginning of the next line. After typing in the nursery rhyme you should get something like this (Figure 6-5):

Figure 6-5. *Mary had a little lamb, nano style*

We've shrunk nano's window down a bit so that we don't take up vast quantities of paper with blank white space. It also acts as a pretty good example of why you might want to resize a window and how it looks when you actually do. In this case everything looks just fine although admittedly for writing anything of a reasonable length you'd need something a bit bigger than this.

You may have noticed that the status line seems to have disappeared. This is because the file stops being a new file once any content has been added to it. Our modified warning is still up in the top right hand corner though. It's time to get rid of that and get Mary safely on to disk.

Looking at the shortcut bar you can see the options we have available to use. The most common ones you'll use are "WriteOut" which really just means "Save File" and "Exit". Exit actually doubles as WriteOut because if you try to exit nano with unsaved changes, it will ask you if you want to save your changes.

Let's start with the WriteOut command. Hold down the control key and press the O key. Nano should now look something like this (Figure 6-6):

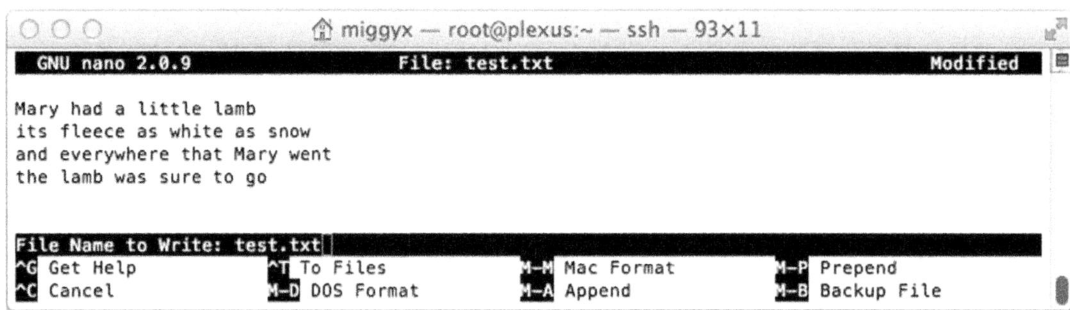

Figure 6-6. *Using the WriteOut command*

You'll notice that we have two changes here. The first is that our status line has made a come back. This time it's asking for information or at least it wants us to confirm it. Now that it's time to save the file, nano is asking us to confirm what the name should be. As we passed it a name when we originally started nano, this is the name that nano will provide by default. If we press the enter key now, it will save the file but before we do that, let's take a look at the shortcut bar.

You can see that it's changed to a whole new set of options. This is because the shortcut bar is actually contextual, that is it will show you the most relevant things based on what it is you're doing at the time. These options are only useful (or even available) when saving a file and so this is when you get to see them. We've never actually had to use any of these options apart from Cancel (when you suddenly decide that saving is not what you wanted to do at all).

Okay, back to saving the file. If you like you can change the name that the file will be saved as and nano will not only save it under your new name but will continue using that name when you go back to editing which is the same file and you should get a message like this (Figure 6-7):

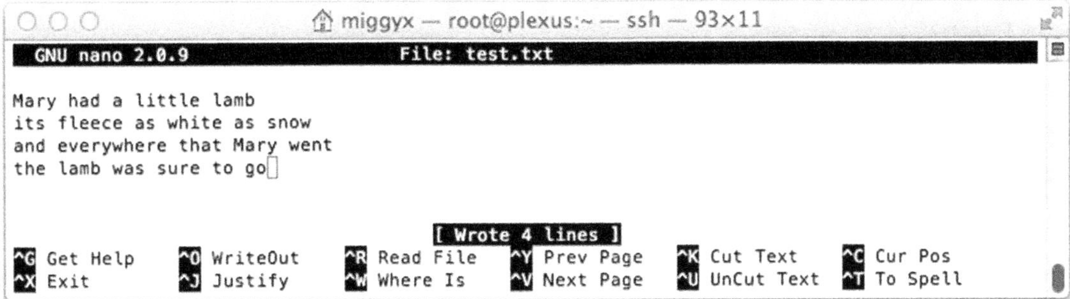

Figure 6-7. *File has been written to disk*

You can see that the shortcut bar has gone back to its usual look and we have a new message in our status line. You'll also have spotted that the Modified status has vanished. So far so good.

Let's quickly look at what happens if you try to exit nano whilst you have an edited file (Figure 6-8):

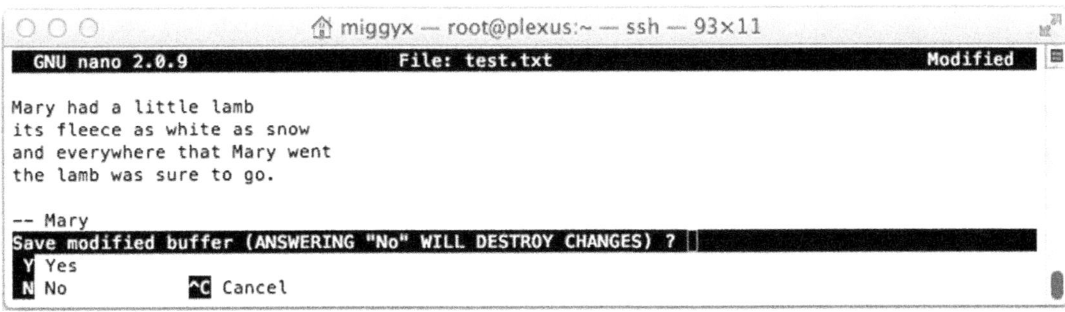

Figure 6-8. *Exiting before saving*

All we did here was add a signature to the file (although admittedly it probably wasn't Mary who wrote it) and then tried to exit nano by using control and X. This time the status line gives us a scary warning and the shortcut bar gives us a somewhat reduced number of choices. We can say yes in which case nano will save the changes before it exits or we can say no in which case nano will still exit but we will lose all the changes we made since the last time we saved the file. We can also think better of exiting and change our minds. In this case we can use control plus C to cancel our exit request which will just take us back to nano.

Moving Around in Nano

You can move around your text just by using the cursor keys as you're probably used to from your word processor of choice. In fact the only reason we mention this here is because some editors don't use those keys at all because they take your hands too far off the home row (that is, they're slow to use because you have to move your hands a long distance to reach them). So rather than explaining cursor keys, we'll show you the two features we use most in nano which are both coincidentally related to finding things.

The first thing you will probably want to use is the search feature which is somewhat oddly named as "Where Is" under nano. We can issue that command by pressing the control and W keys to get to the next step (Figure 6-9):

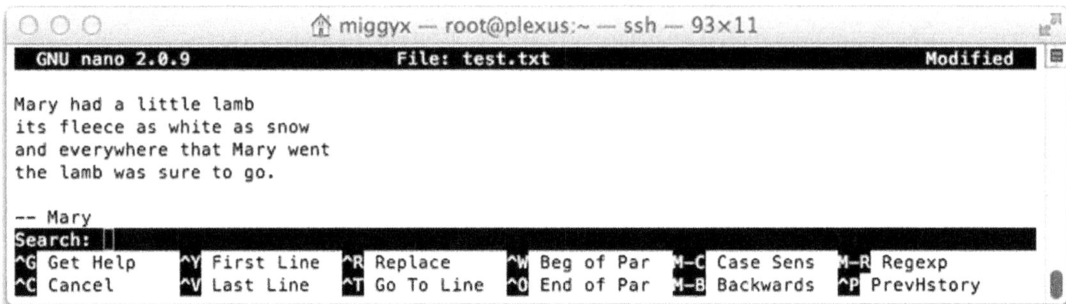

Figure 6-9. *Searching for some text*

Once again we have some new options available to us. The most common task though is to simply find a word. So let's search for Mary and see what happens (Figure 6-10):

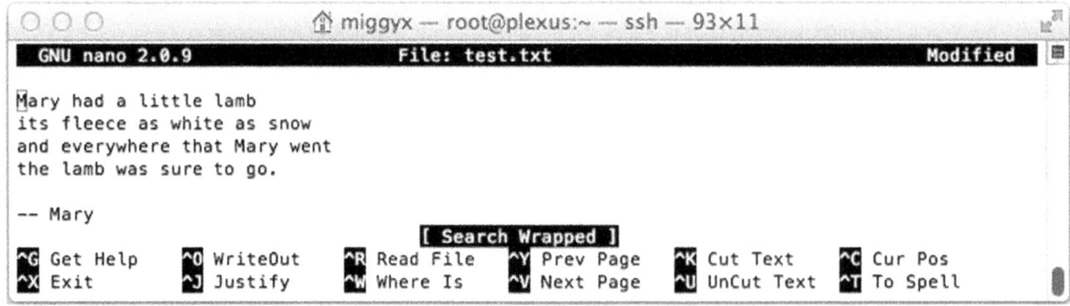

Figure 6-10. *Nano found Mary*

After pressing the enter key, nano will try to find the text you searched for. In our example, we were already at the end of the file and that's why you can see "Search Wrapped" in the status bar - nano reached the end of the file and wrapped around to continue the search from the beginning. This is a really handy feature!

It's quite common that there will be more than one occurrence of the word that you're looking for. If you wanted the second Mary, you would want to repeat your search. You can do this by just pressing control and W and then immediately pressing the enter key. Nano remembers what you searched for last time and if you don't supply a new word, it will simply search again with the old word. This means you can easily cycle through the document to find the specific entry that you're looking for.

The last feature that we'll cover is a slightly more specific form of search. Rather than searching for a word, we want to go to a specific line number. In day-to-day text editing this is not something that you'll actually do all that often. However when you start writing scripts and they generate errors, you will generally be told which line that error occurred on. For short programs it often doesn't matter but if you're building something fairly epic, you'll want to be able to get to the line quickly. This is true even in medium length programs because if you have a particularly tricky problem, you'll have to keep revisiting a specific piece of code and you certainly don't want to have to use the cursor keys to find it each time.

To go to a specific line number, you need to start the search as you did before by using control plus W but rather than typing any text, you should then do control + T. This will change the status line to read (Figure 6-11):

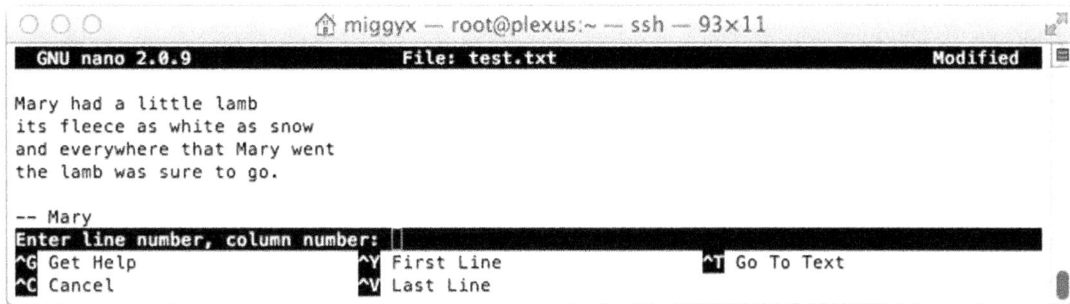

Figure 6-11. *Go to a specific line number*

All you have to do here is enter the line number that you want to go to and press enter. You can also see there are some other useful options here that allow you to go to the start of the file and the end of the file respectively. You can also press command and T to go back to searching for text or you can press command and C and cancel the search.

Wrapping Up Nano

That's all we're going to cover for nano but as you can see, even the limited amount of functionality we've covered has already given you the ability to edit configuration files or even compose your own book. Nano is great for these kinds of tasks where you don't want distractions and you just want to get the job done. As it happens a good deal of this book was written in nano so it just goes to show that this tool is certainly not just a toy! That being said, let's move on now to look at what the vim editor can offer you instead...

Getting Started with Vim

Vim is a bit more advanced than nano. Whereas nano was specifically designed to be simple, vim is designed to be a fully featured environment for doing all sorts of tasks. You can even integrate other applications (such as the shell and source code control) directly with vim and this means you can do huge amounts of work without ever leaving your text editor.

The downside to this raw power is that you're going to have to learn how to use it. Unlike nano which is basically ready to use right away, vim has the concept of modes. Generally speaking you're either in the normal or insert modes and those are the ones that we'll focus on in this section.

However we do want to point out that even though we use vim ourselves on a regular basis, we're not what you would call vim experts. We know how to use the functionality that helps us with our work, but there's a huge number of features that we don't use or even know about. As this is just a primer on vim, we don't feel that this is an issue, but if you think vim is the tool for you, there are a wealth of books dedicated solely to vim as well as numerous video tutorials on some of its more advanced and powerful features.

Rather than having to type in yet another poem, let's give Mary an encore and bring her back to the stage with vim:

```
[pi@raspberrypi ~] $ vim test.txt
```

Needless to say, starting vim is as straight forward as starting nano, but it does look a little different once it has started (Figure 6-12):

```
miggyx — root@plexus:~ — ssh — 93×11
Mary had a little lamb
its fleece as white as snow
and everywhere that Mary went
the lamb was sure to go.

-- Mary
~
~
~
~
"test.txt" 6L, 115C                                          1,1           All
```

Figure 6-12. *Starting up vim*

Gone are the nice headers, status lines and shortcut bars. In the land of vim, like Linux itself, we're expected to know what we're doing. In the bottom left of the screen you can see the name of the file that we're editing. Next to that we have 6L which tells us how many lines are in the file followed by 115C which tells us the number of characters. On the other side of the screen we have another useful piece of information 1,1. This tells us the line that we're currently on and the column that we're in. At present it is telling us that we're on line 1 and in the first column. That makes sense because we only just opened the file and if you look at the cursor, sure enough we've sitting on top of the first M.

■ **Note** Depending on the version of vim and how it is configured, it will usually take you to the location you were at when you last stopped editing that file. This is really useful when programming because it gets you immediately to where the action is.

You can also see seveal lines of tildes "~" beneath the last line in our file. These are here to remind us that although the screen is a certain size there is no content below Mary. This is especially useful when doing certain types of programming and you want to make sure there's no additional white space. It's really just a visual clue and won't get in your way.

Vim's Modes

Vim comes across as being a bit querky because unlike word processors and more basic text editors, with vim you can't start typing right away. This is because vim has different modes or personalities. When you first start vim, it is in command mode. Unlike nano where you give commands by using key combos, vim has a wide range of commands that are single or double letters. You might think that this would be hellishly confusing and well, you'd be right. Once you know the magic keypresses to make vim do your bidding, then you'll love this way of controlling your text editor. Until then however it's likely to drive you to distraction.

So let's get out of command mode and into slip into something more comfortable. We can replicate a nano-esque environment in vim by pressing the 'i' key. This will take us out of command mode and place us in insert mode. You can tell when you're in this mode because you get --INSERT—in the bottom left hand corner (Figure 6-13):

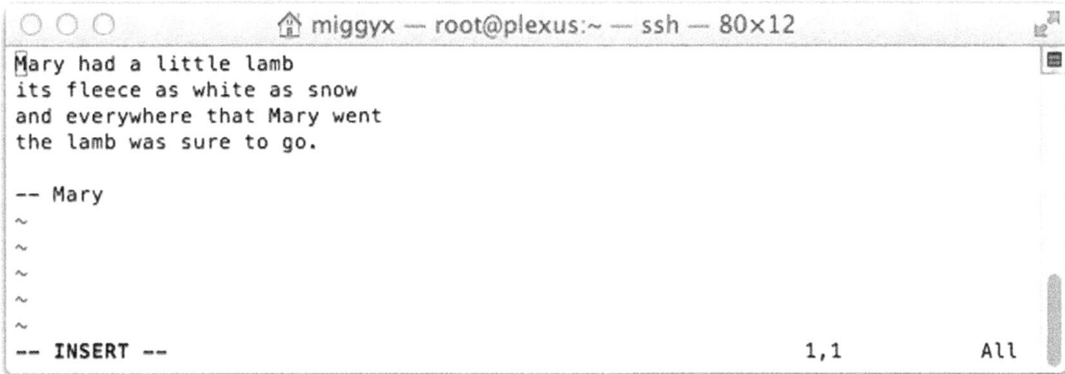

Figure 6-13. *Vim in insert mode*

At this point you can move around your text file just like you did with nano. The cursor keys work as expected and you can add and delete text as you did under nano. The differences start when you want to do something other than writing text though. How do you save your changes?

Saving Your Changes

To save your changes in vim the first thing you need to do is exit from insert mode. This takes you back to normal mode where you can issue commands and consequently where you can save your document. First though let's change the signatory to say John instead. This will give us the much-needed change for the document. To actually save the document we use this command:

```
:w
```

The command really is a colon followed by a lowercase W. Vim is case sensitive so if you tried to do: W you would get an error message that it isn't valid command (Figure 6-14):

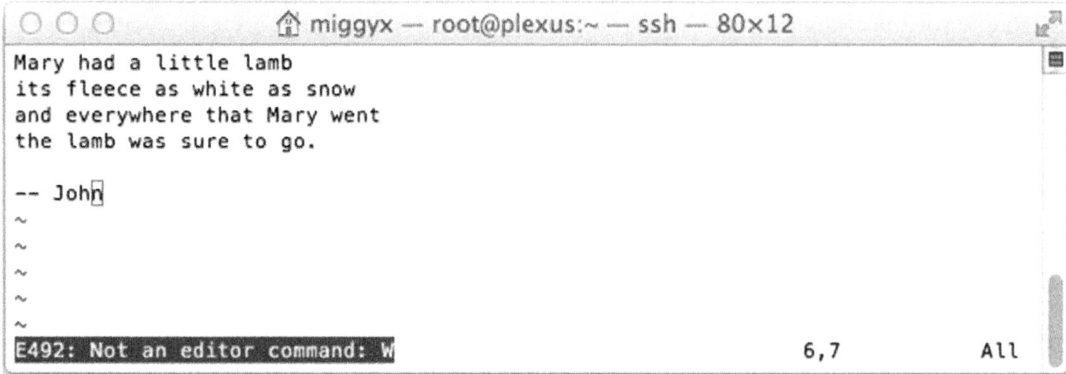

Figure 6-14. *Whoops, W isn't a command*

There's no need to panic though, just try the command again and you'll be fine (Figure 6-15):

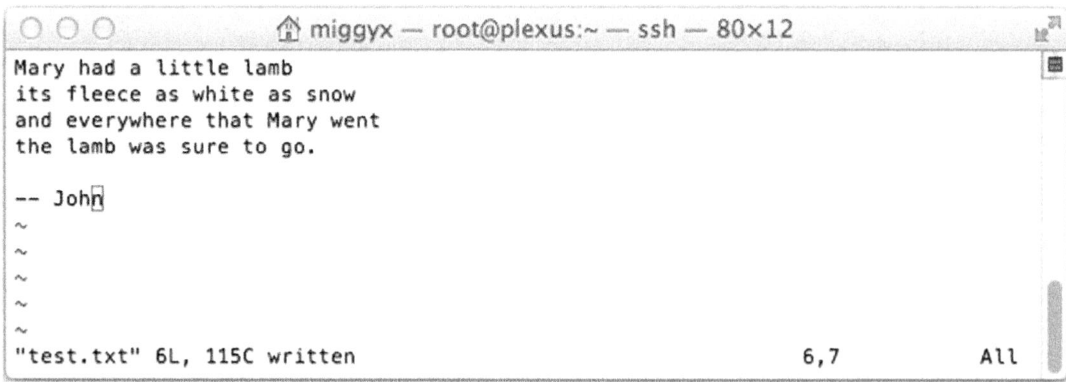

Figure 6-15. *:w on the other hand works like a charm*

If you wanted to change the file name whilst you were saving, you can simply type in the file name you want to use after the command like so:

```
:w test2.txt
```

This will then save the changes to the new file name and will then continue to edit the new file.

Getting Out of Vim

This leaves us with just one more feature to bring you to the same basic level that you had with nano (we'll cover searching in just a moment). Once you've done all your editing and you've saved your files you'll want to exit. The command for this is:

```
:q
```

As long as you haven't made any changes, vim will immediately exit and you'll be back at the command line. However if you had made some changes and you try to do this, you'll once again catch the wrath of vim (Figure 6-16):

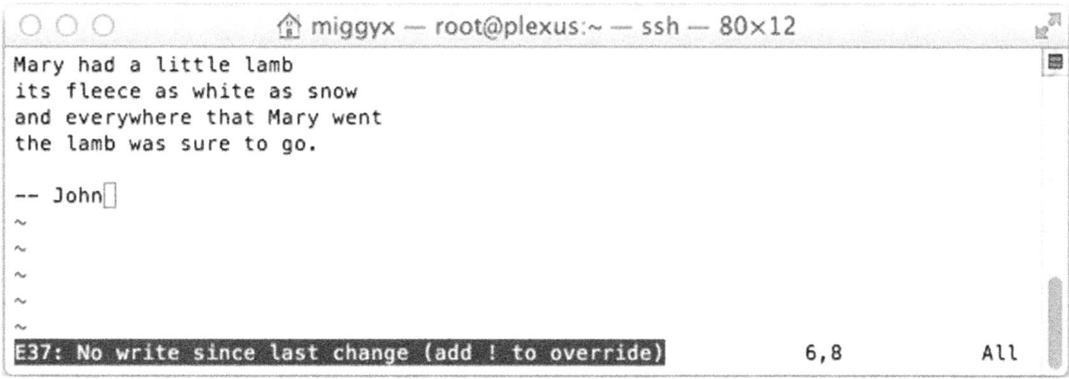

Figure 6-16. *To quit without saving you'll need an override*

Fortunately vim has already told us how to fix the problem, but basically if you want to quit without having your changes saved, you'll need to explicitly tell vim that's what you want to do with:

```
:q!
```

And that's all there is to leaving vim!

Searching in Vim

In this section we're only going to cover the basics and show you how to do the same sort of searches that you did in nano. In actual fact vim has very advanced search capabilities (you can use regular expressions for a start - see boxout) but while you might come to depend on these features as you become more advanced in your usage, you'll still probably find that you spend most of your time doing the simple things.

To search for a word in vim, all you need to do is prefix it with a forward slash. To give this a try, whilst in command mode (tap the escape key twice to ensure that you're in the right mode) type:

```
/Mary
```

This should then find all instances of Mary and highlight them for you (Figure 6-17):

```
miggyx — root@plexus:~ — ssh — 80×12
Mary had a little lamb
its fleece as white as snow
and everywhere that Mary went
the lamb was sure to go.

-- John
~
~
~
~
~
search hit BOTTOM, continuing at TOP                    1,1           All
```

Figure 6-17. *Vim found Mary*

You can see the “search hit BOTTOM, continuing at TOP” message, which is equivilant to nano’s “Search Wrapped”. One thing to watch out for with vim is that because it uses regular expressions for searching, it’s also case sensitive by default. That means if you search for mary rather than Mary, expect to receive a complaint (Figure 6-18):

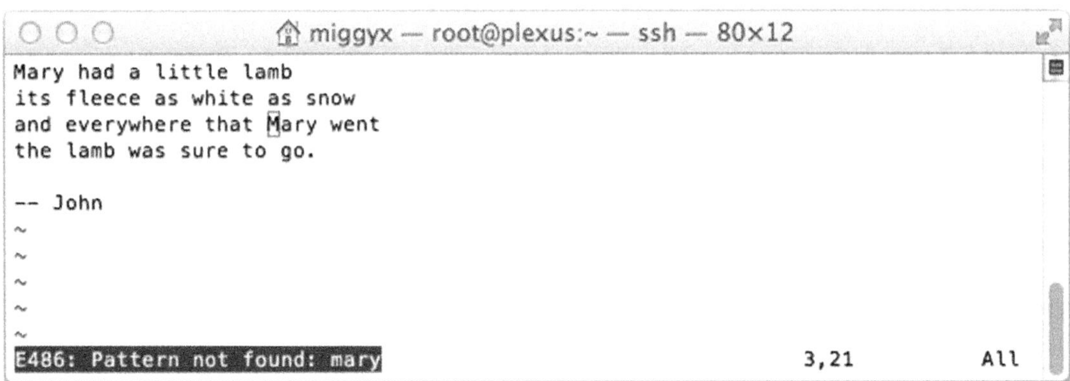

Figure 6-18. *Vim can’t find mary*

One area that vim has over nano is how to do repeated searches. To move to the next search result, all you need to do is press the ‘n’ key. In our example text above, if you search for Mary with /Mary and then keep pressing the ‘n’ you will see vim will cycle through the search results for you. We can’t really demonstrate that affect in print, but it’s a nice distraction for a few seconds if you’d rather not be doing something else. If you’d like to search in the opposite direction (i.e. towards the top of the file rather than the bottom) simple use a capital ‘N’ instead.

REGULAR EXPRESSIONS

Regular expressions in the right hands are like magic. They slice through complex text processing tasks like a hot chainsaw through warm butter. They are also frequently used to give system administrators bed-wetting nightmares and to scare small children. Regular Expressions are very powerful once you know how to use them but boy does that power come with a cost. Be that as it may, a basic knowledge of regular expressions will be very useful to you and you can use them directly in vim for searching, replacing and otherwise manipulating your text.

We don't have enough space to go into regular expressions here (often referred to solely as regex) but there are some fantastic resources available on the Internet to get you started, not to mention complete books on the topic. A great starting place is Jan Goyvaerts' website `http://www.regular-expressions.info/`. Not only is this site full of useful and helpful information (it is very often our first port of call) but Jan has also written some very powerful software. We bought RegexBuddy many years ago and it's still our first port of call when we're trying to debug some complicated regex. If you want a simpler tool for testing out your regular expressions, check out `http://rubular.com/` which does real time regex parsing in Ruby.

The last thing we covered in nano was moving to a specific line number. This is actually much easier in vim, probably because it's something that programmers have to do all the time. To jump to a specific line number, all you need to do is place the line number after the colon. For example to jump to the 5th line all you'd need to do is this:

```
:5
```

Once you hit the enter key, you'll be taken directly to the 5th line. As before this feature isn't particularly useful for normal editing, but it comes very much in handy when you're fiddling about with a program that simplify refuses to work the way you know it should!

Moving About in Vim

Although we've already shown you how to move around your text file, we haven't been leveraging the power of vim. Vim provides additional commands that can allow us to navigate through text more quickly.

In command mode you can still move around your text using the cursor keys, which is nice and convenient. In effect you can do the same thing using two other commands, the 'h' and 'l' keys. The h key will move the cursor back one character and the l key will move the cursor forward one character. Admittedly that's not very exciting, but we can now introduce the 'b' and 'w' commands. They work just like the previous commands only rather than stepping back just one character, they jump to the beginning of words. Suddenly that's more useful because now if you have a long line of text rather than pressing and holding down the cursor key for extended periods of time (tempting though isn't it?), you can greatly speed up the process by hopping a word at a time.

We can take this one step further though. If you want to jump to the beginning of a line you can press the '0' (zero) key. To get to the end of the line, you simply use $ (in our case that means holding down the shift key and pressing the 4 key). This is surprisingly useful because there will be lots of times when you want to get to either the beginning or the end of the line and now you can do so with a single key press.

Let's put this in a table to make it a bit clearer:

Start of line	Back one word	Back one letter	Forward one letter	Forward one word	End of line
0	b	h	l	w	$

So what we have now is a progressive way to move our cursor from one end of the line to the other. No longer do we have to fiddle about with the enter or back space keys or fall asleep waiting for the cursor to trundle across the screen. That's just the beginning though because these keys can be used for a lot more than just moving around your file, they can also be used to specify the scope of the commands you feed to vim.

Deleting in Vim

To delete a single character all you need to do is press the 'x' key. This will remove whichever letter happened to be under the cursor at the time. This is sometimes useful in its own right (usually when tweaking a typo) but it doesn't really offer you any great advantages over dropping into insert mode. The 'd' key however provides a very powerful delete command, that you can now combine with your newly acquired knowledge of moving the cursor to do some pretty impressive things.

The first delete command we're going to try is 'dd.' Let's start out by deleting the first line in our file. To make sure we're all in the right place, use the following command to get back to the first line:

```
:1
```

Now we're going to delete the current line by typing:

```
dd
```

Your poem should now be somewhat shorter and look like this (Figure 6-19):

```
miggyx — root@plexus:~ — ssh — 93×11
its fleece as white as snow
and everywhere that Mary went
the lamb was sure to go.

-- Mary
~
~
~
~
~
                                                    1,1           All
```

Figure 6-19. *Deleting the first line*

Now that we've ruined our poem, now would be a great time to introduce another very useful feature in vim, the "undo" command. To undo the change we just made, simply press the 'u' key and Mary will be restored to her former glory. This not only prevents panic attacks when accidentally deleting the wrong line, but it also means we can delete parts of this line in numerous fascinating ways.

If you have more than one line that you want to remove, you can tell vim how many times you want it to execute a particular command by prefixing the command with a number. For example if we wanted to remove three lines from our poem, we could do this:

```
3dd
```

This is equivilant to pressing the d key six times and gives you this happy result (Figure 6-20):

```
miggyx — root@plexus:~ — ssh — 93×11
the lamb was sure to go.

-- Mary
~
~
~
~
~
~
~
3 fewer lines                                    1,1          All
```

Figure 6-20. *Deleting three lines in one go*

You can see in the bottom left corner that there are now "3 fewer lines" just as we'd hoped. Let's restore Mary with the 'u' key and try something else. With our cursor at the beginning of the first line, try executing this command:

```
dw
```

This command combines the delete command with movement commands that we saw earlier. In this case we combined it with 'w' which means "one word to the right". We can see the effect of that command here (Figure 6-21):

```
miggyx — root@plexus:~ — ssh — 93×11
had a little lamb
its fleece as white as snow
and everywhere that Mary went
the lamb was sure to go.

-- John
~
~
~
~
"test.txt" 6L, 115C                              1,1          All
```

Figure 6-21. *Deleting a single word*

Rather than moving the cursor itself, we have effectively selected text that we wanted to delete. In this case, 'd' will start deleting from the cursor's current location, up to the first letter of the next word. We could have achieved this effect easily enough simply by pressing the 'x' key multiple times, but using 'dw' is clearly faster and more precise. Let's take this to the next level again and combine what we know. We know that we can make vim execute a command multiple times by prefixing the command with a number. We also know that we can combine the 'd' command with 'w' to delete a complete word. Let's revive Mary (another press of the 'u' key) and try this new improved command (Figure 6-22):

```
2dw
```

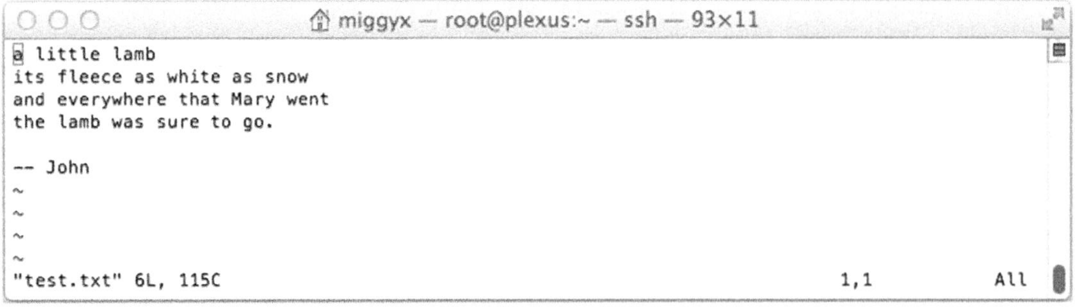

```
a little lamb
its fleece as white as snow
and everywhere that Mary went
the lamb was sure to go.

-- John
~
~
~
~
"test.txt" 6L, 115C                                               1,1           All
```

Figure 6-22. *Deleting two words at once*

Well isn't that interesting? We've been able to combine a serious of commands to express some reasonably complicated tasks. You can of course combine these in any way. For example if you wanted to delete everything to the end of the line, you could use d$. If you wanted to delete everything from the start of the line, you can use d0. It's being able to combine commands in this way that makes vim such a powerful tool for working with text. Although these features are of fairly limited used when working with English prose, when you start working with programming languages, they become very useful indeed.

Misc Little Commands

Before we move on to look at some of the features of Vim's visual mode, we're going to provide a very quick overview of some other simple commands that will come in handy. The 'i' enters into insert mode but sometimes you want to write immediately above or below the current line. You can get this affect by using O and o respectively. These will both insert a new line and then switch to insert mode. Sometimes you don't need to actually edit the content of a file but you just need to change a single letter. This could be because of a typo or maybe you just want to increment a number. You can do this with the 'r' key. This allows you to replace the character under the cursor with any other character. Simply press 'r' and then type the character you want to replace it with. Simple but very effective!

Visual Mode

Visual mode is not something we use very often ourselves but when we do use it, it often saves us a huge amount of time and effort. This mode allows you to select or highlight blocks of text for further processing. This is akin to highlighting text with your mouse in a word processor. There are two ways you can enter visual mode, by pressing either the 'V' key or the 'v' key. If you use the upper-case V, you will be able to select a block of text based on lines. With the lower-case v, you gain extra precision as you can select based on single letters rather than entire lines. The overall result is the same and the option you choose depends only on which one would be most convenient to you.

So what exactly can you do with visual mode? Well it really doesn't do anything in and of itself, it just provides an easy way for you to tell vim what text the following command should be applied to. In keeping with our previous examples, let's select a chunk of Mary's poem. You don't need to highlight the exact text that we have, but try to get a fairly random chunk (Figure 6-23):

Figure 6-23. *Highlighting text in visual mode*

As you can see from the highlight, we used the lower case 'v' option as we wanted to highlight within a particular word. There's no real reason for that apart from a sense of the dramatic, so it could easily have been a bunch of lines selected with 'V'. Now let's apply our favourite command, the delete command. By pressing 'd' you will find that the highlight text magically disapears. In this case you don't need to provide additional information to vim to tell it what to delete because in effect you've already told it by highlighting the text in the first place.

Of course you can do other interesting things apart from deleting text (though deleting text is fun). For example, if you want to indent the first two lines of the poem, you can highlight the first two lines with V and then use the greater than and less than signs (> and < respectively) as appropriate. We can't show you how that would look in print (honestly moving huge chunks of text back and forth is surprisingly theraputic) but we can show you the end result of this command (Figure 6-24):

```
miggyx — root@plexus:~ — ssh — 93×11
        Mary had a little lamb
        its fleece as white as snow
and everywhere that Mary went
the lamb was sure to go.

-- John
~
~
~
~
                                                   1,2-9          All
```

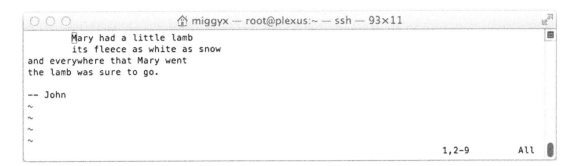

Figure 6-24. *Indenting highlighted text*

There is one more terribly useful feature that we haven't covered yet that works very nicely with visual mode - copy and paste.

Copy and Paste Vim Style

Copy and paste in a terminal is something of an iffy proposition. The reason for that is an application running in the terminal effectively lives in its own little world. If you copy text from the terminal on your laptop for example, that text is copied into your laptop's clipboard. The remote application (in this case vim) has no idea that you did that. Likewise if you paste content in to vim from your laptop, vim will simply receive it as a set of key strokes, it won't have a clue that it came from a clipboard. Generally speaking this is okay. If you just want to move a bit of text about, then using the clipboard in this way is probably fine.

There are times when this doesn't do what you want. For example, if you have a split screen and you have two files side by side and you want to select the first paragraph on the left, you're now a bit stuck. The terminal just shows you a representation of what's on the server, it's just a display and as such the terminal has no real understanding of what it's displaying. If you try to copy and paste the left hand side, you'll find the right hand side comes along for the ride. That's far from ideal (not to mention highly irritating).

Another issue you might come across is that you might want vim to do something with the text. If you just want to paste it once, no big deal, but what if you want to paste exactly 10,004 times? Vim can't help you there because it has no concept of your local clipboard. You'll find that when these issues do crop up they'll be fairly niche and you can work around them. However it is likely to really irritate you because you will think "if only I could just copy this text!" whilst you're sat there trying to work around the problem.

What we need then is a remote clipboard, somewhere for the remote application to store data for processing. There's no standard for this as such but many terminal based applications offer a solution and in the case of vim, it's the yank and paste feature. To yank some content you need to use the 'y' key. This takes the same modifiers that the 'd' command uses so you can quite happily copy an entire line with 'yy' (remember, the letter just doubles up), and a single word with 'yw'. Also like the delete command we can also use this with the visual mode.

First, simply highlight the text that you want to copy. For simplicity, let's go for the top two lines again. Once you've highlighted that with the 'V' key, press the 'y' to yank it into the clipboard. That's phase one complete, now all we have to do is paste it back into our file. There are two ways you can use the paste command with either 'P' or 'p'. As with the 'V' and 'v' commands, the upper and lower case versions are usually related in some way. In this case, the 'P' key inserts the content before the current line whereas the 'p' key inserts it after. Feel free to move your cursor to any location location in the file before hitting one of those keys. The effect is really what you'd expect and vim will just paste content in. You can of course combine these commands with the numeric prefixes to repeat the number of times something is inserted. Here's what happens if you end 40p (Figure 6-25):

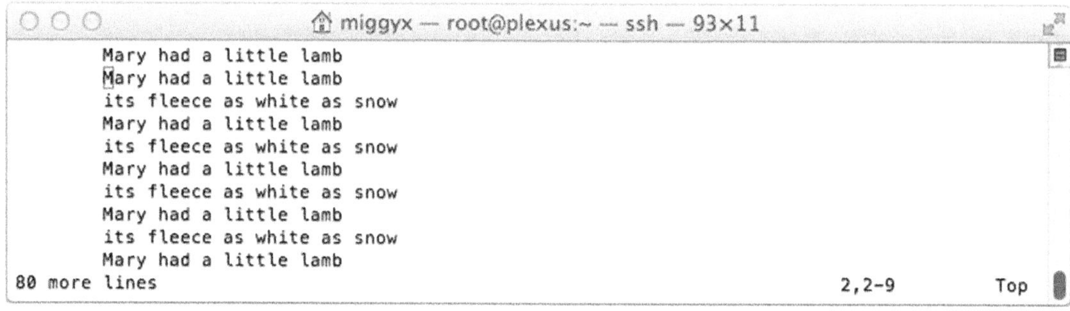

Figure 6-25. *Mass pasting*

Although you don't know it yet, you actually learned to cut as well as copy text. Whenever you use the 'd' key, you delete the text from the file, but a copy is placed in the clipboard. If you select a line and delete it with 'dd', you can restore it with 'P'. Bear in mind that if you use the 'p' key instead, because you've removed the line, you'll actually be inserting the original line after the line you're currently on. If you want to restore it to its original location, you must use the 'P' key to paste before the current line.

Summary

In this chapter we've looked at what separates a text file from a binary file and why text files are the lingua-franca when it comes to configuring software. We've covered two of the key text editors that you are likely to come across in your travels and we've given you a good grounding in both of them. Certainly we have not been able to show you everything that is possible, but now you should be in a good position to explore and try new things yourself.

In the next chapter we're going to cover the BASH shell and show you some of the more important things that a system administrator needs to know...

CHAPTER 7

Managing Your Pi

So now you have this magical Pi, installed Raspbian, logged in and got your Pi the way you like it, and even have a few things in mind to do with it. Although you are becoming familiar with Linux, the problem is that every time your Pi is switched off or loses power, you need to go over to it, log in and physically set things up before you can use it again. Well, no more!

This chapter is about systems administration and some of the basic application functions that will allow you to manage the way your system functions at boot. To help, we will also give you a crash course in coding with the BASH language so that you can create start scripts of your own to initiate applications (we'll cover just what a script is, too). Finally, we will cover some basic security for your system, including user management, so you can change your password and add new users to your system.

Remotely Accessing the Pi

Probably one of the hardest things to get used to when working in a Linux environment when coming from a Windows or an OSX environment is working in the shell. For starters, it's not pretty, but more importantly humans are creatures who are very much used to manipulating things to achieve an outcome. This means that a GUI-based environment is much more intuitive—at first. Having come from a Windows environment, I can say for certain that the command line is such a great environment to work in. The amount you can do with a few deft keystrokes—compared with keyboard and mouse work, clicking, dragging, and performing context actions is amazing. Being able to work within a system purely from the command line is a great asset indeed. But you need to become familiar with it, and the only way to do this is practice!

Why am I talking about the command line when we need to talk about managing your Pi? Because most Linux management is achieved through the command line, with most if not all of the system functions you want to use being available from the command line. Moreover, it is far easier and less resource-intensive to access your system via the command line than it is to access it via the GUI. To access your system remotely via the command line, you simply need to use Secure Shell (or SSH for short), which you first saw in Chapter 3. You also need to ensure that your system's network access is available on boot as well. These two functions serve the basics of being able to manage your system from anywhere as you have network enabled and then can use SSH to connect to your system. So, let's examine these two functions a little more closely so that you understand how to ensure you can always access your Pi to manage it.

Networking

If you are like most people and have a router to provide multiple devices on your system with network access, you will probably be aware that your router automatically provides network IP addresses to all your devices. It doesn't do this through any sort of magic, but rather through a special protocol called DHCP, which stands for Dynamic Host Control Protocol. The purpose of DHCP is to automatically assign an IP address to a machine, which means there is no need to manually assign it one. DHCP is invoked automatically by the network service when it is configured to do so. We cover how to configure networking in much more detail within Chapter 9 WiPi.

However, if for some reason you need to manually invoke DHCP to assign you an IP address and get you connected to the network, you need to use the `dhclient` command. You will need to run it as root, as you will need to do with most of these commands, because you are changing core system functionality. If you just run `dhclient` as is, you will try and get a new IP address for every interface on the system, which may not be desirable. You can actually specify a specific interface for `dhclient` to work with by simply adding it as the first argument of the command (i.e., `dhclient eth0`).

DNS

Probably one of the most important things to keep in mind when working with your systems networking is DNS, which is short for Domain Name System. DNS is the way that every system on the Internet is able to turn URLs (e.g., `www.apress.com`) into an IP address (e.g., `173.203.147.183`). DNS on your Linux machine works by knowing where it should direct its queries. This is governed by the file `/etc/resolv.conf`, which contains a name server directive that tells your system where the name server it should query is located. Normally this is your router, but it can be an Internet DNS server such as Google's 8.8.8.8. These will appear in `resolv.conf` like this:

```
nameserver 10.0.0.1
```

SSH

SSH is a way that you can remotely gain a secure and encrypted connection to your Pi's shell without needing to physically do anything to it. Getting SSH installed and running, along with basic commands to access your system, are covered in Chapter 3 so we won't go into much detail and will instead be diving deep into the function of SSH. SSH is provided by the `sshd` daemon that is run at boot time on your Pi. You can start and stop this command in the same way that your system does, which is to use the `sshd` init script. All system init scripts are normally located in `/etc/init.d/` and they are normally run as root. To use them, add the action you want to take (start, stop, and restart) to the first argument of the script. So to restart SSH, run `/etc/init.d/ssh restart`. Additionally, these scripts are the ones your system uses to run programs or commands on boot. So let's have a look at how we can leverage this to write your own init scripts.

BASH: Basic Coding

Besides "Hey can you fix my computer?" the most common computing question I am asked is "Can you teach me how to write this application in C?". Not a month goes by without someone I am working with, a friend, or a relative comes and asks me to teach them how to write software. Normally, they ask for a quick rundown of how to write applications in C. This is not an unreasonable question for the most part, but often when I ask them what they want to do, they want to do something simple. And while I would happily advocate learning C, there is a much simpler way for them to get introduced to the wonderful world of software design, without taking on the task of learning C (which for what they are normally after is a lot of overkill).

That is the goal of this part of the chapter. We aim to introduce you to coding, to basic logic structures, and to some of the basic software design principles so that you can get the job done. We will achieve this by introducing you to BASH. While many people will scoff, BASH is a perfect way to introduce the core fundamentals of what programming is about. BASH is also one of the most widely used languages for software in the world because most applications on Linux systems will have some level of BASH software performing some kind of intermediary functions somewhere along the route.

What Is BASH?

As covered in Chapter 3, BASH is short for Bourne Again Shell and is the default shell environment for most Linux and UNIX environments. When you log in to your system via the command line and are presented with your prompt, this prompt is provided to you by the BASH shell. The shell will take commands and instructions and process them to perform system functions. Most of the commands you normally issue when working with or administering your system via the command line are ones to invoke other applications so that you can generate output.

While this seems like a very obvious and simple way to go about things, it is also a fantastic way of demonstrating the core precept of how any software application works. You take a given input, perform some kind of computation upon it, a response (called the *output*) is generated. This process is, in fact, the basic process of so many functions of life and work that many people take for granted. It is this basic model of input, compute, output that will form the basic model of how we go about understanding how programming functions.

So back to the first question: what is BASH? BASH is a shell, and a shell is a method for taking inputs and computing against them to generate an output. BASH has a number of tools that allow you to use the same basic logic constructs of just about all programming languages. This is how BASH works as a programming language as well as a shell—you can write a number of these logical operations and commands and then use them to form a computation. Now you have a rudimentary understanding of what BASH is, what a shell is, what the broad purpose of any computer program is, and how all these functions are available to perform the basic action of input, compute, and output. Now that you have a very broad overview of what we want to achieve, we can use this knowledge as the starting block for learning how to write a program with BASH.

Starting in BASH

So you know what BASH is and what a shell is and how the rudimentary logic of a program works that's often considered by many to be head and shoulders above the pack. In fact, several interviewers commented that while their employers had rigorous questioning of potential software engineers who could all espouse what we have covered, they complained that many employees and graduates could not form the logic for a basic program on a piece of paper. They went forward to propose a coding test, a very simple test that any software engineer should be able to solve quickly. This test, which is called the *FizzBuzz test*, is based on a children's game of the same name. The basic principle is that you must count from 1 to 100 and say *Fizz* for every number that is a multiple of 3, you must say *Buzz* for every number that is a multiple of 5, and finally you must say *FizzBuzz* for every number that is a multiple of both 3 and 5. It sounds simple; that's because it is. After all, most coding is simply building small blocks of logic and attaching them to other blocks of logic; mashing together lots and lots of little input, compute, and output nodes to form a larger computing system that does a much larger input, compute, and output process.

To this end, we will start by writing our own solution to the FizzBuzz problem in BASH so that you all can pass the basic software engineer competency test! That's right; we will be programming in BASH. The BASH interpreter provides commands that have the same function as common programmatic logic elements. These can be combined with normal shell commands to form whole programs. So, let's start writing (we covered text editors in Chapter 6, so you can use any you like). All you need is to be able to edit a file and execute it on the command line afterward. Go ahead and open up your favorite text editor and write the following:

```
#!/bin/bash
```

This is the first thing that anyone wanting to write a program in BASH should write. This is called the *shebang*, and it is a special symbol that when placed on the first line of any file means that it is the path to the script interpreting engine we are to use. In this case, we will be using the interpreter for BASH that is located in `/bin/bash` on your Pi and on just about every other Linux and UNIX operating system. This will tell the outside command prompt shell that when it is running this program, it should use the `/bin/bash` interpreter to execute it. You should always include some form of shebang at the start of your given program for any interpreted language.

Interpreted versus Compiled

This brings me nicely to the next point of order: interpreted vs. compiled languages. For these purposes, you won't need to have a deep knowledge of compiled languages, but it is always good to know that they exist and to be aware of some of the differences between an interpreted language and a compiled language. So while both sets of languages allow you to write your own programs for the computer to execute, they go about this in fundamentally different ways.

Interpreted languages (sometimes called *scripting languages*) write down a series of programmatic commands that are fed to an interpreting engine (as given by the shebang, for example) that will extrapolate their computational meaning and perform the functions that the program intended. This is the pen-and-paper equivalent of a recipe for a cake, whereby you write down the exact method for how to make the cake, and the interpreter cooks it for you and outputs tasty delicious cake.

■ **Note** This recipe nature is also much like a script for a play in that as long as you have the script and can read it you will perform the same actions each time. This is why interpreted languages are often known as scripting languages: their ultimate output is a collection of text that can be used to create the programmatic output the same way each time.

Compiled languages take a different approach. They also have a recipe (called *source code*), but instead of the recipe running, it will be taken to a specialized piece of software called a *compiler* that will take the recipe and create an executable package (called a *binary*) from it. This binary package is written in the computer's own machine language so when executed it performs all the actions itself. This is the equivalent of writing the plans for a specialized cake-making system and then installing it in your system and having it make the cake. In both cases you get cake, but the interpreted one may take a little longer to make from the moment you say go. The flip side of this is that creating the specialized cake-making machinery takes much more effort. Now you should understand why I said languages like C were overkill for small problems—C is a compiled language.

Output in BASH

Back to our application: if you were to save and run your program, it would not do anything for you. So the first order of business should be to make your program output something. This is accomplished with the `echo` statement, which is also available from your command prompt shell; you use `echo` to make the system output a given set of text. So let's add an output to your script to have it say hello to everyone out there in the big wide world. Modify your script so it looks like this:

```
#!/bin/bash
echo "Hello World!"
```

Now go ahead and execute your script; to do this, you will need to change the script's file permissions to allow it to be executed. My script is called `fizzbuzz.sh`, so the commands needed to make it executable and then to execute it are these:

```
$ chmod +x fizzbuzz.sh
$ ./fizzbuzz.sh
```

This code will generate the following output:

```
Hello World!
```

Congratulations! You have just written the world's most simple program, the *Hello World program*, which is the first program most software engineering students are given to create. It shows how to begin building a small piece of software and accomplishes the basic task of any software program: it generates output. In this case, the chain was that we gave it an input of "Please output 'Hello World!'" and the system computed that and then gave us the desired output: `Hello World!` I wrapped `Hello World!` in a pair of quotation marks. (This is done so that the line of `Hello World!` is treated as a string of characters instead of other commands to execute.) All languages need to make the distinction between what is a piece of data and what is an actual piece of programmatic logic. The quotation marks in this instance show that everything within them is considered to be a string of text.

You may ask, "So what if I want to output a quotation mark? Suppose I want to output `"Hello World!"` like that in quotation marks." Well, not a problem, we have you covered! All systems have the concept of what is called an *escape*. An escape is a special character that tells the interpreter or compiler to ignore the special properties of the next character and just treat it as part of a given string. In most systems, the escape character is a backslash (\). So if we wanted to make our `Hello World!` have quotation marks, we would modify it to be as follows:

```
#!/bin/bash
echo "\"Hello World!\""
```

This shows that we want to escape those inner pair of quotation marks, so if we execute, we should see the following:

```
$ ./fizzbuzz.sh
"Hello World!"
```

Fantastic! You can even escape an escape if you want to print a backslash as the output of something in your code. Remember this as you are writing software because this is one of the most common mistakes people make—having unescaped characters in their code, which causes the rest of their software to have issues because the strings are mixed up.

■ **Note** Probably the most commonly escaped character is `\n`, which is short for *newline*. This can be used to output text on the next line.

As an aside, this is where text editors that have syntax highlighting come into a realm of their own because they are an immense help in displaying which characters are part of a string and which aren't. Vim has syntax highlighting, as does nano (but not over SSH); unfortunately, the default GUI editor LeafPad doesn't, but there are a number of editors out there that do you simply need to find one that suits you. They also have other functions such as bracket matching and brace matching, but they won't help us much at this stage.

Recap

So what have we learned so far? We have covered how to start off a BASH application using the shebang so we can pick out the right interpreter. You learned how to print basic output to the screen and also how to use the escape character within a string. This brings us nicely to the next point on our list: variables.

Variables

Variables are an abstract representation of a given piece of data. Come again? A variable is a way that a computer can store a given piece on information so that it can be retrieved again. This is the way that most information within a program is stored and manipulated because most programs do not work like our simple `Hello World!` They take various forms of information and turn it into other information. So let's depart from our first example and return to the problem of writing a FizzBuzz application. We need to start by counting from 1 to 100.

We could simply write each of the numbers, one per line, and then perform the FizzBuzz calculations on each, but that's no really a good and logical way of going about writing this program. What we need is an abstract variable that can contain the "number"; we can then run the FizzBuzz tests against this "number" and then we will simply increase the "number" by one and rinse and repeat until the number 100 has been tested. Then we are done!

So now you should have some understanding of what a variable is. It's a way that we can represent any single piece of information. We don't have to have a specific piece of information because the variable is just that—variable in nature? However, there are a few limitations of variables to consider. First, there are many different types of variables defined in the wider world of programming, such as Boolean, integer, double precision integer, long integer, character, string, floating point integer, vector, array, and so on. For BASH, there are only a few variable types, but we should be aware of the most important of the other types of variables because this can come into play with other programming languages:

- First is the *integer*, which is a numeric variable that is designed to represent only a number (and in most cases only a whole number). This type is defined to allow easy use of mathematical and other numeric functions such as addition, subtraction, multiplication, and so on.
- Second is the *string*, which is a type of written data and represents a long stream of written characters. Strings are normally related to user input and output because they are far too cumbersome to work with inside an application due to the highly variant nature of what can be included in a string of text.
- Third is the *array*, which is a special type of variable because it is a metavariable and is basically a carrier for a number of other variables. The subvariables within an array are called *elements* and are referenced by adding a pair of square brackets to the end of the array variable and a number that corresponds to the element of the array in question. Arrays do not start at 1; they instead start at 0 because 0 is logically the first number in the counting sequence. So if you want to retrieve the fourth element from an array you would be adding `[3]` to the end of your array variable.

So now that you know what a variable is, we can start to form our basic program logic for solving the FizzBuzz problem.

Logical Operation: if

Now we have both the ability to output something and to store something, which covers the first and last portions of what one needs to do with a computer program input and output. What we need to do now is to actually perform some calculations on our variables so that we can have our program do something meaningful. This is where we break out into logical operations. In programming there are two basic logical operations that you will need to become intimate with. These two logical operations form the basis of most of the programming that will be done anywhere. They do this because they allow people to perform tests and take divergent actions depending on the outcome of the test.

The first of these statements is the `if` statement. An `if` statement performs just as its name implies—if something is true, an action is performed. It is the test nature of an `if` statement that provides it with all its power because when combined with the use of variables we can test just about anything we want. So looking at the FizzBuzz example, we know we have our initial variable "number" that will represent the counting numbers between 1 and 100. We will need to perform tests on "number" to see if it is divisible by 3, divisible by 5, or divisible by both 3 and 5. If it matches one of these conditions, we need to output the correct word.

So now you need to understand how an `if` statement is written into a program. In BASH, the basic syntax is this:

```
if [ <TEST> ]; then
        DO SOMETHING
fi
```

The preceding is a simple BASH `if` statement and it really isn't that complex. You will notice that along with the `if` and the test and doing something, there is also a `fi`. The `fi` denotes the end of things that are to be performed, as you can perform multiple actions within an `if` statement. So, now we have our `if` statement, so we need to make it do things. So let's have a quick look at some mathematical operations.

■ **Note** Remember to leave a space on either side of the open square bracket, a space before the close square bracket, and a space after the semicolon; otherwise, you will get a syntax error.

Test Based Arithmetic

We know that we need to have a test for equality, so how does someone confirm if any given number is divisible by another given number? The simple answer is to check that when divided by a given number, the result is a "whole" number without any "remainder." This is, in fact, as hard a concept to program as it sounds. Whereas multiplication, addition, subtraction, and even division will give finite answers that can be tested upon, checking whether something is divisible by another number requires a different operation. Thankfully, there is a specialized mathematical operation designed for just this issue: the *modulus*. The modulus returns the remainder of a division of any two numbers and is denoted by the symbol %. So the modulus gives you results like these:

```
12 % 3 = 0
12 % 5 = 2
```

And suddenly our test has appeared: if number modulus 3 is equal to 0 we output Fizz, if number modulus 5 is equal to 0, we output Buzz, and if number modulus 3 and 5 is equal to 0, we output FizzBuzz. So, if we combine all of these, we get the following:

```
if [ number % 3 = 0 ]; then
    echo "Fizz"
fi
if [ number % 5 = 0 ]; then
    echo "Buzz"
fi
if [ number % 3 = 0 ]; then
    if [ number % 5 = 0 ]; then
        echo "FizzBuzz"
   fi
fi
```

Okay, that's a good-looking attempt, but there are a number of problems that relate to things about BASH we still need to cover in order to make this into valid executable BASH.

Let's start with the simple variables. In BASH, there are two modes that variables operate in. First is *assignment mode*, which occurs when we are creating a new variable and giving it a value. In these instances, the variables work just like the previous number, so we could create our `number` variable as 1 this way:

```
number=1
```

This is fine and looks like our example, but when we want to use the current value of the `number` variable, we need to access the variable, which is done in *dereferencing mode*. In BASH, this means adding a dollar sign (`$`) to the front of every variable for which we want to use the value.

To recap, there are two modes for a variable: one for loading the variable (called *assigning*) and one for pulling the values out of the variable (called *dereferencing*). In the first mode, we use the variable as is; in the second, we use a $ in front of the variable. Okay, not a problem. Let's update the code:

```
if [ $number % 3 = 0 ]; then
    echo "Fizz"
fi
if [ $number % 5 = 0 ]; then
    echo "Buzz"
fi
if [ $number % 3 = 0 ]; then
    if [ $number % 5 = 0 ]; then
        echo "FizzBuzz"
   fi
fi
```

So our code looks a bit better, but you may have noticed the next problem that occurred when we assigned a number the value of 1. The use of the equal sign (=) is used to assign values to variables, so in this context it looks like we are trying to assign the variable 5 with the number 0, which will cause all kinds of problems with the test in the `if`. Most languages handle this using a pair of equal signs (==) to denote a test for equality, but in BASH there are a number of special arithmetic testing operators we are given to test this:

- `-eq` for equality
- `-ne` for not equal
- `-gt` for greater than
- `-lt` for less that
- `-ge` for greater than or equal to
- `-le` for less than or equal to

We can take advantage of these operators in our code to do the comparison of the result of our modulus and 0. So make these changes to your code again and you should have the following:

```
if [ $number % 3 -eq 0 ]; then
    echo "Fizz"
fi
if [ $number % 5 -eq 0 ]; then
    echo "Buzz"
```

```
fi
if [ $number % 3 -eq 0 ]; then
    if [ $number % 5 -eq 0 ]; then
        echo "FizzBuzz"
   fi
fi
```

Finally, when doing an arithmetic operation (such as modulus), we need to tell BASH that this is meant as an arithmetic operation. To do this, we use a `$` and a pair of parentheses around the actual bit of arithmetic so the operation of `5 % 3` means that we need `$((5 % 4))`, and we can make the change:

```
if [ $(($number % 3)) -eq 0 ]; then
    echo "Fizz"
fi
if [ $(($number % 5)) -eq 0 ]; then
    echo "Buzz"
fi
if [ $(($number % 3)) -eq 0 ]; then
    if [ $(($number % 5)) -eq 0 ]; then
        echo "FizzBuzz"
   fi
fi
```

There you have it; you have written three simple tests for the FizzBuzz application; and used `if` statements, a variable, the print, and the special arithmetic operator. That's a lot of code, so let's test it and make sure what we have got now works!

We can do this simple test by creating the `number` variable with a single value for now. Let's assign it to 15 so we can guarantee some output. With the `number` variable added, your script should look like this:

```
#!/bin/bash
number=15
if [ $(($number % 3)) -eq 0 ]; then
    echo "Fizz"
fi
if [ $(($number % 5)) -eq 0 ]; then
    echo "Buzz"
fi
if [ $(($number % 3)) -eq 0 ]; then
    if [ $(($number % 5)) -eq 0 ]; then
        echo "FizzBuzz"
   fi
fi
```

When executed, the output will be this:

```
$ ./fizzbuzz.sh
Fizz
Buzz
FizzBuzz
```

Troubleshooting

Oh dear. That output is a problem. We said all three words at once, not just the FizzBuzz when the number was divisible by both 3 and 5. We just failed! Argh! Okay, take a few deep breaths; this isn't the end of the world. In fact, it's a great time to introduce a new feature. The `if` statement does something when the test is true, but there is also another part we can add: the `else`. The `else` is the flip side of the `if`, and the logic flows like this: *if* the test is true, do something, *else* do a different thing. We can use a combination of these two to perform our tests for FizzBuzz. The syntax of an `if`, `else` statement is as follows:

```
if [ TEST ]; then
    DO SOMETHING
else
    DO A DIFFERENT THING
fi
```

The syntax is almost identical to the original `if` statement, so it is easy to make a few changes to make your `if` statements into `if`, `else` statements. But now we run into the much bigger problem—and one that is the cause of most people's problems with programming; it's the logical order flow. We need to create a sequence of tests so that we can determine if something is divisible by 3, divisible by 5, or divisible by both; and perform a wholly different action in each case. This kind of thinking is what makes programming so hard for so many people, and there is no trick to it: you simply have to work it out. So let's have a go at working this one out together.

If we find something that is divisible by 3 or 5, and output something before checking whether it is divisible by both, we run into the potential for outputting a Fizz, a Buzz, and a FizzBuzz, which is not what we want. So let's start with a test for both:

```
 if [ $(($number % 3)) -eq 0 ]; then
    if [ $(($number % 5)) -eq 0 ]; then
        echo "FizzBuzz"
    fi
fi
```

Okay, now we have FizzBuzz, but what if the answer *is* divisible by 3 but not by 5 (which is the case for Fizz)? Then we can just output the Fizz. Thus, if we add an `else` to the divisible by 5 tests, we will be guaranteed a number that is divisible by 3 and not by 5. This means we avoid the issue when we output both Fizz and FizzBuzz at once. We can use the new `else` statement here to accomplish this, so when we add the `else` to the divisible by 5 test, we get this:

```
if [ $(($number % 3)) -eq 0 ]; then
    if [ $(($number % 5)) -eq 0 ]; then
        echo "FizzBuzz"
    else
           echo "Fizz"
    fi
fi
```

Fantastic. Now we only have one case left: when a number is not divisible by 3 but is divisible by 5. We can do this test in another else statement off the divisible by 3 test. By doing this as part of an else statement and adding a second divisible by 5 test, we can ensure that a number is not already divisible by 3 when we output when it is divisible by 5. This means we avoid running into the issue from before, so add this test in and your code becomes the following:

```
if [ $(($number % 3)) -eq 0 ]; then
    if [ $(($number % 5)) -eq 0 ]; then
        echo "FizzBuzz"
    else
           echo "Fizz"
    fi
else
    if [ $(($number % 5)) -eq 0 ]; then
        echo "Buzz"
    fi
fi
```

And that should do it! We have ourselves a new series of tests to run. Go ahead and replace the old statement in your script and run this new one:

```
$ ./fizzbuzz.sh
FizzBuzz
```

Perfect! That's the correct result for 15! You can change the value of number and execute a few more times to test, but this test should stand up well because we have thought through our programming. Now we need to have the numbers from 1 to 100 counted. To do this, we will use the second logical operation!

Logical Operation: Loop

A loop is a special type of logical operation that functions at its core like an if statement, but instead of running the code if a statement is true, it will run the statement over and over again as long as the statement is true. This is how we will be able to increase the value of number by 1 over and over again to count to 100. A loop in BASH uses the following syntax:

```
while [ TEST ]; do
    DO SOMETHING
done
```

A loop is very similar to an if statement by design. Both are testing that some condition is true and both will then execute a section of code. The difference is that an if statement will execute only once and a while loop will execute until something is no longer true. This brings be to the first and biggest warning about loops: if you forget to have a leaving condition for your loop, then you won't EVER leave it. This is called an *infinite loop*, in which your program will get stuck, do nothing, and run forever. There are a few situations when this is desirable but not many. Luckily for us we have the Ctrl+C shortcut that will send a terminate signal to whichever program we are running and we can use it to snap programs out of their infinite loops.

You might be thinking, "Oh, so that's why so many programs get stuck!" This is 100% true. Sometimes cases that you may not have considered arise, and your program can wind up running in a loop forever, so consider yourself warned.

For our FizzBuzz program, we want to count the numbers 1 to 100, so we can do a simple test of numbers less than or equal to 100. So for all situations in which our number is less than or equal to 100, we will execute the loop. So let's go ahead and write the loop around our existing block of tests. When done, it should look like the following. *Don't execute it* yet because we have no way to increase the number from 1 to 100 (which means we'll get an infinite loop because we can never reach 100 and leave the loop).

```
#!/bin/bash
number=1
while [ $number -le 100 ]; do
if [ $(($number % 3)) -eq 0 ]; then
    if [ $(($number % 5)) -eq 0 ]; then
        echo "FizzBuzz"
    else
           echo "Fizz"
    fi
else
    if [ $(($number % 5)) -eq 0 ]; then
        echo "Buzz"
    fi
fi
done
```

Okay, we have our code block, now we need to add the increasing number. We simply need to increase the value of `number` by 1 each time it goes around the loop. But we also want to perform all the calculations prior to changing the number. We can do this by using the arithmetic operations and assignment operation we have already. And we can add this block to the bottom of the code before the `done` statement:

```
number=$(($number +1))
```

Once you have made this change, execute your script! It will run and give you an output like this:

```
Fizz
Buzz
Fizz
Fizz
Buzz
Fizz
FizzBuzz
...
```

This is great, and it looks like it worked, but we should go ahead and print the current value of `number` for each trip round the loop. We could output the value at the start before we Fizz or Buzz or FizzBuzz, but that means we will have numbers on each line. Better if we can integrate it into our `echo` statements. To do this, we simply add the `$number` variable within the string of text to print. You learned earlier that the quotation marks mean everything is treated like a string of text, but there is one marker that supersedes it: the $ sign operator. This operator is used to make your life easier when you want to print out data from a variable in a block of text.

We should also add one final else statement, which will take care of the output of all the “other” numbers. Try and work it out for yourself; then check against this code:

```
#!/bin/bash
number=1
while [ $number -le 100 ]; do
if [ $(($number % 3)) -eq 0 ]; then
    if [ $(($number % 5)) -eq 0 ]; then
        echo "$number - FizzBuzz"
    else
           echo "$number - Fizz"
    fi
else
    if [ $(($number % 5)) -eq 0 ]; then
        echo "$number - Buzz"
    else
        echo $number
    fi
fi
number=$(($number +1))
done
```

And there you have it! A working FizzBuzz solution. Congratulations!

Troubleshooting

Having trouble with your code can be a bit of a nightmare. Probably the best tool at your disposal is the echo command. You can output anything you want, so if you are unsure of where your application is within your code, write an echo to output stuff and then check. Are you not entering the loop correctly? Output the variables that go into the test and compare by hand. Not sure why the if statement didn't work? Add an else, output the full test case, and see if you went in correctly. Using these outputs to trace where you are in your code is the best way of doing diagnostics. Otherwise, pay attention to any errors; most should provide a line number and will tell you (in a manner of speaking) what's wrong with what line. If you are in doubt, feel free to Google around because it's almost certain someone, somewhere has had the same error before you and asked for a solution.

Practical BASH: An Init Script

You should be aware by now that most Linux applications are started by a special script called an init script. These scripts aren't magic; they are simply scripts in BASH that take a given value and perform a series of actions based on what they are told to do—just as any good program does. The init scripts do have a small amount of special information in them, but none of this is actually program logic.

Let's go through one together and examine exactly how one of these init scripts works. Following is the init script for XBMC, which you will see again later in this book:

```
#! /bin/bash
### BEGIN INIT INFO
# Provides:          xbmc
# Required-Start:    $all
# Required-Stop:     $all
```

```
# Default-Start:     2 3 4 5
# Default-Stop:      0 1 6
# Short-Description: Start XBMC
# Description:       Start XBMC
### END INIT INFO
DAEMON=/usr/bin/xinit
DAEMON_OPTS="/usr/lib/xbmc/xbmc.bin"
NAME=xbmc
DESC=XBMC
RUN_AS=root
PID_FILE=/var/run/xbmc.pid
test -x $DAEMON || exit 0
set -e
case "$1" in
  start)
        echo "Starting $DESC"
        start-stop-daemon --start -c $RUN_AS --background --pidfile $PID_FILE
        --make-pidfile --exec $DAEMON -- $DAEMON_OPTS
        ;;
  stop)
        echo "Stopping $DESC"
        start-stop-daemon --stop --pidfile $PID_FILE
        ;;
  restart|force-reload)
        echo "Restarting $DESC"
        start-stop-daemon --stop --pidfile $PID_FILE
        sleep 5
        start-stop-daemon --start -c $RUN_AS --background --pidfile $PID_FILE
        --make-pidfile --exec $DAEMON -- $DAEMON_OPTS
        ;;
  *)
        echo "Usage: /etc/init.d/$NAME{start|stop|restart|force-reload}" >&2
        exit 1
        ;;
esac
exit 0
```

The first thing you will notice is there are a lot of lines that start with #. These lines are comments; because # is the comment symbol in BASH, any line that starts with a # will not be executed as part of the application. The top lines of `INIT INFO` are in fact very important for an `init` script. These are special comments that can be processed to show how the application controlled by the script is to be run. The blocks look like this:

```
### BEGIN INIT INFO
# Provides:          xbmc
# Required-Start:    $all
# Required-Stop:     $all
# Default-Start:     2 3 4 5
# Default-Stop:      0 1 6
# Short-Description: Start XBMC
# Description:       Start XBMC
### END INIT INFO
```

These blocks provide a few bits of description and say for which application they provide a function; in this case, the application provided is `XBMC`. They also mention what applications are needed to be running before this application can start or stop. The `$all` symbol means that this application will be started last, so that it is guaranteed that all other applications on which it can depend are started before it. Probably the more important set of operators are `Default-Start` and `Default-Stop`. These operators correlate with the Linux system's *run levels*, which govern the various stages of the Linux system boot process.

The Linux specification defines the following run levels:

- *Level 0*: Halt; shut down and power off
- *Level 1*: Single User Mode; only basic system functionality (used for repairs)
- *Levels 2 % 3*: Multi User; adds networking and multiple user functionality
- *Level 4*: User Defined
- *Level 5*: Normal System running state
- *Level 6*: Reboot

The numbers next to the start and stop switches correlate to these levels, so `XBMC` will start in run levels 2–5 and will shut down in levels 0, 1, and 6.

Pick and Match with the case Statement

Once all the initialization is done and the script has set some initial variables, it performs a few quick tests and then moves on to the `case` statement. A `case` statement is very much like a series of running `if` statements against the same variable. Insofar as you take a given variable and for each of a series of given values for said variable, you perform a function. In most `init` scripts, this is used to confirm which action it is to perform.

The `case` statement in this `start` script is working on the special `$1` variable. This variable represents the first thing passed to the script from the command line; so when trying to start the `xbmc` application, you will execute with this:

```
/etc/init.d/xbmc start
```

This gives the `$1` variable the value of `start`. The `case` statement offers a number of different options of the potential value of the `case` statement:

- `start`: Self-explanatory.
- `stop`: Self-explanatory.
- `restart|force-reload`: The values of `restart` or `force-reload`, which perform the stop application and then the start application in one process. The pipe (`|`) between them is used to denote an OR operation, which means that if either of the values here match, we treat this as having been a match.
- *: Anything else.

After each `case` value, there is a small block of code that is executed in that case, followed by a pair of semicolons. These semicolons are like a `fi` and are used to denote the end of a block of `case` statement code.

Application within Application: Forking

Once within the case statement, you can see that each line will perform some action with the start-stop-daemon. But this isn't a variable or anything special; it's another program. The most powerful part of BASH is the bit we haven't gotten to yet. BASH has the capability to execute any command-line process from within your programs just by using their names. Because BASH is the shell we use most of the rest of the time, this actually makes a lot of sense.

The last function of an init script: it will use the start-stop-daemon to create a new process for you. This action is called *forking* because you are forking something off of the currently running application. The start-stop-daemon is a small application that is used to fork off processes and will manage their running for you. The start script corrals the arguments for it, works out what action needs to be performed, and then tells start-stop-daemon which action needs to be taken against which application.

Now that you are armed with this knowledge, you should be able to write your own simple init scripts to start and stop any process you want by providing the starting comment block to describe how the script should be loaded, having a case statement determine which action to take, and finally executing the start-stop-daemon process to launch and manage your application!

Update the Run Files

Now you have a fully working script ready to go. You need to use chmod to set the executable flag on your file and then you can test it with the start and stop commands. It does as intended—fantastic! Now we need to add it into the system's boot logic. Historically, this involved linking the file in a special way into the various run levels. However, this has been made much easier with the update-rc.d application. The update-rc.d application takes advantage of those special comment headers we added to our BASH scripts in order to know which run levels should have which shortcuts.

All we need to do to add the init script to the boot sequence is to issue the update-rc.d command with the name of the init script we want, which is xbmc in the example. Then we need to add the argument to say that we should use the defaults from the comments in the script; the argument unsurprisingly defaults. This gives us the command update-rc.d xbmc defaults, which will need to be executed as root. When run, the outputs should be as follows:

```
$ sudo update-rc.d xbmc defaults
update-rc.d: using dependency based boot sequencing
```

And that's it; if you reboot, your application should run on boot!

Creating Your Own init Script

We have covered how init scripts are created; now we can create one. The process is relatively simple because we simply need to re-create the structure and input our own code in the correct place to perform the functions we need. You can have these init scripts do quite literally whatever you want, but for this example I will be creating a file with the touch command and then deleting it with rm when done. The touch command is used to simply create a file on disk with nothing in it; if it runs on an existing file, it will change the last modified time of the file. As mentioned earlier, you can have your programs managed by start-stop-daemon or you can simply perform system functions, as I will do in my example.

As you will recall, the first thing we need in this script is the shebang, which is the starting point for all BASH scripts and is thus the best place to start.

```
#! /bin/bash
```

Now that we have our shebang, recall the XBMC start script we worked with earlier: the first thing in that script is the opening comment block that gives us details about which init levels will run this script, and so on. So let's add that next. You should fill in all your own details here. My script will be called touchfile.sh and will provide the Touch File service. My opening block of script will look like this:

```
### BEGIN INIT INFO
# Provides:          touchfile
# Required-Start:    $all
# Required-Stop:     $all
# Default-Start:     2 3 4 5
# Default-Stop:      0 1 6
# Short-Description: Run TouchFile
# Description:       Run TouchFile
### END INIT INFO
```

Now that I have defined the comment block, I can define my variables. They will be the variables that will cover what my application does. Anything you can think of needing in order to start this that can be configured should be defined as a variable. In the case of my touchfile command the thing I need to have defined as a variable is the filename of my touchfile. Remember that this is your code, and thus you can define literally anything you desire as a variable. My variable is this:

```
TOUCHFILE="/var/tmp/touch.file"
```

Now that my touchfile is defined, I need to add the case statement to cover the available actions. In this case, I want to have the following actions:

- Start: Touch the file
- Stop: Remove the touched file
- Restart: Remove and then re-touch the file
- Reload: Touch the file
- Default Case: Tell people about how to use this file

This means I will have four case statements within my case. I will define the case statements (sans code to perform actions) as such:

```
case "$1" in
  start)
;;
  stop)
;;
  restart)
;;
  reload)
;;
  *)
;;
esac
exit 0
```

Now that we have the case entries, we just need to make them do something. I mentioned earlier what I want to do in each of the cases, so let's write out the commands into each block and combine them into the script we have already. This will give us the following script:

```
#!/bin/bash
### BEGIN INIT INFO
# Provides:          touchfile
# Required-Start:    $all
# Required-Stop:     $all
# Default-Start:     2 3 4 5
# Default-Stop:      0 1 6
# Short-Description: Run TouchFile
# Description:       Run TouchFile
### END INIT INFO
TOUCHFILE="/var/tmp/touch.file"
case "$1" in
  start)
        echo "Creating $TOUCHFILE"
        touch $TOUCHFILE
;;
  stop)
        echo "Removing $TOUCHFILE"
        rm $TOUCHFILE
;;
  restart)
        echo "Recreating $TOUCHFILE"
        rm $TOUCHFILE
        touch $TOUCHFILE
;;
  reload)
        echo "Re-Touching $TOUCHFILE"
        touch $TOUCHFILE
;;
  *)
        echo " Usage: touchfile.sh <start|stop|restart|reload>"
;;
esac
exit 0
```

And that's it. The code is a simple `init` script, which accepts the `start`, `stop`, `restart`, and `reload` commands and outputs what it is doing and performs actions based on what arguments we provide it. This can be placed in `/etc/init.d` and can be set to be executable with `chmod +x`. Once they are done, you can test the script to ensure that it works. Finally, you can use `update-rc.d` to add this to your system boot process as we did earlier. It is in this fashion that you can write your own start scripts to run applications as you design.

Security and User Management

Security is one of the most neglected areas of systems administration. Because it is perceived as a black art to many, it often gets neglected.

The Rules of Raspbian Security

There are some very simple ways to make your system secure; just follow a few rules:

- Don't log in as root, but if you must, log out when done.
- Use `sudo` whenever possible for admin tasks.
- Choose a nontrivial password—one that is long enough and complex enough that it cannot be readily guessed or worked out by hand without taking a long time.
- Change your password regularly.
- Review your system logs regularly, specifically `/var/log/auth.log` because it lists all user authentications to your system.
- If you don't need an application running, don't run it.
- Expose as little of your system to the Internet as possible.
- Restrict file permissions whenever possible.

Most of these rules will seem like common sense and that is because they are. Yet most people seem to fall into the trap of thinking that they won't be attacked and ignore most of this advice. Now that you know these rules, you are probably saying, "I will change my password if only you would show me how!" Changing your password from the Linux command line is relatively easy: you simply use the `passwd` command and you will be prompted to enter a new password (twice, so that you can't misspell it by accident the first time).

You can also change the password for other users as root. To do this, you simply append the name of the user whose name you are changing as the first argument of the command. This is incredibly useful when configuring new user details or resetting passwords.

Adding a New User

Because you aren't supposed to use root at all times, it's important to be able to create new users and understand how user creation takes place. In Linux operating systems, the users are governed by the file `/etc/passwd`. You can have a look for yourself and you will see a number of lines like this:

```
root:x:0:0:root:/root:/bin/bash
daemon:x:1:1:daemon:/usr/sbin:/bin/sh
```

These lines show the user, X for the password, the user's ID number, the user's group ID number, the user's group identifier, the path of the user's home directory, and the user's shell. These are the basics of what is needed for a user to function within the Linux environment.

While this file has a password field, it is no longer used and normally contains a placeholder (in this case, `X`). The passwords are stored in the shadow file, `/etc/shadow`. The shadow file was separated so that only root could access password data and all the more common user data could be read by other more generic system applications.

Now that you understand how Linux stores users, add a new one called raspberry. To add this user, we will use the useradd command and a few arguments. There is another command, adduser, which performs user additions, but instead of being supplied with arguments will prompt you for details. adduser is a great command to use in a pinch when you forget a necessary argument for useradd.

First we want to specify the user's home directory, which is done with the -d flag and the full path of the directory we want to use. Most home directories for users are /home/<username>, and we will do this for raspberry. Currently, /home/raspberry doesn't exist, but before you rush out and add it, we can use the -m flag to tell useradd to do it for us! This gives us this command:

```
$ sudo useradd -d /home/raspberry -m raspberry
```

We could go a step further and even specify the group with -g <groupname> to set the primary group for the user. Or even specify the shell that the user would use with -s <shell path> or finally a password with -p <password>. Once you have executed your command, you can go and inspect the changes to /etc/passwd, where you should see something like this at the bottom of your file:

```
raspberry:x:1001:1001::/home/raspberry:/bin/sh
```

That's it; you have now successfully added a new user! If you didn't specify a password, you can use the passwd command we covered earlier to change your new user's password and then you're set to go. However, let's say that you forgot to set the shell path with -s earlier and you want to change that so you start with /bin/bash rather than /bin/sh. Well, first you could edit the passwd file to change the shell or you can use the usermod command. The usermod command functions exactly the same as the useradd command, right down to the arguments; it simply adjusts the values. So run the following:

```
$ sudo usermod -s /bin/bash raspberry
```

We can expect the shadow file to be changed and, yes it is:

```
raspberry:x:1001:1001::/home/raspberry:/bin/bash
```

Fantastic! With these tools, you should be capable of creating new user accounts to allow people to access your Pi.

Summary

This chapter covered quite a number of things. We introduced SSH, DHCP and DNS. We covered some of the basics of how these systems function and how daemons are launched via init scripts. We then dove deep into learning BASH so that we could write our own init scripts. Finally, we covered some common security do's and don'ts; then went on to cover how the basics of Linux systems manage users and their passwords. We even went so far as to create a whole new user ready for use.

These skills should enable you to manage the startup and networking of your Pi and should have given you an introduction into the wonderful world of software development!

CHAPTER 8

A LAMP of Your Own

One of the key things that many people who come to Linux want to know is how to establish themselves by setting up a small website of their own. And many have difficulty finding a place to start. Which OS, which applications, what hardware, and how exactly to do all this? All these are legitimate questions as there are so many facets to the greater Linux environment that it is very easy to get lost.

Our goal is to provide the first few stepping stones on your way to being able to navigate the Linux environment. One of the key stepping stones on this path is to show you how to install, configure, and maintain a web server. Although you will be able to connect this server to the Internet, in these examples we will only cover using your Pi as a local network server (in other words, for running an intranet). In addition, there is also the extra challenge of learning how to make a basic interactive website. While this may seem a lot to take on, and others devoted entire books and lives to finding the absolute optimum solution this problem, we aim to cover it for the Raspberry Pi in one chapter.

To this end we will be using a LAMP. No, not one of those bedroom luminescence devices, but a Linux, Apache, MySQL, and PHP system designed to make delivering web content easy. This is one of the easiest ways to create your own web server and there are a number of variations on the original LAMP, which include, but are not limited to, the following:

- WAMP (Windows, Apache, MySQL, PHP)
- MAMP (Mac OS, Apache, MySQL, PHP)
- Replacement Ps with Python or Perl
- Replacement M with MariaDB

So, as you can gather from the amount of mixing, matching, and improving that people have done, it is a great way to get a powerful web server up and going. Best of all, it is simple to set up and can be run on just about any hardware.

One of the most regularly cited potential uses of the Pi is to enable the ability to build, run, and maintain a website. What better way to inspire a generation of young developers than to teach them how to make their own websites with a minimum of cost!

First Steps

Now it is time to get real about what we can accomplish here. Within this chapter, we will provide you the skills to set up a full website stack and show you how to integrate the functions of a MySQL database into a website using PHP to dynamically generate website content. However, there are a few things we won't be able to do for you here:

- Set up and configure a DNS or domain naming
- Advanced SQL and database administration

- Full coverage of HTML and HTML development methods
- Full coverage of PHP development and PHP development methods
- JavaScript
- CSS

There are a number of resources that you can take advantage of to get help with these other areas, including other great and weighty texts by Apress. We still have our work cut out for us, so let's get started.

L is for Linux

There are only a few prerequisites for setting up a LAMP stack. You will need to

- Have the Raspbian OS (the *L* of LAMP) installed and configured
- Have the memory split set to 240/16 (run `sudo raspi-config`)
- Be familiar with working within the Raspbian OS using the command line
- Have a basic understanding of how to write simple software
- Have your Pi connected to a network and the Internet (how else can we serve content if we aren't?)

There are only a few other provisos for Raspberry LAMP. We will be doing all of this from a shell. Given that the website will be viewed from outside the Pi, there is no need to use any extra resources to run the GUI. Now that we know what we need to get going, let's do it.

A is for Apache

Probably the most important part of any web server is the web server application. A web server is an application that will take requests for a website and then return the requested web page content. Most web servers can also provide a large number of other functions that can help enhance their capability to provide web content to end users. For our LAMP stack, we will be using the Apache web server.

Apache is considered by many to be the world's premiere web server. It was first released in 1995 and has become renowned for playing a role in the growth of the World Wide Web by providing a simple, powerful, and free web server to the masses.

As reinforcement of this fact, it is estimated that Apache delivers between an estimated 54 to 58 percent of the world's websites.

There are two stories that are told about how Apache came to be named:

- The first is that it was named for it being "A patchy web server" when first developed all those years ago.
- The second (and much better from a storytelling perspective) is that Apache is said to be named for the Apache tribes of America.

Being named for a tribe is not even a misnomer as acting like a tribe is one of the key features of Apache. Apache's first task when it starts is to create its own small tribe of "workers" that are tasked with the actual serving up of your website's content. Now that you have a clearer understanding of what Apache does, the first step becomes to get Apache installed, up and running.

For our installs, we will rely (as ever) on the ever-faithful apt-get tool:

```
$ sudo apt-get install apache2
Reading package lists... Done
Building dependency tree
Reading state information... Done
The following extra packages will be installed:
  apache2-mpm-worker apache2-utils apache2.2-bin apache2.2-common libapr1
  libaprutil1 libaprutil1-dbd-sqlite3 libaprutil1-ldap ssl-cert
Suggested packages:
  apache2-doc apache2-suexec apache2-suexec-custom openssl-blacklist
The following NEW packages will be installed:
  apache2 apache2-mpm-worker apache2-utils apache2.2-bin apache2.2-common
  libapr1 libaprutil1 libaprutil1-dbd-sqlite3 libaprutil1-ldap ssl-cert
0 upgraded, 10 newly installed, 0 to remove and 71 not upgraded.
Need to get 1,348 kB of archives.
After this operation, 4,990 kB of additional disk space will be used.
Do you want to continue [Y/n]?
```

Now that you have installed Apache, we should go and validate that it is all up and running. There are a few ways we can do this. First, run this:

```
$ ps -ef | grep apache
root      2306     1  0 Sep17 ?        00:00:09 /usr/sbin/apache2 -k start
www-data  2309  2306  0 Sep17 ?        00:00:00 /usr/sbin/apache2 -k start
www-data  2311  2306  0 Sep17 ?        00:00:00 /usr/sbin/apache2 -k start
www-data  2315  2306  0 Sep17 ?        00:00:00 /usr/sbin/apache2 -k start
```

From this output, you can see that Apache is indeed up and running. From this point, there are another few important things to note. The first process listed with the following line is different from the others:

```
root 2306 1 0 Sep17 ? 00:00:09 /usr/sbin/apache2 -k start
```

This is the chief of the Apache tribe mentioned earlier. It is owned by root (as indicated in the first column), and its process ID (PID) is 2306. The other three are owned by a user called `www-data`, which is a user specifically for Apache. While each worker has a different PID, they all have a PPID (parent process ID) of 2306, meaning that the Apache chief process made them (its PID is 2306).

Now for the second and by far more fun test; on this test, we will actually get Apache to display its default starting web page! For this, you can either log in to the GUI or you can get the system's IP address using `ifconfig`. Your output should look like the one following with the relevant IP addresses highlighted:

```
$ ifconfig
eth0      Link encap:Ethernet  HWaddr b8:27:eb:8a:46:ba
          inet addr:10.0.0.20  Bcast:10.0.0.255  Mask:255.255.255.0
          UP BROADCAST RUNNING MULTICAST  MTU:1500  Metric:1
          RX packets:213812 errors:0 dropped:0 overruns:0 frame:0
          TX packets:5119 errors:0 dropped:0 overruns:0 carrier:0
          collisions:0 txqueuelen:1000
          RX bytes:19226371 (18.3 MiB)  TX bytes:495394 (483.7 KiB)
```

```
lo        Link encap:Local Loopback
          inet addr:127.0.0.1  Mask:255.0.0.0
          UP LOOPBACK RUNNING  MTU:16436  Metric:1
          RX packets:8 errors:0 dropped:0 overruns:0 frame:0
          TX packets:8 errors:0 dropped:0 overruns:0 carrier:0
          collisions:0 txqueuelen:0
          RX bytes:1104 (1.0 KiB)  TX bytes:1104 (1.0 KiB)
```

Assuming your system is (like mine) attached to a network, you can use the first IP address (10.0.0.20). This address in the eth0 block represents its network port. The address in lo block is the loopback address, which is used for internal self-reference and is always 127.0.0.1.

The next test is to access the Apache default web page; and to do so, you simply need to input one of those IP addresses into a browser (assuming that you are on the same network as the Pi, of course!). If you want to test using the Pi's onboard browser, that's completely fine, too, and you can choose between either address (10.0.0.20 or 127.0.0.1). So what are you waiting for? Open a browser window and have a look at the default web page, as shown in Figure 8-1.

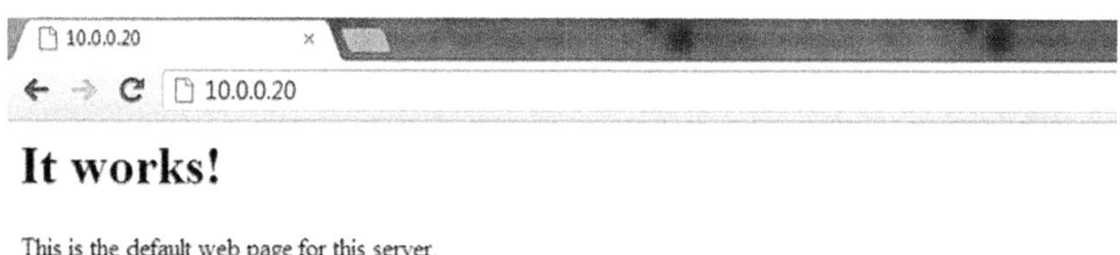

Figure 8-1. *It works!*

As you should by now be aware, it works! This is the default web page for the Apache web server and as it suggests there is no content added yet, we will be getting to that later. For now, let's have a look at how that one default page is generated, as this will give you some insight into how Apache truly works.

Apache Configuration

Getting your head around the Apache config is, to be frank, a bit of a nightmare. If you're game, go ahead and have a look in /etc/apache2 for an idea of what I mean. There are a number of folders in there with different meanings and how those folders interrelate changes how your Apache server instance works. Thankfully, though, once you understand where you need to make changes, everything becomes much easier.

The first file of note in the Apache configuration is the apache2.conf file. This is the governing config file that says where each of the other separate pieces are located, and how the application should load them. The second things to be aware of are the mods-available and mods-enabled folders. If you have a look at the mods-available file, you will see that there are a large number of .load and .conf files. These files represent where Apache should load a module from and any configuration information this module needs, respectively.

Next is mods-enabled, an initial look over this folder will make it seem just like mods-available. However, if you run an ls -l on this directory, you will see this:

```
$ ls -l /etc/apache2/mods-enabled/
total 0
lrwxrwxrwx 1 root root 28 Sep 17 21:44 alias.conf -> ../mods-available/alias.conf
lrwxrwxrwx 1 root root 28 Sep 17 21:44 alias.load -> ../mods-available/alias.load
lrwxrwxrwx 1 root root 33 Sep 17 21:44 auth_basic.load -> ../mods-available/auth_basic.load
lrwxrwxrwx 1 root root 33 Sep 17 21:44 authn_file.load -> ../mods-available/authn_file.load
...
```

This shows that, in fact, each of the files in mods-enabled is actually a link to a file in mods-available! This is the first intricacy of the Apache configuration, while there are a number of available modules at any given time only a certain number are actually loaded. Using symlinks like this means that only one copy of the configuration needs to be kept and maintained at a given time. And more to the point, any changes made to one will be made to both.

If you look inside the sites-available and sites-enabled folders, you will see the same layout, except there might be fewer sites. This brings us to the true object of our search: the first default site that is available within the Apache system. So open up either /etc/apache2/sites-available/default or /etc/apache2/sites-enabled/000-default because it doesn't matter; they are the same thing! So, now that you're inside, go over what everything in the config means. Many of them will be important for you later on if you wish to add additional websites or modify how websites are displayed.

```
<VirtualHost *:80>
        ServerAdmin webmaster@localhost
        DocumentRoot /var/www
        <Directory />
                Options FollowSymLinks
                AllowOverride None
        </Directory>
        <Directory /var/www/>
                Options Indexes FollowSymLinks MultiViews
                AllowOverride None
                Order allow,deny
                allow from all
        </Directory>
        ScriptAlias /cgi-bin/ /usr/lib/cgi-bin/
        <Directory "/usr/lib/cgi-bin">
                AllowOverride None
                Options +ExecCGI -MultiViews +SymLinksIfOwnerMatch
                Order allow,deny
                Allow from all
        </Directory>
        ErrorLog ${APACHE_LOG_DIR}/error.log
        # Possible values include: debug, info, notice, warn, error, crit,
        # alert, emerg.
        LogLevel warn

        CustomLog ${APACHE_LOG_DIR}/access.log combined
</VirtualHost>
```

The first line is probably one of the most important; it specifies that this web server is available to any incoming address on port 80. Changing this means you can run multiple web servers on the same site by using different ports to reference each.

■ **Note** You can specify a port when connecting to just about any application by adding `:<port number>` at the end of the URL.

Following the `VirtualHost` address, the next relevant thing is the `DocumentRoot`. This is critical as it says where Apache will load all the web server content from. This means that anything that is in the `/var/www` folder will become available via the basic website on port 80. For example, if you go into the `/var/www` folder, you will see one file: `index.html`. If you examine this file, you will see some very familiar content:

```
<html><body><h1>It works!</h1>
<p>This is the default web page for this server.</p>
<p>The web server software is running but no content has been added, yet.</p>
</body></html>
```

Yep, that's the website content that is used to generate the basic start page that Apache is currently showing. I try to think of it this way: the web server is providing you access to that folder (and all subfolders and documents within it). As proof of this, try executing the following command as root:

```
$ echo "Hello World" > /var/www/foo
```

■ **Note** You can gain root by executing `sudo su -`.

Once you have successfully executed this command, direct your browser to `http://<IP Address>/foo` and you should see `hello world` displayed there. You may be wondering why we didn't need to use `index.html` in the first request to our website (i.e., use `http://10.0.0.2/index.html`). This is because files named "index" are special ones. They are the default page displayed if no other content is available.

The next portions of the config you should be aware of are the `Directory` config sections. These are a list of directories that can provide special rules as to how they are accessed and even who can access them. In this instance, there are two directories that Apache has configuration settings for: the / root directory and `/var/www`. While there are a number of very interesting things you can do with the directory values, there isn't much we need to do with them here. For more information, you should head over to the Apache website and read through the far more detailed documentation available there.

After the directory details comes `ScriptAlias`, which governs how CGI scripts are accessed by the application. The `ScriptAlias` is a special directory in which these CGI programs live and are executed from. As PHP is a scripting system much like BASH (covered in Chapter 7), you may think this has a direct bearing, but it is not the case. PHP is run by a special interpreter module (`modphp`) rather than by a single CGI program.

The directory value below the `ScriptAlias` is related to it. The quick give away is that both reference `/usr/lib/cgi-bin/`. This directory contains the `+ExecCGI` directive. Again, this relates to how scripts and things such as PHP are executed. Finally, the configuration file comes to a close with a few very useful config lines. These values are the logfile directives for the Apache server; they say where the logfiles will go and which files they will write to. Both access logs (so you can spy on everyone who visits you) and the much more standard error logs are covered here. The `LogLevel` directive in the middle governs at which level logs regarding the running of the server should be output, and right now it is set at `WARN`, which is sensible.

Given that you will probably need to take advantage of these logs later when working with PHP, you should become familiar with them now. But first let's make a small change to the log that we will make Apache incorporate. Let's change that logging level to notice, so go ahead and change it then save the newly edited file. Once the file has been changed, we need to tell Apache this so it will reload the config. Unlike making a content change to your website, we need to inform Apache of config changes. Thankfully, Apache makes this easy by including a reload function that we can issue to it. Go ahead and issue this:

```
$ sudo /etc/init.d/apache2 reload
[....] Reloading web server config: apache2apache2: Could not reliably determine the
server's fully qualified domain name, using 127.0.1.1 for ServerName
. ok
```

This has told Apache to reload its config and get going again. Now have a look at the logfiles to see the changes we made. The Apache log directory is `/var/log/apache2`, and the file we are interested in is the `error.log`. Once you are looking inside, you should see something like this:

```
[Tue Sep 18 22:46:56 2012] [notice] SIGUSR1 received.  Doing graceful restart
apache2: Could not reliably determine the server's fully qualified domain name, using
127.0.1.1 for ServerName
[Tue Sep 18 22:46:56 2012] [notice] Apache/2.2.22 (Debian) configured -- resuming normal
operations
```

This says that my Apache instance was given a signal and it performed a graceful restart; then it resumed normal operation within the same second. This is the configuration reload we performed just now. We can also look at the access log and see ourselves accessing content off the web server, go ahead and open up the `access.log` file in `/var/log/apache2` and have a look. You should see something like this:

```
10.0.0.104 - - [18/Sep/2012:20:31:17 +1000] "GET / HTTP/1.1" 200 482 "-" "Mozilla/5.0
(Windows NT 6.1; WOW64) AppleWebKit/537.10 (KHTML, like Gecko) Chrome/23.0.1262.0
Safari/537.10"
10.0.0.104 - - [18/Sep/2012:22:21:22 +1000] "GET /favicon.ico HTTP/1.1" 404 498
"-" "Mozilla/5.0 (Windows NT 6.1; WOW64) AppleWebKit/537.10 (KHTML, like Gecko)
Chrome/23.0.1262.0 Safari/537.10"
10.0.0.104 - - [18/Sep/2012:22:28:36 +1000] "GET /foo HTTP/1.1" 200 274 "-" "Mozilla/5.0
(Windows NT 6.1; WOW64) AppleWebKit/537.10 (KHTML, like Gecko) Chrome/23.0.1262.0
Safari/537.10"
```

These lines show that someone on IP 10.0.0.104 made a `GET` request on the / of the web server, which is the `/var/www` folder and the `index.html` file within (because index is the default file). It also shows someone accessing the foo file within this directory. They were both me accessing the website in sequence. You will also notice that there is a request in the middle, which is for a `favicon.ico`. This represents my browser trying to request the favorite's icon of this website; there is not one, unfortunately.

Troubleshooting

For the most part, setting up an Apache server is a breeze. It's only when you start making a lot of changes that you might run into trouble. However, if you did find yourself running into issues, try the following. Check that you can see the Apache process running with `ps -ef`. If Apache is not running, try and start it. If that fails, try examining the error logfile as this will contain information on any errors that Apache has suffered. Most of the entries in the error log are fairly self-explanatory. However, if you find yourself at a loss, head over to the Apache website where there is a large amount of help available there for those in need.

M is for MySQL

Now that you have your web server up and running, you are probably asking, "I see that you can make a website by just writing content into a web server and it will be displayed. What more software could I possibly need?" And it's true; right now, you could write a web page in basic HyperText Markup Language (HTML) and be done with it. The problem with writing in HTML alone is that HTML is static, meaning that any time you wish to change what is displayed, you need to open up and edit the file to change what is said. This is not going to make for very good management when you want to display different things to different people. You would need to be manually sitting there and editing a whole bunch of things—that's pointless.

This is where we begin to see the power of the full LAMP stack. We have Apache to serve content, PHP will handle the dynamic portion, and the MySQL database will actually contain the various different bits of information you want to display. It is only when you have all these components in and working together that you begin to see the true power of a LAMP system.

Installing MySQL

A database (DB) is a system for the easy storage and retrieval of data. They take large volumes of input and then structure the data so that information can be easily retrieved with a query. All SQL databases are named for the Structured Query Language, which they use to process requests for information retrieval. MySQL is the world's most widely deployed open source database. It is what is called a *relational database system* that is used because it is easy to set up and to work with, thus its wide adoption. To install MySQL, we will again turn to our old friend `apt-get`; this time, we will be installing the `mysql-server` package. Execute the following:

```
$ sudo apt-get install mysql-server
Reading package lists... Done
Building dependency tree
Reading state information... Done
The following extra packages will be installed:
  heirloom-mailx libaio1 libdbd-mysql-perl libdbi-perl libhtml-template-perl
  libmysqlclient16 libnet-daemon-perl libplrpc-perl mysql-client-5.5
  mysql-common mysql-server-5.5 mysql-server-core-5.5
Suggested packages:
  libipc-sharedcache-perl libterm-readkey-perl tinyca
The following NEW packages will be installed:
  heirloom-mailx libaio1 libdbd-mysql-perl libdbi-perl libhtml-template-perl
  libmysqlclient16 libnet-daemon-perl libplrpc-perl mysql-client-5.5
  mysql-common mysql-server mysql-server-5.5 mysql-server-core-5.5
0 upgraded, 13 newly installed, 0 to remove and 84 not upgraded.
Need to get 9,770 kB of archives.
After this operation, 91.5 MB of additional disk space will be used.
Do you want to continue [Y/n]?
```

Once the actual MySQL install has finished, you will be asked to provide a root password for your DB; this is the master admin password for your database. Make sure you remember it; you will need it later. Now that the installation has finished, confirm that the process has started with this:

```
$ ps -ef | grep mysql
```

The output should show a few different things, including the MySQL daemon, which is highlighted here:

```
root       5254     1  0 20:23 ?        00:00:00 /bin/sh /usr/bin/mysqld_safe
mysql      5592  5254  3 20:23 ?        00:00:03 /usr/sbin/mysqld --basedir=/usr --datadir=/
var/lib/mysql --plugin-dir=/usr/lib/mysql/plugin --user=mysql --pid-file=/var/run/mysqld/
mysqld.pid --socket=/var/run/mysqld/mysqld.sock --port=3306
root       5593  5254  0 20:23 ?        00:00:00 logger -t mysqld -p daemon.error
```

That's one big process command, but it does show that MySQL is up and running. We can go over the MySQL config, but thankfully the system will work for all our basic needs without the need to modify the configuration. Given that, let's start working on some basic ways to both insert data and retrieve it.

Structured Query Language

Structured Query Language (SQL) is a language for inserting and retrieving information from an SQL database. In SQL, there are a number of different queries you can do, ranging from the simple to the extremely complex. Given that there are (as with everything) a number of other resources that spend much more time and go into far more detail about syntax and origin and whatever, we won't cover those here. Besides, for our purposes there should only be five types of queries we need:

- Basic admin commands
- Insert new data
- Find data
- Update data
- Delete data

While it sounds incredibly simple, it is very easy to get lost in the syntax if you wish to do something more complex. If that is the case, and you wish to do something slightly more complex than what we have covered here please head over to the MySQL web page as they have full documentation on how exactly to perform each query and what the large number of options on each command entail. If you want something a little more focused on web development with all the Apress niceties, have a look at *Beginning PHP and MySQL 5*, by Jason W. Gilmore.

Anyway, enough product placement; let's start with the basic administration stuff and make a database. The syntax for this one is dead simple:

```
create database <database name>
```

To perform commands on your MySQL instance, you need to connect to it and get into the `mysql` shell. This is the command to do this:

```
mysql -uroot -p
```

So jump into the shell, provide your root password, and execute `create database pi;` which should generate the following output:

```
mysql> create database pi;
Query OK, 1 row affected (0.00 sec)
```

Okay, awesome. We have a database called `pi`. In an SQL database system, a database is the highest-level construct. Underneath that is a *table*, which is the object that holds your data (a database holds multiple tables). Each of these items of data in a table is called a *row*. So our next step is to create a table; the problem is that we need to give our table some structure. We need to tell it what kind of data it should hold and how we will lay out that data, which means we need a project. The most obvious for now is a simple to-do list, so let's make one of those.

■ **Note** All MySQL commands end with a semicolon (`;`). It signifies that this is the end of a statement. This is done as you can put lines in for one command over multiple lines to make it easier to follow.

Creating Tables

Just stepping aside quickly, I have departed from the normal project planning method a little here so that we can run through a basic database setup together. When undertaking a big project, it is far better to plan ahead and fully understand what will be going into a database long before any data is ever added to it.

So, for our to-do list, we want to keep the following information for each "thing to do":

- Description
- Person doing the task (owner)
- Date to be done by (date)
- Location
- Importance
- Who set the task (creator)

Okay, so with this information, we have our rough table structure; so now let's go ahead and create it. The syntax for a table creation is this:

```
create table <tablename> (
<column name> <column type>,
<column name> <column type>,
...
<column name> <column type>
);
```

That's the basic syntax, but there is one final thing we need to make sure we have when creating our table: a key. Given that we need to ensure we are getting the right value back each time, we need to have something unique about each individual piece of data. Many of these tasks could wind up almost identical, excluding one or two minor variations. For this reason, we will need what is called a ***primary key***, which is a unique identifier for each row. In this case, it's best just to use a simple count that will automatically go up for each row we add. Now we know what we want; let's flesh it out into the syntax from before and see what we have.

```
create table todolist (
idnumber <column type>,
description <column type>,
owner <column type>,
date <colunm type>,
```

```
location <column type>,
importance <column type>,
creator <column type
);
```

Well, looking better, but we still don't have those `<column types>`, nor do we have anything that will say that our `idnumber` is the primary key, or should be automatically updated for each new row. This brings us nicely to what the column types are about. MySQL will need to know what kind of values each of our data elements will be so it can know how to store them and what kind of queries they can be involved in. There are at least 30 different data types in MySQL, which can perform all kinds of operations, but for our simple purposes there are only three we need to be concerned with: one is text or a string of text that is known as a `VARCHAR` and is given a maximum number of characters, the second is a number or integer known as an `INT`, and the last is a date value that is known as a `DATE`. Given that we now know some data types, we can set them out into our `create table` command. Go ahead and do that now and remember that text strings (`VARCHAR`) need to be given a maximum number of characters long:

```
create table todolist (
idnumber INT,
description VARCHAR(200),
owner VARCHAR(40),
date DATE,
location VARCHAR(40),
importance VARCHAR(10),
creator VARCHAR(40)
) ;
```

That looks much better and will probably run, but remember we wanted to have that number be our unique identifier and be automatically updated for us to make our lives easier. The syntax for the `idnumber` being automatically incremented (updated to be +1) is `PRIMARY KEY NOT NULL AUTO_INCREMENT`. This gives us a final command of this:

```
create table todolist (
idnumber INT PRIMARY KEY NOT NULL AUTO_INCREMENT,
description VARCHAR(200),
owner VARCHAR(40),
date DATE,
location VARCHAR(40),
importance VARCHAR(10),
creator VARCHAR(40)
);
```

So, go ahead and run it:

```
ERROR 1046 (3D000): No database selected
```

Oh, whoops. We need to tell MySQL which database we are using, and thus under which database this table will reside. To change which database we are using, we need to use the USE command. To change to using the Pi database we simply execute USE pi; and MySQL will tell us that the database has changed. If you have forgotten your database name, you can use the SHOW command to see things, SHOW DATABASES; will show you all the databases on your system. Now go ahead and execute the table creation again. This time you should see this:

```
Query OK, 0 rows affected (0.91 sec)
```

Fantastic, we have a table. Let's have a look and see if we can see it. Issue the SHOW command, but this time for tables. You should see the following output, which lists off all the tables within the Pi database:

```
mysql> SHOW TABLES;
+--------------+
| Tables_in_pi |
+--------------+
| todolist     |
+--------------+
1 row in set (0.00 sec)
```

Yahoo! Now, say for example that you have forgotten what exactly the table looks like; you will want MySQL to describe how the table is made up. You can use the DESCRIBE command to do just this, so let's try describing our new todolist table so we can see how MySQL understands it.

```
mysql> DESCRIBE todolist;
+-------------+--------------+------+-----+---------+----------------+
| Field       | Type         | Null | Key | Default | Extra          |
+-------------+--------------+------+-----+---------+----------------+
| idnumber    | int(11)      | NO   | PRI | NULL    | auto_increment |
| description | varchar(200) | YES  |     | NULL    |                |
| owner       | varchar(40)  | YES  |     | NULL    |                |
| date        | date         | YES  |     | NULL    |                |
| location    | varchar(40)  | YES  |     | NULL    |                |
| importance  | varchar(10)  | YES  |     | NULL    |                |
| creator     | varchar(40)  | YES  |     | NULL    |                |
+-------------+--------------+------+-----+---------+----------------+
7 rows in set (0.00 sec)
```

Awesome; you can even see that our idnumber is the PRI key and has automatic incrementing on the end! Everything registered successfully. We have successfully created a database and a table. We have given structure to our table. Now it is time to put it to good use, but before we start playing with data there's one last admin command I want to cover: creating a user other than root. This way, we don't have to constantly use the root user, which will cut down the potential security risk. The syntax for this command (called a GRANT) is this:

```
GRANT ALL ON <databse>.<table> TO '<username>'@'<user location>' IDENTIFIED BY '<password>';
```

So, let's say we want to grant the default pi user on our system access to our todolist table with the password *raspberry*. The command will become this:

```
GRANT ALL ON pi.todolist TO 'pi'@'localhost' IDENTIFIED BY 'raspberry';
```

Run this command and then quit MySQL shell by typing `quit`. Now try logging back in with your new username and password. Remember, the syntax for this:

```
$ mysql -u<username> -p
```

■ **Note** Quotation marks are needed when putting in any text data in MySQL that is not for something that MySQL already "understands" (i.e., table names and column names).

Inserting Data

Now you're logged back in as the `pi` user, let's start learning some actual commands to insert data into MySQL. The first command to cover is one for inserting data. How else can we be expected to work with MySQL data if there is no data available! The command for inserting data is the aptly named `INSERT` command. The basic syntax for `INSERT` is this:

```
INSERT INTO <TABLE> (<FIELD1>, <FIELD2>, ... <FIELDX>) VALUES ('<VAL1>',
'<VAL2>', ... '<VALX>');
```

So, now that we know how an insert is supposed to look, let's go ahead and make one into the database. Let's insert a pair of tasks into our to-do list. The first one will be my writing of this chapter. So the command will be this (after ensuring we typed `USE pi`):

```
INSERT INTO todolist (description, owner, date, location, importance, creator) VALUES
('Finish LAMP Chapter', 'David', '2012-09-22', 'Australia', 'HIGH', 'David');
Query OK, 1 row affected (0.43 sec)
```

That worked. Let's add another, just for good measure. Let's make Peter do something now:

```
INSERT INTO todolist (description, owner, date, location, importance, creator) VALUES
('Finish GUI Chapter', 'Peter', '2012-09-22', 'Hong Kong', 'HIGH', 'David');
Query OK, 1 row affected (0.48 sec)
```

Now that we have a pair of records to play with. But how are we certain that they are correct? How can we check that the `idnumbers` are incremented, given that we didn't even add them into our `insert` statement? For that we will need to issue a query to our SQL database!

Querying a Database

Unlike most of the other statements, a data query is not done with a `QUERY` command. This is because all of the commands we have been executing are considered to be queries themselves. The command for retrieving data is called a `SELECT` and its syntax is as follows:

```
SELECT <Fields1>, <Field2>... <FieldX> FROM <TABLENAME> WHERE <INFORMATION QUERY>
```

Yes, I know that syntax is a little strange, but once we fill it out you will get more of an idea of why it is the way it is. For starters let's just grab everything. Normally you put field names that you wish to get, which limits the amount of excess data being transmitted, but in this case we can use the special wildcard *. Thus to query everything from our `todolist` table, we will execute this:

```
mysql> SELECT * FROM todolist;
+----------+---------------------+-------+------------+-----------+------------+---------+
| idnumber | description         | owner | date       | location  | importance | creator |
+----------+---------------------+-------+------------+-----------+------------+---------+
|        1 | Finish LAMP Chapter | David | 2012-09-22 | Australia | HIGH       | David   |
|        2 | Finish GUI Chapter  | Peter | 2012-09-22 | Hong Kong | HIGH       | David   |
+----------+---------------------+-------+------------+-----------+------------+---------+
2 rows in set (0.00 sec)
```

You will notice that I left off the `WHERE`, this is done, as there is no actual limitation of what we want, we want everything. After this, you can see that everything else we entered is in the format we gave it and more importantly the ID numbers are incrementing! This validates everything that we inserted before. Now that you understand the very basic syntax we can do some slightly more advanced queries. Let's say I want to find out whom to blame for assigning me (David) a task. The relevant information in this case is the creator as that's all we want, whom to blame. This will give us the first half of a query:

```
SELECT creator FROM todolist
```

Now the next part we need is the portion in which we specify that the owner must be David. The syntax for this is a very simple `WHERE owner = "David"` giving us the final query:

```
SELECT creator FROM todolist WHERE owner = "David";
+---------+
| creator |
+---------+
| David   |
+---------+
1 row in set (0.00 sec)
```

Beautiful. I now know that I have only myself to blame for this mess. In the same vein, let's try another. I want to know the description and priority of all tasks that are due after today (which, in this example, is the 20th of September). So again we start building our query. We want the description and importance fields this time, so in they go. We also want a date greater than 2012-09-20. Thankfully, MySQL understands date data, so all we need to do is give it our date and the greater-than symbol, which is >. This will give you the query:

```
mysql> SELECT description, importance FROM todolist WHERE date > "2012-09-20";
+---------------------+------------+
| description         | importance |
+---------------------+------------+
| Finish LAMP Chapter | HIGH       |
| Finish GUI Chapter  | HIGH       |
+---------------------+------------+
2 rows in set (0.01 sec)
```

There is one last simple part of a SELECT query that will likely be relevant later. This is the ORDER BY statement that can be added to the end of a query. Take our last one for instance; let's say we want them ordered by the order in which they were added (by idnumber). This will make our query into this:

```
mysql> SELECT description, importance, idnumber FROM todolist WHERE date > "2012-09-20"
ORDER BY idnumber;
+--------------------+------------+----------+
| description        | importance | idnumber |
+--------------------+------------+----------+
| Finish LAMP Chapter | HIGH      |        1 |
| Finish GUI Chapter  | HIGH      |        2 |
+--------------------+------------+----------+
2 rows in set (0.00 sec)
```

And there it is, sorted. Okay, so we can't see it as it is in ascending order and has been previously displayed as such. To reverse (or force) an order, we can add an ASC or DESC to the end of the statement, so let's try that with the same query as before and watch the change:

```
mysql> SELECT description, importance, idnumber FROM todolist WHERE date > "2012-09-20"
ORDER BY idnumber DESC;
+--------------------+------------+----------+
| description        | importance | idnumber |
+--------------------+------------+----------+
| Finish GUI Chapter  | HIGH      |        2 |
| Finish LAMP Chapter | HIGH      |        1 |
+--------------------+------------+----------+
2 rows in set (0.00 sec)
```

That's better; you can see the change in order now! Having things returned in order is great as this means the database system is doing the sort for you—something that it is programmed to do very easily. If we were to attempt to write this sort, it would likely take us much longer than the database to perform. Now we have covered our second basic command, and we can insert and retrieve data. The next command we will look into is one to update our data.

Updating a Database

Now that we are past the slight silliness of the SELECT command to query, we are back into named-as-they-mean territory with the UPDATE command. An update is somewhat of a hybrid of both the INSERT and SELECT queries, and rightfully so, given that we need to both find something and then update that something. The basic syntax of an UPDATE is this:

```
UPDATE <table name> SET <column name1> = "<value1>",<column name2> = "<value2>"... <column
nameX> = "<valueX>" WHERE <Information Query>
```

Let's work our way through an example. Let's say I need a deadline extension on this chapter because I'm working way too hard and want to take it easy for a night. This means I will want to increase my deadline to the 23rd instead of the 22nd. So we know what we want to update, which gives us this command:

```
UPDATE todolist SET date="2012-09-23" WHERE
```

Now we just need a query; we can't pick something on the 22nd as there are two things using that date; the same with severity and creator. We could use owner or description or idnumber. In this case I would choose ID number, as we have set this as the primary key and thus totally unique identifier. This makes our UPDATE query into

```
mysql> UPDATE todolist SET date="2012-09-23" WHERE idnumber=1;
Query OK, 1 row affected, 1 warning (0.48 sec)
Rows matched: 1  Changed: 1  Warnings: 0
```

You will notice that I did not add quotation marks around number 1 on the end. This is because MySQL treats numbers as INT differently to numbers as a VARCHAR; while this seems semantic. it is an important distinction as mathematical operations cannot be carried out against a VARCHAR, but can be against an INT. MySQL has not displayed the actual output of the data; to see it we will need to issue another select, so let's go ahead and examine the change:

```
mysql> SELECT * FROM todolist WHERE idnumber=1;
+----------+---------------------+-------+------------+-----------+------------+---------+
| idnumber | description         | owner | date       | location  | importance | creator |
+----------+---------------------+-------+------------+-----------+------------+---------+
|        1 | Finish LAMP Chapter | David | 2012-09-23 | Australia | HIGH       | David   |
+----------+---------------------+-------+------------+-----------+------------+---------+
1 row in set (0.00 sec)
```

And there you have it; I've just given myself a night off. But because of this, Peter and I will both have to work harder on the chapters we have remaining. This means that we will need to set the importance of both our chapters up to highest! The first part is simple:

```
UPDATE todolist SET importance="HIGHEST" WHERE
```

This is where we can look at changing how we do queries again. Do we wish to do everything? And set everything to HIGHEST by removing the WHERE? Let's search for HIGH and make it HIGHEST, which makes our final query:

```
mysql>  UPDATE todolist SET importance="HIGHEST" WHERE importance="HIGH";
Query OK, 2 rows affected (0.49 sec)
Rows matched: 2  Changed: 2  Warnings: 0
```

Again there is no output, so we must retrieve the data again:

```
mysql> SELECT * FROM todolist;
+----------+---------------------+-------+------------+-----------+------------+---------+
| idnumber | description         | owner | date       | location  | importance | creator |
+----------+---------------------+-------+------------+-----------+------------+---------+
|        1 | Finish LAMP Chapter | David | 2012-09-23 | Australia | HIGHEST    | David   |
|        2 | Finish GUI Chapter  | Peter | 2012-09-22 | Hong Kong | HIGHEST    | David   |
+----------+---------------------+-------+------------+-----------+------------+---------+
2 rows in set (0.00 sec)
```

We were able to update both those HIGH values to HIGHEST. Now for the one last remaining task: delete.

Deleting Data

We want to be able to remove tasks as they are finished. The syntax of a DELETE command is constructed almost exactly like a SELECT command:

```
DELETE FROM <table name> WHERE <information query>;
```

Here's one final example. Let's say my reason for a night off wasn't that I was tired; it was because I was finished with this chapter early! Woohoo! So let's build the delete. Again let's go by the idnumber to be certain. The command will be this:

```
mysql> DELETE FROM todolist WHERE idnumber=1;
Query OK, 1 row affected (0.42 sec)
```

As with UPDATE, there is no information returned other than the short output saying that we deleted one row. Let's issue a SELECT again and see what has changed:

```
mysql> SELECT * FROM todolist;
+----------+--------------------+-------+------------+-----------+------------+---------+
| idnumber | description        | owner | date       | location  | importance | creator |
+----------+--------------------+-------+------------+-----------+------------+---------+
|        2 | Finish GUI Chapter | Peter | 2012-09-22 | Hong Kong | HIGHEST    | David   |
+----------+--------------------+-------+------------+-----------+------------+---------+
1 row in set (0.01 sec)
```

Only Peter's chapter remains, and he has to work the hardest since it's on highest. Okay, let's be kind—one last command. This one gets rid of a table; it's called the DROP command and is very simple:

```
DROP TABLE <table name>;
```

Let's drop our todolist table since we are done with these MySQL examples and we don't want it taking up room:

```
mysql> DROP TABLE todolist;
Query OK, 0 rows affected (0.49 sec)
```

Okay, now we only have our pi database left. If you wish to delete it, you simply need to replace the world TABLE with the word DATABASE in the DROP command. It's up to you; we will be reusing this one later. For now, let's head on to the last part of our LAMP stack: PHP.

P is for PHP

PHP is a system for allowing you to add dynamic functions into your web page. Originally, all web pages were made from HTML alone, which doesn't allow for much flexibility based on inputs and actions. HTML just displays a static page of content that needs to be modified to show something different. To solve this initial issue, the Common Gateway Interface (CGI) was developed. This provided a way for web servers to take requests that would allow them to return content.

Originally, most CGIs were full-blown applications that output various pieces of HTML depending on their input, and whole portions of these applications were dedicated to outputting large chunks of the same HTML over and over. This is where the development of PHP came in. PHP was designed to be a language in which one could add snippets of actual dynamic code into the static HTML and presto: a dynamic web page would be formed.

Since its creation, PHP has become widespread with installation figures of 20 million being cited. This success is in no small part due to the ease in which PHP can be used as a CGI compared with the original application form CGIs. Now that you have an understanding of what PHP is, let's install it on the Raspberry Pi. As ever, we will rely on the services of `apt-get` to fetch and install PHP for us. The command to run is this:

```
$ sudo apt-get install php5
Reading package lists... Done
Building dependency tree
Reading state information... Done
The following extra packages will be installed:
  apache2-mpm-prefork libapache2-mod-php5 libonig2 libqdbm14 php5-cli php5-common
Suggested packages:
  php-pear
The following packages will be REMOVED:
  apache2-mpm-worker
The following NEW packages will be installed:
  apache2-mpm-prefork libapache2-mod-php5 libonig2 libqdbm14 php5 php5-cli php5-common
0 upgraded, 7 newly installed, 1 to remove and 84 not upgraded.
Need to get 5,707 kB of archives.
After this operation, 16.3 MB of additional disk space will be used.
Do you want to continue [Y/n]?
```

Notice that PHP is making a modification to our Apache installation. This is to replace the Apache tribesman modules with ones that are preferred for utilizing PHP. Once the PHP has finished installing, we want to go ahead and test that it is working. There is a simple PHP page that we can write, which will show all our installation settings and confirm that PHP is up and running. To test this first page, we need to replace `index.html` in `/var/www` with a new `index.php` that has the following line inside it:

```
<?php phpinfo(); ?>
```

Once you have removed `index.html` and added `index.php`, direct your browser to your Apache server. Figure 8-2 will be your reward.

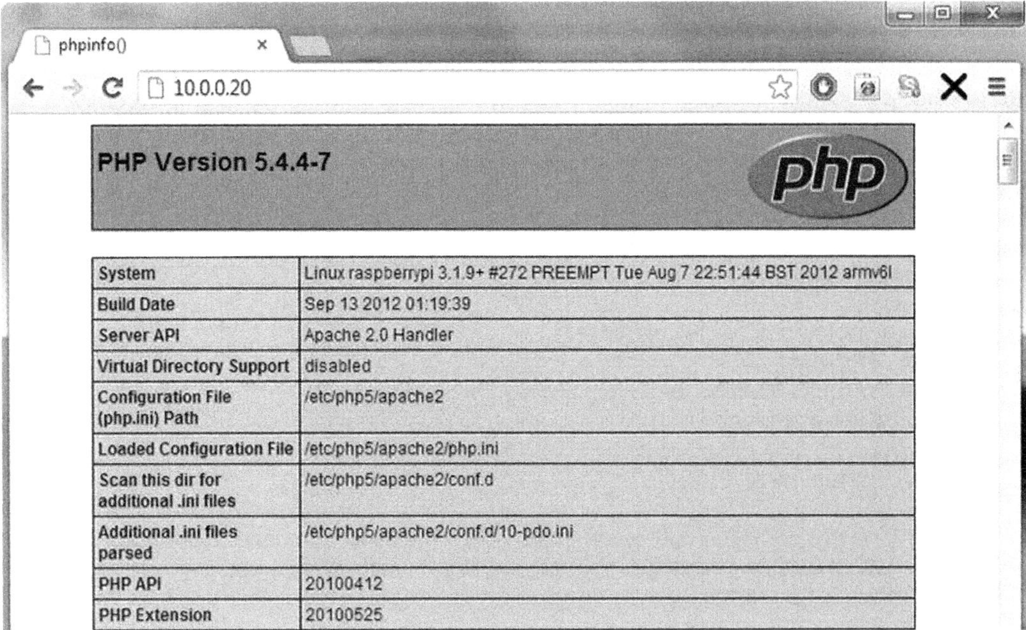

Figure 8-2. *PHP info page*

This is the PHP info page, which describes the entire current configuration of your newly installed PHP instance. Since we are viewing it, it also proves that the PHP interpreter is working correctly. It also shows that `index.php` has been picked up as a default page by Apache. The code that we added to generate this was the following:

```
<?php phpinfo(); ?>
```

This is a great example of PHP code; first we have the opening markers that show that this is PHP and to be interpreted as such (`<?php` and `?>` to close) and we have a single function call inside to `phpinfo();` that displays all our data.

A function is a reference to a predefined piece of code that we run by invoking the function name. Functions always end with a pair of parentheses, which can contain data (variables that will be passed into the function for use there). In addition to functions, PHP uses arrays, much like the arrays you saw in Chapter 7. To recap, arrays are variables that contain a number of values rather than one. An array can be manipulated as a whole array or by each of its individual elements. To access the array elements, you need to add a pair of square brackets to the end of the array variable and enter the number of the element you wish to access. These element numbers start from 0 as the first element and increment.

The other important things one needs to know for PHP are these:

- All PHP statements end with a semicolon
- All PHP variables start with a $ sign (recall variables from BASH in Chapter 7; PHP variables are used for the same thing)
- All PHP array variables start with an @ sign
- All PHP function's internal code are surrounded with curly braces { and }

Next we need to have a look through the PHJP Info page; start by searching for MySQL. Oh dear, there's no mention of it. PHP will need to understand how to communicate with MySQL in order for us to be able to display database content on our web page. Thankfully, apt-get comes to the rescue again. This time, we need to install the php5-mysql package:

```
$ sudo apt-get install php5-mysql
Reading package lists... Done
Building dependency tree
Reading state information... Done
The following extra packages will be installed:
  libmysqlclient18
The following NEW packages will be installed:
  libmysqlclient18 php5-mysql
0 upgraded, 2 newly installed, 0 to remove and 84 not upgraded.
Need to get 711 kB of archives.
After this operation, 3,547 kB of additional disk space will be used.
Do you want to continue [Y/n]?
```

Again, you will see that this install adds a new MySQL client library for communications and the new PHP MySQL interleave. It will also automatically restart your Apache web server and change several PHP configuration files for you. Once again, open up and direct your browser to the Apache web page and search for MySQL, and there we go! (See Figure 8-3).

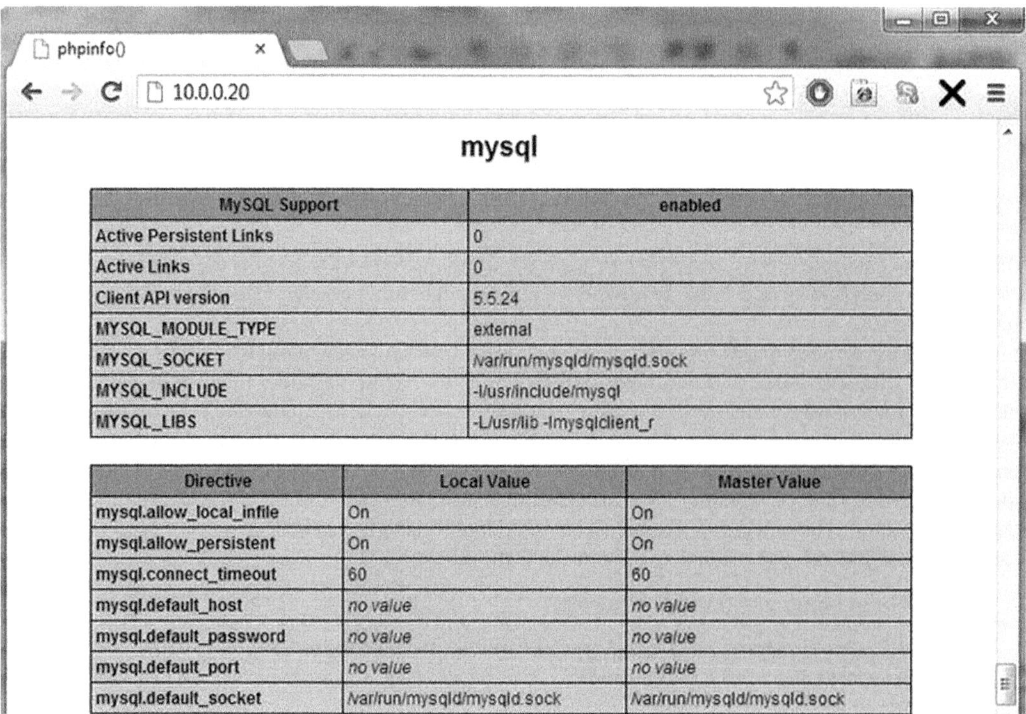

MySQL Support	enabled
Active Persistent Links	0
Active Links	0
Client API version	5.5.24
MYSQL_MODULE_TYPE	external
MYSQL_SOCKET	/var/run/mysqld/mysqld.sock
MYSQL_INCLUDE	-I/usr/include/mysql
MYSQL_LIBS	-L/usr/lib -lmysqlclient_r

Directive	Local Value	Master Value
mysql.allow_local_infile	On	On
mysql.allow_persistent	On	On
mysql.connect_timeout	60	60
mysql.default_host	no value	no value
mysql.default_password	no value	no value
mysql.default_port	no value	no value
mysql.default_socket	/var/run/mysqld/mysqld.sock	/var/run/mysqld/mysqld.sock

Figure 8-3. *PHP MySQL config info*

We have confirmed the following:

- We have a working PHP system
- Apache can render the PHP
- MySQL and PHP know how to communicate

This means that we have just accomplished creating a working LAMP setup! Now let's put it to use.

Simple Web App

Now that we have built our new LAMP stack and it is up and running on your Pi, it is time to make good use of it. Good use can be literally anything you want as you now have a web server of your own that you can write web applications on. For many of you, however, this may seem a daunting task, as you are unfamiliar with PHP or even HTML. Fear not; like Linux in general this seems daunting at first and there are intricacies, but nothing insurmountable and nothing that you can't get over with a little help. I've always found that the best way to learn is to actually do it, which means we can undertake a project together, which will illustrate how you can use your new LAMP stack to create a web application.

In order to build a web application, we need to understand both HTML and PHP. One final thing: this will be a bare-bones web page and may look a little rough. There are so many ways to improve the visual aspect of your web page, but there are whole books dedicated to this, which will cover a larger amount of content and interactions. So with this in mind, let's have a look at understanding HTML.

HTML

Hyper Text Markup Language (HTML) is the language that makes the Internet. HTML provides the basis for all transmitted web application content, it is made up as a series of tags and they are sent as a HTML document to your browser. Your browser then uses these tags to assemble its version of your web page. This means that web content can be very small and can be viewed by any system that has the capacity to decode HTML tags. The downside here is that different software can display websites with slight differences in them.

HTML tags are words surrounded by angle brackets. These tags are written in what is called a markup language. HTML tags come in two varieties, on their own or in pairs, with pairs being the much more common. Here are two sets of HTML tags.

- `<html></html>`: An open and a close HTML tag (these tags tell your browser where the HTML page starts and finishes)
- `<hr/>`: An `hr` tag on its own (`<hr/>` will draw a line across your web page because it stands for headed rule)

The slashes at the front of the second HTML tag show that this is the close of this tag. The slash at the end of the `hr` tag shows it is meant to be on its own. Have a look at a very basic website:

```
<html>
        <head>
              <title>Pi Brand - Todo List App</title>
        </head>
        <body>
              <h1>Pi Todo List App</h1>
        </body>
</html>
```

If you place this into index.php on your Pi, open up your browser you should see a basic white page with the phrase Pi Todo List App in large black text. Additionally up the top of your browser should say the same. This website is wholly generated by the HTML tags we just entered. Let's go over these as an explanation of how the website works:

- First you will see that all the content is wrapped within a pair of HTML tags, which say that all the content within them is HTML.
- At the next level are the head and body tags, which represent the next level of tags, the heading information of the page and the actual body of the page.
- The title tags are used to set the title bar at the top of the page.
- And within the body is one pair of h1 tags that are the big block of text. The h1 is short for *header 1*, which represents the largest size of header tags. There are an almost unlimited number of hx tags you can use; as long as they are defined, most browsers will only go as far as h4 or h5 without one being defined separately.

So we have now covered five basic HTML tags but there are many, many more. For a reference of a host of the common HTML tags, some examples and great tutorials, head over to wc3schools.com or have a look at "Beginning HTML with CSS and XHTML," by Craig Cook and David Schultz.

Here are a few more HTML tags and how they are used:

- <p>: Paragraph tag, used to create text into a paragraph block
-
: Break tag, used to insert a break into the page
- <hr>: Horizontal rule, creates a horizontal line across the screen
- <a>: Hyperlink tag, for a link to another page
- <img>: Image tag, for adding images to a page
- Table tags
  - <table>: Top-level tag of a table
  - <th>: Element of the tables heading row
  - <tr>: Row for the table
  - <td>: Cell of a table within a row
- Form tags
  - <form>: Top-level element of a form
  - <input>: Input element of a form

These are some of the basic HTML tags we will use in our project to create output and drive input to the to-do list. In addition to the raw tags, there are a number of different options you can use to change the various aspects of how these elements are displayed; unfortunately, it would take more than the rest of this book to cover each element, so we will have to discuss them as they come along. Now that you're familiar with what HTML can do and what some of these tags look like, we can move on to trying to add some PHP into the mix here. But first, let's have a look at actually designing our page.

Starting Our Page

The basic concept for our page will be a website in two parts; first will be a page that contains a to-do list, listing off all the elements in the database. Next will be a form for the submission of new elements to the database down the bottom. We will also add a check box that will allow you to delete elements you no longer need. Now that we have the basic layout, there are some functional decisions that need to be made regarding how the processing of the page should occur. Since the design and output will remain constant with just some processing to connect to the database to load the elements or remove elements, we can just go ahead and have one page, which will attempt to perform any of the actions it needs (the additions and deletions before displaying the page.

Now we can start actually writing the page out. To start, add all the content to the page and get the output going. However, first we need to have our database set up so we have data to display. We have already created the Pi database and we have the to-do list table structure from earlier, so let's use them. The `create` statement for this table was as follows:

```
create table todolist (
idnumber INT PRIMARY KEY NOT NULL AUTO_INCREMENT,
description VARCHAR(200),
owner VARCHAR(40),
date DATE,
location VARCHAR(40),
importance VARCHAR(10),
creator VARCHAR(40)
);
```

Now that we have a dataset to work with and a layout for our data, we can begin to add display elements. Since our data is tabular, we can use the table elements to display it. This will make arranging the data much easier. So, we have our basic page layout from earlier; next we should set up our data connection. A MySQL PHP connection uses the `mysqli` interface. Thus to establish a connection to the database we must create a new `mysqli` that has the details of our database and connection:

```
<?php
$mysqli = new mysqli('localhost', 'pi', 'raspberry', 'pi');
if ($mysqli->connect_error) {
    die('Connect Error (' . $mysqli->connect_errno . ') '
            . $mysqli->connect_error);
}

$mysqli->close();
?>
```

The preceding is a small segment of PHP code, which does the following:

- Creates a new `mysqli` object to connect to the system, which is available on the local machine using the username `pi` and password `raspberry`.
- Checks that the connection to the database was successful; and if not, displays an error message.
- Closes the connection as we don't want to leave a potentially open connection there unused.

Now that we have this block of code for database connectivity, add this to the original block of code in `index.php`:

```
<html>
<head>
<title>Pi Brand - Todo List App</title>
</head>
<body>
<h1>Pi Todo List App</h1>
<?php
$mysqli = new mysqli('localhost', 'pi', 'raspberry', 'pi');
if ($mysqli->connect_error) {
    die('Connect Error (' . $mysqli->connect_errno . ') '
            . $mysqli->connect_error);
}
$mysqli->close();
?>
</body>
</html>
```

Display the Database Content

We now have that original piece of HTML from before, with the addition of one little `mysqli` connection object. This won't do much unless there is an error because nothing else will be displayed. Now it's time to add another block of code to display the to-do list. This will take two forms: the table block and the table head. Then we will need to display everything within the MySQL table. Displaying them means creating a loop that will display the content of each row, and placing it within the correct set of HTML tags. Let's start with the basic HTML table layout:

```
<table>
<tr>
<th>Description</th>
<th>Owner</th>
<th>Due Date</th>
<th>Location</th>
<th>Importance</th>
<th>Creator</th>
</tr>
...
</table>
```

This code sets out the table and its first row, which are all tagged as being table header elements. Now add the PHP to display all the content from the MySQL table:

```
<?php
$result = $mysqli->query("SELECT * FROM todolist");
while($row = $result->fetch_assoc()){
        print "<tr>";
        print "<td>".$row["description"]."</td>";
        print "<td>".$row["owner"]."</td>";
        print "<td>".$row["date"]."</td>";
        print "<td>".$row["location"]."</td>";
        print "<td>".$row["importance"]."</td>";
        print "<td>".$row["creator"]."</td>";
        print "</tr>";
}
?>
```

The PHP section performs this nicely. First, it creates a new variable, `$result`, which contains the output of executing a query on `mysqli`. The query is, of course, `SELECT * FROM todolist`. Each line of the result is then passed out one by one in the `while` loop by the `$result->fetch_assoc()` call and assigned to the `row` variable. For each row that comes out, we print the row value for each field we request. You can see the resemblance between the output section of the PHP and the raw HTML. This is deliberate as we want the output of the PHP to marry up with the table header.

Now we should add this back to the original code block, but when doing so we need to make one more change, which is to move the `$mysqli->close();` to the bottom of the new block, just before the close of the PHP segment. This move needs to occur because otherwise we will have closed off the database connection before we have actually pulled the data out of the database.

```
...
<body>
<h1>Pi Todo List App</h1>
<?php
$mysqli = new mysqli('localhost', 'pi', 'raspberry', 'pi');
if ($mysqli->connect_error) {
    die('Connect Error (' . $mysqli->connect_errno . ') '
            . $mysqli->connect_error);
}
?>
<table>
<tr>
<th>Description</th>
<th>Owner</th>
<th>Due Date</th>
<th>Location</th>
<th>Importance</th>
<th>Creator</th>
</tr>
```

```
<?php
$result = $mysqli->query("SELECT * FROM todolist");
while($row = $result->fetch_assoc()){
        print "<tr>";
        print "<td>".$row["description"]."</td>";
        print "<td>".$row["owner"]."</td>";
        print "<td>".$row["date"]."</td>";
        print "<td>".$row["location"]."</td>";
        print "<td>".$row["importance"]."</td>";
        print "<td>".$row["creator"]."</td>";
        print "</tr>";
}
$mysqli->close();
?>
</table>
</body>
</html>
```

Website Data Insertion

This HTML is now working in concert with the PHP to generate a full page of content. The static HTML provides a framework and then we have two pieces of PHP: one piece to establish a connection and a second to pull the results out of the to-do list table and add them to the page. Now that we have the basic display working, we need to add a form to give ourselves a form to submit new content. This basic form should have an input stream for each of the elements we will insert into the table. We will also need one more element, a special hidden one that will tell our processor what kind of things it is to do with the data. In this case, I like to use a variable called `"action"` and assign it as needed. The final element we will need is a submission one, which allows us to push the data to the server to be processed. In addition to all these elements, we need to give the form an `action` and `method` variable, which says how it is to invoke CGI on our web server and what method it should use. This block when it is put together looks like this:

```
...
</table>
<form action="index.php" method="POST">
<input type="hidden" name="action" value="insert" />
Description: <input name="description" /><br/>
Owner: <input name="owner" /><br/>
Date: <input name="date" /><br/>
Location: <input name="location" /><br/>
Importance: <input name="importance" /><br/>
Creator: <input name="creator" /><br/>
<input type="submit" />
</form>
</body>
</html>
```

This code block can then be added below the table and even separated with an `<hr />` tag, which means that you will have a table of display content and a section below it that will give you the ability to add new content. When put together and installed into the web server, the content that it generates will look like Figure 8-4.

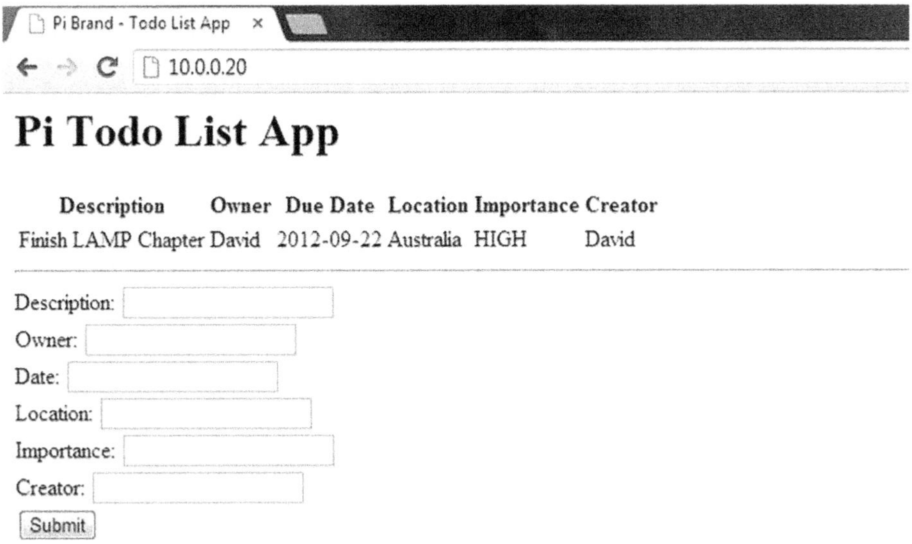

Pi Brand - Todo List App

10.0.0.20

Pi Todo List App

Description	Owner	Due Date	Location	Importance	Creator
Finish LAMP Chapter	David	2012-09-22	Australia	HIGH	David

Description:

Owner:

Date:

Location:

Importance:

Creator:

Submit

Figure 8-4. *To-do list app with insert table*

If you press the submit button, you will wind up right back on the page, but you can see that the page is referenced in the URL. This is the action block sending the CGI command to run on this page. So now we will need to add some CGI processing to our PHP in order to process this data.

Recall that we set a method of `POST` earlier, which is one of two methods that we can use to pass data from our page into the CGI system to be processed. The other method is `GET`, and the difference between the two is limited as both pass data in basically the same manner. For all practical purposes, the only difference is that `GET` will display the content data on the web address, whereas `POST` will keep it hidden. You can check this out for yourself by changing the `POST` to `GET` and then pressing the submit button. Your URL will look something like `http://10.0.0.20/index.php?action=insert&description=&owner=&date=&location=&importance=&creator=`

There is actually a large amount of data being transmitted that will need to be processed. Thankfully, PHP has methods to make this much easier; it has special variables that are automatically populated with the data from CGI requests. There are three special variables that you can access (as we did with the SQL assoc variables): `_POST`, `_GET`, and `_REQUEST`.

To process our CGI, we need to do quite a few things. First, check if the `action` variable is set and contains data; that it will when we press the submit button as we have it set to insert (and later have an action of remove). Once we have ensured that action is set, we can check what it is set to. Once we know which action we are performing, we can simply pull apart the remainder of the output and then perform the required actions on the database. Finally, if we do this before the main page load, we will actually have the latest version of the data displayed automatically!

Our CGI should start looking like this:

```
if(isset($_REQUEST["action"])){
switch($_REQUEST["action"]){
        case "insert":
                $SQL="INSERT INTO todolist (description, owner, date, location, importance, 
creator) VALUES (";
                $SQL=$SQL."'".$_REQUEST["description"]."',";
                $SQL=$SQL."'".$_REQUEST["owner"]."',";
                $SQL=$SQL."'".$_REQUEST["date"]."',";
                $SQL=$SQL."'".$_REQUEST["location"]."',";
                $SQL=$SQL."'".$_REQUEST["importance"]."',";
                $SQL=$SQL."'".$_REQUEST["creator"]."'";
                $SQL=$SQL.");";
if ($mysqli->query($SQL)=== FALSE) {
    printf("Error - Unable to insert data to table " . $mysqli->error);
}

                break;
        case "delete":
                print "Delete function yet to be added!";
                break;
}
}
```

The first thing is to see whether the `action` variable specified in the hidden field within the form is set. If it is, we can be reliably certain that an action needs to be performed. Next, if action is set, we go into a `switch` (or `case`) statement to work out which function we are performing. I've added a case for both insert and delete, but the delete function is just printing that we will add it later. Besides, how would we access it without a `submit` method for it and an action field in a form?

Inserting to the Database

In the insert case, we simply need to create and the build the SQL command. The command we are trying to build is exactly like the previous SQL inserts. First, I laid out the static content: the frame of the `INSERT` statement, the table name, and which fields we will be writing into. Then I have started adding variable by variable to that statement. You can see that the additions have a lot of funny stuff around them because each of these variables will need to be surrounded by single quotation marks and have a comma on the end. Each of these little pieces of text needs to be treated as such, which means wrapping them in a pair of double quotation marks like so:

```
$SQL=$SQL."'".$_REQUEST["description"]."',";
```

This assigns the `SQL` variable the value of the current `SQL` value (given by `$SQL=$SQL`) and then adds to it (marked by the period) a single quote (given by `"'"`) and the value of the `REQUEST` variable description, then a single quote, and then a comma. I know it seems a lot of work, but we have been able to pull out each of the variables we need and have the whole SQL statement in one tiny variable.

■ **Caution** It's also important to note at this point that the above is not to be considered secure. Those variables can quite literally be anything and there are special functions that you can use to perform some sanity checking on those values. The recommended function for performing a good selection of these sanity checks is the `mysqli_real_escape_string`.

Once we have created the SQL variable, we need to insert it by simply invoking the `mysqli` query function again. In this example, I've also added a check to see that the execution of the query failed. And that's it; this block of code will process the CGI insert into our database from our PHP. All that remains is to insert the block correctly into the right place in our code. I have chosen to append this to the first block of PHP we added instead of giving it its own. This means the flow of the page becomes first to draw the header of the page, then to create the database connection and perform any CGI actions, then to display the actual content of our to-do list, and then to display the final form. Once the code is in, you can test that it works by placing values into the form and pressing submit. This should go ahead and add an extra row that will show up in your table, as shown in Figure 8-5.

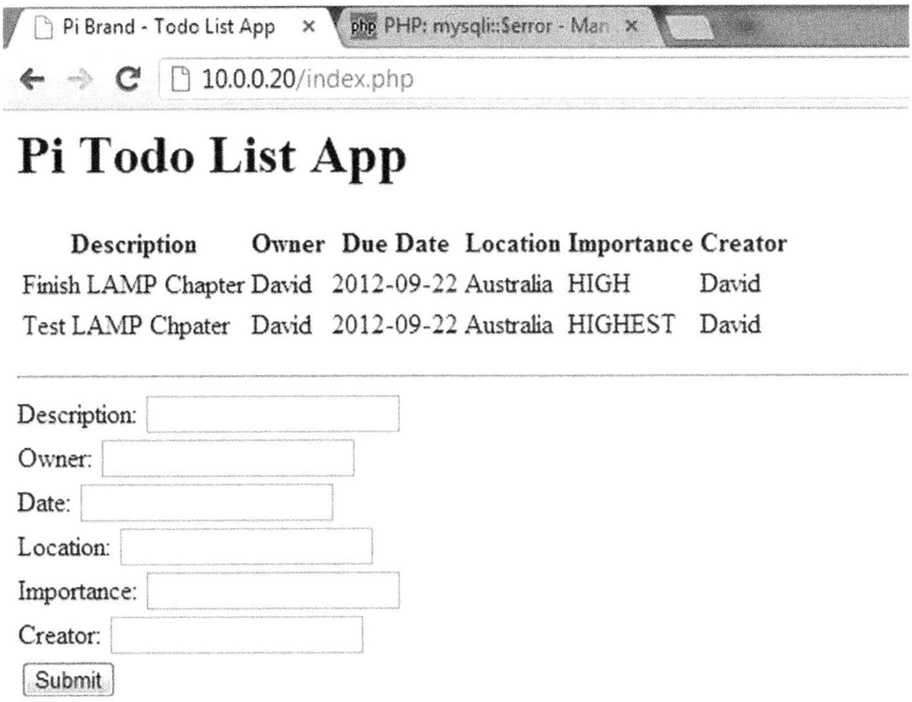

Figure 8-5. *All work and no play...*

Remove Entries

Now that the add functionality is working, we need to create a delete functionality. As with all things in life, there are a number of ways to can approach it. The easiest is to simply add a form and delete option for each individual row, which means that if you want to delete, you need to issue them one at a time. The second option is to have a series of check boxes that will delete all the ticked elements. I am a fan of the second option as it gives a lot more flexibility with the deletions.

We need to make two changes for this process to work. The first change is to add a form around the table that will be the delete form, a hidden field with the action delete, a submission button below the form, and check boxes to each element. To add the check boxes, we will also need to add an empty element to the start of the table header row. Figure 8-6 is what your page should look like with the added check boxes and submit button.

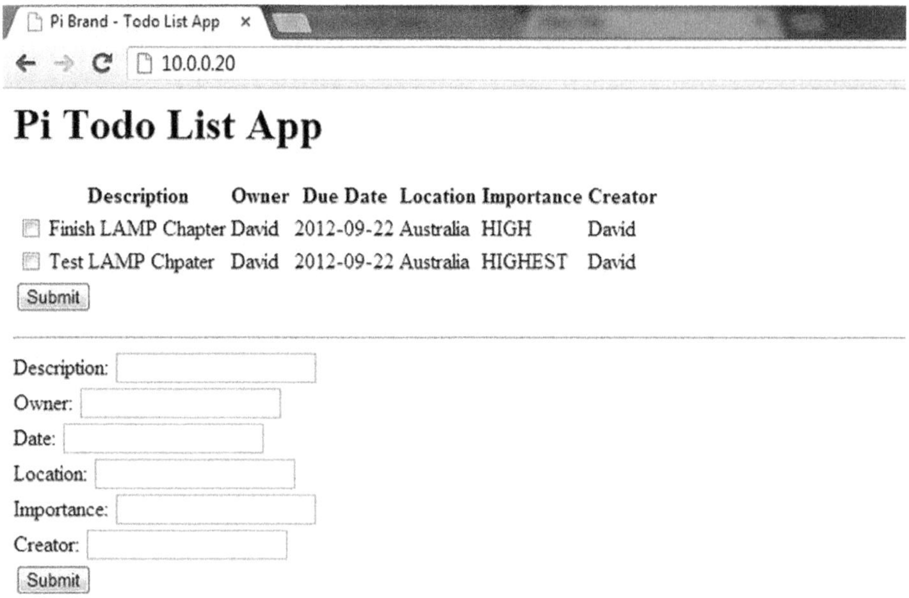

Figure 8-6. *Now with extra check boxes*

The code section for the form content generation is shown following. You can see that there is another form wrapping the table that has the same method and action. Next is the new hidden input value that sets the action to delete, allowing us to access the correct section in our `case` statement. Probably the most important change is the addition of the empty `td` pair and the additional input of type check box. This check box is probably the most complex set of elements we have added—it contains the type of check box, the value that is specially configured to be accessible as an array that is done by adding the square brackets before and after. The final element is the value, which I have set to be the value of the check box. This means that when we go into CGI mode, we will take the array value of check boxes and it will contain a list of the `idnumber` values for the elements we wish to delete.

Here is a short summary of all the changes we have made to the form to add the check boxes:

```
...
<h1>Pi Todo List App</h1>
<form action="index.php" method="POST">
<input type="hidden" name="action" value="delete" />
<table>
<tr>
<td></td>
...
</tr>
<?php
$result = $mysqli->query("SELECT * FROM todolist");
while($row= $result->fetch_assoc()){
        print "<tr>";
        print "<td><input type='checkbox' name='checkboxes[]'
        value='".$row["idnumber"]."' /></td>";
        print "<td>".$row["description"]."</td>";
        print "<td>".$row["owner"]."</td>";
        print "<td>".$row["date"]."</td>";
        print "<td>".$row["location"]."</td>";
        print "<td>".$row["importance"]."</td>";
        print "<td>".$row["creator"]."</td>";
        print "</tr>";
}
$mysqli->close();
?>
</table>
<input type="submit"/>
</form>
...
```

Remove Data from DB

We have one final change to make, which is adding the delete processing in the `case` statement. We can use a similar logic to the `insert` statement, whereby we create a SQL variable and then iteratively add the remove for the `idnumbers` one after another. In this case, we will need to have a `for` loop that will run through each element of the `_REQUEST['checkboxes']` variable that we can get from the count function being run on the variable. This gives us a full `for` loop as follows:

```
for($i=0; $i < count($_REQUEST['checkboxes']); $i++){
```

Once we are within the loop, we simply need to pull out the `$i`'th element of the `_REQUEST['checkboxes']` array each time in the loop. In addition, we will need to add an `or` to the end of each of them so that we will delete each of the elements by `idnumber`; we use `or` because we want it to delete the variable if the `idnumber` is the first number, the second number, or the third, and so on.

However, we will have one issue with the or: we will add it to the end of the last element that we don't want. We will need to use the rtrim function to trim off the or from the end. The rtrim function will trim off a given value from the right side of a string, which will give us the SQL we want. Finally, we perform the same query action as in the insert and will again check to see whether there is an error. This will give us a code block like this:

```
$SQL="DELETE FROM todolist WHERE";
for($i=0; $i < count($_REQUEST['checkboxes']); $i++){
        $SQL=$SQL . " idnumber=" . $_REQUEST['checkboxes'][$i] . " or";
}
$SQL= rtrim($SQL, "or");
if ($mysqli->query($SQL)== FALSE) {
         printf("Error Unable to delete value " . $mysqli->error);
}
```

Figure 8-7 is the final result. I have used the delete to remove the original entry so we are just left with the one. Remember that all examples from this book are available online via the Apress website. If you are unsure about how all this code is assembled, please download a copy and have a look!

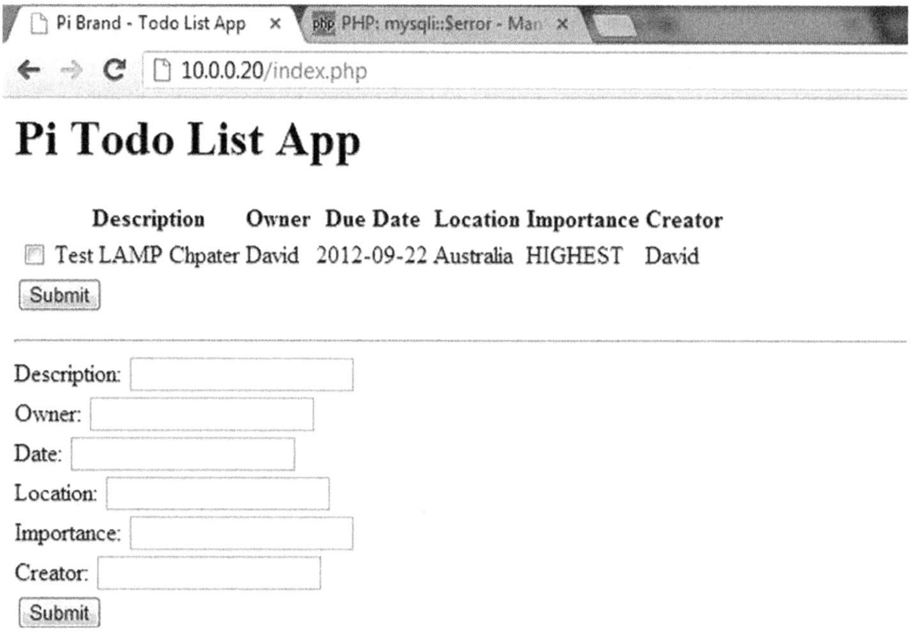

Figure 8-7. Lowering my workload

Troubleshooting

Now let's go over some ways to troubleshoot some issues. First, try making each code change in sequence and then reload the page. You can use the `view source` command to see the full HTML that is being generated by the PHP and see whether the values are showing up correctly. If you can't get that far, have a look at the error log, (the one from right back at the start when we configured Apache). This file will list all of the PHP errors that occur. Have a look to ensure that your quotation marks are open and closed correctly and you haven't left any dangling. Check that you have a semicolon on the end of each of your statements (I always forget this one). Check that your parentheses, square brackets, and circle brackets are opened and closed correctly with no overlap.

Much of the stuff in PHP and web development is trial and error. You should check that each statement or block of code that you add functions and generates as expected. You can use a `print` statement to output variables as they are generated to see what exactly you are doing, which is a great way to diagnose any problems with your SQL statements. Finally, remember that you have access to the full system, go ahead and test inserting values into your SQL and delete them as needed; use the system to work out what it is doing and what causes your problems.

Where From Here?

We've done all this development and we have a functional to-do list that you can use to display, add, and delete entries with. We have used a variety of different programming tools to do things, but there are a lot of things we can do from here. These are some of the changes you could make to your to-do list:

- Add `isset();` checks to each of the insert values to check that you are actually inserting values, not just blank spaces.
- Wrap each of the inserted values with the `mysqli_real_escape_string` function. This will increase the security of the to-do list because it prevents people writing "nasty" values into your application that will execute as separate SQL queries.
- Change the `value` option of each of the submit elements, so that they say what we are using them for: inserting or deleting.
- Create a table around the form elements for inserting and give each of the labels and insert fields their own row and own cell. Wrapping them in a table makes the display much more uniform.
- Start looking into CSS because it can make a big difference in how your to-do list looks. Twitters "bootstrap" is a great starting point.

Summary

So we've come a long way since we started. We've done a lot. We have installed and configured Apache, MySQL, and PHP. You have learned how to create simple SQL statements to create and delete databases and tables and then learned how to insert and delete data from these tables. Finally, you have learned how web content is displayed from an Apache web server. Then we combined all and went through some PHP and HTML to generate a whole application that provides access to a database to-do list table.

This has been a monumental undertaking because we have not only gone and installed three different applications and created an interconnected application stack but also gone over three languages to create an application on top of the application stack.

Congratulations—job well done!

CHAPTER 9

WiPi: Wireless Computing

One of the biggest advantages of the Raspberry Pi is that it is tiny and can fit in just about any small nook or cranny you care to think of. This is why it is constantly touted as a great choice for people to use when designing—it can be placed just about anywhere and, with the right peripherals, can do almost any task. Additionally, its low power consumption means that there is less of a barrier to its usage in these situations as it doesn't need a large amount of electrical plumbing to "just work." Which is to say that Raspberry Pi is a super tiny machine that provides a monumental bang for your buck!

However, this is not without some strings attached (see Figure 9-1)! All that power is for naught without a small supply of external electricity. While 5 volts isn't much, it does need to somehow magically enter your Raspberry Pi to turn the lights on. In addition to requiring power, the Pi is almost useless on its own as there is little you can do with the Pi on 5 volts alone beyond making the power LED go on and off. You need to attach devices to make the Pi useful. To use the Pi as a simple home computer you need the following (at a minimum):

- HDMI or composite cable for video
- Ethernet cable for Internet and network access
- A keyboard to enter data with
- An SD card to provide storage

Figure 9-1. *Constrained Pi*

Suddenly, you see what I'm getting at; the Raspberry Pi, the tiny unattached super machine is actually quite tied down. Tied down with the needs of human usability and interactiveness, these constraints mean running a large number of cables to your Pi just to get some of the basic functionality out of it. As you can probably guess, all is not lost! There are a number of ways you can detach your Pi and make it a lot more mobile and give yourself a lot more flexibility in what you can do with it. That's the purpose of this chapter: to provide you with the tools and some background to remove the wires constraining your Raspberry Pi.

Preparing for WiPi

In addition to having your SD card loaded with a copy of Raspbian, you will want to ensure that your version of Raspbian has been upgraded because the September release included significant improvements in how WiFi access is managed. To get this system up, you first need to run a few quick commands:

```
$ sudo apt-get update
$ sudo apt-get upgrade
```

These two commands will first tell your `apt-get` instance to update to know which versions of the software are available to you for usage. The second will tell `apt-get` to compare and then install every upgraded version of all software currently installed on the system. As you can imagine, running these commands on a regular basis is a very good idea because it allows you to keep your system running the latest version of the software.

Simple Constraint Removal

Before you begin chopping off cables willy-nilly, you need to understand what you want to achieve with your Pi. This will automatically place a number of constraints on what you want to do with it. I can't presuppose what you want to do with your Pi because there are genuinely so many options. So given this, what I will try and provide here are individual ways that you can cut the cord (not literally) and unconstrain your Pi. You may well be able to make use of your newfound cable-cutting skills with some of the content in later chapters to improve on the designs or to make them better suit your purpose.

Removing Human Input Devices

Start with the easiest and lowest hanging of fruits: the monitor, keyboard, and audio cables. I know it sounds funny to say that cutting out three peripherals at once is easiest, but you really are cutting something much different out of the equation: you. By far, the easiest set of connections to cut is that of the human interaction devices. Much of this book is, in fact, geared toward giving you the skills to work with your Pi without the aid of a monitor, a keyboard, or speakers. This is not to say you can't ever go without; you can always plug them back in as needed to diagnose any really critical issues, but you can start by removing them and managing your Pi remotely. The use of SSH is key here because you can use SSH to remotely connect to your Pi over your network connection. Once you have connected to your Pi, you have full command-line access to perform whatever tasks you need. There is also the added benefit that you can go and change the memory distribution within your Pi using `sudo raspi-config` and set the `memory_split` value to 240/16, which puts most of the memory into free RAM for your system to use and as little as possible into the Graphics display, which you won't normally be using.

Before you assume that this means no use of monitor and keyboard ever, stop. All the things you want to do with your Pi should be tested and configured in a working environment with keyboard, monitor, mouse, and so on, all available for usage. Once you have your system to a state where it works without your interference, you can power on and off without needing to jump back in and manage each time you know you should be able to remove all the human interface devices. This is a great start for anyone: being able to remove all the cables and interface with your system remotely. This is also means you can do other things such as manage your Raspberry Pi via your phone or from a system at work across the Internet. Once you get the feeling for jumping across the Internet to manage your machine, I guarantee you will ask yourself how you did without it before.

Adding a Remote GUI

Alright, while I will readily admit that there are some true benefits from working within a console-only remote environment there are some people who just cannot get their head around it. And there are a number of cases where it is impractical for whatever reason. In these situations, it's best to use a tool called Virtual Network Computing (VNC) to give you the ability to interact with your Pi's desktop from another machine.

To do this, you will need to install a VNC server on your Pi and you will need a client on your machine. There are numerous different VNC solutions out there, and as long as they obey the VNC protocol, they should all be compatible. For your Pi, you will be using tightvnc because it aims to be efficient and "tight." You can download the clients for both Windows and Linux systems at `www.tightvnc.com`. But before you go jumping into clients, start by installing the server on your Pi. Run the following command:

```
$ sudo apt-get install tightvncserver
```

This command will install tightvnc with the package management tool; your output should be similar to the following:

```
Reading package lists... Done
Building dependency tree
Reading state information... Done
The following extra packages will be installed:
  x11-xserver-utils xfonts-base xfonts-encodings xfonts-utils
Suggested packages:
  tightvnc-java nickle cairo-5c xorg-docs-core
The following NEW packages will be installed:
  tightvncserver x11-xserver-utils xfonts-base xfonts-encodings xfonts-utils
0 upgraded, 5 newly installed, 0 to remove and 91 not upgraded.
Need to get 7,824 kB of archives.
After this operation, 11.7 MB of additional disk space will be used.
Do you want to continue [Y/n]?
```

Once you have Tight VNC Server installed, you need to power it up and start it running so you can connect. So go ahead and execute this command:

```
$ tightvncserver
```

You will then be prompted for a pair of passwords: one is the actual VNC password that allows you to use the mouse and keyboard to manipulate the screen; the second is the optional "View Only" password that allows you to view what's on the screen but not interact. This is what you should expect to see after executing:

```
You will require a password to access your desktops.
Password:
Warning: password truncated to the length of 8.
```

```
Verify:
Would you like to enter a view-only password (y/n)? n
New 'X' desktop is raspberrypi:1
Creating default startup script /home/pi/.vnc/xstartup
Starting applications specified in /home/pi/.vnc/xstartup
Log file is /home/pi/.vnc/raspberrypi:1.log
```

Now all you need to do is go ahead and connect with the tightvnc client on the machine you wish to browse from. Go ahead and fire up the client. I am working from a Windows environment, and you should see a screen like in Figure 9-2.

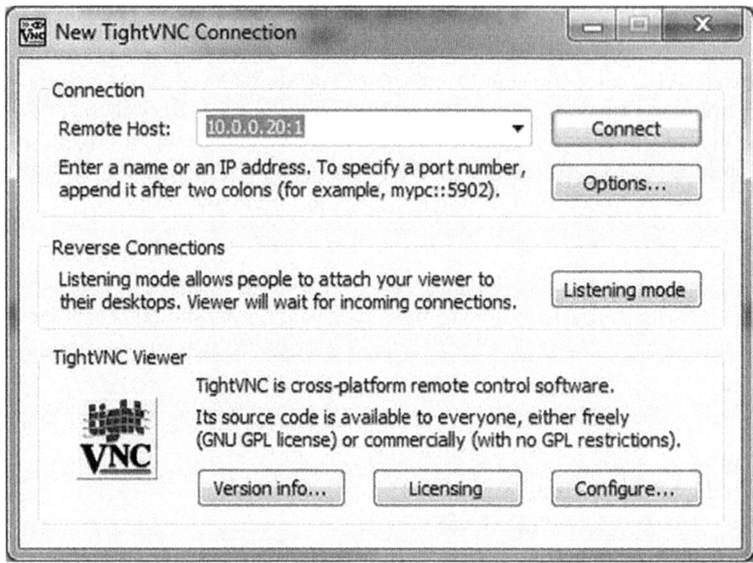

Figure 9-2. *TightVNC Client*

In Figure 9-2, you can see that I have entered my Raspberry Pi's IP address and :1. Normally a single colon after an IP address designates a port number, but in this case it designates a screen number. If you go back over the output from the tight VNC startup, you can see that it says it created a new desktop of `raspberrypi:1`, which is what I have connected to. Now press Connect and boom, there is the lovely pink raspberry displayed on your screen and you are able to move around in the Raspberry Pi environment.

If you were to restart, however, you would be without a VNC server again, and running `tightvncserver` will ask you for credentials again. This is not the optimal way to do this, so instead you will run the following command if you wish to restart the server:

```
$ vncserver :1 -geometry 1920x1080 -depth 24
```

This command says to run a `vncserver` on screen `:1` with the dimensions 1920 x 1080, which is the maximum resolution of your Pi (full 1080p high definition) and set the color depth to 24 bits. You can lower these values if need be to fit the dimensions of your client screen or to lower the number of resources used by your Pi in hosting a VNC connection. In addition to this, you may wish to run your VNC server on boot so you don't need to SSH in to set up a video connection. After all, that's just redundant! The simple way is to add the `vncserver` command to `/etc/rc.local` as everything in this file gets executed during the boot process.

By default, your `rc.local` file will look like this:

```
#!/bin/sh -e
#
# rc.local
#
# This script is executed at the end of each multiuser runlevel.
# Make sure that the script will "exit 0" on success or any other
# value on error.
#
# In order to enable or disable this script just change the execution
# bits.
#
# By default this script does nothing.

# Print the IP address
_IP=$(hostname -I) || true
if [ "$_IP" ]; then
  printf "My IP address is %s\n" "$_IP"
fi

exit 0
```

You can then add the following line to start tightvnc just before the `exit 0`:

```
vncserver :1 -geometry 1920x1080 -depth 24
```

If you want a proper start process, you can use something like the following script as the file `/etc/init.d/tightvnc`:

```
### BEGIN INIT INFO
# Provides: tightvnc
# Required-Start: $remote_fs $syslog
# Required-Stop: $remote_fs $syslog
# Default-Start: 2 3 4 5
# Default-Stop: 0 1 6
# Short-Description: Start Tight VNC Server at boot time
# Description: Start Tight VNC Server at boot time.
### END INIT INFO
#! /bin/sh
# /etc/init.d/tightvnc

USER=pi
HOME=/home/pi
export USER HOME

case "$1" in
 start)
   echo "Starting Tight VNC Server"
   /usr/bin/vncserver :1 -geometry 1920x1080 -depth 24
;;
```

```
 stop)
   echo "Stopping Tight VNC Server"
   /usr/bin/vncserver -kill :1
   ;;

 *)
   echo "Usage: /etc/init.d/tightvnc {start|stop}"
   exit 1
   ;;
esac

exit 0
```

Once you have created this file, you need to execute the following command to allow the script to be executed:

```
$ sudo chmod +x /etc/init.d/tightvnc
```

Then you can start and stop the script with /etc/init.d/tightvnc. Be aware that the first time you run this script you will have to enter a VNC password again as this script is being run as root, rather than the Pi user. Finally, you can set the script to automatically boot with this:

```
$ sudo update-rc.d tightvnc defaults:
update-rc.d: using dependency based boot sequencing
```

Now that you have installed and configured VNC on your Pi and been able to remove the dependency on human input devices for working with the Pi, you can move into the next area.

True WiPi with WiFi

From your earlier work with VNC and SSH, you will have come to realize that in removing human input devices, you have increased the dependency on your network connection. This dependency comes in the form of management because you can't interact directly via keyboard and monitor anymore; you need to have another access method: the Ethernet network connection. Of course, this is still a wire, so you may as well keep the input devices, right? There is a very obvious solution here—WiFi—but to the chagrin of many people the Raspberry Pi doesn't come with WiFi on the board itself. You will need to go out and purchase a wireless adapter for your Pi if you wish to use one.

Okay, simple enough, you say, and off you pop down to the local computer hardware store to pick up a wireless adapter. You look around and urgh. There are so many wireless adapters available! So which of the dozens available is best for the Pi? Will all of them even work with the Pi? While most people would intuitively go and pick up the cheapest that will fit in with their WiFi setup at home, this is not the correct thing to do here as there are other factors at play.

First, all USB devices require power, and, as you are well aware, the Raspberry Pi runs on 5 volts of power. This means that you will need to get a wireless device that runs on a lower amount of power (if you place too much draw on your Pi's USB you can crash it), or you will need to invest in a powered USB device that connects to an external power source (not good for your purposes, but I will cover this later because there are other uses for them). So you need to be mindful of power; you also need to be mindful of compatibility as some of the stranger wireless adapters may not have support within Linux systems. I have included some data from the Raspberry Pi community on their experiences with various wireless adapters to supplement my own.

As you can see in Figure 9-3, I chose to use a D-Link DWA-131 wireless adapter purchased from my local tech store. The rest of this example will cover some of the basics of getting your Pi to communicate with your local wireless network using the DWA-131.

***Figure 9-3.** D-Link DWA-131 802.11n wireless N nano adapter*

■ **Note** Your Pi may restart when you connect the wireless adapter, so save any work beforehand.

This doesn't mean you need to use this particular adapter alone; the setup of most wireless adapters to work with your Pi should be the same process once you have managed to get it to register correctly. So without further ado, start and plug in the wireless adapter and get to work. The current state of the board is shown in Figure 9-4.

***Figure 9-4.** Three down, two to go!*

As you can see, I have still got my Ethernet cable attached for now. I will show you how to configure wireless on your Pi from both the command line and the GUI. Before you jump straight into configuration, you need to know exactly what you are working with, so jump into the shell and run the `lsusb` command, which is just like the `ls` command, but for USB devices.

```
$ lsusb
Bus 001 Device 001: ID 1d6b:0002 Linux Foundation 2.0 root hub
Bus 001 Device 002: ID 0424:9512 Standard Microsystems Corp.
Bus 001 Device 003: ID 0424:ec00 Standard Microsystems Corp.
Bus 001 Device 004: ID 07d1:3303 D-Link System DWA-131 802.11n Wireless N Nano Adapter(rev.A1)
[Realtek RTL8192SU]
```

Perfect! You can see from this command that my wireless adapter has been recognized by the system and should be able to function—fantastic. If not, don't fear; you will simply need to install the driver for your particular network card. A small amount of Google research and you should be able to find the chipset of the WiFi card. The *chipset* refers to the small silicon chip inside the wireless adapter that "runs" the wireless adapter. The chipset is often manufactured by an entirely different company from the one whose badge appears on the device, and it is the chipset with which you need to interface and is thus what determines which drivers you need to find. Once you have found the chipset, a quick search on this should point out what driver packages you will need to install. Once you have installed your driver packages and you can see your wireless adapter in `lsusb`, you can move to the next step.

Since you have the device installed and registered, you should check that the device has registered correctly as a network device. When working with Linux, the most common tool for network management is `ifconfig`. So go ahead and run `ifconfig` and examine the output:

```
$ ifconfig
eth0      Link encap:Ethernet  HWaddr b8:27:eb:8a:46:ba
          inet addr:10.0.0.20  Bcast:10.0.0.255  Mask:255.255.255.0
          UP BROADCAST RUNNING MULTICAST  MTU:1500  Metric:1
          RX packets:6558 errors:0 dropped:0 overruns:0 frame:0
          TX packets:268 errors:0 dropped:0 overruns:0 carrier:0
          collisions:0 txqueuelen:1000
          RX bytes:374403 (365.6 KiB)  TX bytes:28129 (27.4 KiB)

lo        Link encap:Local Loopback
          inet addr:127.0.0.1  Mask:255.0.0.0
          UP LOOPBACK RUNNING  MTU:16436  Metric:1
          RX packets:0 errors:0 dropped:0 overruns:0 frame:0
          TX packets:0 errors:0 dropped:0 overruns:0 carrier:0
          collisions:0 txqueuelen:0
          RX bytes:0 (0.0 B)  TX bytes:0 (0.0 B)

wlan0     Link encap:Ethernet  HWaddr 90:94:e4:51:81:7a
          UP BROADCAST RUNNING MULTICAST  MTU:1500  Metric:1
          RX packets:0 errors:0 dropped:0 overruns:0 frame:0
          TX packets:0 errors:0 dropped:0 overruns:0 carrier:0
          collisions:0 txqueuelen:1000
          RX bytes:0 (0.0 B)  TX bytes:0 (0.0 B)
```

The previous configuration actually shows information for three devices rather than just the wireless adapter (two of which you saw in Chapter 3):

- It shows first the eth0 device that is the physical Ethernet device.
- Next is the lo adapter; recall that this is the system's internal self-reference device that is used when you want to address traffic to within the Pi (or any system) from itself.
- Finally you have wlan0, which is the wireless device. You should be able to notice a few differences between the eth0 and lo devices and the wlan device—it doesn't have an IP address (denoted by inet addr) or a mask. These are things you will need to configure to get it talking with your wireless network—along with the details of your wireless networks SSID and security arrangements. So that will be your next step.

If your adapter didn't show up, but did register in the lsusb, reboot and perform the same troubleshooting steps. The system may be able to recognize your device, but be unable to interface with it correctly. Installing a driver package for your system will likely be the solution here.

To begin with, make this easy and do the configuration via the GUI, which ironically involves installing something via the command line. Go ahead and fire up apt-get to install wpa-gui. WPA GUI is an application that has recently been added to Raspbian to make the installation and configuration of wireless devices much, much simpler. It is so recent, in fact, that this chapter needed to be rewritten to include it because the version of Raspbian that was used during the first round of the writing did not include it! If you're unsure about whether you have the correct version, you should run this command because there is no harm in doing so. The command to install this application is the following:

```
$ sudo apt-get install wpagui
```

If you have the latest version of Raspbian, which includes wpagui, you will see the following output stating that the package is already installed:

```
Reading package lists... Done
Building dependency tree
Reading state information... Done
wpagui is already the newest version.
0 upgraded, 0 newly installed, 0 to remove and 0 not upgraded.
```

If you have not installed the package, your installation will look something like this:

```
Reading package lists... Done
Building dependency tree
Reading state information... Done
The following extra packages will be installed:
  libaudio2 liblcms1 libmng1 libqt4-svg libqtcore4 libqtgui4 menu
Suggested packages:
  nas liblcms-utils qt4-qtconfig menu-l10n
The following NEW packages will be installed:
  libaudio2 liblcms1 libmng1 libqt4-svg libqtcore4 libqtgui4 menu wpagui
0 upgraded, 8 newly installed, 0 to remove and 96 not upgraded.
Need to get 8,921 kB of archives.
After this operation, 22.6 MB of additional disk space will be used.
Do you want to continue [Y/n]?
```

Fantastic! Now that you have installed `wpagui`, you should be able to make good use of it via the user interface. But before you jump in, go ahead and reboot your Pi because you have made a major change to how the Pi manages your network connections and you want to make sure it's bombproof before continuing. Booted okay? You can run `ifconfig` and the output looks the same, great.

Now you can begin configuring your wireless adapter. You'll start with the GUI and then see how to do it over the command line.

■ **Note** If you notice your Pi slowing or failing to connect to WiFi, it may be your keyboard drawing too much power. Try removing it and using VNC or SSH to configure your wireless.

GUI WiFi Configuration

Log in to the GUI and there should be a new icon called WiFi Config, as shown in Figure 9-5.

Figure 9-5. *WiFi Config icon*

Double-click this icon to open the application and you should be presented with the wpagui window, as shown in Figure 9-6.

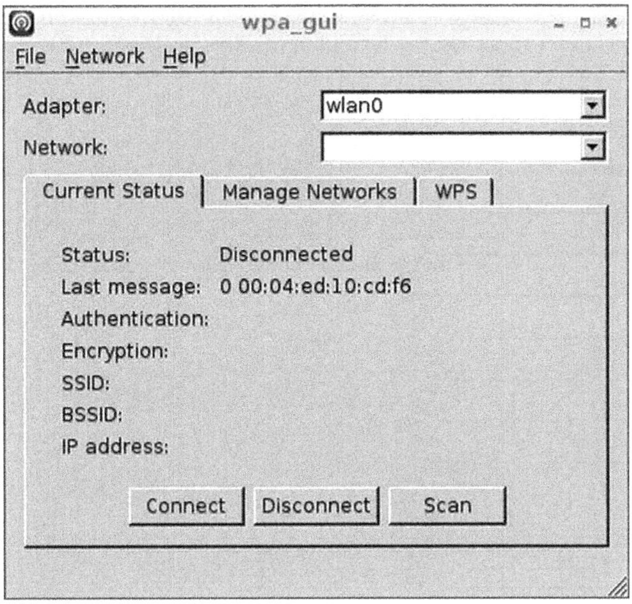

wpa_gui
File Network Help
Adapter: wlan0
Network:
Current Status
Manage Networks
WPS
Status: Disconnected
Last message: 0 00:04:ed:10:cd:f6
Authentication:
Encryption:
SSID:
BSSID:
IP address:
Connect
Disconnect
Scan

Figure 9-6. *wpa_gui window*

From within the wpagui window, press the Scan button. It will take a few moments, but another window will pop up, as shown in Figure 9-7.

wpa_gui
File Network Help
Scan results
SSID BSSID frequency signal flag
wlan-daveh 00:04:ed:10:... 2417 -156 dBm [WP
TawaloWireless 00:24:01:7a:... 2427 -230 dBm [WP
RTA1046VW b4:82:fe:d1:... 2462 -214 dBm [WP
NETGEAR50 84:1b:5e:35:... 2412 -213 dBm [WP
buddha7 34:08:04:a7:... 2452 -200 dBm [WP
Scan
Close

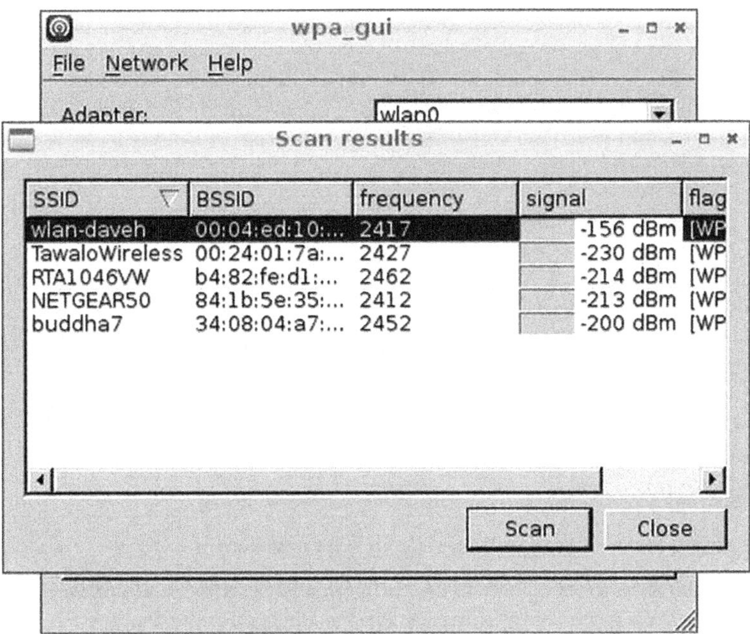

Figure 9-7. *Scan results window*

This window should look familiar to everyone. This is the window for selecting your wireless network. Find your particular network and then double-click it to open the configuration window (see Figure 9-8).

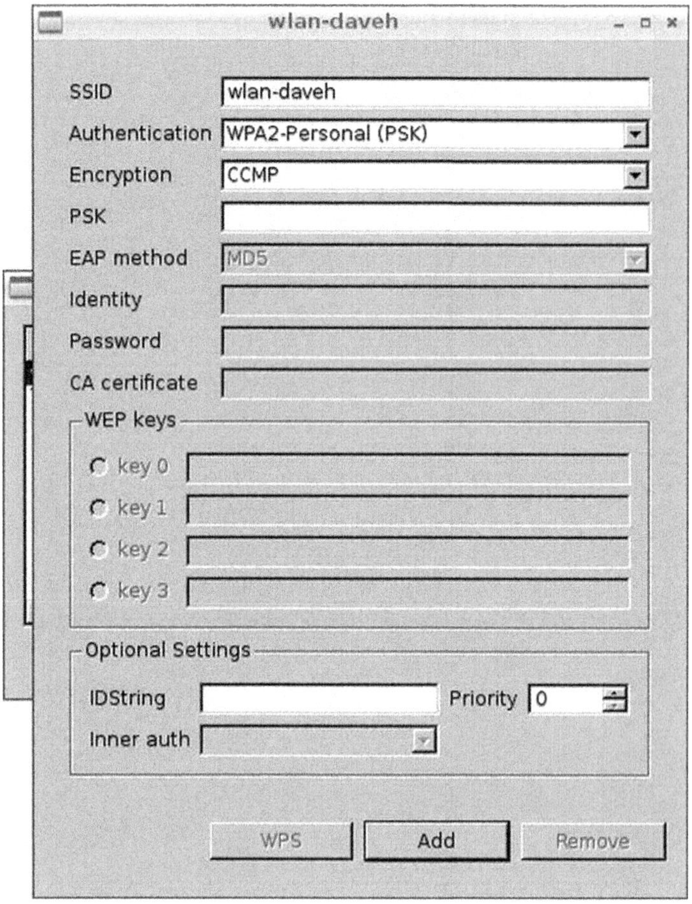

Figure 9-8. *Network details*

I am assuming that you should have your details available to set up your configuration. Most of this is intuitive, but there are a few things you need to be aware of:

- SSID is the "name" given to your wireless network, so you need to type this name.
- Next is Authentication, which specifies the type of authentication that you are using: WEP, WPA, WPA2, and so on.
- Next is Encryption, which selects the encryption mode that you will be using.
- The last is PSK, which stands for preshared key. This is your WiFi password.

Now change to the Wireless Security tab and set up whichever authentication method, encryption method, and password you are using for your WiFi. This information is normally inside your router's configuration system, but can also be written on the router itself or within the router manual. Now click Add. Your wireless settings should be saved into the system and it will pick these up and begin attempting to connect to your adapter; after a few moments, you should expect to see something like Figure 9-9.

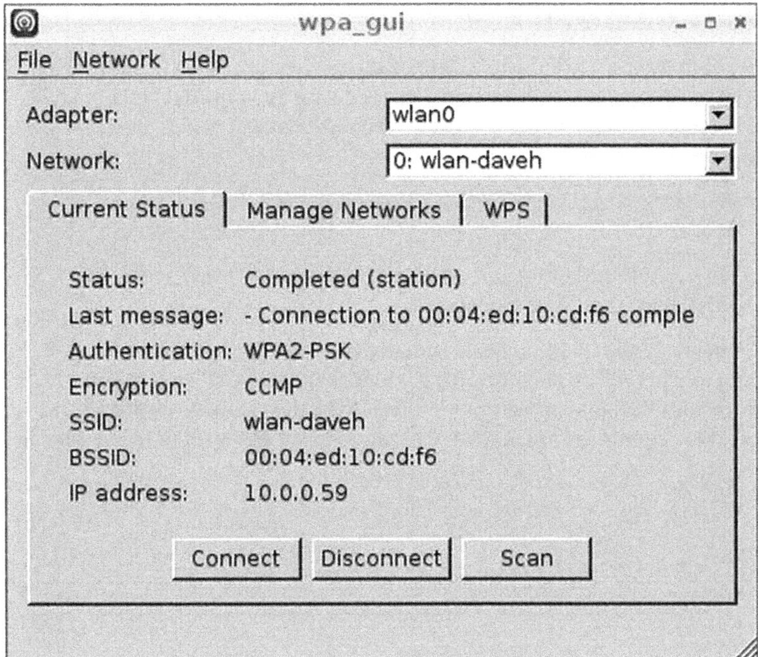

Figure 9-9. *WiFi connected!*

If you didn't see this, have a look at the mouse-over message it should give you an idea of what is going wrong with your connection. Check that your settings are correct and that you have picked the right security method. If in doubt, open your router configuration to double-check. Finally, you can go back into the console and issue `ifconfig` again to check out your wireless adapter settings!

```
wlan0     Link encap:Ethernet  HWaddr 90:94:e4:51:81:7a
          inet addr:10.0.0.59  Bcast:10.0.0.255  Mask:255.255.255.0
          UP BROADCAST RUNNING MULTICAST  MTU:1500  Metric:1
          RX packets:772 errors:0 dropped:10 overruns:0 frame:0
          TX packets:35 errors:0 dropped:0 overruns:0 carrier:0
          collisions:0 txqueuelen:1000
          RX bytes:100749 (98.3 KiB)  TX bytes:4254 (4.1 KiB)
```

That looks much more like what you expect; it has an IP address, mask, and so on. It also shows that it has been sending and receiving packets (those are the RX and TX packet numbers) without error. The final test is to ping that IP address from a second machine, and that's it. You can now go ahead and remove that Ethernet cable. As a final test, go ahead and reboot; you should be able to ping your system on the `wlan0` IP address after the reboot, showing that you have successfully kept the wireless adapter details stored across a reboot. Now you can go ahead and remove that next cable and reboot as you want to ensure your system is using the wireless adapter by default.

Managing WiFi from the Command Line

For those of you who don't really want to use the GUI or who consider themselves purists to the true Linux tradition of using only the command line to manage your systems, this is the bit for you! To do this, you will be modifying the NetworkManager configuration. The basic way the NetworkManager system decides how it should manage your Ethernet devices is twofold:

- It checks to see whether the managed flag in /etc/NetworkManager/NetworkManager.conf is set.
- It takes over management of anything configured within /etc/network/interfaces; these settings say how this device should be managed.

You don't want the NetworkManager system to jump in and take over your settings from above, so you need to ensure that it's not going to. This will be an issue only if you installed the GUI earlier, or if NetworkManager came bundled with your Raspbian image, but it is best to be thorough. So go ahead and check /etc/NetworkManager/NetworkManager.conf and ensure that the managed flag is set to false. The file should look like:

```
[main]
plugins=ifupdown,keyfile

[ifupdown]
managed=false
```

Once this is done, go ahead and reboot your Pi; you want to ensure that the Pi comes up correctly and all existing Ethernet connections are working after this first reboot. Now you need to add the configuration into /etc/network/interfaces so that it knows how to manage the device and connect to your WiFi. So go ahead and open up /etc/network/interfaces. You will see that the file is already partially populated with the following lines:

```
auto lo

iface lo inet loopback
iface eth0 inet dhcp
```

You may also see the following lines in your file, depending on whether your system has already done some wireless configuration or not.

```
allow-hotplug wlan0
iface wlan0 inet manual
wpa-roam /etc/wpa_supplicant/wpa_supplicant.conf
iface default inet dhcp
```

These lines correspond to the loopback and eth0 devices, respectively, and provide some simple details about their management; is in this case, the loopback is an automatically managed loopback device, and the eth0 device is given an IP address via DHCP. There may also be some existing configuration for your wlan0 device; if they exist, you should comment them out by adding a # to the front of them or delete them from the file. You now need to add a new configuration for the wlan0 wireless device, so go ahead and add the following to your config below the existing content:

```
auto wlan0
iface wlan0 inet dhcp
    wpa-ssid <Your WiFi SSID>
    wpa-psk <Your WiFi password>
```

This block says that you will have an automatically managed wlan0 device, which gets its connection information via DHCP. You also pass it the SSID and PSK. This configuration will work for both WPA and WPA2 network security implementations. Once you've finished, it's time to test your new device, so go ahead and run the following, which will start the interface. It may take a few moments, but your output should resemble mine:

```
$ sudo ifdown wlan0
$ sudo ifup wlan0
Internet Systems Consortium DHCP Client 4.2.2
Copyright 2004-2011 Internet Systems Consortium.
All rights reserved.
For info, please visit https://www.isc.org/software/dhcp/

Listening on LPF/wlan0/90:94:e4:51:81:7a
Sending on   LPF/wlan0/90:94:e4:51:81:7a
Sending on   Socket/fallback
DHCPDISCOVER on wlan0 to 255.255.255.255 port 67 interval 8
DHCPDISCOVER on wlan0 to 255.255.255.255 port 67 interval 15
DHCPDISCOVER on wlan0 to 255.255.255.255 port 67 interval 9
DHCPREQUEST on wlan0 to 255.255.255.255 port 67
DHCPOFFER from 10.0.0.1
DHCPACK from 10.0.0.1
bound to 10.0.0.59 -- renewal in 444671 seconds.
```

All this shows that the device has connected to my wireless network and has been given an IP address via DHCP, which is exactly what you told it to do! Now suppose that you don't want to use DHCP, but would rather give your WiFi adapter a static IP address. You simply need to change the iface line to read static rather than dhcp and then add details for your IP address, subnetmask and gateway. Your config will look like this instead:

```
auto wlan0
iface wlan0 inet static
    address 10.0.0.57
    netmask 255.255.255.0
    gateway 10.0.0.1
    wpa-ssid <Your WiFi SSID>
    wpa-psk <Your WiFi password>
```

Now that you have successfully configured wireless on your system, you can go ahead and reboot your Pi to check that the wireless adapter automatically comes up. If not, go back and ensure that you set auto wlan0 and that you enabled the managed=false flag in the NetworkManager config file.

If that doesn't work, go over your configuration settings for SSID and WiFi password. You can confirm whether or not you can start your wireless adapter with `ifup wlan0`; if there are problems connecting and getting an IP address your system should show them here giving you a chance to work out what's going wrong. Finally, if you just can't get it to run, try removing any other attached USB devices; they can draw valuable power away from your WiFi adapter.

One last thing on the command line that may help you is the `iw` series of commands:

- You can run `iwlist` with the `scan` option to get a scan of information about nearby wireless hotspots.
- Or you can use `iwconfig` to get configuration details about your wireless adapter.

Down to One

Congratulations, you are on your way to a fully wireless Raspberry Pi! You have successfully removed the need for an Ethernet cable and you can now access your Pi wirelessly. It should now be down to just one cable! (See Figure 9-10).

Figure 9-10. *Last cable standing*

Removing the Need for Power

There is very little you can do to shortcut the need to provide your Raspberry Pi with power; it needs it, and there are only a finite number of solutions to this problem. By far the most easy and convenient is to get a large USB battery. These are available just about everywhere these days for charging any of the many devices people commonly carry on the go. The simple solution here is to attach your Pi to one of these batteries for use because this kind of battery should guarantee the correct level of power output to your Pi—as they are designed to power USB devices. The important thing when looking at batteries to power your Pi is to be certain they can provide the full 1 amp of power, as some USB batteries are okay for charging but don't pack quite enough juice to power a Pi. Figure 9-11 shows the final WiPi.

Figure 9-11. *WiPi at long last!*

There are a few hacks out there with a combination of rechargeable batteries and solar panels, which will go much further for you, but those are well beyond the scope of this book.

Powered USB Adapters

I made mention earlier that if you place too much draw on your Pi's USB, you can crash it as it has only got a limited power supply of its own. The solution is to get your hands on a powered USB hub. These powered hubs normally have one connection out and a number of connections in and will also have a mains connection with which to supply power. The principle with these is that people rarely use the full data transmission volume of a USB but will often run out of power, so having a way to supplement the power of a USB device with a mains power source is a good way to give people more flexibility with their devices. If you find that when you attach your device your Pi switches itself off, it's a fair bet that you will need something like one of these to help spread out the power load (see Figure 9-12).

Figure 9-12. *Powered USB hub in action*

Summary

After all that work, you should have seen a large payoff. You should now know how to configure your Pi to make it wireless. You should be able to set up and connect to your Pi via a VNC client in addition to the normal SSH connections. You have learned how to configure your Raspberry Pi to take a wireless adapter and can attach it to your existing wireless network. Finally, you should be aware of some of the limitations of your Pi with regard to power consumption and how you can resolve these issues.

CHAPTER 10

The Raspberry sPi

Everyone wants to be James Bond. Or at least I know I do. He seems to get into all sorts of situations; then whips out a handy gadget to save the day. The Raspberry Pi is, as we have shown, supremely versatile for such a tiny little piece of hardware. This makes it the perfect tool for a secret agent because with just a little bit of energy you can provide a fully-fledged technological solution at a fraction of the expense of employing John Cleese (admittedly the Pi is not as funny). So, with this in mind, we can now don our tuxedos and get down to secret agent business.

All good secret agents know that you need to be able to detect and be alerted to intruders in your secret hideout. So this makes it the perfect time to introduce you to the Raspberry sPi! The Raspberry sPi is a combination spy camera and alerting system, the perfect solution for spotting dastardly intruders into your inner sanctum! Or for monitoring your pets over the Internet. The basic concept here is that we will be configuring our Raspberry Pi. So without further ado, let's get started.

Materials Needed

Here are the materials needed for this project (also shown in Figure 10-1):

- 1x Raspberry Pi
- 1x Micro USB cable (for power)
- 1x Ethernet cable
- 1x USB webcam
- 1x SD card

Figure 10-1. *The Raspberry sPi kit*

At this point, you should note that not all webcams are compatible with the Raspberry Pi. This document was created with a Logitech C525 webcam. Thankfully, the Pi community maintains a list of compatible hardware, which is available at `http://elinux.org/RPi_VerifiedPeripherals#USB_Webcams`. If you are in doubt, please check there to see which peripherals will work with your Pi.

Presetup

Nothing special here; just attach your micro USB for power, attach the Ethernet for network access, attach the SD for storage, and make sure you leave the camera unattached—we will do that later. The rest of this process assumes you are familiar with the following:

- Installing the Raspbian OS
- Knowledge of how to work within a Raspbian Linux environment

If you aren't familiar with either of these two, that's perfectly okay. That's what this book is for after all, so please go back and read Chapter 1 for how to get started with Raspbian and Part 2 of this book to gain familiarity with working in a Raspbian Linux environment.

Getting Started

So, without further ado, let's get started. Go ahead and load up Raspbian and connect your Pi to your network. Go through the Raspbian setup procedures and make sure to enable SSH because you will need to remote in later. (We don't see James Bond carrying round a keyboard, HDMI cable, and a monitor, do we?) Once you are set up, go ahead and SSH into your Pi (covered in Chapter 3).

Okay, once you're logged in, go ahead and issue the command `dmesg` and have a look at the output.

dmesg

The dmesg command is a tool called a *driver message* that shows a logged output of all the messages to the kernel, which includes messages from devices and the drivers that are attached to your system. dmesg is infinitely useful in determining which devices are attached, and where and how you should interface with them. It also lists driver and kernel messages that are incredibly useful when diagnosing low-level problems. So, let's have a look at the relevant section of the output.

■ **Note** less is more. If you find that the output for a command is running over the top of the screen and you can't see it any more, reissue the command and then pipe it to less (i.e., dmesg | less). This should allow you to navigate the output of just about any command using the arrow keys and spacebar to page down.

```
[    1.998581] Waiting for root device /dev/mmcblk0p2...
[    2.071268] mmc0: new high speed SD card at address 7d37
[    2.079917] mmcblk0: mmc0:7d37 SD02G 1.83 GiB
[    2.088723]  mmcblk0: p1 p2
[    2.132278] EXT4-fs (mmcblk0p2): mounted filesystem with ordered data mode. Opts: (null)
[    2.145275] VFS: Mounted root (ext4 filesystem) on device 179:2.
[    2.155272] Freeing init memory: 200K
[    2.187333] usb 1-1: new high speed USB device number 2 using dwc_otg
[    2.418045] usb 1-1: New USB device found, idVendor=0424, idProduct=9512
[    2.427750] usb 1-1: New USB device strings: Mfr=0, Product=0, SerialNumber=0
[    2.438708] hub 1-1:1.0: USB hub found
[    2.445041] hub 1-1:1.0: 3 ports detected
[    2.727674] usb 1-1.1: new high speed USB device number 3 using dwc_otg
[    2.837920] usb 1-1.1: New USB device found, idVendor=0424, idProduct=ec00
[    2.857413] usb 1-1.1: New USB device strings: Mfr=0, Product=0, SerialNumber=0
[    2.878968] smsc95xx v1.0.4
[    2.942985] smsc95xx 1-1.1:1.0: eth0: register 'smsc95xx' at usb-bcm2708_usb-1.1,
               smsc95xx USB 2.0 Ethernet, b8:27:eb:8a:46:ba
[   11.006171] EXT4-fs (mmcblk0p2): re-mounted. Opts: (null)
[   11.426960] ### snd_bcm2835_alsa_probe c05c88e0 ############### PROBING FOR bcm2835 ALSA
               device (0):(1) ###############
[   11.442869] Creating card...
[   11.448268] Creating device/chip ..
[   11.454771] Adding controls ..
[   11.460340] Registering card ....
[   11.475463] bcm2835 ALSA CARD CREATED!
[   11.487786] ### BCM2835 ALSA driver init OK ###
[   18.493739] smsc95xx 1-1.1:1.0: eth0: link up, 100Mbps, full-duplex, lpa 0x45E1
[   24.672322] Adding 102396k swap on /var/swap.  Priority:-1 extents:1 across:102396k SS
```

As you can see, the output from dmesg is a little offputting and hard to understand. Much of the information relies on understanding a few basic tenets of how the dmesg system works. First is the numerical values within the square brackets [and]. This value is a timer value that registers the amount of time that has passed since system launch. This is a good way to follow the sequence of events in your system and to tell recent ones from those that occurred in the past.

Next is the content itself. Most of these lines are diagnostically useless alone, but together they form a very interesting picture of what exactly has gone on in my Pi. Let's start with the first line:

```
waiting on root device /dev/mmcblk0p2
```

The first few lines are obvious: the system is waiting for something, but what is /dev/mmcblk0p2? Well, the first giveaway is the /dev; this is where the Linux OS lists all its devices so we know /dev/mmcblk0p2 is a device. Second is the mmcblk0p2, which looks like a string of garbage but is actually a series of abbreviations.

- mmc means multimediacard (the flash device standard)
- blk means a block storage device
- 0 means the first logical device of this type
- p2 means partition two of the device

So we are waiting for the SD card. The second through fourth lines are what we are waiting for: the SD card to register as you can see it actually registers as each of the subdevices we mentioned, in order no less! After that, the next two lines are the device mounting the filesystem on this device as readable. Continuing down, you can see the registration of the Pi's USB devices (lines 8-15), its Ethernet port (lines 16, 17, and 26) and finally an Advanced Linux Sound Architecture (ALSA) device, which is the audio port (lines 19-25).

Now that you understand why we didn't just attach the webcam to begin with, I wanted to view the dmesg output. Given that you know what to look for, now go ahead and attach your webcam and run dmesg again. Have a look at the new lines that have shown up. These should all be related to your newly attached webcam! Here is the output from me attaching mine:

```
[ 8168.793423] usb 1-1.2: new high speed USB device number 4 using dwc_otg
[ 8169.147691] usb 1-1.2: New USB device found, idVendor=046d, idProduct=081d
[ 8169.147736] usb 1-1.2: New USB device strings: Mfr=0, Product=0, SerialNumber=1
[ 8169.147758] usb 1-1.2: SerialNumber: 8627F4C0
[ 8169.314171] Linux video capture interface: v2.00
[ 8169.336482] uvcvideo: Found UVC 1.00 device <unnamed> (046d:081d)
[ 8169.402071] input: UVC Camera (046d:081d) as /devices/platform/bcm2708_usb/usb1/1-1/1-
               1.2/1-1.2:1.2/input/input0
[ 8169.402280] usbcore: registered new interface driver uvcvideo
[ 8169.402299] USB Video Class driver (1.1.1)
[ 8169.460903] usbcore: registered new interface driver snd-usb-audio
```

So, what can you tell from these lines? For starters, you can see a large difference in timing for this particular entry in the dmesg log, which represents the delay from start up until I connected my device. Next, you will recognize that the first four lines represent the USB ports picking up a new attached device; in fact, the first line references the module used to do this dwc_otg (short for DesignWare Cores—On The Go). Line 5 shows that it's a video capture interface, and line 6 shows that the module uvcvideo found a USB Video Class (UVC) device that it identifies and registers. Finally, we can also see that the webcam's microphone has also been registered on the last line as a snd-usb-audio device. From this we can see that my webcam has been attached and has registered itself with a driver into the OS.

Now that the device has been registered, we need a way to reference it so it can be used by an application. You will notice that the dmesg output didn't actually specify which device we added, so let's have a look and see if we can't match it the other way. Let's start by listing the contents of /dev (results shown in Figure 10-2).

```
$ ls /dev/
```

```
pi@raspberrypi ~ $ ls /dev/
autofs           loop0          network_latency     ram4     tty0   tty23  tty38  tty52  ttyAMA0    vcs5
block            loop1          network_throughput  ram5     tty1   tty24  tty39  tty53  ttyprintk  vcs6
btrfs-control    loop2          null                ram6     tty10  tty25  tty4   tty54  uinput     vcsa
bus              loop3          ppp                 ram7     tty11  tty26  tty40  tty55  urandom    vcsa1
cachefiles       loop4          ptmx                ram8     tty12  tty27  tty41  tty56  usbdev1.1  vcsa2
char             loop5          pts                 ram9     tty13  tty28  tty42  tty57  usbdev1.2  vcsa3
console          loop6          ram0                random   tty14  tty29  tty43  tty58  usbdev1.3  vcsa4
cpu_dma_latency  loop7          ram1                raw      tty15  tty3   tty44  tty59  usbdev1.4  vcsa5
disk             loop-control   ram10               root     tty16  tty30  tty45  tty6   v4l        vcsa6
fb0              MAKEDEV        ram11               shm      tty17  tty31  tty46  tty60  vchiq      video0
fd               mapper         ram12               snd      tty18  tty32  tty47  tty61  vc-mem     xconsole
full             mem            ram13               sndstat  tty19  tty33  tty48  tty62  vcs        zero
fuse             mmcblk0        ram14               stderr   tty2   tty34  tty49  tty63  vcs1
input            mmcblk0p1      ram15               stdin    tty20  tty35  tty5   tty7   vcs2
kmsg             mmcblk0p2      ram2                stdout   tty21  tty36  tty50  tty8   vcs3
log              net            ram3                tty      tty22  tty37  tty51  tty9   vcs4
pi@raspberrypi ~ $
```

Figure 10-2. *Contents of /dev directory*

That is a few devices. We can quickly eliminate a few right off the bat: all the `tty` devices because they are teletype devices, all the `ram` devices because that's the Pi's RAM, all the `loop` devices because they are loop back connectors, all the `memblck` devices because they relate to the SD card, and all the `vcs` devices because they are virtual consoles. There are still a few, but the best looking is `video0`. We are looking for a webcam, right? It registered as a video capture device didn't it? Okay, so we think that's right—but how can we tell?

udev, more specifically the `udev` administration function, is the device manager for the Linux kernel. It governs how and where devices register themselves so that they can be accessed as part of the OS by applications. In Debian (and thus Raspbian), the inner workings of `udev` can be accessed with the `udevadm` command, so let's go ahead and use it. Execute the following:

```
$ udevadm info -a -p  $(udevadm info -q path -n /dev/video0)
P: /devices/platform/bcm2708_usb/usb1/1-1/1-1.2/1-1.2:1.2/video4linux/video0
N: video0
S: v4l/by-id/usb-046d_081d_8627F4C0-video-index0
S: v4l/by-path/platform-bcm2708_usb-usb-0:1.2:1.2-video-index0
E: DEVLINKS=/dev/v4l/by-id/usb-046d_081d_8627F4C0-video-index0 /dev/v4l/by-path/platform-
   bcm2708_usb-usb-0:1.2:1.2-video-index0
E: DEVNAME=/dev/video0
E: DEVPATH=/devices/platform/bcm2708_usb/usb1/1-1/1-1.2/1-1.2:1.2/video4linux/video0
E: ID_BUS=usb
E: ID_MODEL=081d
E: ID_MODEL_ENC=081d
E: ID_MODEL_ID=081d
E: ID_PATH=platform-bcm2708_usb-usb-0:1.2:1.2
E: ID_PATH_TAG=platform-bcm2708_usb-usb-0_1_2_1_2
E: ID_REVISION=0010
E: ID_SERIAL=046d_081d_8627F4C0
E: ID_SERIAL_SHORT=8627F4C0
E: ID_TYPE=video
E: ID_USB_DRIVER=uvcvideo
E: ID_USB_INTERFACES=:010100:010200:0e0100:0e0200:
E: ID_USB_INTERFACE_NUM=02
E: ID_V4L_CAPABILITIES=:capture:
E: ID_V4L_PRODUCT=UVC Camera (046d:081d)
E: ID_V4L_VERSION=2
```

```
E: ID_VENDOR=046d
E: ID_VENDOR_ENC=046d
E: ID_VENDOR_ID=046d
E: MAJOR=81
E: MINOR=0
E: SUBSYSTEM=video4linux
E: TAGS=:udev-acl:
E: UDEV_LOG=3
E: USEC_INITIALIZED=8168852755
```

Wow, okay, that's a big block of scary looking output. As I'm sure you've guessed by now, we just asked the udev system to give us an info query for all info relevant to the device with name /dev/video0, which it well and truly has. However, before hyperventilation sets in, actually have a look at the first few lines. The first line should spring out as familiar—it's the device identifier that we saw in dmesg from when the webcam was attached! In fact, most of the information in here is all data that was referenced somewhere in the dmesg block. Okay, so given that we can match the device from dmesg to the device here in our system, it's safe to say that the USB webcam we attached is available on the filesystem as /dev/video0.

Troubleshooting

If, unlike mine, your webcam had issues when registering with the kernel in dmesg, you may need to install a driver. You should check with the manufacturer and online to see whether there is a driver that's available for your webcam. If so, install the driver and then try reattaching your webcam to see if it can be registered. You may even get lucky, and your device driver will have the kernel list where the webcam is registered in /dev in dmesg—as it did with my SD card in the preceding example.

Additionally, if you don't have a device such as /dev/video0 listed, you should check to see whether any of the other devices match up with output that relates to your device from dmesg. While Linux tries to be sensible in how the /dev filesystem is laid out, manufacturers and software engineers can do funny things to try and stand out—with the upshot that you sit there screaming about how you cannot find a device. So just be patient and have a look around and use the process of elimination to try and work out where your device has been attached. The goal here is to ensure that you know which /dev file references your webcam.

Motion Capture

Okay, system configured, check. Webcam attached, check. Now let's make all this actually do something! To do the webcam capture, we will be using the Linux motion capture ironically named *motion*. So let's go ahead and install it. Run the following command to direct apt-get to download and install the motion package:

```
$ sudo apt-get install motion
```

Your output should resemble the following:

```
Reading package lists... Done
Building dependency tree
Reading state information... Done
The following extra packages will be installed:
  ffmpeg libav-tools libavcodec53 libavdevice53 libavfilter2 libavformat53 libavutil51
libdc1394-22 libdirac-You
  libjack-jackd2-0 libmp3lame0 libpostproc52 libpq5 libraw1394-11 libschroedinger-1.0-0
libspeex1 libswscale2 libtheora0 libva1
```

```
  libvpx1 libx264-123 libxvidcore4
Suggested packages:
  jackd2 libraw1394-doc speex mysql-client postgresql-client
The following NEW packages will be installed:
  ffmpeg libav-tools libavcodec53 libavdevice53 libavfilter2 libavformat53 libavutil51
libdc1394-22 libdirac-encoder0 libgsm1
  libjack-jackd2-0 libmp3lame0 libpostproc52 libpq5 libraw1394-11 libschroedinger-1.0-0
libspeex1 libswscale2 libtheora0 libva1
  libvpx1 libx264-123 libxvidcore4 motion
0 upgraded, 24 newly installed, 0 to remove and 71 not upgraded.
Need to get 8,365 kB of archives.
After this operation, 17.6 MB of additional disk space will be used.
Do you want to continue [Y/n]? y
```

I don't know about you, but I'm way too excited to bother with all the setup and config; let's just fire up motion and see what it does! Start it up with this:

```
$ motion -s
```

The light on the camera goes on and action! Start waving and moving about, because you want it to capture you!

```
[1] Changes:  3374 - noise level: 15
[1] Changes:  3198 - noise level: 15
[1] Changes:  3011 - noise level: 15
[1] Changes:  2922 - noise level: 15
[1] Changes:  2555 - noise level: 15
[1] Changes:  2390 - noise level: 15
[1] Changes:  2491 - noise level: 15
[1] Changes:  2874 - noise level: 15
[1] Changes:  2817 - noise level: 15
[1] Changes:  3238 - noise level: 15
[1] Changes:  3093 - noise level: 15
[1] Motion detected - starting event 1
[1] File of type 1 saved to: ./01-20120910203217-05.jpg
[1] Changes:  2912 - noise level: 15
[1] File of type 1 saved to: ./01-20120910203217-06.jpg
[1] Changes:  2480 - noise level: 15
[1] File of type 1 saved to: ./01-20120910203217-07.jpg
```

There you go, you can see it capturing changes in the image and registering any changes in noise level as you move. And finally, it's capturing images! If it may take a moment to write the image file out, depending on your SD card speed—so be patient. Awesome, works like a charm, to cancel out of the application you can go ahead and press Ctrl+C. If you want, you can go ahead and log in with console to have a look at any images it's captured. Inspecting the output is generally a good idea because your webcam driver may need fine tuning or may not generate valid output. If you don't want to get out a cable and HDMI, you can copy these images off with tools such as scp. From a Windows machine, you can use a tool such as winscp to copy any files off. If you are copying to a Mac or Linux system, you just need to copy the files by issuing the following command:

```
$ scp <raspberry pi's ip>:/home/pi/*.jpg.
```

■ **Note** Please remember the period on the end of the scp command It's important because it is the destination identifier for the command.

This command says to copy from the server on the Raspberry Pi identified by IP in the directory /home/pi the home directory of the pi user and the first place you will be when you log in (I said I was excited, didn't I?) and match any file that ends in .jpg. The final period on the end is the destination: in Linux a period is a reference to the current directory, so that's where we are copying.

OK, now that we have had fun with the pictures, let's get down to business. The aim for the Raspberry sPi is to have it function with no intervention; this means we will need to have the motion application function without us telling it to. Raspbian has handled most of this for us already, but there are still a few little things we need to do.

■ **Note** You will need to edit these files as root, so remember to start your text editor with sudo.

First, open and edit the file /etc/default/motion and change the line start_motion_daemon=no to be start_motion_daemon=yes; this file governs whether the daemon will start when we issue the daemon's start command, and having it run on command is exactly what we want. Now we tackle the config, so go ahead and open it. The file is /etc/motion/motion.conf, so open it up. First thing you will note is that daemon mode will be set to off, so go ahead and set that to on because we want motion to be started as a daemon, which means it will run in the background. Next thing to check is the videodevice line and ensure that the listed device matches the devices we confirmed earlier (for most of us, that should be /dev/video0).

Following this, we begin getting into the nuts and bolts of the situation. First we can modify the height, width, and framerate. The defaults are to capture two images per second at a resolution of 320 x 240. This creates a file about 12 Kb in size—you can check by examining the files that we generated earlier during our testing of the motion capture. You can increase this as you see fit; just remember not to exceed the maximum available resolution of your webcam and also that each file will increase in size as resolution increases.

Next is threshold. The threshold value is the amount of change that needs to occur so that an image will be captured. You can leave this value for now, but remember it later because you may want to make the capture more or less sensitive.

Next is ffmpeg_cap_new, which determines whether or not you want to capture a video file. I have turned this one off, but you can keep it on if you want to generate video files of your motion captures. These files are generated as .swf files now (think YouTube) but you can change them by editing the ffmpeg_video_codec variable.

Finally, you can change the target_dir, which says where you will output the image files when running as a daemon. This one is important because you will need to know where you are to copy your files from. Additionally, it's important to be aware that the /tmp directory is just that, a temporary space. This temporary space is emptied each time your OS is restarted.

This kind of functionality is perfect for what we intend because we don't want to have to deal with extra files that will stay on the disk until we clean it out; simply reboot your Raspberry sPi and off you go again. However, there are cases where we may want these files to be saved beyond a restart of the system—but more on them later.

Finally, save all your changes and exit so we can test the new config! My config is displayed here for your reference:

```
daemon on
process_id_file /var/run/motion/motion.pid
setup_mode off
videodevice /dev/video0
```

```
v4l2_palette 8
input 8
norm 0
frequency 0
rotate 0
width 320
height 240
framerate 2
minimum_frame_time 0
netcam_tolerant_check off
auto_brightness off
brightness 0
contrast 0
saturation 0
hue 0
roundrobin_frames 1
roundrobin_skip 1
switchfilter off
threshold 1500
threshold_tune off
noise_level 32
noise_tune on
despeckle EedDl
smart_mask_speed 0
lightswitch 0
minimum_motion_frames 1
pre_capture 0
post_capture 0
gap 60
max_mpeg_time 0
output_all off
output_normal on
output_motion off
quality 75
ppm off
ffmpeg_cap_new off
ffmpeg_cap_motion off
ffmpeg_timelapse 0
ffmpeg_timelapse_mode daily
ffmpeg_bps 500000
ffmpeg_variable_bitrate 0
ffmpeg_video_codec swf
ffmpeg_deinterlace off
snapshot_interval 0
locate off
text_right %Y-%m-%d\n%T-%q
text_changes off
text_event %Y%m%d%H%M%S
target_dir /tmp/motion
snapshot_filename %v-%Y%m%d%H%M%S-snapshot
jpeg_filename %v-%Y%m%d%H%M%S-%q
```

```
movie_filename %v-%Y%m%d%H%M%S
timelapse_filename %Y%m%d-timelapse
webcam_port 8081
webcam_quality 50
webcam_motion off
webcam_maxrate 1
webcam_localhost on
webcam_limit 0
control_port 8080
control_localhost on
control_html_output on
track_type 0
track_auto off
track_motorx 0
track_motory 0
track_maxx 0
track_maxy 0
track_iomojo_id 0
track_step_angle_x 10
track_step_angle_y 10
track_move_wait 10
track_speed 255
track_stepsize 40
```

This test will be just like the one before; we simply want to start motion and check that it will run and capture images. This time, however, we want to use the config file and the Linux start commands because it allows us to emulate a power on of our Raspberry sPi. So go ahead and execute `sudo /etc/init.d/motion start` this should start motion. You should see your camera light come on and if you move about, you should start seeing image captures appear almost immediately in `/tmp/motion` (or wherever you pointed target_dir). You can also check that the process is running by typing the following to check for a running motion process:

```
$ ps -ef | grep motion
```

Troubleshooting

Still not working? Go back over the section on connecting your webcam, unplug it, plug it back in, and check for the output from `dmesg`. Validate that the output you see in `dmesg` matches what you get from `udev` in examining the device you have said is your webcam. Did the motion package install correctly? examine the output from `apt-get` to see that it did; if not, try installing again or try this:

```
$ apt-get --reinstall install motion
```

Does motion run when you execute it on the command line with `motion -s`? If not, examine the messages on the screen, which will help you understand what has gone wrong.

If all that failed, go over your motion configuration file. Did you accidentally mis-set one of the variables? Did you forget to set the value in `/etc/default/motion` to yes? Is the motion daemon running, but you can't see images appear in your given output directory? If not, examine the files `/var/log/messages` and `/var/log/syslog`, which is a repository of messages from daemons started by the system, including motion. The output that was onscreen before should now be in this file.

One of the problems I ran into when testing this setup was that the motion daemon was unable to write to the /tmp/motion directory as this was initially created by the root user. I found the following line in /var/log/syslog which showed the problem clearly.

```
Mar 24 20:58:22 raspberrypi motion: [1] Error opening file /tmp/motion/01-20150324205822-01.
jpg with mode w: Permission denied
```

To resolve this issue I had to change the permissions of this directory to grant the “motion” user which starts the motion daemon access. This was accomplished with the following chown command

```
sudo chown motion /tmp/motion/
```

Alerting Yourself

Thus far, we have attached a webcam, configured the webcam, installed motion detection software and configured it to start automatically along with your Raspberry sPi. Now we have a fully fledged monitoring system that you can use to spy on your enemies and keep you notified about intruders entering your inner sanctum. Well, almost. You now need to create a system that will allow you to send messages to yourself so that you can be alerted when intruders enter.

To do this, we will be taking advantage of one of the oldest and most efficient messaging systems ever developed: e-mail. We won’t, however, be going as far as to set up our own mail server and domain; that’s a big task and well outside the scope of what we will be doing in this chapter. Instead, we will be aiming to set up a lightweight mail client to forward messages to a mail service in which it can then be sent on to you on whatever handy spy gadget you use to receive e-mail. Now that you understand the plan, let’s begin.

Installing SSMTP

The application we will be using to send our mail to the mail server is called SSMTP. SSMTP is a highly simplified mail transfer agent (MTA) that is used when a system administrator needs to be able to send mail from a server, but doesn’t need to be set up as a fully fledged mail domain. The advantage here should be obvious: a significantly less intensive setup process and much lower overhead—all of which should scream Raspberry Pi to you.

With all this in mind, let’s begin. Start by issuing the command to download and install the SSMTP application and install it:

```
$ sudo apt-get install ssmtp
```

Your output should look like mine:

```
$ sudo apt-get install ssmtp
Reading package lists... Done
Building dependency tree
Reading state information... Done
The following extra packages will be installed:
  libgnutls-openssl27
The following NEW packages will be installed:
  libgnutls-openssl27 ssmtp
0 upgraded, 2 newly installed, 0 to remove and 71 not upgraded.
Need to get 272 kB of archives.
After this operation, 279 kB of additional disk space will be used.
Do you want to continue [Y/n]?
```

Once we have installed SSMTP we need to configure it. The SSMTP configuration file is `/etc/ssmtp/ssmtp.conf`. Open it up with your favorite text editor and get started.

The first thing we need to configure is where the mail is destined to go. Most people who read this book will have some different and specific location they want their mail to go. Although all good spies want to be as efficient as possible, I can deal only with what's in front of me, so we will be configuring this for the most generic and free option available to everyone: Gmail.

So we need to configure where the mail is to be sent; in SSMTP, this is governed by the `mailhub` value. This value is the DNS name of the mail server for the domain we will use to send outbound mail. This name is traditionally *mail.<yourdomain>.<whatever>*, but for us it will be `smtp.gmail.com:587`, which is Google's SMTP server.

Having set the Gmail server, you may have noticed that we included a `:587` on the end. The studious among you will recognize this as a port number. The even more studious would be aware that 587 is not the default port for SMTP (it is port 25). It is the port dedicated for Transport Layer Security (TLS) e-mail, (secure e-mail over SSL). This means we need to add another pair of options to ensure that we have encrypted communications:

```
UseTLS=YES
UseSTARTTLS=YES
```

The next option to configure is the `hostname` option, which is the hostname listed by the Raspberry sPi. Go ahead and list a hostname for the sPi if you have a domain. If not, just give it something like `raspberry.spi`. The next option should be `FromLineOverride=yes`, which allows us to set the "from" field on an e-mail if we so desire.

Finally, the last sets of options are related to authentication. There are three options you need to configure here. The first two are the most obvious: username and password. So go ahead and add `AuthUser=username@gmail.com` and `AuthPass=password`. The third, which is a little more circuitous, is the `AuthMethod` option, which is used to specify which authentication method will be used to allow users to register with the server. The method we will be using for Google is the `LOGIN` method. Although other mail servers may not require this to be specified, with Google we should set `AuthMethod=LOGIN`.

That's it; your config should now look something like this:

```
root=
Mailhub=smtp.gmail.com:587
UseTLS=YES
UseSTARTTLS=YES
Hostname=raspberry.spi
FromLineOverride=yes
AuthUser=username@gmail.com
AuthPass=password
AuthMethod=LOGIN
```

■ **Note** It should go without saying, but you should always have a secure root password.

One final change to make is to secure this data so that nobody except those that we intend can read the file. This is incredibly important because you have put your precious GMail password in the file! The solution is to change permissions so that nobody but the intended users can read it. Execute the following:

```
$ sudo chmod 640 /etc/ssmtp/ssmtp.conf
```

This will change the file so that the only user who can access it is root, and the only users who can are members of the mail group.

Once SSMTP is configured, all you need to do is invoke it to send the e-mail and get it to send the captured... Wait. There's something more we need; we need a way to invoke SSMTP so that we can tell it to send the file to our e-mail and alert us to the intruders. And we need a tool that can do all this from the command line. The best tool here is one called `mutt`.

Installing and Using mutt

The `mutt` tool is a text-based e-mail client with the fantastic motto of "All mail clients suck. This one just sucks less." (Isn't it obvious why we are using it?) The other benefit of `mutt` over other mail clients is that it is happy to send attachments from files on the filesystem—which is key to what we need to make the sPi send images of our intruders.

Now you know that it is `mutt` that we are installing, go ahead and install it by using the following:

```
$ sudo apt-get install mutt
```

Your output should look like this:

```
Reading package lists... Done
Building dependency tree
Reading state information... Done
The following extra packages will be installed:
  libgpgme11 libpth20 libtokyocabinet9
Suggested packages:
  gpgsm gnupg2 urlview mixmaster
The following NEW packages will be installed:
  libgpgme11 libpth20 libtokyocabinet9 mutt
0 upgraded, 4 newly installed, 0 to remove and 71 not upgraded.
Need to get 1,985 kB of archives.
After this operation, 7,181 kB of additional disk space will be used.
```

Did `mutt` install okay? Good. As I mentioned earlier, `mutt` is designed to be small, simple, and easy to use and configure—lofty goals. With that in mind, the setup process for mutt is incredibly simple: we just need to tell `mutt` how to use our MTA (which is SSMTP). To do this, we need to create a file that will live hidden in the Pi users' home directory. The file is `.muttrc`, which will contain only one line:

```
set sendmail="/usr/sbin/ssmtp""
```

Instead of using a text editor we will use a "cheat" to do this. Run the following command:

```
$ echo "set sendmail=\"/usr/sbin/ssmtp\"" > ~/.muttrc
```

That's it.

■ **Note** The backslashes before the quotation marks are escapes.

You can go and look in the root user's home directory for the file `.muttrc` and check the contents. Yep, it's there and exactly as expected. The `.muttrc` file is a config file used by `mutt` to load important configuration options automatically on startup. Many different applications use hidden files that end in rc, so if you are wondering how an application is storing certain configuration options, have a look in your home directory for files starting with a period and ending in rc.

Testing the Alerting System

Now that we have installed and configured SSMTP and mutt, we need to test them in combination. The way to use mutt is, strangely enough, to run the mutt command. The syntax is rather simple, so send yourself an e-mail from the command line. Execute the following command:

```
$ echo "the quick brown fox jumps over the lazy dog" | sudo mutt -s "[INTRUDER ALERT] Test
of intruder system" <your email>@gmail.com
```

I know it's a long command, but don't worry because I will explain it in a moment. Go ahead and check your e-mail; you should have one there from the user root just as shown in Figure 10-3!

Now I'll explain the syntax and how we will use this to send alert messages from the sPi. The preceding message can be broken down into a few much smaller segments. The basic syntax that I use is this:

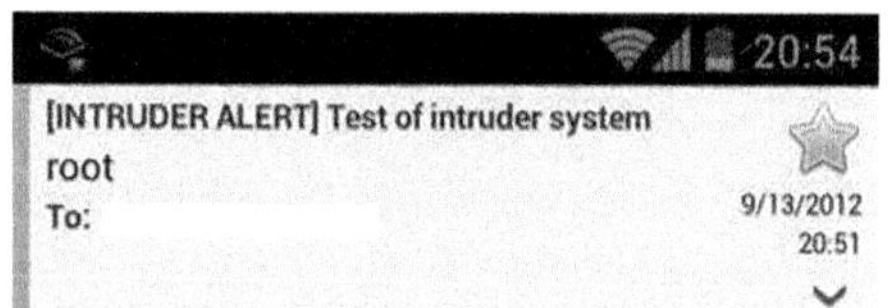

the quick brown fox jumps over the lazy dog

Figure 10-3. *E-mail from the Rasperry sPi*

```
echo <mail content> | mutt -s <subject> <recipient>
```

You may be wondering about the use of echo. You need to generate the value that will be passed as output and then have the pipe direct it into mutt, rather than providing it as an argument.

■ **Note** You can include whole sentences with spaces in a shell command by enclosing the whole thing in quotation marks. You can even escape quotes within a command to create quotes within quotes!

We need to also be able to send attachments with our e-mail. mutt has us covered here because it provides the capability to attach files to its outgoing e-mail. The reason why I elected to use mutt to create the Raspberry sPi is because it is not only easy to configure but also provides the capability to send attachments.

The syntax to send an attachment with the e-mail we just sent is as follows:

```
echo <mail content> | mutt -s <subject> -a <filename> -- <recipient>
```

Yes, it's as easy as that! The -a signifies attachments, and the -- is used to separate attachments from recipients.

Troubleshooting

Did everything work as expected? If not, try configuring both SSMTP and mutt from scratch. When you send an e-mail, does it output an error regarding login details? If so, double-check your username and password. Is it an error regarding unsupported login type? If so check the TLS settings and the AuthMethod setting. Did you spell your mail server incorrectly? Is their trailing whitespace? That is spaces or tabs at the end of any of your entries. When you changed permissions did you move them too far so that now you can no longer read the file?

You may also encounter an error if you try and send an e-mail as the pi user, without sudo because the pi user is not a member of the mail group on your system. If you wish to allow the pi user or any other user for that matter, you need to add them using gpasswd, the syntax is this:

```
$ gpasswd -a <username> mail
```

Okay, so all sorted? You can capture the presence of intruders. You can alert yourself from the Raspberry sPi. You can send the captured images of your intruders to yourself from your sPi. So what's left? Automating it all.

Bringing It All Together

So far we have done the following:

- Attached a webcam to the Raspberry sPi
- Installed and configured the monitor application to use the webcam
- Used the webcam and monitor application to function as a motion sensor and capture images
- Installed and configured SSMTP as an MTA

- Installed and configured `mutt` mail application to use SSMTP
- Sent e-mail from the command line to ourselves using SSMTP and `mutt`

The remaining problem is that we have done most of this with human intervention. We need a solution that enables the capture of images to automatically trigger an e-mail being set to us, with the image attached. Although I'm sure that someone has dreamed up a software solution to this problem, there is no reason why we can't write a solution ourselves!

Understanding the Problem

The first step in any software design problem, no matter how small a job, is to understand what the exact needs of the software solution are. So let's start by listing our goals:

- Capture of a new image should trigger the solution
- An e-mail should be sent with any new captured image(s)
- Should function automatically without needing to be started manually

Okay, that seems like the solution we need. But there are a few other things that having those two main requirements brings into play. These extra requirements are these:

- Only new images should be sent
- Only images captured by motion should be sent
- The application should always be running and not need to be manually started, just like motion

Okay, that seems a bit better; we are now pretty firm on what exactly our software solution should do. But what about how it should do it? Maybe we should be a little specific on how the application we are to write will achieve its goal.

Some things we should consider when developing the application include these:

- We should send the time that the image was captured
- We should check and send regularly, but given that e-mail has a delay, a semiregular check should be enough

Okay, now we're cooking. Those are looking like some good requirements to remember when building our application. We were specific in what we wanted and about how we should achieve it. Now that we know exactly what we want in our application, we can move on to the next step.

Making Decisions

The next step after working out what we want to achieve is to make some decisions about how it should be achieved. So, first decision: how should we write this? Well, much of what we want to achieve here is manipulation of shell commands. We want to list image files and then use those image files within another shell command to send us the e-mail alert. Additionally, you learned bash earlier in this book, so that makes it a perfect fit for what we want to develop.

Okay, we know what language we will be working in. Next, how will we start this one? I see two options here and both will inform which direction we take:

- One is to have the application executed from within the start script for `motion` because we want them to run together. This means that we can ensure that they are both running at the same time and that the script would need to be always running and then check periodically.
- The second option is to have the script automatically executed regularly. This means we wouldn't need to start it and keep the script running permanently. It also means that if the worst happens and the script dies, we don't need to deal with that and reboot it because it will be automatically started again. It does mean that we need to have something that will execute the script on a timer, but that can be handled by the cron daemon.

So, we have two options to decide from, but let's put off that decision for a moment because there is another thing we need to look at first.

What will we do with the images? We have two options again:

- First is to delete each image after we send it. This is good because it means we can save on space as we clean up after ourselves.
- The second option is to keep track of all the images that we have and send only the new ones. This means keeping a running track of which images we have in stock so we can determine which ones to send out.

So, now that you understand the options, it is time to make decisions. I know that it's hard to decide, so let me make it easier for you. Instead of four possible scripts, let's narrow it down to two:

- A script that will be run from `cron` and will search for images, send them, and then remove them
- A script that will start with the `motion` daemon and will monitor all the files, keep a running count and then recognize when there is a new image.

Okay, now that we have two working designs, let's head on to the next step.

Designing Solution

"Wait; you have two solutions and you didn't actually pick one. You giant flake." I hear you say that and it's true; I didn't. Because we had two very different ways to achieve our one goal we felt it would be best to cover both, give you the options, and share some guidance. So, let's start by looking at the commonalities between the two; first, they will both need to have a reference for the folder where `motion`'s captured files will be going. We could keep this in a variable and just edit it when we change the output folder, but that is a lot of effort to go to, changing two whole files. That's not the Linux way. So let's just load it from the `motion` config file and be done with it. It means that we need two variables: a variable that will contain the `motion` config file and the second that we will create dynamically to contain the file location. The variable that will contain the filename is simple enough with `MOTIONCONF=/etc/motion/motion.conf`.

■ **Note** All the following is being done as the root user (you can `sudo su` to get a root shell) because it is the root user who will spawn `motion`.

The next step is to pull the variable out, and the best way to do this is with a combination of two commands: one is grep, which will find any information in a file that contains a particular pattern, in this case any line that contains the line target_dir, but we also need to ensure that we avoid comments, so we need to grab lines that start with target_dir. This is achieved by simply adding one extra symbol so that grep can know that we are looking for a value that starts with our desired value. This gives us a command of grep "^target_dir" $MOTIONCONF. If you execute this command you will see the following result:

```
root @raspberrypi ~ $ grep "^target_dir" $MOTIONCONF
target_dir /tmp/motion
```

Now the next problem with our command rears its head: we need to get rid of the target_dir portion so we only have the location we are after. To remove the first part, we need to use the awk command, which will split the given data at whitespace values by default. This is perfect and then we just need to print the second value that results. So building this on to our command, we get this: ″

```
root@raspberrypi ~ $ grep "^target_dir" $MOTIONCONF | awk '{ print $2}'
/tmp/motion
```

Now all that's left is to push the result into a variable, which is accomplished with the back-tick symbol, giving us a final result of this:

```
MOTIONDIR=' grep "^target_dir" $MOTIONCONF | awk '{ print $2}''
```

Now, one thing that you may not have considered: if this directory is not created, motion will create it when it captures its first image, but that can take hours. We need it now, so let's go ahead and do a check to see whether it exists and if not, create it. The check to see whether a directory exists is if [-d *<directory name>*]. We also need to add a note to see if the directory doesn't exist, so go ahead and add an exclamation point before the -d, which means *not*. Finally, mix this with a mkdir and you should have the following if statement:

```
if [ ! -d $MOTIONDIR ]; then
        mkdir $MOTIONDIR
fi
```

Along with making the directory, you need to ensure that it is owned by the correct user. The motion daemon is run by root, but this ownership is passed to motion, so you need to add a chown to this command, which gives this value:

```
if [ ! -d $MOTIONDIR ]; then
        mkdir $MOTIONDIR
        chown motion $MOTIONDIR
fi
```

Okay, so now we have the directory where the files will be found, and we need to write some code to check it and count the number of files. Normally, you would think "Sweet, let's just use ls to list the files in the directory." But this won't help in the event that there are no files because ls will give us an error. To do this, we need to use the find command. To find all the .jpg files within only that directory, we need to add a pair of arguments to find the following:

- -maxdepth 1 says not to go within any subdirectories to search
- -type f to tell it to only search for files

I also wrapped the command in a pair of parentheses, which means that the file is meant to be treated as an array. This gives us this command:

```
LISTFILES=('find $MOTIONDIR -maxdepth 1 -type f')
```

Now, in case there are non-image files, we should also add in a grep to pull out only the .jpg files. A simple grep for anything ending in .jpg (using the $ operator) should suffice. This will give us the following:

```
LISTFILES=('find $MOTIONDIR -maxdepth 1 -type f | grep jpg$')
```

Now we need to get the count of files in our list using the `wc -l` command. This will list all the files in a directory and if we pipe that to `wc` with the `-l` argument, we get the number of files within a given folder. This gives us our next line:

```
NUMFILES=' find $MOTIONDIR -maxdepth 1 -type f | grep jpg$ | wc -l'
```

There is one final common piece of code that will be common to both scripts that we can work up now: the `mutt` mailer line that will send the image file and a message. The original one we sent was good, but I've modified it slightly here to include a variable name for the attachment that is the variable `IMAGEFILE`. I've also added a new `-F /root/.muttrc` option, which forces `mutt` to use the root `muttrc` file we created. The new mail line is this:

```
echo -e "Warning,\nAn intruder was detected at 'date'\nPlease see the image attached for
details"| mutt -F /root/.muttrc -s "[INTURDER ALERT] Intruder Detected" -a $IMAGEFILE --
you@gmail.com
```

As you can see, it's a bit of a mouthful. I've added some nice body text that will come out as follows:

```
Warning,
An intruder was detected at Sat Sep 15 22:50:32 EST 2012
Please see the image attached for details
```

You may be asking yourself how I got those newlines in there, and how I was able to get a very nice date and time output in the e-mail. The date and time come from the shell `date` command, which I have encased in back-ticks to give us the output. I've also added some `\n`s, which are references to newlines, but only when you give echo the `-e` argument to tell it to interpret special escape values. Now that we have a block of code to work from, let's start with script number 1, the cron executed run once script.

Script 1

To begin, let's go over what we have so far; we can get the number of files in the correct working directory. The next step then is to check whether that number shows that there are indeed files to work with, which is to say > 0. This means we need the following `if` statement:

```
if [ $NUMFILES -gt 0 ]; then
```

With our `if` statement in place, we should now know whether there are any files we need to send urgently. Now we just need to iterate through the list and send each as an e-mail and then delete it. To iterate through anything, you need to use a loop; in this case, we will be using a `for` loop. This loop will split each image off from the list as its own variable, allowing us to take action on each one after another. The loop will look like the following, where IMAGEFILE is the current image from the list; this image changes to the next one in the list each time the for loop starts again. The for loop will finish when there are no more images to process from the list.

```
for IMAGEFILE in $LISTFILES
```

■ **Note** Remember to chmod +x your script so it can be executed!

Okay, that's it. We have all our code blocks, so let's assemble. The final script should look something like this:

```
#!/bin/bash
MOTIONCONF=/etc/motion/motion.conf
MOTIONDIR=' sudo grep "^target_dir" $MOTIONCONF | awk '{ print $2}''
if [ ! -d $MOTIONDIR ]; then
        mkdir $MOTIONDIR
        chown motion $MOTIONDIR
fi
LISTFILES=('find $MOTIONDIR -maxdepth 1 -type f | grep jpg$')
NUMFILES=' find $MOTIONDIR -maxdepth 1 -type f | grep jpg$ | wc -l'
if [ $NUMFILES -gt 0 ]; then
        for IMAGEFILE in $LISTFILES
        do
                echo -e "Warning,\nAn intruder was detected at 'date'\nPlease see the image
                attached for details" \
                | mutt -s "[INTURDER ALERT] Intruder Detected" \
                -F /root/.muttrc \
                -a $IMAGEFILE -- <your email>
                rm $IMAGEFILE
        done
fi
```

Script 2

Because we have finished discussing script 1, let's work on script 2. This one is slightly more complex. The first thing we need to do is add a counter that will tell us how many images we have dealt with already. Initially, we can set this to 0. So let's initialize this variable with LASTCOUNT=$ NUMFILES. Next is to create a simple loop that will keep the application running forever; this is, in fact, the easiest kind of loop and is simply while true (for more on while loops, see Chapter 7).

Now within the loop we need to update LASTCOUNT and NUMFILES, so have those commands run again to update their values. We need to compare to see if we have had anything new added (i.e., that NUMFILES is greater than LASTCOUNT). If it is, we need to read off the latest files and send them. Normally, this sounds like the place for an if statement, but in this case we will use a while loop because we want to do things while LASTCOUNT is greater than NUMFILES, so our second inner while loop is this:

```
while [ $LASTCOUNT -lt $NUMFILES ]
```

Now we simply need to update; first we need to get each new image a filename. Thankfully they are found in order because the motion package names them sequentially. This means that we simply need to pull off the top X to make up the difference. This means we will need an iterator value so we can count each of the top X as we go. So create an ITERATOR set to 0 outside the second loop but inside the first, so we reset it every round.

Now that we have this iterator, we can use it with the LISTFILES to pull off each of the numbers. Because we are treating LISTFILES as an array, we just need to use the ITERATOR to access that array element. We need to wrap the whole array output within a pair of curly braces because this will perform the array dereferencing and give us the output value:

```
IMAGEFILE=${LISTFILES[$ITERATOR]}
```

Finally, we need to increment LASTCOUNT and ITERATOR so that they can count off each image as we process it. This is done with the following:

```
LASTCOUNT='expr $LASTCOUNT + 1' and ITERATOR='expr $ITERATOR + 1'
```

The expr function treats given values as mathematical expressions and returns their result, which is perfect when we want to increment a value by 1.

So, now we need to assemble each of these items of code. When put together, they should look like this:

```
#!/bin/bash
MOTIONCONF=/etc/motion/motion.conf
MOTIONDIR=' sudo grep "^target_dir" $MOTIONCONF | awk '{ print $2}''
if [ ! -d $MOTIONDIR ]; then
        mkdir $MOTIONDIR
        chown motion $MOTIONDIR
fi
LISTFILES='find $MOTIONDIR -maxdepth 1 -type f | grep jpg$'
NUMFILES='find $MOTIONDIR -maxdepth 1 -type f | grep jpg$ | wc -l'
LASTCOUNT=0
while true
do
        LISTFILES=('find $MOTIONDIR -maxdepth 1 -type f | grep jpg$')
        NUMFILES='find $MOTIONDIR -maxdepth 1 -type f | grep jpg$ | wc -l'
        ITERATOR=0
        while [ $LASTCOUNT -lt $NUMFILES ];
        do
                IMAGEFILE=${LISTFILES[$ITERATOR]}
                echo -e "Warning,\nAn intruder was detected at 'date'\nPlease see the image
                attached for details" \
                | mutt -F /root/.muttrc \
                -s "[INTURDER ALERT] Intruder Detected" \
                -a $IMAGEFILE -- <your email> LASTCOUNT='expr $LASTCOUNT + 1' ITERATOR='expr
                $ITERATOR + 1' done sleep 1
done
```

Testing

So, let's take this super script for a spin. Ensure that motion is up and running and execute your script.

■ **Note** To cancel running the script, press Ctrl + c to stop execution. This is the only way to stop script 2.

You shouldn't expect to see any output, so just watch your e-mail inbox (see Figure 10-4).

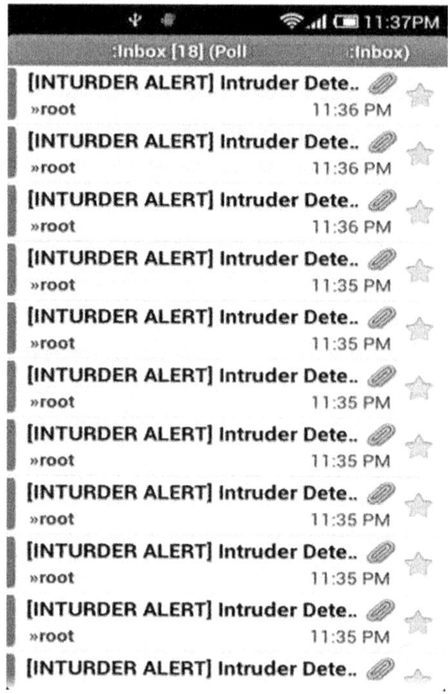

Figure 10-4. *One full inbox!*

As you can see, it works. In fact, it works rather well; I have 18 unread e-mails from the intruder detection system. Perfect! Now that we have tested that the script will function in sending us e-mails of new images from motion, we need to configure the script so that it will start automatically—the one final requirement that remains unmet. Looking back, we decided that we would start each of the two scripts in different ways: script 1 would be added to `cron` and script 2 would be added to the motion start script, so that it would run with motion!

For script 1, things are fairly simple. `cron` will automatically evaluate if it should run something once a minute, so all we need to do is have a `cron` job that will run at all times. So as root (since we want to run this as root), open up the `cron` table with `crontab -e` and enter the following:

```
* * * * * /root/script1.sh
```

That's it; we have no added script 1 to start and run from a `crontab` entry every minute. So that every minute we will check to see if there are any files in `/tmp/motion`, send them to us and then delete them, which fulfills all our requirements.

The second script's `launch` method requires modification to the `launch` script for motion `/etc/init.d/motion`, so go ahead and open that up to be edited as root. The basic format of any of these start scripts is to have a large case statement that processes the given action it is to perform be that start, stop, restart, or any other number of required cases. So look for the line `start`, which is the action we want to enhance. Within this, we can see that there are a number of nested checks and preliminaries; we want our script only to be started after motion, which is invoked by the `start-stop-daemon` command.

So go ahead and add a link to your script after that; then add a & on the end. The ampersand says "run this script and then let it go in the background." If we don't do this, the start script will assume that its next function is to wait for that script to end, which it won't! Your final updated start section should look like this:

```
start)
    if check_daemon_enabled ; then
        if ! [ -d /var/run/motion ]; then
                mkdir /var/run/motion
        fi
        chown motion:motion /var/run/motion

        log_daemon_msg "Starting $DESC" "$NAME"
if start-stop-daemon --start --oknodo --exec $DAEMON -b --chuid motion ; then
             /root/script2.sh &
            log_end_msg 0
        else
            log_end_msg 1
            RET=1
        fi
    fi
    ;;
```

Once you've finished editing, go and restart your Pi; then log back in and execute a check to see if the script is running! It is? Fantastic, you now have a fully automated Raspberry sPi of your very own!

```
$ ps -ef | grep script
root      2058     1  0 11:23 pts/0    00:00:00 /bin/bash /home/pi/script2.sh
```

Troubleshooting

As I'm sure you're aware by now, there are so many things that can go wrong when doing software development. So there is plenty of space for troubleshooting. and it makes my giving you advice about where to look a little difficult. That being said, there are a number of things you can do to make diagnosis easier.

There's a reason why I started off scripting by writing out each little section of code and then adding it. This is a version of what's called *isolation testing*, which involves doing as much as you can to isolate a particular section of code to execute it with controlled inputs and then evaluating the outputs to see that they work as you intend.

As you can imagine, doing this block by block means that you can test each little bit of an application as it grows.

The next thing is to take advantage of the `echo` command to output a working value or a location in the code. You can see what an application is working with and where within the code it is running, which lets you pick up on unexpected values and where your software is failing.

Finally, if all else fails, change the shell from `#!/bin/bash` to `#!/bin/bash -x`. Adding the `-x` will put your instance of bash into debug mode and it will output every variable, every manipulation, and every change it goes through. While there can be a lot of output this is the ideal way to see what's going on within a troublesome application.

Where to Go from Here

Wow. We've come a long way from where we started. We have:

- Attached a webcam to our Raspberry sPi
- Installed and configured the monitor application to use the webcam
- Used the webcam and monitor application to function as a motion sensor and capture images
- Installed and configured ssmtp as an MTA
- Installed and configured `mutt` mail application to use SSMTP
- Send an e-mail from the command line to ourselves using SSMTP and `mutt`
- Written two scripts to automatically pick up any new image files and then e-mail them to ourselves using all of the above

This is quite an accomplishment, but what now? As spies, you all know how adaptability is the key to success. What we have gone through here should be a guide on how you can take advantage of software like motion, `SSMTP` and `mutt`. You should now also be familiar with using `dmesg` and how to locate newly loaded devices and integrate them into your system. Finally, you should see how you can use scripts written in bash to fill a gap in your application stack and solve complex problems. So what can you do from here?

- You can add a wireless adapter, so you don't need to be cabled in, giving you a wireless Raspberry sPi that you can hide in the most innocuous of places.
- You can add a USB battery pack to remove the need for access to a power point.
- You can change which directory the files are stored in out of `/tmp`. That way, you can have your images persisted to disk, where you can review them at a later date.
- Or you can go full Bond. I've taken my inspiration further afield, modified the software to capture full video, and disabled the image capture. I changed the storage location to be away from `/tmp` and I've attached a USB battery pack. I then added a little tape to hold this all together and mounted the webcam inside a hat (see Figure 10-5).

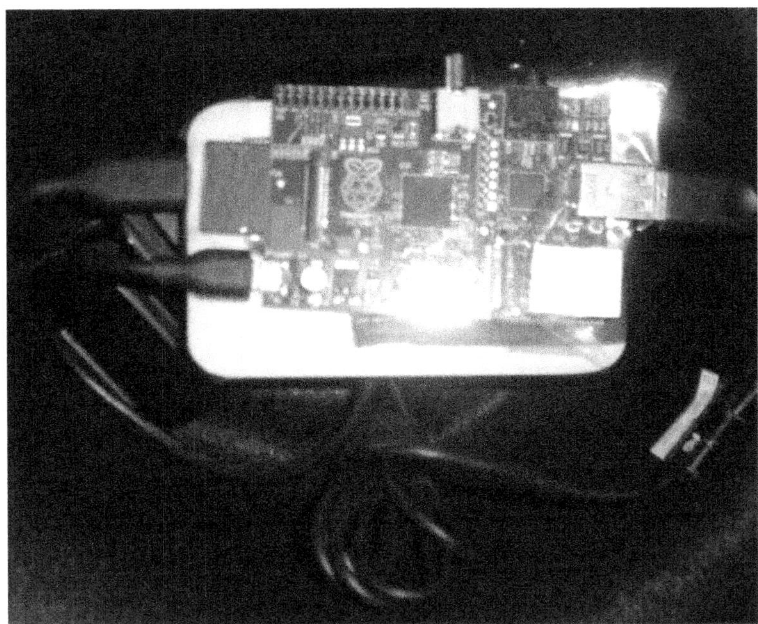

Figure 10-5. *Maybe I should have invested in a stetson!*

Summary

You should be able to understand the output of `dmesg` and know how `udev` works. You should also be able to configure the motion application, SSMTP application, and `mutt` application. Finally, you should be able to send e-mail with different recipients, body text, subjects, and attachments.

CHAPTER 11

Pi Media Center

The beautiful things about a Raspberry Pi are that it is so flexible a device and its potential uses are nearly limitless. You can do just about anything with Pi, and it has an array of peripheral input ports that can be used to great effect.

You should also be aware that while your Pi can display through a standard HDMI, the power of the device doesn't end there. It can display at a full 1920 x 1080 resolution, commonly called 1080P, which is the benchmark level for high definition. Your tiny little Raspberry Pi is capable of displaying video at full high-definition resolution, and thanks to the sound interleave of HDMI it can also play back audio on the same channel as video. That is the goal of this chapter; we are going to take advantage of the Pi's media playback capabilities to create two different varieties of Pi media center. One is a video playback center that you can use to play videos over your network. It can sit attached to your TV and allow you to tap into the Internet for video. The second is a wireless playback device that enables you to remotely stream your music collection and play back across a network.

Video with XBMC

As mentioned earlier, one big advantage of Raspberry Pi is that it can play back in full high definition, but we need a way to take advantage of this, which is where XBMC comes in.

XBMC (which is short for *XBox Media Center*) was originally designed as a media center for the original (Fat) XBox. People liked the project so much that it has subsequently been ported to just about every operating system under the sun, including but not limited to Windows, Android, OS X, and iOS. There is even a full-blown, stand-alone version called XMBCbuntu that is a port of Ubuntu that has XBMC installed, preconfigured, and ready to go out of the box. Given its wide use, open source nature, and easy-to-work-with nature, it has been ported and forked many times with its progeny, including MediaPortal, Plex, Voddlern, and Boxee. This goes to show how popular media center systems are; as a further example, Boxee makes a small device called the Boxee Box that costs upward of $200. What we are creating is a tool that is just as powerful and only costs $35—the price of the Pi. So now that you're all excited about the bright and shiny media center future, it's time to take advantage of it.

You've reached the end of the book, so it's time to crack out the big guns and do a proper Linux install from the application source. While most applications come prepackaged via `apt-get`, there are some that do not and they need to be compiled. Installing XBMC from source is a somewhat involved process and is very time-consuming. We have chosen to compile it from source because not only does it help you through one of the more complex ways of getting an application running in Linux but it also means that our installation of XBMC is optimized for our system because we have built it on our own system. Historically, compiling from source was considered to be an arduous process, but as the number of people using Linux has grown so has the need for simple-to-use installation tools and the rise of precompiled binary installation systems such as `apt-get`. But as with everything, there are still times when using a prebuild is never as good as doing it from scratch, and as time as gone on, tools for compilation have grown and become much more approachable. It's also easier to do when someone steps you through the process—which is what this book is all about.

So let's get started. First, I have stepped away from the primary build of Raspbian to use one of the slightly cut-down versions of Raspbian called Pisces that is available from Raspbian at `www.raspbian.org/PiscesImages`. I am using Pisces because it has been cut down and doesn't include as much overhead, which means more power for doing what we want: playing movies! Download and install this image on an SD card (you will need one with 4 GB of space) and then boot up and get the OS attached to the Internet so you can work with it. The default user is `raspbian` and the password is also `raspbian`, which is also the root password.

OSMC

There is a much more simple way to get XBMC working on your Pi: using a prebuilt version of Raspbian called OSMC (previously RaspMC). You can download a OSMC installer and push the image onto an SD card just as you did with Raspbian. You can download this image from `https://osmc.tv/`. This installation is very simple and will take between 15–25 minutes. You simply attach your Pi to your network, turn it on, and off the installer goes. It will download everything it needs from the Internet and then set itself up. This is by far the easiest way to get XBMC running on your Pi. For those of you who take the path of using OSMC, you can skip to the "Starting and Using XBMC" section of this chapter.

■ **Note** If `ifconfig` is missing, install the `net-tools` package using `apt-get`. See Chapter 3 for more on `apt-get`.

Once you are inside the operating system, it's time to issue some commands and start getting XBMC installed. This is a very long process: the compiler is much slower than using `apt-get` because all the software installed by `apt-get` is precompiled, thus cutting out some steps. The compile in this case takes about 12 hours—yes hours, half a day. I find it best to leave the final compile to run overnight so I won't be tempted to sit there for hours on end and watch it.

The process takes such a long time because of the nature of the ARM processor and the speed at which it can work. This means that compiling takes longer, but we can do as much work on a lower level of power.

Setup to Build

Let's start with the build. The first step is to ensure that we can divert as much power and memory to the compile as possible. In the core Raspbian we did this with the `rapsi-config` command, but Pisces doesn't have that control script, so you have to change this manually by replacing the `start.elf` file with a different one that will change how the system's resources are allocated. Run this command:

```
$ sudo cp /boot/arm224_start.elf /boot/start.elf
```

This will copy the version that allocates 224 MB to system RAM and 32 MB to graphics into the system to be used. Now we need to make this configuration change registered within the system and then reboot so that the changes can take effect by issuing the following two commands:

```
$ sudo rpi-update
$ sudo reboot
```

Once your system has rebooted, and you are back up and running, it is best if you upgrade the OS to ensure it is running the latest versions of software. To do this, we will leverage `apt-get` by telling it to update itself with the latest version of its configuration from the Internet and then upgrade all available packages on your system. To do this, issue the following commands:

```
$ sudo apt-get update
$ sudo apt-get upgrade
```

This execution will take a little bit of time because it needs to download, unpack, and replace a large number of system components. So get this up and running and then go have a coffee; it should be done when you return, and you can move on to the next step.

■ **Note** Some of these packages might already be installed on your system. We include them as they might not be installed for everyone.

The next step is to install packages to give us the ability to compile; they include the essential build tools, automatic configuration tools, zip and unzip tools, and so on. To install these tools, run the following command:

```
$ sudo apt-get install build-essential autoconf ccache gawk gperf mesa-utils zip unzip
Reading package lists... Done
Building dependency tree
Reading state information... Done
build-essential is already the newest version.
The following packages were automatically installed and are no longer required:
  libcdio-cdda0 libcdio-paranoia0 libcdio10 libcelt0-0 libdb4.8 librpmio2
Use 'apt-get autoremove' to remove them.
The following extra packages will be installed:
  automake autotools-dev libglew1.7 libsigsegv2
Suggested packages:
  autoconf2.13 autoconf-archive gnu-standards autoconf-doc libtool gettext distcc gawk-doc
  glew-utils
The following NEW packages will be installed:
  autoconf automake autotools-dev ccache gawk gperf libglew1.7 libsigsegv2 mesa-utils
The following packages will be upgraded:
  unzip zip
2 upgraded, 9 newly installed, 0 to remove and 187 not upgraded.
Need to get 2,647 kB/3,174 kB of archives.
After this operation, 7,143 kB of additional disk space will be used.
Do you want to continue [Y/n]?
```

Once you have installed these basic packages, move on to the far bigger install job. We now need to install a number of packages that will install video and decoder libraries and specialized graphics libraries. In addition to all these, you will need to install a few other packages to enable you to connect remotely to the XBMC. This command is very long, so I recommend you download the source code from the Apress website. There is a script within that package that will execute these commands for you. The command to install this giant number of packages is as follows:

```
$ sudo apt-get install autotools-dev comerr-dev dpkg-dev libalsaplayer-dev \
libapt-pkg-dev libasound2-dev libass-dev libatk1.0-dev \
libavahi-client-dev libavahi-common-dev libavcodec-dev libavformat-dev \
libavutil-dev libbison-dev libbluray-dev libboost1.49-dev \
libbz2-dev libc-dev-bin libc6-dev libcaca-dev libcairo2-dev \
libcdio-dev libclalsadrv-dev libcrypto++-dev libcups2-dev libcurl3-gnutls-dev \
libdbus-1-dev libdbus-glib-1-dev libdirectfb-dev libdrm-dev libegl1-mesa-dev \
libelf-dev libenca-dev libept-dev libevent-dev libexpat1-dev libflac-dev \
libfontconfig1-dev libfreetype6-dev libfribidi-dev libgconf2-dev \
libgcrypt11-dev libgdk-pixbuf2.0-dev libgl1-mesa-dev libgles2-mesa-dev \
libglew-dev libglewmx-dev libglib2.0-dev libglu1-mesa-dev \
libgnome-keyring-dev libgnutls-dev libgpg-error-dev libgtk2.0-dev libhal-dev \
libhunspell-dev libice-dev libicu-dev libidn11-dev libiso9660-dev \
libjasper-dev libjbig-dev libjconv-dev libjpeg8-dev libkrb5-dev \
libldap2-dev libltdl-dev liblzo2-dev libmad0-dev libmicrohttpd-dev \
libmodplug-dev libmp3lame-dev libmpeg2-4-dev libmysqlclient-dev \
libncurses5-dev libnspr4-dev libnss3-dev libogg-dev libopenal-dev \
libp11-kit-dev libpam0g-dev libpango1.0-dev libpcre++-dev libpcre3-dev \
libpixman-1-dev libpng12-dev libprotobuf-dev libpthread-stubs0-dev \
libpulse-dev librtmp-dev libsamplerate0-dev \
libsdl-image1.2-dev libsdl1.2-dev libslang2-dev \
libsm-dev libsmbclient-dev libspeex-dev \
libsqlite3-dev libssh-dev libssh2-1-dev libssl-dev libstdc++6-4.6-dev \
libtagcoll2-dev libtasn1-3-dev libtiff4-dev libtinfo-dev libtinyxml-dev \
libts-dev libudev-dev libv8-dev libva-dev libvdpau-dev \
libvorbis-dev libvpx-dev libwebp-dev libwibble-dev \
libx11-dev libx11-xcb-dev libxapian-dev libxau-dev \
libxcb-glx0-dev libxcb-render0-dev libxcb-shm0-dev \
libxcb1-dev libxcomposite-dev libxcursor-dev libxdamage-dev \
libxdmcp-dev libxext-dev libxfixes-dev libxft-dev libxi-dev \
libxinerama-dev libxml2-dev libxmu-dev libxrandr-dev \
libxrender-dev libxslt1-dev libxss-dev libxt-dev \
libxtst-dev libxxf86vm-dev libyajl-dev libzip-dev linux-libc-dev \
lzma-dev mesa-common-dev python-dev python2.7-dev x11proto-composite-dev \
x11proto-core-dev x11proto-damage-dev x11proto-dri2-dev x11proto-fixes-dev \
x11proto-gl-dev x11proto-input-dev x11proto-kb-dev x11proto-randr-dev \
x11proto-record-dev x11proto-render-dev x11proto-scrnsaver-dev \
x11proto-xext-dev x11proto-xf86vidmode-dev x11proto-xinerama-dev xtrans-dev \
zlib1g-dev
```

This list of packages has a number of slashes on the end; they are line breaks that say that the current command should be executed and that there will be another line of command following. Line breaks are very useful when you need to break up long commands over a large number of lines, as I have done here. This command will take a while to run because there are is a large number of packages to be downloaded and installed. So execute this command, go cook dinner, and then come back.

Once you have installed all these packages, you need to copy some special files into place and create other ones that are linked into the correct location so they can be used. Again, they will be included within the script that we have created to help ease the execution of these commands.

The first of these is to copy the VideCoreIV include files from the Raspberry Pi firmware into `/usr/include`. This directory is a special directory from which the compiler will search for libraries and files that are to be included within a build. To copy all these files into the correct place, execute the following commands:

```
$ sudo cp -R /opt/vc/include/* /usr/include
$ sudo cp /opt/vc/include/interface/vcos/pthreads/* /usr/include/interface/vcos
```

Now in addition to copying these files into place, there are a number we need to link correctly into the right location so they can be read. While in the last step we copied include files that are predominantly source code, this time we need to link in precompiled portions of the firmware into the correct spot to be read by the compiler at compile time. Instead of copying, we are linking because we are happy to use the files in their current location and save on some space. Run the following:

```
$ sudo ln -fs /opt/vc/lib/libEGL.so /usr/lib/libEGL.so
$ sudo ln -fs /opt/vc/lib/libEGL.so /usr/lib/arm-linux-gnueabihf/libEGL.so
$ sudo ln -fs /opt/vc/lib/libEGL.so /usr/lib/arm-linux-gnueabihf/libEGL.so.1
$ sudo ln -fs /opt/vc/lib/libEGL_static.a /usr/lib/libEGL_static.a
$ sudo ln -fs /opt/vc/lib/libEGL_static.a /usr/lib/arm-linux-gnueabihf/libEGL_static.a
$ sudo ln -fs /opt/vc/lib/libGLESv2.so /usr/lib/libGLESv2.so
$ sudo ln -fs /opt/vc/lib/libGLESv2.so /usr/lib/arm-linux-gnueabihf/libGLESv2.so
$ sudo ln -fs /opt/vc/lib/libGLESv2.so /usr/lib/arm-linux-gnueabihf/libGLESv2.so.2
$ sudo ln -fs /opt/vc/lib/libGLESv2_static.a /usr/lib/libGLESv2_static.a
$ sudo ln -fs /opt/vc/lib/libGLESv2_static.a /usr/lib/arm-linux-gnueabihf/libGLESv2_static.a
$ sudo ln -fs /opt/vc/lib/libbcm_host.so /usr/lib/libbcm_host.so
$ sudo ln -fs /opt/vc/lib/libbcm_host.so /usr/lib/arm-linux-gnueabihf/libbcm_host.so
$ sudo ln -fs /opt/vc/lib/libvchiq_arm.a /usr/lib/libvchiq_arm.a
$ sudo ln -fs /opt/vc/lib/libvchiq_arm.a /usr/lib/arm-linux-gnueabihf/libvchiq_arm.a
$ sudo ln -fs /opt/vc/lib/libvchiq_arm.so /usr/lib/libvchiq_arm.so
$ sudo ln -fs /opt/vc/lib/libvchiq_arm.so /usr/lib/arm-linux-gnueabihf/libvchiq_arm.so
$ sudo ln -fs /opt/vc/lib/libvcos.a /usr/lib/libvcos.a
$ sudo ln -fs /opt/vc/lib/libvcos.a /usr/lib/arm-linux-gnueabihf/libvcos.a
$ sudo ln -fs /opt/vc/lib/libvcos.so /usr/lib/libvcos.so
$ sudo ln -fs /opt/vc/lib/libvcos.so /usr/lib/arm-linux-gnueabihf/libvcos.so
```

▒ **Note** We found that these links can be removed by other processes and sometimes by rebooting; if they do, you need to re-create them.

Now that you have linked all the files into the correct place, go ahead and get the source code. Change the directory into your home directory with this:

```
$ cd ~
```

If you can't type a tilde (~), you can try reconfiguring the Pi keyboard layout with `dpkg-reconfigure keyboard-configuration` and then rebooting the Pi. You can also just use `cd` with no arguments because it will also take you to your home directory. The tilde is just a symbol to reference the current user's home directory.

Now that you have changed into your home directory, it is time to download the source code so you can work with it and correctly compile everything. Thankfully, a modern tool has appeared that makes doing source code downloads much easier: Git, which is named for Linus Torvalds of Linux Kernel fame. Git is used for source code management and version control; all users can download the current source version of a set of source code and submit modifications back to the central repository.

■ **Note** This means that we always download the latest version, but we might get a less stable build if something is wrong with the current version in Git. Most developers strive to keep their Git repositories in good working order, but it is something to be aware of.

All we want to do at this point is download the source code into our home directory to work with it. To do this, use the `git` command and tell it to clone the repository of source code onto the system. We have also added the `--depth 1` to the command to say that we only want to clone the most recent 1 revision of the source code (the absolute latest version of the code) and avoid getting a lot of extra and unwanted historical code.

Start your clone by running the following:

```
$ git clone --depth 1 git://github.com/xbmc/xbmc-rbp.git
Cloning into 'xbmc-rbp'...
remote: Counting objects: 35172, done.
remote: Compressing objects: 100% (22895/22895), done.
remote: Total 35172 (delta 15265), reused 27885 (delta 10698)
Receiving objects: 100% (35172/35172), 158.26 MiB | 385 KiB/s, done.
Resolving deltas: 100% (15265/15265), done.
```

Now that we have cloned the source code of XBMC, we need to start building the application. This is the part that will take the longest by far. Change the directory into the newly created `xbmc-rbp` directory because there are a few last steps we need to take.

Changing Files with Sed and Regular Expressions

Before we go ahead and kick off the build of our XBMC application, we need to make a few minor adjustments to the source code so that it compiles in the exact manner we want it to. Instead of making these changes by hand, we will use a tool called *Sed* (short for *Stream Editor*). It does just as its name implies: it takes a stream of text and then performs edits on that text. The tricky part of Sed is that it makes use of a highly specialized language called *regular expressions*, which are used to perform the equivalent of a find-and-replace function.

Regular expressions evolved out of the need to validate a given set of data to see if it conforms to a given standard and to edit when the given example is found. While a simple find and replace is enough for most people when editing text, how do you perform a find-and-replace when you want to edit only words that start with *T* as the third letter in a given sentence? Probably one of the easiest cases for a regular expression is e-mail. You want to confirm that a given string is a valid e-mail: an e-mail will contain a username (who it's from), a domain (where it's from, e.g., Hotmail or Gmail), and there will be an *at* (`@`) symbol in between. Okay, we can do that with just a wildcard like *. So something that looks like *@* will be an e-mail, right?

Well the * that we use to denote anything will pick up anything. Even spaces, numbers, strange symbols, and so on. So we need a way to pick up something that is made up of a string of valid e-mail characters (letters, numbers, period, underscores) and then `@`, and finally a valid domain. This will be a collection of letters, followed by a period and then perhaps another set (or a few sets) of letters. Describing this is exhausting, which is why we have a specialized language for performing them.

Now that you understand what we are trying to achieve, run the following two commands to alter the file `tools/rbp/setup-sdk.sh`. These `sed` commands make use of the `-i` option, which says to edit the given file:

```
$ sed -i 's/USE_BUILDROOT=1/USE_BUILDROOT=0/' tools/rbp/setup-sdk.sh
```

$ sed -i 's/TOOLCHAIN=\/usr\/local\/bcm-gcc/TOOLCHAIN=\/usr/' tools/rbp/setup-sdk.sh. These commands change the `USE_BUILDROOT` variable from a value of `1` to a value of `0` wherever it is found within that file and to replace any instance of the phrase `TOOLCHAIN=/usr/local/bcm-gcc` with `TOOLCHAIN=/usr`. Once you have edited the `tools/rbp/setup-sdk.sh` file, you should execute it with the following command:

```
$ sudo sh tools/rbp/setup-sdk.sh
```

The command will generate a makefile, but won't display anything onscreen. Once it is finished it's time to edit the newly created `tools/rbp/depends/xbmc/Makefile`. All you need to do then is run one last `sed` on the file to add a # to the start of any instance of `cd $(SOURCE); $(CONFIGURE)`:

```
$ sed -i 's/cd $(SOURCE); $(CONFIGURE)/#cd $(SOURCE); $(CONFIGURE)/' tools/rbp/depends/xbmc/
Makefile
$ sudo sed -i 's/#include "vchost_config.h"/#include "linux\/vchost_config.h"/' \ /usr/
include/interface/vmcs_host/vcgencmd.h
$ sed -i 's/-DSQUISH_USE_SSE=2 -msse2//' lib/libsquish/Makefile.in
$ sed -i 's/-DSQUISH_USE_SSE=2 -msse2//' lib/libsquish/Makefile
```

What we did is change the way our system will compile the XBMC software and make it use some of our system libraries rather than use the ones that can be found within the XBMC source code.

Now that the Makefile is created, it is time to compile!

Compiling Source Code

Most compilations use a very simple logic: you run the command `./configure` to generate a configuration file that knows about the makeup of your system. This generates a file that is called a *makefile*. This file is in a slightly specialized language that describes the way in which a compile for a collection should be performed. It is not a script that executes code in and of itself; it is a collection of directions that will be used by the make application.

Unfortunately, this compile is slightly more advanced. We need to make our configuration tools to match the setup we are trying to do before we run the configuration and the compile. This will take a little while to execute, so kick off and go have another cuppa.

The command to execute is this:

```
$ make -C tools/rbp/depends/xbmc/
```

This command will run the make within the directory `tools/rbp/depends/xbmc/`, which will generate the config file. The output for this is very long, but when it's done successfully, you should see something like this on your console window:

```
examples/Makefile.am: installing './depcomp'
Makefile.am: installing './INSTALL'
autoreconf: Leaving directory 'lib/libdvd/libdvdnav'
Please (re)run configure...
#cd ../../../../; ./configure --prefix=/opt/xbmc-bcm/xbmc-bin --build=i686-linux --host=arm-
bcm2708-linux-gnueabi --enable-gles --disable-sdl --disable-x11 --disable-xrandr --disable-
openmax --disable-optical-drive --disable-dvdcss --disable-joystick --disable-debug
--disable-crystalhd --disable-vtbdecoder --disable-vaapi --disable-vdpau --disable-pulse
--disable-projectm --with-platform=raspberry-pi --disable-optimizations --enable-rpi-cec-api
#cd ../../../../; make -j 1
#cd ../../../../; make install
make: Leaving directory '/home/raspbian/xbmc-rbp/tools/rbp/depends/xbmc'
```

Now that the compile of the configuration utility has gone through its time to perform the configure. This `configure` command is very long and again, you will find code that will perform this for you in the Apress source code repository, the `configure` command is this:

```
$ ./configure --prefix=/usr --build=arm-linux-gnueabihf --host=arm-linux-gnueabihf \
--localstatedir=/var/lib --with-platform=raspberry-pi --disable-gl --enable-gles \
--disable-x11 --disable-sdl --enable-ccache --enable-optimizations \
--enable-external-libraries --disable-goom --disable-hal --disable-pulse \
--disable-vaapi --disable-vdpau --disable-xrandr --disable-airplay \
--disable-alsa --enable-avahi --disable-libbluray --disable-dvdcss \
--disable-debug --disable-joystick --enable-mid --disable-nfs --disable-profiling \
--disable-projectm --enable-rsxs --enable-rtmp --disable-vaapi \
--disable-vdadecoder --disable-external-ffmpeg  --disable-optical-drive
```

Specify a number of arguments to the `configure` command that specifies where this installation should go (`--prefix=/usr`), which architecture to build (`--build=arm-linux-gnueabihf`), where to keep its running files (`--localstatedir=/var/lib`), and which platform (`--with-platform=raspberry-pi`), along with a whole host of disable and e-mail options to remove features such as CD drives and joysticks and enable things such as optimizations and Avahi automated detection of peripherals. Ultimately, when the command has finished executing, the output on your screen should look like this:

```
------------------------------------------------------------------------
  XBMC Configuration:
------------------------------------------------------------------------
  Debugging:     No
  Profiling:     No
  Optimization: Yes
  Crosscomp.:    No
  target ARCH:   arm
  target CPU:    arm1176jzf-s
  OpenGLES:      Yes
  ALSA:          No
  DBUS:          Yes
  VDPAU:         No
  VAAPI:         No
  CrystalHD:     No
```

```
VDADecoder:    No
VTBDecoder:    No
OpenMax:       No
Joystick:      No
XRandR:        No
GOOM:          No
RSXS:          Yes
ProjectM:      No
Skin Touched: No
X11:           No
Bluray:        No
TexturePacker:Yes
MID Support:  Yes
ccache:        Yes
ALSA Support: No
PulseAudio:   No
HAL Support:  No
DVDCSS:        No
Avahi:         Yes
Non-free:      Yes
ASAP Codec:   No
MySQL:         Yes
Webserver:    Yes
libRTMP support:       Yes
libsmbclient support: Yes
libnfs client support:No
libafpclient support: No
AirPLay support:       No
AirTunes support:      No
Optical drive:         No
libudev support:       Yes
libusb support:        No
libcec support:        No
libmp3lame support:    Yes
libvorbisenc support: Yes
libcap support:        No
External FFmpeg:       No
prefix:        /usr
```

This configuration specifies all the flags we asked for in our installation, which is designed to get the best from the Raspberry Pi. So, now we have done our configure onto the actual compilation. The command itself *highly* anticlimactic for what it will do: tell the system to spend the next 12 hours generating code for our system. All these other jobs taking a little time is nothing compared to how long this compile will run for. So saddle up, and execute this simple four-letter command `m a k e`:

```
$ make
```

Don't be alarmed if you see lines such as the following:

```
/tmp/ccGvUe1g.s:507: Warning: swp{b} use is deprecated for this architecture
```

The only thing that will stop the compile is a critical error or success. These warnings are related to some of the functions being used within the XBMC compile being a bit old for our Pi. When the compile has succeeded, you should expect to see this:

```
XBMC built successfully
```

This shows that we have successfully build XBMC and can do the last step in this process, which is to install our newly compiled software. The make system will actually take care of installation, too. To install, you simply run `make install`, which copies all the freshly compiled binaries into the correct spot in your OS. You will need to prefix this with `sudo` because the location we are copying too (`/usr`) is a system location, and only root is given write access. Your output should look like this:

```
$ sudo make install
Copying XBMC binary to /usr/lib/xbmc/xbmc.bin
You can run XBMC with the command 'xbmc'
Copying support and legal files...
Done!
Copying system files to /usr/share/xbmc
```

And we are done! While it was long and required a little bit of work to begin with, the actual process of compiling is relatively pain-free, you know, beyond the pain of waiting. So now that the XBMC is installed, how do we use it?

Troubleshooting

Before we jump ahead and run XBMC, we should have a look at some of the issues you could have run into. Most of these steps should take care of themselves because this setup is generic and meant to work on any Pi because they all share the same hardware. If you are ever in doubt, remove the xbmc-rbp directory and start over. Ensure that you execute the copies and the linking in full. I found that when doing the git clone, things could sometimes get stuck and not move.

When this is the case, it is best to stop the current job with Ctrl + C, remove the directory, reboot, and start again. It was also better to remove peripherals from the system during the compile and install stages because having too many peripheral devices caused load issues on my system. Additionally, you should ensure that your output for commands such as `configure` match the ones given as these flags can play a much bigger role when compiling and save you a nasty headache and another 12-hour compile job. Finally, ensure that all your `apt-gets` run and complete successfully because these packages are required to provide the libraries that your Pi will use when building XBMC.

Starting and Using XBMC

Now that we have gone through that mega compile process, it is time to start up XBMC and get going! First, though, we need to reset the options we set earlier, directing a larger amount of memory into system RAM. We will need to go to the graphics device because we want to do some serious display work with XBMC. Execute the following command to change over the Pi boot system:

```
$ sudo cp /boot/arm128_start.elf /boot/start.elf
```

Go back and check that the linked files mentioned earlier are correct. Now we can also make some changes to the `/boot/config.txt` file because it governs how the Pi's low-level hardware runs. The most simple change to make is to add the line `disable_overscan=1` as it will remove the need to do overscan processing because overscan processing will make the amount of video we play back larger, thus consuming more resources. Once you have made these changes, issue the following commands to reconfigure and reboot your Pi one last time:

```
$ sudo rpi-update
$ sudo reboot
```

Now that you have changed the settings back to 50/50 resource allocation, start XBMC by logging in as root and issuing the following command:

```
$ /usr/lib/xbmc/xbmc.bin
```

Your screen will freeze for a moment, and Figure 11-1 will greet you.

Figure 11-1. *XBMC boot screen*

You should get to the XBMC menu, which looks like Figure 11-2.

Figure 11-2. *XBMC main menu*

From within the main menu, there are options to select different types of playback, and XBMC is a fully graphical system that will present you with options and locations for getting files from when you are within it. As long as your media are accessible on a network, XBMC should be able to access it and play it back! Now on the topic of playback, you will probably be sitting there thinking, "Will I be stuck with this keyboard for all my playback?" The answer is a resounding *no*! There are two solutions:

- Purchase a USB remote and attach it to your Pi.
- The second is much sneakier: use your smartphone!

Most smartphones have the capability to download an XBMC remote control application that simply needs to be paired with your XBMC system to function. To do this, we need to enable two options within XBMC to allow it to receive remote control. Go into the settings menu and then into services, and change the remote control settings to "Allow programs on other systems to control XBMC." Once you have allowed remote control, you need to go into Webserver and set "Allow control of XBMC via HTTP"; you should also go ahead and set a username and password so that only people with the password can control your XMBC instance, not just anyone on your network with an XBMC app!

Once you have enabled these remote control options, it is simply a matter of downloading the application from your favorite app store and then setting the options within the application. You should only need to give the application the local address of your Pi, which you can see via the System ➤ System info menu, set the port to 8080, and furnish an instance name for the XBMC and the username/password, as shown in Figure 11-3.

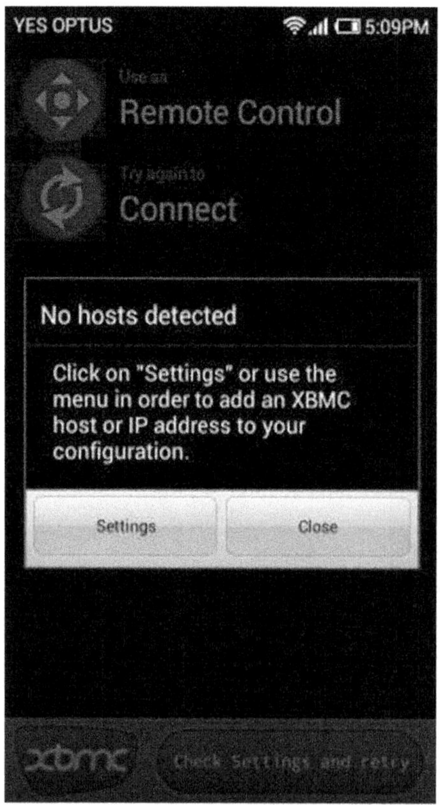

Figure 11-3. *XBMC remote application*

Once you have given all the details, your phone should turn into a remote for your XBMC instance! Complete with a whole host of directional buttons and playback controls, as shown in Figure 11-4.

Figure 11-4. *XBMC remote in action!*

XBMC on Boot

Although we have started XBMC by hand thus far, most people will want it to occur automatically because what is the point of a media center that you need to plug a keyboard into each time you want to start it up?

The following is a simple `start` script that will allow you to execute XBMC using a `start` script. Create this in the file `/etc/init.d/xbmc` (like all other long files, it can be found in the Apress repository for this book):

```
#! /bin/sh
### BEGIN INIT INFO
# Provides:          xbmc
# Required-Start:    $all
# Required-Stop:     $all
# Default-Start:     2 3 4 5
# Default-Stop:      0 1 6
# Short-Description: Start XBMC
# Description:       Start XBMC
### END INIT INFO
DAEMON=/usr/bin/xinit
DAEMON_OPTS="/usr/lib/xbmc/xbmc.bin"
NAME=xbmc
DESC=XBMC
RUN_AS=root
PID_FILE=/var/run/xbmc.pid
test -x $DAEMON || exit 0
set -e
```

```
case "$1" in
  start)
        echo "Starting $DESC"
        start-stop-daemon --start -c $RUN_AS --background --pidfile $PID_FILE
        --make-pidfile --exec $DAEMON -- $DAEMON_OPTS
        ;;
  stop)
        echo "Stopping $DESC"
        start-stop-daemon --stop --pidfile $PID_FILE
        ;;
  restart|force-reload)
        echo "Restarting $DESC"
        start-stop-daemon --stop --pidfile $PID_FILE
        sleep 5
        start-stop-daemon --start -c $RUN_AS --background --pidfile $PID_FILE
        --make-pidfile --exec $DAEMON -- $DAEMON_OPTS
        ;;
  *)
        echo "Usage: /etc/init.d/$NAME{start|stop|restart|force-reload}" >&2
        exit 1
        ;;
esac
exit 0
```

Once this file is created, run the following commands to make it executable and have it loaded into the Pi's boot process:

```
$ sudo chmod +x /etc/init.d/xbmc
$ sudo update-rc.d xbmc defaults
```

Now go ahead and reboot your system; it will bring you automatically into XBMC! Congratulations; at this point, you should have a fully functional XBMC instance complete with working smartphone remote!

Troubleshooting

Because you compiled from source successfully, there shouldn't be any issues with getting your XBMC instance up and going. The first thing to check is that the compile did indeed complete fully and so did the install. They are the two most likely culprits. If you start your XBMC instance, you might see warnings like the following:

```
libEGL warning: DRI2: xcb_connect failed
```

If you do, you have to re-run the previous copy and linking commands. This issue relates to being unable to load those library files.

Stream Music with Airplay

People often want to use the Raspberry Pi as a streaming music system, which means that it is connected to a set of speakers and can be remotely controlled and has music streamed to it from a central controlling system. There are already a large number of systems out there for doing this kind of playback, but for us the plan is to take advantage of the Apple AirPlay protocol. You can continue working in this on Pisces or you can revert to the original Raspbian. This install will work the same way on both devices.

This setup is much easier to do than the video update; we still need to do some compiling to get things to work, but we won't need to run a `./configure` because there are far fewer moving parts. Additionally, we want to have the ability to play audio out to a given device, so you need to ensure you have speakers attached.

The first thing to do is to install the following precursor packages:

```
$ sudo apt-get install build-essential libssl-dev libcrypt-openssl-rsa-perl libao-dev libio-
socket-inet6-perl libwww-perl avahi-utils pkg-config alsa-utils libwww-perl avahi-utils
Reading package lists... Done
Building dependency tree
Reading state information... Done
build-essential is already the newest version.
libio-socket-inet6-perl is already the newest version.
libio-socket-inet6-perl set to manually installed.
libssl-dev is already the newest version.
libwww-perl is already the newest version.
libwww-perl set to manually installed.
pkg-config is already the newest version.
pkg-config set to manually installed.
The following packages were automatically installed and are no longer required:
  libcdio-cdda0 libcdio-paranoia0 libcdio10 libcelt0-0 libdb4.8 librpmio2
Use 'apt-get autoremove' to remove them.
The following extra packages will be installed:
  alsa-base avahi-daemon libao-common libao4 libavahi-core7 libcrypt-openssl-bignum-perl
  libdaemon0 libnss-mdns
Suggested packages:
  alsa-oss oss-compat avahi-autoipd libaudio2 libesd0 libesd-alsa0
The following NEW packages will be installed:
  alsa-base alsa-utils avahi-daemon avahi-utils libao-common libao-dev libao4 libavahi-core7
  libcrypt-openssl-bignum-perl libcrypt-openssl-rsa-perl libdaemon0
  libnss-mdns
0 upgraded, 12 newly installed, 0 to remove and 139 not upgraded.
Need to get 1,699 kB of archives.
After this operation, 3,702 kB of additional disk space will be used.
Do you want to continue [Y/n]?
```

Once you have installed all these packages, load the sound module into the system to take advantage of it. To load a module, use the `modprobe` command. In this instance, load the `snd_bcm2835` module, which is the Broadcom sound adapter in the Pi. Issue this command:

```
$ sudo modprobe snd_bcm2835
```

The command will run, but it doesn't generate any output to tell us the status of the execution or just about anything else. We need to check and see whether the module has been loaded. Just like the `ls` command for directories and `lsusb` for listing USB devices, there is an `lsmod` command for listing the modules that are currently installed within your system. Issue the `lsmod` command and check that you can see the `snd_bcm2835` module loaded within your system (like mine):

```
$ lsmod
Module                  Size  Used by
snd_bcm2835            21485  0
snd_pcm                82208  1 snd_bcm2835
snd_page_alloc          5383  1 snd_pcm
snd_seq                59808  0
snd_seq_device          6920  1 snd_seq
snd_timer              21905  2 snd_seq,snd_pcm
snd                    57668  5 snd_timer,snd_seq_device,snd_seq,snd_pcm,snd_bcm2835
ipv6                  290227  34
r8712u                182646  0
spi_bcm2708             4815  0
i2c_bcm2708             3818  0
```

Because you are loading the sound module for the first time, you also need to select which audio device is being used (because none was used before). To change the device, use the `amixer` command as follows:

```
$ sudo amixer cset numid=3 1
numid=3,iface=MIXER,name='PCM Playback Route'
  ; type=INTEGER,access=rw------,values=1,min=0,max=3,step=0
  : values=1
```

We changed the `numid=3` value, which is the PCM Playback Route, to be equal to `1`, which is the value of the 3.5 jack. You can change the `1` on the end to a `2`, which signifies that you should use the HDMI's inbuilt audio channel to send the sound.

Now that the hardware is sorted out, it is time to take care of the software by downloading the shairport software from its repository on the Internet. By far the easiest way to do this is by using the `wget` (short for *Web GET*) command to download all the available contents on a given URL. In this manner, we can download a whole software package from the Internet with a simple URL. Execute the following:

```
$ wget https://github.com/albertz/shairport/zipball/master
--2012-09-30 18:13:36--  https://github.com/albertz/shairport/zipball/master
Resolving github.com (github.com)... 207.97.227.239
Connecting to github.com (github.com)|207.97.227.239|:443... connected.
HTTP request sent, awaiting response... 302 Found
Location: https://nodeload.github.com/albertz/shairport/zipball/master [following]
--2012-09-30 18:13:42--  https://nodeload.github.com/albertz/shairport/zipball/master
Resolving nodeload.github.com (nodeload.github.com)... 207.97.227.252
Connecting to nodeload.github.com (nodeload.github.com)|207.97.227.252|:443... connected.
HTTP request sent, awaiting response... 200 OK
Length: 46413 (45K) [application/zip]
Saving to: 'master'
100%[===================================================>] 46,413      60.1K/s   in 0.8s
2012-09-30 18:13:50 (60.1 KB/s) - 'master' saved [46413/46413]
```

Now that we have downloaded the shairport software we need to work with it. The file is called `master`, so let's neaten it up and name it correctly. Just use the `move` command to change the filename. Once you have moved the file, unzip it with the `unzip` command and `cd` into the newly created `albertz-shairport-b58f156` directory:

```
$ mv master albertz-shairport-b58f156.zip
$ unzip albertz-shairport-b58f156.zip
$ cd albertz-shairport-3892180
```

Now you need to build the application, so run the `make` command. Thankfully this application is far simpler than the XBMC one and thus doesn't need to be preconfigured.

```
$ make
cc -O2 -Wall   -c alac.c -o alac.o
cc -O2 -Wall   -DHAIRTUNES_STANDALONE hairtunes.c alac.o -o hairtunes -lm -lpthread
-lssl -lcrypto -lao
cc -O2 -Wall   -c socketlib.c -o socketlib.o
cc -O2 -Wall   -c shairport.c -o shairport.o
cc -O2 -Wall   -c hairtunes.c -o hairtunes.o
cc -O2 -Wall   socketlib.o shairport.o alac.o hairtunes.o -o shairport -lm -lpthread
-lssl -lcrypto -lao
```

Once the compile is finished, it is time to test; shairport is run by executing the `shairport.pl` file. So execute it as such:

```
$ ./shairport.pl
Can't locate Net/SDP.pm in @INC (@INC contains: /usr/lib/perl5/site_perl
/usr/share/perl5/site_perl /usr/lib/perl5/vendor_perl /usr/share/perl5/vendor_perl /usr/lib/
perl5/core_perl /usr/share/perl5/core_perl .) at ./shairport.pl line 45.
```

Whoops! There's an error related to a particular module of code not being available to the Perl system that it needs to perform the install. In this case, it is the Net/SDP module that we need to install.

Unfortunately, `apt-get` cannot fix this one, so you have to get it working by downloading the module from the Perl CPAN library (which is much like a giant `apt-get` repository for Perl software that developers can borrow and use) and then install it. You will again use `wget` to download the file from the Internet. Issue the following command:

```
$ wget http://search.cpan.org/CPAN/authors/id/N/NJ/NJH/Net-SDP-0.07.tar.gz
--2012-09-30 19:01:11--  http://search.cpan.org/CPAN/authors/id/N/NJ/NJH/Net-SDP-0.07.tar.gz
Resolving search.cpan.org (search.cpan.org)... 199.15.176.161
Connecting to search.cpan.org (search.cpan.org)|199.15.176.161|:80... connected.
HTTP request sent, awaiting response... 302 Found
Location: http://mirror.westfield.com.au/cpan/authors/id/N/NJ/NJH/Net-SDP-0.07.tar.gz
[following]
--2012-09-30 19:01:11--  http://mirror.westfield.com.au/cpan/authors/id/N/NJ/NJH/Net-
SDP-0.07.tar.gz
Resolving mirror.westfield.com.au (mirror.westfield.com.au)... 203.42.62.21
Connecting to mirror.westfield.com.au (mirror.westfield.com.au)|203.42.62.21|:80... connected.
HTTP request sent, awaiting response... 200 OK
Length: 20679 (20K) [application/x-gzip]
```

```
Saving to: 'Net-SDP-0.07.tar.gz'
100%[===========================================================================>]
20,679      --.-K/s   in 0.05s
2012-09-30 19:01:12 (382 KB/s) - 'Net-SDP-0.07.tar.gz' saved [20679/20679]
```

Once the file is downloaded, you need to extract it with the `tar` command. Issue a `tar` command to unpack the file with the arguments `-zxvf` to unzip and extract this tarball. Then change into the newly created `Net-SDP-0.07` directory:

```
$ tar -zxvf Net-SDP-0.07.tar.gz
$ cd Net-SDP-0.07
```

Now that the package is here, you just need to issue commands to the Perl build system here. The first is to execute the `Build.PL` script to generate the build file:

```
$ perl Build.PL
Created MYMETA.yml and MYMETA.json
Creating new 'Build' script for 'Net-SDP' version '0.07'
```

Once the build file is created, you need to run it with this:

```
$ ./Build
Building Net-SDP
```

And once the build is finished, run the inbuilt tests to ensure there are no problems by issuing the `test` command to the `build` script:

```
$ ./Build test
t/00use.t ....... ok
t/10generate.t .. ok
t/10parse.t ..... ok
t/20repeat.t .... ok
t/30asstring.t .. ok
All tests successful.
Files=5, Tests=69,  5 wallclock secs ( 0.97 usr  0.05 sys +  3.40 cusr  0.29 csys =
4.71 CPU)
Result: PASS
```

Finally, you need to install the modules, so issue the `install` command to the `build` script (you might need to press Enter after the command to get the install to finish and display):

```
$ sudo ./Build install
[sudo] password for raspbian:
Building Net-SDP
Installing /usr/local/man/man1/sdp2rat.1p
Installing /usr/local/share/perl/5.14.2/Net/SDP.pm
Installing /usr/local/share/perl/5.14.2/Net/SDP/Time.pm
Installing /usr/local/share/perl/5.14.2/Net/SDP/Media.pm
Installing /usr/local/man/man3/Net::SDP::Media.3pm
Installing /usr/local/man/man3/Net::SDP::Time.3pm
Installing /usr/local/man/man3/Net::SDP.3pm
Installing /usr/local/bin/sdp2rat
```

Once the build is done, it is a simple matter to run the `shairport.pl` script again, and this time it should work! The output should look like this:

```
$ cd..
$ ./shairport.pl
Established under name '891BEA3BF8A1@ShairPort 2113 on pisces'
```

Now you need to establish connectivity with the application and test that you can send music to it. Open up iTunes and then change the output destination in the bottom-right corner of iTunes (see Figure 11-5). You should see a shairport name there. Select it and press Play on your favorite song and presto: streaming music!

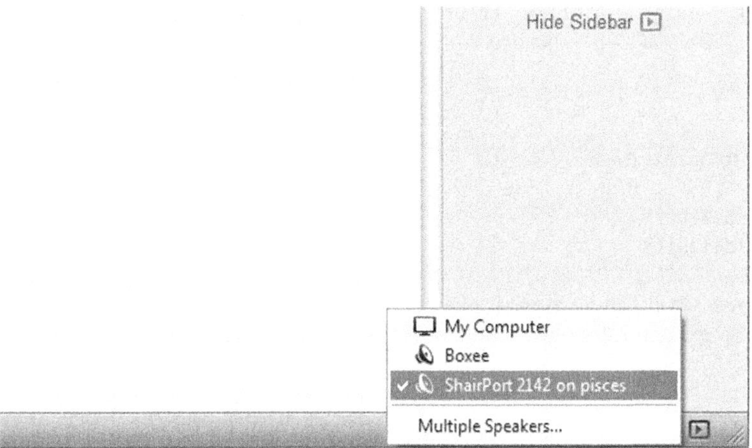

Figure 11-5. *ShairPort enabled*

Troubleshooting

As with XBMC, this process is fairly painless because the Raspberry Pi has a fixed hardware platform, and without all these variables there is not as much to worry about—things should just work.

If you find that no sound is coming out of your speakers when they are attached, check that you correctly issued both the `modprobe` and the `amixer` commands because both are needed to make the audio function.

Other than this issue, most of the commands should work. If not, you should delete any downloaded content and start over.

Airport on Boot

As with using the XBMC instance, most people won't want to have shairport started with their system without needing to manually log in to your Pi and start the application. This is easy for us because the shairport install has all the files needed to do this bundled with it! To perform this, first install the shairport system: run `sudo make install`, and your output should look like this:

```
$ sudo make install
install -D -m 0755 hairtunes /usr/local/bin/hairtunes
install -D -m 0755 shairport.pl /usr/local/bin/shairport.pl
install -D -m 0755 shairport /usr/local/bin/shairport
```

Once the install is finished, you can copy the provided init script into the correct location:

```
$ sudo cp shairport.init.sample /etc/init.d/shairport
```

Now that the file is copied, you need to make one small modification: add the modprobe command from earlier—modprobe snd_bcm2835—into the /etc/init.d/shairport file just before you start the shairport application. The start section should look like this:

```
start() {
    echo -n "Starting shairport: "
    modprobe snd_bcm2835
    start-stop-daemon --start --quiet --pidfile "$PIDFILE" \
                      --exec "$DAEMON" -b --oknodo -- $DAEMON_ARGS
    log_end_msg $?
}
```

The last commands we need to run are these:

```
$ sudo chmod +x /etc/init.d/shairport
$ sudo update-rc.d shairport defaults
```

These commands make the new start script writeable and update the boot sequence to include the new shairport scripts! Reboot your Pi, and shairport should be up and running for you on boot! Congratulations.

Summary

In this comprehensive chapter, you installed a whole course of precursor applications and learned how to download source code, configure it, and compile from it. This is quite a lot of work and the XBMC compile took in excess of 12 hours!

You also created and installed start scripts to get these new media playback systems to run on the Pi at boot, avoiding the need to manually intervene.

Finally, you connected the XBMC instance to the remote control application for smartphones. This has been an incredible amount of work for one chapter, so well done!

CHAPTER 12

Installing Windows 10!

Wait what? Windows 10? Isn't this a Linux book? Well, yes, the focus of this book is firmly on learning Linux with the Raspberry Pi, but one of the neat features that has a lot of people excited is its new found ability to run Windows 10. Now if you're starting to think that we're being just a little bit heretical, then don't worry, we're only going to scratch the surface in this book. In fact we're going to show you how to install it, get it up and running, and that's basically it.

So why then are we taking up precious space with this? Well, we want you to be aware of all the capabilities of the Raspberry Pi, and even though you might not want to use Windows 10 now, who knows what Microsoft will come out with in the future? In short, as much as we love Linux and Open Source, we are also pragmatic and that means using the best tools at our disposal. In this chapter, we're simply providing you with a new tool for your toolbox.

I Thought Windows couldn't Run on the Pi?

For those of you that have read the first edition (thank you by the way!), you might recall that we spent quite a bit of time in the Introduction explaining that although the Raspberry Pi is an ARM based device, it can't actually run Windows RT (Microsoft's ARM based version of Windows commonly found on tablets and the like). Needless to say if you check the Introduction in this edition that particular boxout has been replaced!

Now before you get too excited about running Windows on a Pi, the first thing you need to know is that the version of Windows that supports the Pi is not the one that you may be looking forward to running on your PC (especially if you have previously "upgraded" to Windows 8). Instead it is a highly cut down version of Windows that really just makes the basics available to you. You get a powerful API for writing software but it's really meant to be powering data collection devices or remote sensors - not a desktop.

Okay, so the lack of a full on desktop environment is a bit disappointing. I'm not a big Windows user, and even I was disappointed that I wouldn't be able to turn my Pi into a handy remote desktop machine. However there is some good news to be had - the Internet of Things edition of Windows 10 will be completely free to download and use on the Pi!

■ **Note** All of this stuff covered in this chapter has been taken from the Internet and is based on what is believed to be the best current sources. It's quite possible that by the time you read any of this the platform will have moved on and this won't be so relevant.

Why include it? Well, this turn of events (Windows on the Pi) deserves mentioning and from what I can tell, some of the instructions and requirements listed on Microsoft's own page aren't actually correct. So use this as a guide, but you may find newer and more accurate stuff available by the time you get to read this.

Check out their main site for the latest and greatest:

`https://dev.windows.com/en-us/iot`

The Internet of what Now?

The Internet of Things (or IoT for short) has been taking the world by storm, especially in the last year or so. Previously the Internet was full of data. You could search for restaurants, send and receive messages and do some online banking without any trouble at all but ultimately you were just moving bits of data around. Useful for sure but not terribly exciting.

Step in the IoT. With this way of looking at the Internet, rather than it being simply machines sharing data, it instead a collection of things such as sensors or devices that can be communicated with and controller over the network.

For example, you could add a temperature sensor to your Raspberry Pi, put it in a cupboard somewhere and it will happily sit there reporting the current temperature. That might be useful if you're doing something like brewing your own beer where you want to track and control temperature. In fact I actually use the Pi I bought for the first edition of this book to control the boiler in a building using a solid state relay.

So when we talk about the Internet of Things, what we're really talking about is letting computers interact with the world around them. From sensing (such as temperature, light and even radiation) to doing (turning a boiler on and off or opening or closing a gate), this opens a whole new way of using the Internet.

One of the challenges with the IoT is the fact that you need things to actually do the sensing or do the doing. You could use a big box PC, but that's not really ideal. They draw a lot of power (especially if you just want to read a temperature sensor), require cooling, are generally noisy, take up a lot of space and are well, somewhat unsightly in modern homes. Add to that the fact they're heavy, they're really not the kind of thing you want to place in a tree or the top shelf in the garage.

What you need is something small, portable and reliable. Ideally you want no moving parts (so no fan that can die on you in the middle of the night, 50 miles from where you live), low power requirements and given that it could be in a harsh environment, you don't really want to be paying too much for it. If that sounds like a Raspberry Pi, then you're not the only one who thinks so - in fact the Pi's ability to interface with such a wide range of sensors and devices has made it a very popular system for IoT development. Not only do you get access to all those devices but you also get to do it with a full operating system, something that something like Arduino can't offer you.

But why Windows?

Personally, I'd be unlikely to use Windows but that's because I've been working with Linux for nearly two decades. I'm comfortable with Linux and I like how it works. However one of my best friends didn't follow my lead and stayed with Windows. Now he's a Windows expert, he's unlikely to want to use Linux, and especially when starting out with something new people are keen to use something that's familiar to them.

If you don't buy that as a good enough reason, perhaps the fact that the IoT version of Windows provides a full and comprehensive API (.NET access to hardware anyone?) and integrates very nicely with Microsoft's Azure cloud platform could persuade you. One of the key benefits that you get with this platform is that everything comes available out of the box (or at least will by the time the full version is released). With Linux, you need to piece the bits together yourself. Now that might not be an issue for you, but there's something to be said for having someone else take care of all of that for you.

Microsoft is also putting a lot of effort into building a community around the Internet of Things. Even though it's still in the tech preview stage, there are projects online that you can try out already. We're not going to cover those here, but if for no other reason than knowing your enemy (or getting insights on how other people are solving problems) it's worth checking out.

Getting Started

Like using the Pi itself, we need to get a few things set up if we're going to have any luck in getting your Pi to boot up with Windows. Here's a quick list of what you're going to need (adapted from the developer site):

- Machine running Windows 8
- Your Pi 2
- An 8GB mico SD card (at least 8GB) - class 10
- HDMI cable
- Ethernet cable

Windows 8

Now if you look at the developer's site, it claims that you need Windows 10 on your PC in order to use these tools. It also makes the claim that you must be running directly on hardware rather than running in a virtual machine (i.e. you need Windows as your main operating system - you can't use Virtualbox or VMWare).

This didn't seem to be true from my testing. In fact it the tools ran just fine under Windows 8.1 on VMWare and I had no trouble writing the flash image to the SD card. Thus, you'll probably be fine if you do this as well. It could be that Microsoft changes something in the future that does require Windows 10, but VMWare at least had no trouble dealing with an SD card reader.

Your Pi 2

Okay, this is an important one. Windows 10 needs the latest and greatest Pi. The original Pi (all versions) simple isn't up to the task and Windows won't work. You need at least the Pi 2 although presumably later version of the Pi will continue to be supported. Microsoft seems to be pretty keen on IoT and I expect they'll be supporting the Pi for a long time to come.

8GB SD Card

You should already have this from your initial set up. Of course you're probably quite happy with the way things have been set up and aren't that keen on trashing it just to give Windows a spin. In that case you're going to need a second card.

The minimum requirements from Microsoft state that 8GB is needed and should be at least a class 10. The class refers to the speed of the card, but these days class 10 cards are more the norm than the exception. Most cameras need high speed cards so they can quickly get their large images stored safely, otherwise it makes the camera feel slow. Because of this you really shouldn't have any trouble finding a class 10 card in your favourite local store.

■ **Caution** When I first tried to test this, I used an SD card that apparently isn't a class 10. It was able to write the image, and although it would boot the Pi, it would end up in a black screen and never continue. A bit of web searching later, I discovered this is a known issue with slow SD cards, which is why a class 10 is required. So save yourself a lot of frustration and make sure your card is a class 10 before you spend a few hours trying to debug it.

HDMI Cable

Not too much to say about this one. If you've been following along with this book you already have it and if not, well, you only need it to "see" that Windows has booted on the Pi. There is a tool included with the Windows IoT download that lets you detect a Pi on your local network, so if your cable is busy elsewhere, you can get away with just using Ethernet.

Ethernet Cable

Similar to the HDMI cable, you can get away with this one if you don't really care about seeing the Pi on the network and you're really just curious to see if a Pi can really boot Windows. If you don't have an HDMI cable, detecting the Pi on the network will really be the only way to know for sure that it has worked.

Downloading the Tools

For some reason best known to themselves, Microsft has made the IoT download available as an ISO image. This means it looks and feels like a CD or a DVD and in fact you could burn it to a DVD if you wanted to. However it only contains a single executable file, so why they went to all this trouble is beyond me. In any case you're going to need the ISO image and tools to access it. On Windows 8.1, (it won't work on Windows 7 and below) Windows will take care of this for you and will open the ISO image as a virtual DVD - you don't need to actual burn it to disc.

At the time of writing, you can download the image from the Internet of Things dev centre found here:

```
http://go.microsoft.com/fwlink/?LinkId=616847
```

If that link doesn't work for you, searching Google for "Windows 10 Raspberry Pi 2 download" will find the link for you.

Installing the IoT tools

Once you've downloaded the image you should end up with a file that looks like Figure 12-1.

Figure 12-1. *Windows can see it's an ISO image*

If you see this icon then you know that Windows is able to open it. You'll need at least Windows 8.1 to get this to work, though.

When you double click on this icon, Windows will mount the image as a virtual device and will pretend that it's a real DVD. There's only a single file on the image and that's the one that we need to run. You should see something like Figure 12-2:

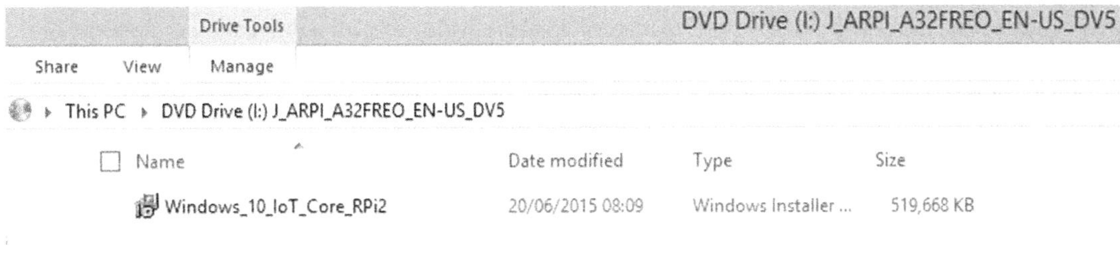

Figure 12-2. *Opening the ISO image*

I don't actually have a DVD drive attached to this machine (it's a virtual machine in any case) so you can see that Windows is taking care of that behind the scenes. Let's get the tools installed by double clicking on the installer. You should get this installer as in Figure 12-3:

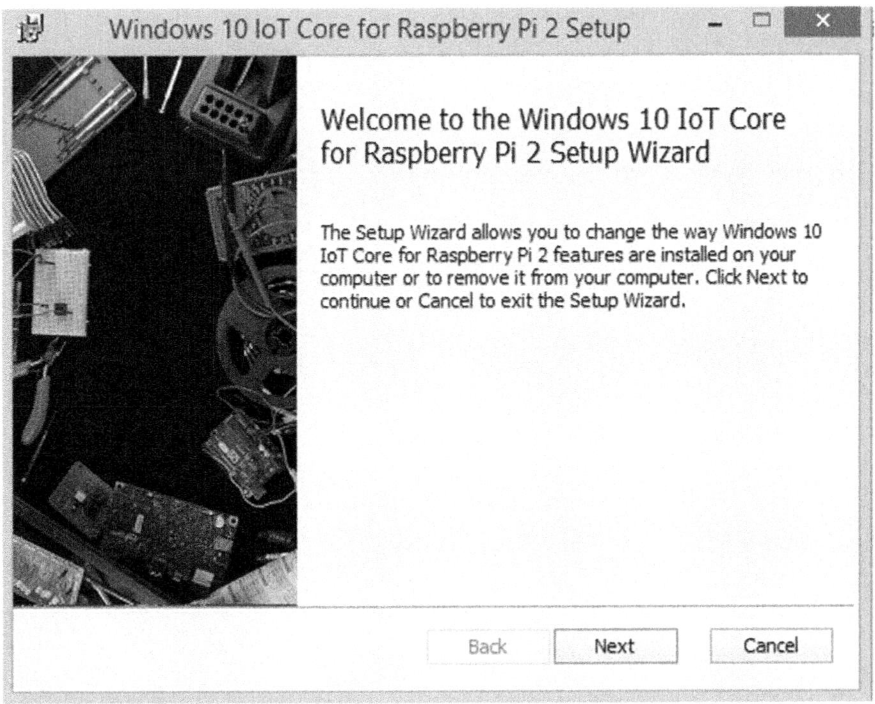

Figure 12-3. *Installing the IoT tool set*

As with most Windows installers (though whether you should or not is debatable) you can get through simply by pressing Next and agreeing to everything. After spinning about for a bit, the installer should tell you that everything has been properly installed and you can exit. Everything is now ready for use.

What do you Get in the Box?

Well so far as I can tell, you get three things of interest. First is a handy tool for writing out the firmware image to your SD card. The second is the firmware image that you want to actually write and contains the IoT version of Windows 10. Lastly is a dinky little tool that detects an IoT Pi on the network and tells you its status.

Let's take them for a spin...

Writing the Firmware to the SD Card

You've already done this under Linux when you initially installed NOOBS or Raspbian onto your Pi. Back then though you were using a different set of (tried and tested) tools and potentially did it under Linux or a Mac. The firmware image seems to be just that, a simple image that we write to the SD card, but just in case Microsoft does something special, we're going to use their tools for this one.

First we need to find it. On my machine, it was installed in the following location:

C:\Program Files (x86)\Microsoft IoT

If you browse to that directory you should see something like Figure 12-4.

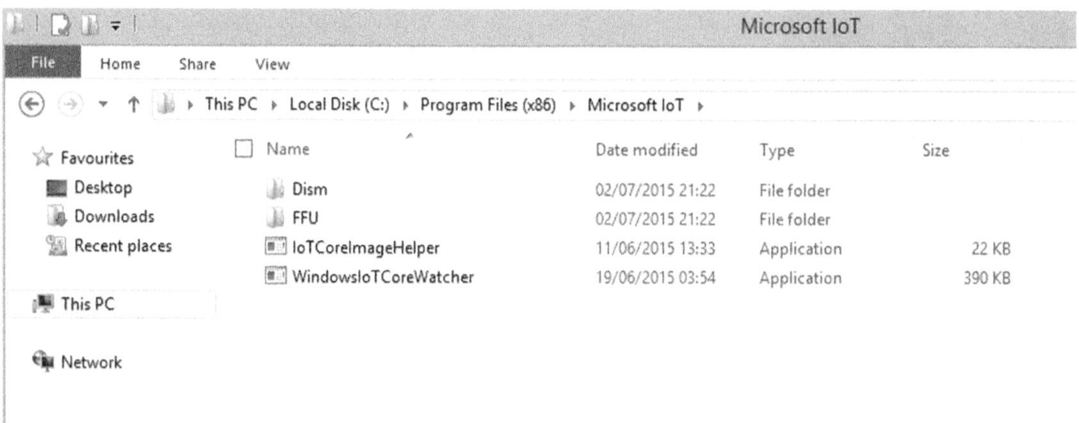

Figure 12-4. *Finding the IoT tools*

The application we're interested in is "IoTCoreImageHelper" which is really just a fancy sounding name for "Image Writer". Double click on this app to start it up and you'll get a nice little app with a simple and clean interface (Figure 12-5):

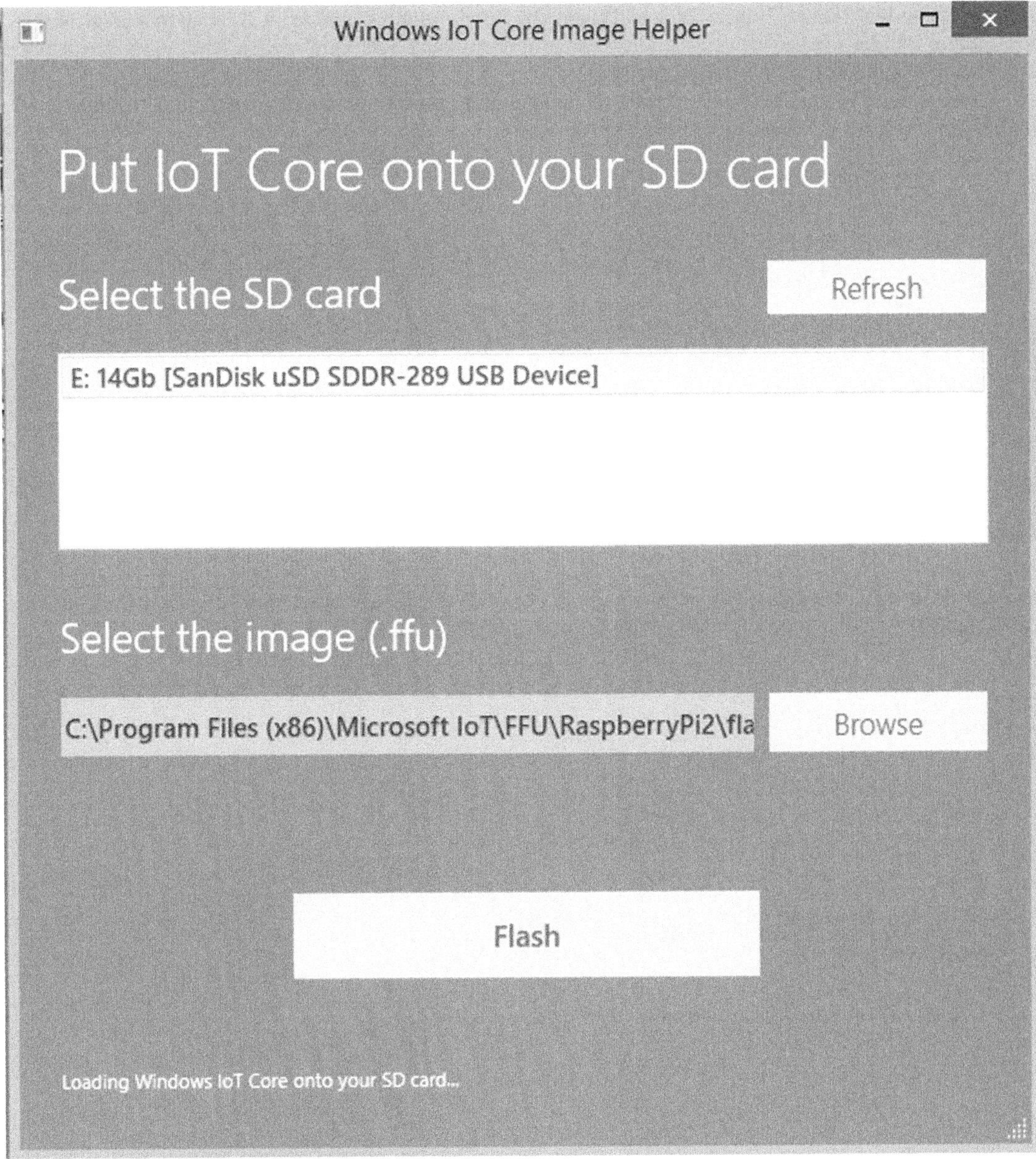

Figure 12-5. *Burning the image onto your SD card*

As you can see, I took the screenshot after I'd already filled in the basics. It's worth noting that originally, the SD card didn't show up and I was beginning to wonder whether the Microsoft site had in fact been correct in that it would require a real physical machine to write to the card. However it turned out that I had simply neglected to plug the SD card reader in (whoops) and as soon as VMWare detected it, I was able to press the Refresh button and see the card right away. So do make sure that Windows can see the device and it shows up under "This PC" (although it will always by "My Computer" for me). I also had to reinsert the SD Card for Windows to see it, even though it had properly detected the card reader. Why? Who knows, but sometimes wiggling the wires actually does fix things.

The last thing you need is to select the flash image file that you want to write to the card. This is located in the same folder as the tools under FFU (Figure 12-6):

C:\Program Files (x86)\Microsoft IoT\FFU\RaspberryPi2

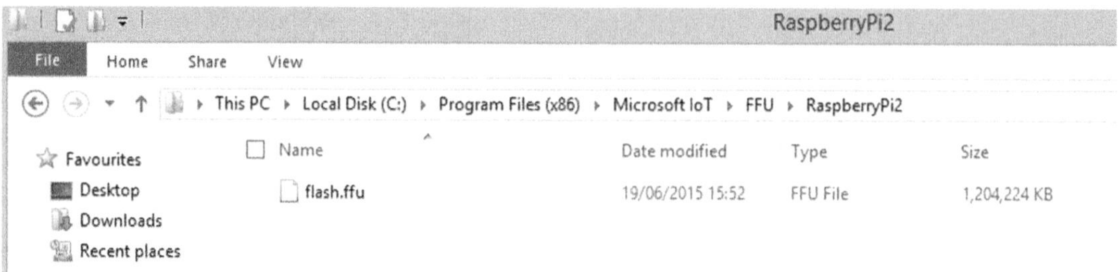

Figure 12-6. *The rather originally named flash file*

Once you've selected the path, all you have to do is press the "Flash" button and it will write to your card. You will get a final reminder that you're about to pulverize your SD card (see Figure 12-7):

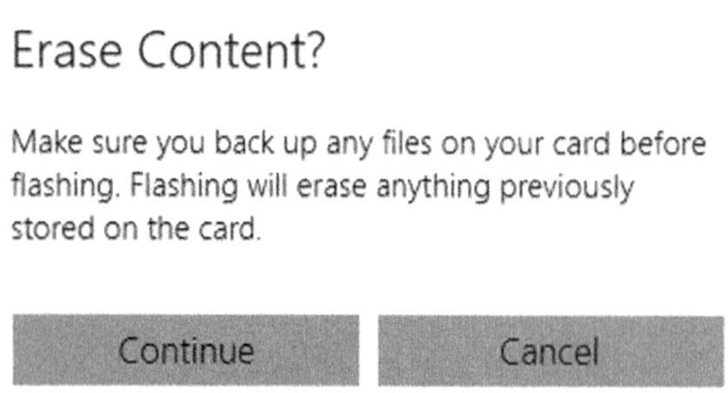

Erase Content?

Make sure you back up any files on your card before flashing. Flashing will erase anything previously stored on the card.

Continue Cancel

Figure 12-7. *Are you sure you want to erase the card?*

Now depending on which version of Windows you're using, you will get an alert asking you if it is okay to "make changes to this computer". In reality it won't change the machine, but it does need elevated privileges in order to write directly to a device (Linux also requires elevated privileges if you want to work directly with devices). So if you get the following warning, just say "Yes" and carry on (Figure 12-8):

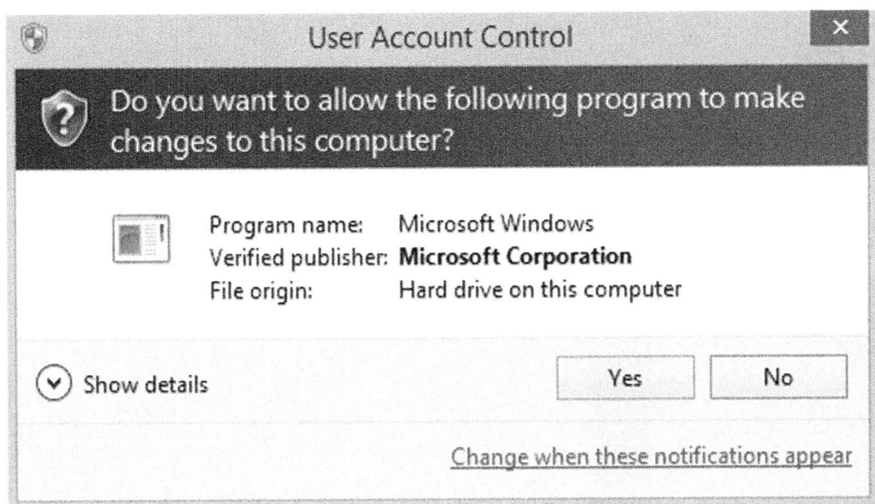

***Figure 12-8.** You need to give the program a higher level of access so it can write directly to the SD Card*

It looks like this shiny new tool is actually a frontend for an older console (text based) application as when it is writing you will see updates in a console screen. Although you can run this command manually yourself and avoid using the graphical interface, you'd need to work out the flags and options by yourself. In any case don't be surprised or concerned when you see the following window pop up (Figure 12-9):

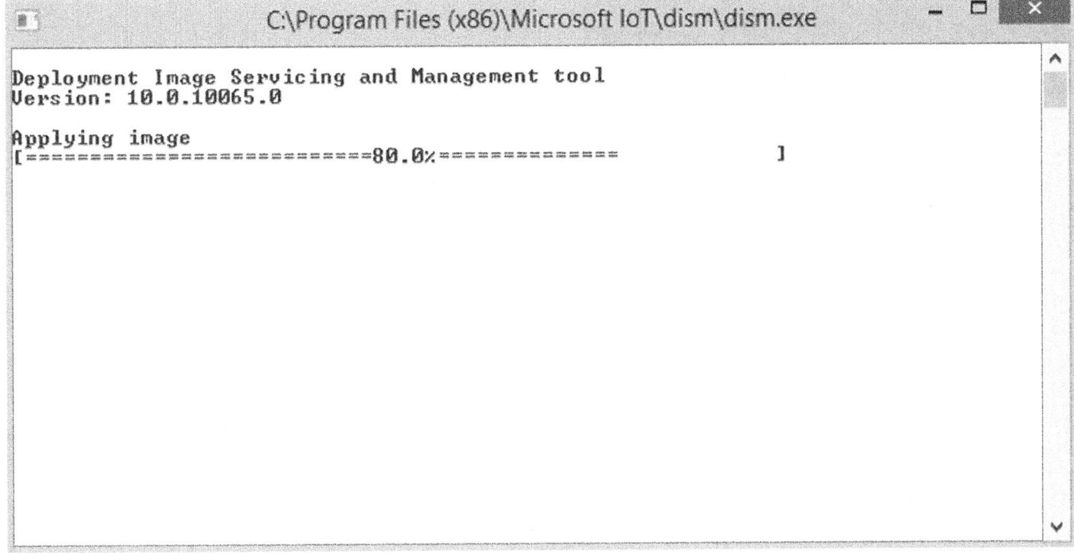

***Figure 12-9.** Writing the image to the SD card*

It can take quite some time to write the image file, especially if you're using USB 2. Even when using USB 3, it still took a good ten minutes for this image to be written successfully. Don't worry if it seems to be taking its time, it'll get there in the end.

Once it is complete, you're now ready to boot up your Pi.

Firing up the Pi

Now that you've got Windows on to the SD card, it's time to actually put it to work. Like NOOBS or Raspbian, this bit is really straight forward - all you have to do is insert the SD card and power up the Pi. That's really all there is to it.

After you power it on you should see a black screen with the following logo in the middle of it and all being well, a little "busy please wait" logo will follow just beneath it (Figure 12-10):

Figure 12-10. *Windows boot logo*

After a bit of spinning the screen will go black for a while. This is perfectly normal and lasts for a couple of minutes. Once it has done what it needs to do (like Raspbian, there is some initial set up done during the first boot such as expanding the partition size), it will reboot and start up the default testing application.

Before we get to that though, there is something else you might encounter. When the screen goes black, rather than rebooting after a few minutes, it instead stays, well, black. Now it's not really clear how long you should wait, but I managed to get through an entire episode of Mythbusters without so much as a peep from the Pi. I decided that I should reboot it and give it another go. This time it did reboot after a minute or so, but instead of loading the default app, it just went back to the same logo, did a bit of spinning before going black and rebooting. Rinse and repeat.

As I mentioned briefly earlier, this turns out to be a known issue if you don't use a high speed (specifically at least a class 10) SD card. I hadn't noticed that the card I was using was not in fact class 10 and as I always buy class 10, I didn't occur to me to check.

So, if you end up with your Pi in a rebooting time loop, or it just sits there in stubborn blackness, it's probably your SD card. As soon as I replaced mine with a real class 10, it worked first time. To paraphrase the Mythbusters, I make these mistakes so you guys don't have to.

Configuration Time

Now assuming you don't get the black screen of death, you should instead end up with a screen that looks something like this (Figure 12-11):

Figure 12-11. *Windows getting things ready*

Given the time wasted with the other SD card, you can probably imagine how happy I was to see this particular screen. If you see this too, then your Pi is only a few minutes away from being ready for you to configure it. Here's the screen that follows this one (Figure 12-12):

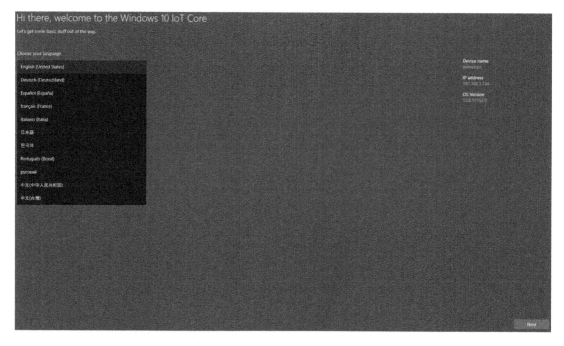

Figure 12-12. *Welcome to Windows on Pi*

Now this screenshot is a little hard to read, but it's here mostly to show you the screens that I went through. On the left we have a list of languages and on the bottom right a next button. Fortunately for me, English is what I wanted and so all I had to do was hit the next button. Of course if you prefer another language this is where you can set it up.

On the top right are some basic pieces of information about the Pi such as its name, IP address and the OS version that it's running. Once you press Next, you'll be take to the final screen which shows your Pi fully operational (Figure 12-13):

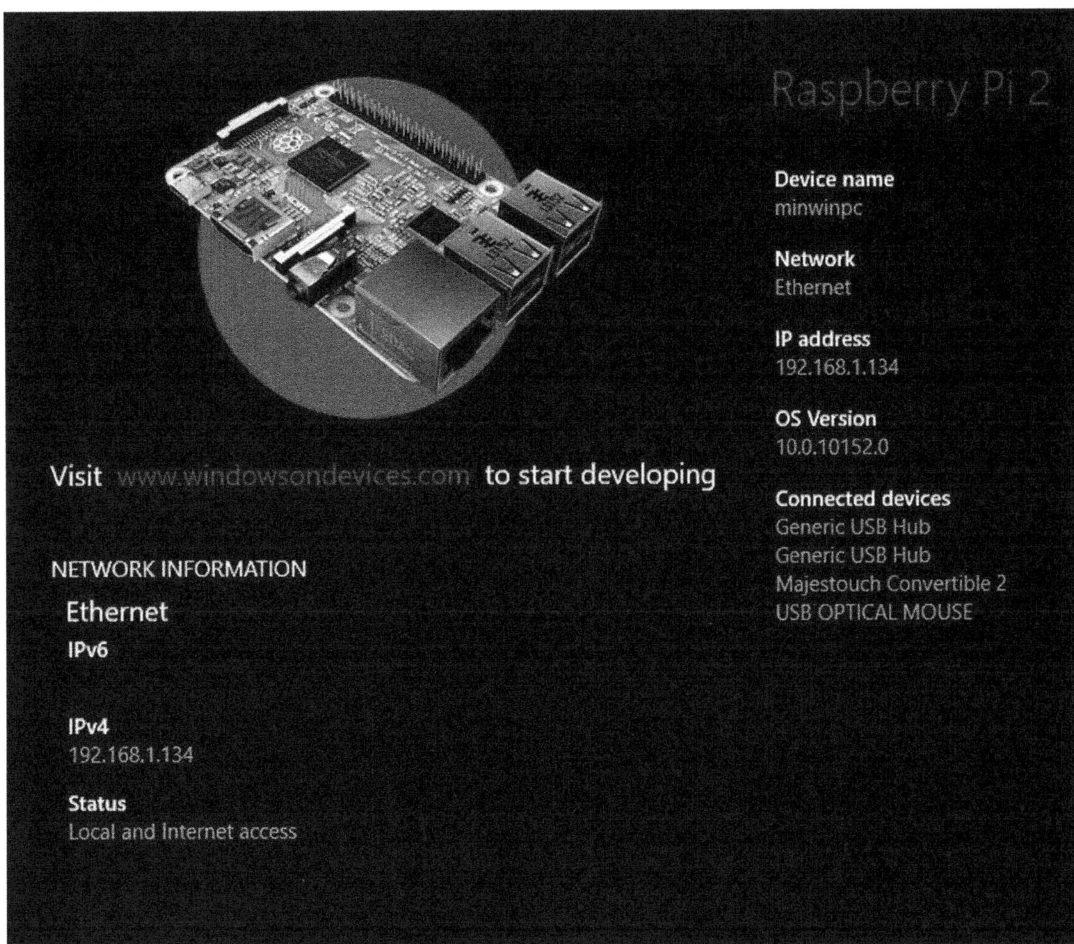

Figure 12-13. *Fully booted Pi*

To save space, I've taken a snippet from the middle of the page. The options on the top are fairly self explanatory, so I will leave those for you to explore. This page gives a little bit more information than the configuration page, but really not that much of interest to us at this stage. In fact the only real difference is a pretty picture of the Pi and a list of connected devices.

One useful feature about this page though is that it provides you with a link to the Microsoft "Windows on Devices" page which will help you get started with developing software for your Pi. Whilst browsing around I even came across tutorials for writing your own device drivers, so there's really something for everyone on there. In any case congratulations are in order - you're one of the first people to run Windows on a Raspberry Pi! I have to admit it was pretty cool to see this booting the first time and even I am interested in seeing where Microsoft takes this platform!

Sensing the Pi on the network.

Before we wrap up, let's take a step back to the other tool in the toolbox, "WindowsIoTCoreWatcher". What it really is is a way for you to detect the Pi over the network. If you go back to the folder (check out the first part of this chapter for a reminder of where it is) you can fire it up by double clicking its icon.

If your Pi is alive and well you should see something similar to this (Figure 12-14):

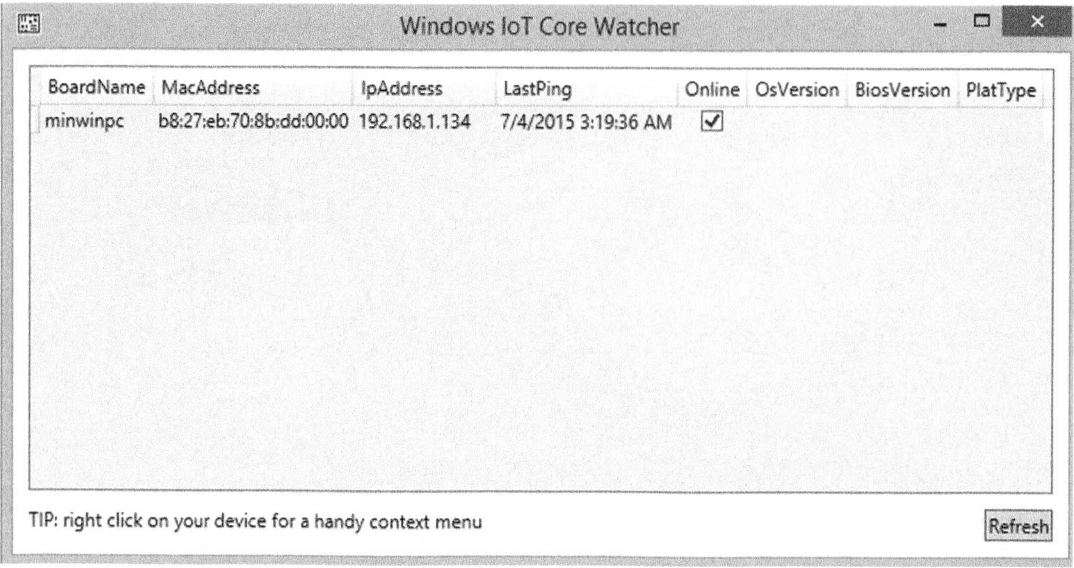

Figure 12-14. *IoT Core Watcher lets you spy on your Pi*

This was how I was able to determine that my Pi was half alive after all the black screen and rebooting issues - it showed up in this list. Now granted it doesn't tell you very much but it does at least let you know that the Pi is up and running and most importantly what its IP address is. Once you develop your own apps and start deploying systems, being able to quickly find your Pi (and specifically finding the right Pi as you could well have a number of them) this application could become very handy indeed.

What next?

So now you have Windows installed what can you do with it? Well with the basic set up, honestly not a lot. However on the main application screen in the top left hand corner there is a tab for "Tutorials". If you click that, you will be able to find some projects that you can try to get yourself started. These are hardware based projects such as "Blinky" which involves turning an LED on and off. There are of course far more complicated projects available.

As mentioned before, there is a developer site that you can visit:

```
https://dev.windows.com/en-us/iot
```

This site contains a wealth of information, tutorials and advice on building devices with Windows. As this is primarily a Linux book we won't go into any more detail on this, but hopefully this piqued your interest in the Internet of Things and just maybe added an extra string to your bow.

Summary

This chapter was a quick walkthrough on setting up Windows 10 for Internet of Things on a Raspberry Pi. This stuff is still in preview and so things are subject to change but the basics are likely to very similar.

We walked through downloading the ISO image containing the toolset and firmware, extracting and installing that toolset and then using the provided tools to write the image to your SD card.

We then booted up the Pi, did some basic configuration and used the IoT watcher application from the toolset to verify that the Pi was up and running. We tied off that section by highlighting the best website to visit for Windows on the Pi.

Windows on the Pi is still a bit controversial but I think it is a big step forward in the adoptance of the Raspberry Pi as a compute platform. Sure it was initially intended just for learning how a computer works but it has far and away exceeded those initial goals. It has great Linux support and now Microsoft is added their own support for the platform. This really can't be bad for the Raspberry Pi or us and users and developers.

CHAPTER 13

TOR

Over the course of this book we have discussed a number of different ways in which you can tailor the Raspberry to be solve problems in your every day life. Many of these projects were about finding ways to use your Raspberry Pi around the home to provide solutions to little problems. In this chapter we are going to talk about the use of Tor software, which can not only be used at home but also while out and about to protect your privacy.

With the aim of protecting your privacy in mind, its probably best to go over what TOR is and how it works. TOR is short for The Onion Router, which is a piece of software designed to allow anonymous internet communications to protect your privacy. Now, many of you will ask "why would I need this at home" and the truth is that under normal circumstances people should not need a privacy protections in the home. Sadly, there are certain circumstances when you may wish to ensure anonymity and privacy. There have recently been a number of publicised cases where ISP's have been using spy software and injecting permenant tracking cookies into their customers internet traffic. This is done as the browsing habbits of users can be sold to advertising companies who are able to use this data to create more targeted avertising profiles.

Outside of the doom and gloom of ISP's spying on you, the next major use of the TOR software would be while traveling. This is really where the Raspberry Pi shines due to its size, portability and low power requirements. Imagine you are traveling and need to connect to your bank to quickly transfer some money to continue your life of enjoyment on the road. Currently, you are staying at a little hotel that has a pair of public computers available for any member of the hotel to use. As you can imagine, these may not be the best computers to use as you cannot know what virsues or other nasties are installed on this PC. Moreover, you cannot know what other things are lurking on the network to capture your banking details for malicious purposes. This is where TOR and your Raspberry Pi come in to save the day, you can quietly connect your Pi in place of the PC, using its USB for power, monitor, ethernet, mouse and keyboard to gain connectivity to your known safe environment. You can then use the TOR system that we will go over installing and configuring within this chapter to browse with anonymity and security.

If the hotel provided WiFi and had a HDMI enabled TV you could connect your Pi to the TV and to the greater internet using a wireless adapter (like the one we covered in Chapter 9: WiPi) and a small portable mouse and keyboard set. This way you can browse from the comfort of your hotel room while still remaining safe and secure.

What is TOR

Up to this point, I can imagine you are all saying "Wow. What is this magical wonderful piece of software and how does it actually work to protect my privacy?". The Onion Router is more than a funny Shrek reference, it gives an insight into how the software works (see Figures 13-1 and 13-2).

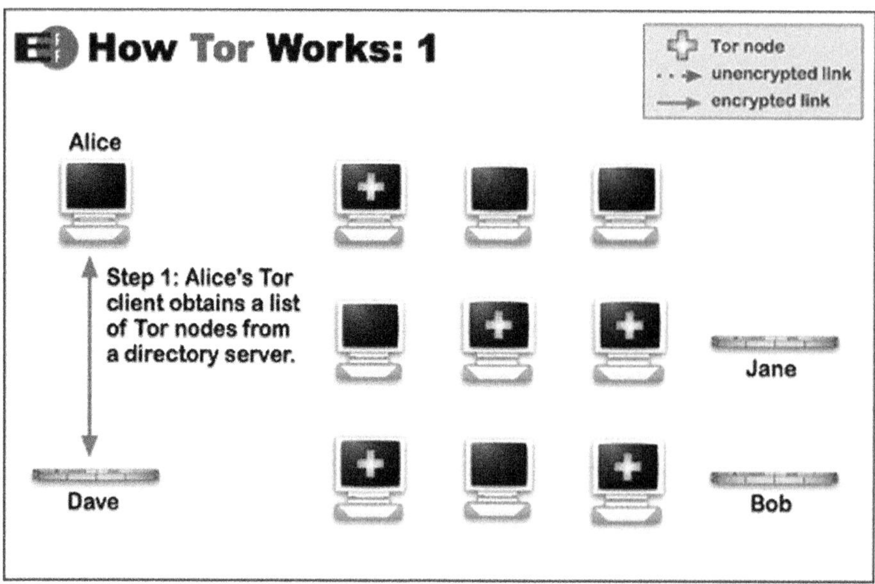

Figure 13-1. *How Tor Works, part 1*

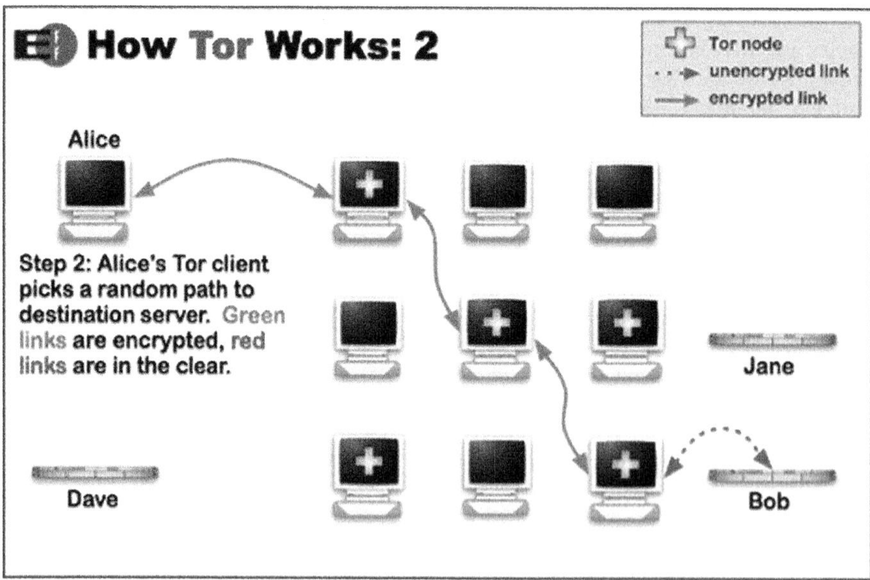

Figure 13-2. *How Tor Works, part 2*

TOR works by there being a number of specialised user run servers (called relays) spread over the internet that you can connect to and a directory server which knows about all of the various relay servers. You (the end user) connect to the directory server, downloads a list of all relays and create a "virtual circuit" of a number of different relays.

The software then takes an internet request and wraps it in a number of layers of encryption (see the onion metaphore coming into play here!). This big blob (onion) of layered encrypted data is then sent on to the first relay in the virtual circuit which removes the top layer of encryption revealing to it the second relay in the circuit. The first relay forwards the now slighly smaller onion onto the second relay and the process repeats until it gets to the last relay in the circuit.

The last relay in the circuit can then send the original unencrypted internet traffic off to the end destination. The traffic can then follow backwards along the same path using the same encryption methods as before. As each node will only ever know the next node in the sequence there is no way for any one relay in the circuit to determine where both the origin and destination are. As all of the traffic between individual relays is encrypted the contents of the communication is safe from eavesdropping.

As you can see, the onion like TOR system provides quite a good solution to granting anonymous and secure internet connectivity. It does have a weakness however; TOR provides adequate security only when there are a number of users on the TOR network at any given time. Unless there are a number of users using the various relays at a given time it is theoretically possible for someone at the end node or destination site to potentially discern the original user. If you think back over the previous examples of how TOR works, imagine if there was only one user in amongst all of those nodes. With knowledge of who is on the network it would be quite easy to see where that one and only person is sending traffic. Thankfully for everyone using TOR there are estimated to be about 2 million people directly connecting to TOR from various countries around the world at any given time of the day.

Installing TOR

As with any piece of software that you wish to use, we first need to install it. And before installing any new package we should look to update your system software to the latest version, so you can go ahead and run the following commands to get your system up to date. Of course, you may not need to run these commands if you have updated recently. Remember that if you have to run rpi-update you may need to reboot following.

```
sudo apt-get update
sudo apt-get upgrade
sudo rpi-update
```

With your system updated we can look to get TOR installed and working. There are a number of ways you can go about getting TOR installed for your use, and by far the easiest way (according to the TOR Projects webpage) is to install the TOR Browser Bundle. This bundle comes with the TOR application installed and a specialised browser that's configured to work with the TOR application. Unfortunately for us, this package is not setup to work with the Raspberry Pi yet, so we have to take a slighly different approach.

To start with, lets install the core TOR application which does all the routing and relay discovery that we disucssed earlier. To do this run the following commands:

```
sudo apt-get install tor
Reading package lists... Done
Building dependency tree
Reading state information... Done
The following extra packages will be installed:
  tor-geoipdb torsocks
Suggested packages:
  mixmaster xul-ext-torbutton socat tor-arm polipo privoxy apparmor-utils
```

```
The following NEW packages will be installed:
  tor tor-geoipdb torsocks
0 upgraded, 3 newly installed, 0 to remove and 4 not upgraded.
Need to get 2,589 kB of archives.
After this operation, 7,024 kB of additional disk space will be used.
Do you want to continue [Y/n]? y
```

Once the install process is finished the TOR application will automatically be booted up and running. The first thing we should do is check that the process is running, so run the following command to list all running processes and search specifically for the to process

```
ps -ef | grep /usr/bin/tor
```

You should see something like the following in your console:

```
109      14591     1  1 22:01 ?        00:00:09 /usr/bin/tor --defaults-torrc
/usr/share/tor/tor-service-defaults-torrc --hush
```

This shows that the TOR application is up and running. Now that we have confirmed that the application is running we should go and investigate the log. You can use the command below to open the log (remember, press q to quit the less application)

```
less /var/log/tor/log
```

When looking over the log you want to see something like this at the bottom of the file. These lines state that TOR has been able to get enough directory information to build a circuit, it was able to connect to the TOR network and successfully open a circuit. These are the basic functions that the TOR application needs to perform and indicate that everything is up and ready for use.

```
Jul 08 22:02:10.000 [notice] We now have enough directory information to build circuits.
Jul 08 22:02:10.000 [notice] Bootstrapped 80%: Connecting to the Tor network.
Jul 08 22:02:10.000 [notice] Bootstrapped 90%: Establishing a Tor circuit.
Jul 08 22:02:12.000 [notice] Tor has successfully opened a circuit. Looks like client
                             functionality is working.
Jul 08 22:02:12.000 [notice] Bootstrapped 100%: Done.
```

Using TOR

So, now that we have TOR installed we need to start using it. As we discussed earlier we cannot get the pre-installed and configured browser to use. As such we need to go and manually configure our browser to use TOR. We will be configuring the default browser that is included with the Raspberry Pi called Epiphany to use TOR with the method suggested by the TOR Project; setting your Linux system up to use TOR as a transparent proxy.

So, the first step to getting this process going is to change the TOR applications settings slighly. We want to setup TOR to be a "Transparent Proxy", which basically means a passthrough to the wider internet. We also want TOR to be doing DNS Resolution, which effectively means allowing TOR to work out how to get to `www.apress.com`. To do this we add the following 4 lines to `/etc/tor/torrc`

```
VirtualAddrNetworkIPv4 10.192.0.0/10
AutomapHostsOnResolve 1
TransPort 9040
DNSPort 53
```

After making these changes we need to restart the TOR application with the following command:

```
sudo /etc/init.d/tor restart
```

Once the TOR daemon has restarted it's a good idea to go back and check the log to confirm all is well. So go back and check /var/log/tor/log for the same messages about successfully bootstrapping that we looked for in the Installing TOR section of this chapter. The next step is to setup the systems DNS to use the TOR proxy, however before we go ahead and change things we need to make a backup of our current settings - for when we want to go back. We create the backup with:

```
sudo cp /etc/resolv.conf /etc/resolv.conf.bkp
```

To go back you can simply replace the resolv file with your original

```
sudo cp /etc/resolv.conf.bkp /etc/resolv.conf
```

Now that the backup is made we can go ahead and change the nameserver entry to be 127.0.0.1 as below:

```
nameserver 127.0.0.1
```

This is a special address in computing and is called a loopback addres - which is effectively a self-reference. The upshot of using this address is that when any DNS resolution is performed it will go to TOR and be routed out. With the loopback address in place we need to setup a method for routing all outbound network connections over TOR. To do this we will use an application called iptables to setup some local firewall rules to route data over TOR. Below is a small script written by the TOR Project designed to rout all outgoing connections over TOR. Before getting going we need to ensure that we exclude any local network addresses from being routed over TOR. This is exceptionally necessary if you are connecting over SSH, as you may end up sending all data intended for your local network out via TOR - where it will fail to work.

This change is only temporary and will vanish upon reboot. If you want to make this change permanent then you need to edit /etc/resolvconf.conf and uncomment the line reading name_servers=127.0.0.1. This will tell your system to read from local name servers upon boot.

To make this change we simply add extra variables to the _non_tor variable in the script below to include your local IP ranges. The script below includes 3 of the most common IP ranges. These are IP's that match 192.168.0.X 192.168.1.X and 10.0.0.X. You can add others if needed.

```
#!/bin/sh

### set variables
#destinations you don't want routed through Tor
_non_tor="192.168.1.0/24 192.168.0.0/24 10.0.0.0/24"
#the UID that Tor runs as (varies from system to system)
_tor_uid=`id -u tor`
#Tor's TransPort
_trans_port="9040"
### flush iptables
iptables -F
iptables -t nat -F
### set iptables *nat
iptables -t nat -A OUTPUT -m owner --uid-owner $_tor_uid -j RETURN
iptables -t nat -A OUTPUT -p udp --dport 53 -j REDIRECT --to-ports 53

#allow clearnet access for hosts in $_non_tor
for _clearnet in $_non_tor 127.0.0.0/9 127.128.0.0/10; do
   iptables -t nat -A OUTPUT -d $_clearnet -j RETURN
done

#redirect all other output to Tor's TransPort
iptables -t nat -A OUTPUT -p tcp --syn -j REDIRECT --to-ports $_trans_port

### set iptables *filter
iptables -A OUTPUT -m state --state ESTABLISHED,RELATED -j ACCEPT

#allow clearnet access for hosts in $_non_tor
for _clearnet in $_non_tor 127.0.0.0/8; do
   iptables -A OUTPUT -d $_clearnet -j ACCEPT
done

#allow only Tor output
iptables -A OUTPUT -m owner --uid-owner $_tor_uid -j ACCEPT
iptables -A OUTPUT -j REJECT
```

Once you have confirmed that all the needed excluded addresses are in the _non_tor variable we can go ahead and run the script to setup TOR. So go ahead and write that script out to a file tor.sh, then execute the script with the following command

```
sudo sh tor.sh
```

Now that TOR has been setup we sould go ahead and check that we are correctly using TOR (Figure 13-3). Again, the TOR Project comes to the rescue, they have provided a great website to visit that you can visit to confirm you are connected to TOR correctly. So go ahead and direct your browser to `https://check.torproject.org/` and confirm that your output matches Figure 13-3.

Congratulations. This browser is configured to use Tor.

Your IP address appears to be: **188.209.52.158**

Please refer to the Tor website for further information about using Tor safely. You are now free to browse the Internet anonymously. For more information about this exit relay, see: Atlas.

Donate to Support Tor

Tor Q&A Site | Volunteer | Run a Relay | Stay Anonymous

The Tor Project is a US 501(c)(3) non-profit dedicated to the research, development, and education of online anonymity and privacy. Learn More »

JavaScript is disabled.

Figure 13-3. *TOR Browser Check*

With this, you should now be up and running in privacy enabled TOR. Congratulations!

Disabling TOR

Disabling TOR is quite a straightforward thing to do. You simply need to reset iptables to remove everything that the script we ran before setup. To do this we simply run the folloing command which will flush everything from iptables:

```
sudo iptables -F
```

This will disable the bulk of the changes made, but will still leave the tor daemon running in background and will also leave the name server changes in tact. You should run the command below to stop the tor daemon.

```
sudo /etc/init.d/tor stop
```

You will also need to reverse the changes made to the resolv.conf file by restoring the backup we took earlier. The command below accomplishes this:

```
sudo cp /etc/resolv.conf.bkp /etc/resolv.conf
```

Errors and Troubleshooting

Over the process of this setup, you may run into a few problems. Here are some of the common problems you may encounter and how to solve them. The first is an issue you may is the following:

```
libkmod: ERROR ../libkmod/libkmod.c:554 kmod_search_moddep: could not open moddep file
'/lib/modules/3.18.7-v7+/modules.dep.bin'
```

This issue is to do with your system being slighlty out of date compared with iptables. The fix here is pretty straightforward, you need to update your Pi's internal system with the following command then retsart:

```
rpi-update
```

Another error you may encouter may be the following:

```
iptables v1.4.14: can't initialize iptables table `filter': Table does not exist
(do you need to insmod?)
```

This is to do with the iptables command being unable to interface correctly with your Pi's Linux Kernel. There are two solution here, the first is to run the following commands to install the kernel module for iptables.

```
sudo modprobe ip_tables
sudo -i
echo 'ip_tables' >> /etc/modules
```

Under newer versions of raspbian this may not work so you should look to run the raspberry pi update and upgrade commands:

```
sudo apt-get update
sudo apt-get upgrade
sudo rpi-update
```

Summary

Over the course of this chapter, you will have learnt what TOR is and how it is a utility for privacy in situations where you may not fully trust the devices you are connecting via. You will have learnt how to setup TOR and how you can configure your raspberry Pi to use it. Lastly you will have learnt how to disable the TOR system from your Pi. Armed with these skills and the portability of your Pi, you should be able to browse in safety regardless of where you are.

APPENDIX A

Doing it by Hand – Writing an SD Card Image

In the first chapter of the book, we highlighted how today it is no longer necessary to write the operating image directly to an SD card because NOOBS will take care of that for you. In fact NOOBS makes it so easy, you might be wondering why we're still including this information at all.

Well, the thing is NOOBS is all well and good when it works and does what you want. Specifically if you're a new user and want to install Raspbian or easily try a different operating system then NOOBS has you covered. But if you want to do anything else such as install a different operating system a number of times without having to redownload the image ten times or you want to put Raspbian on a hundred SD cards (well, who knows, you might), it would be much faster and ironically more straight forward to simply write the SD card yourself and bypass NOOBS altogether. You might recall from Chapter 1 that our Pi refused to play nice with NOOBS and would not go online without a lot of persusion - in this case, downloading the image by hand would probably be your best bet.

Getting Some Images

First before we can write an image to an SD card we need to get our hands on the image. Fortunately the most popular operating systems of choice for the Pi (including of course Raspbian) have images on the main download page here:

```
http://raspberrypi.org/downloads/
```

This is the same place where you downloaded NOOBS from earlier, and you'll find the raw images just below the NOOBS offering. In this example we'll cover Raspbian again, but of course you can do this with any of the choices on the page shown in Figure A-1.

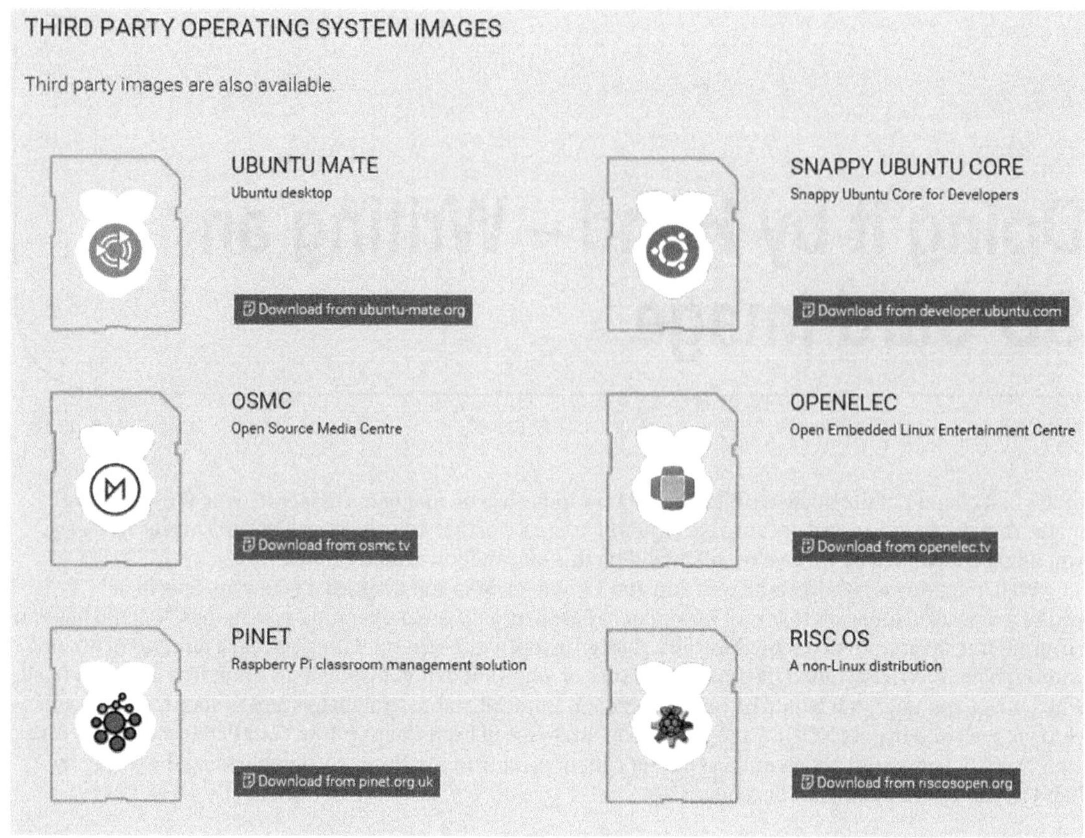

Figure A-1. *Plenty to choose from!*

For Raspbian (not shown in the last screenshot) you can choose to either download it directly or download it via Bit Torrent. Bit Torrent is the preferred means of downloading Raspbian as it eases the load on the project's servers and mirrors. However, you'll need a Bit Torrent client and there are some places where you probably shouldn't be firing one up (i.e., at work), and some connections that tend to perform very badly due to the way BitTorrent works (such as mobile 3G). Also at least in Hong Kong, the download performance is nowhere near as good as a local mirror. If you can, try to use Bit Torrent but otherwise, it's perfectly acceptable to use the direct links.

Remember we are downloading an image that is a direct representation of what should be on the card. If you just copy the image onto the card, it will still just be a card with a copy of the Raspbian image on it. What we need to do is write the image directly to the card, and for that we're going to need some of those handy tools we briefly mentioned earlier.

■ **Note** The image file you downloaded is a compressed ZIP file. On Windows 8.1, double-clicking this file will open a Compressed Folder. You will need to copy the image file itself to another location such as My Documents or your Desktop. On the Mac, simply double-clicking the file will extract the image and place it in the Downloads folder.

Using Image Writer on Windows

The tool recommended for writing images on Windows is the somewhat predictably named Image Writer. You can find the link on the Raspberry Pi downloads page or you can visit this link and select "External Downloads" which will cause it to download automatically (see Figure A-2):

```
https://launchpad.net/win32-image-writer
```

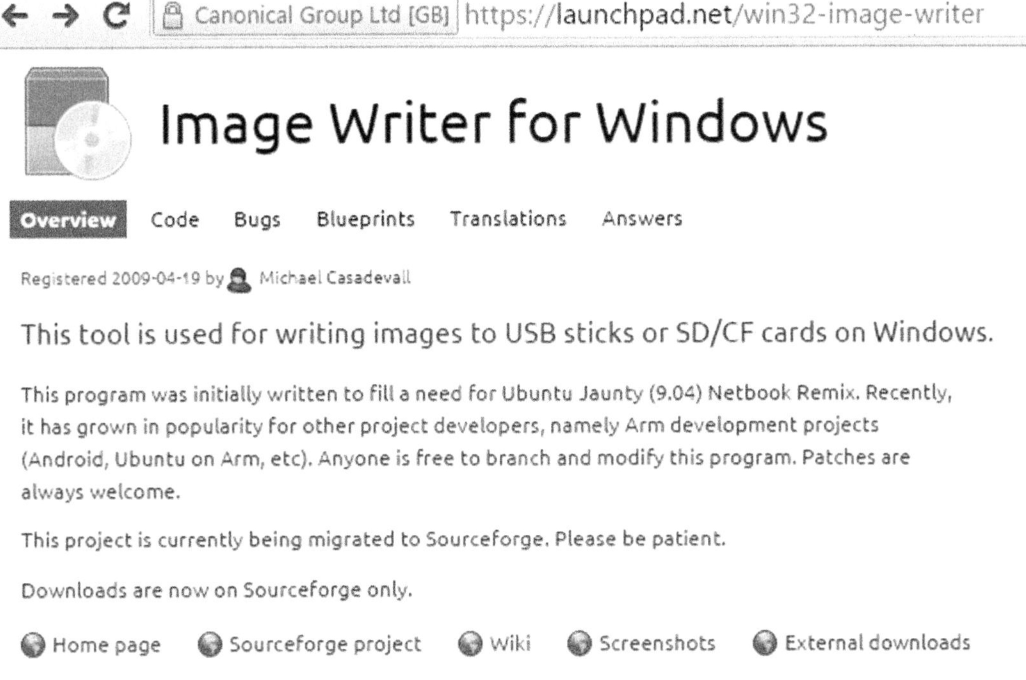

Figure A-2. *Downloading Image Writer*

At the time of writing, Image Writer is known not to work with Windows 10, although this may be resolved by the time you read this. If you need to use Windows 10, you can also take a look at the Windows IoT (Internet of Things) release for the Raspberry Pi 2. This toolkit contains an alternative image writing tool that should be able to write this images to the SD card without any trouble and as it's from Microsoft, it should work without problems on Windows 10.

Once you've downloaded Image Writer, you'll notice that it's an executable ready to run. Previously it was provided as a zip file and needed extracting first, but it looks like they've written a nice installer for you to use instead. So first things first - run the installer to get Image Writer installed. The first thing you'll get is a helpful warning from Windows (see Figure A-3).

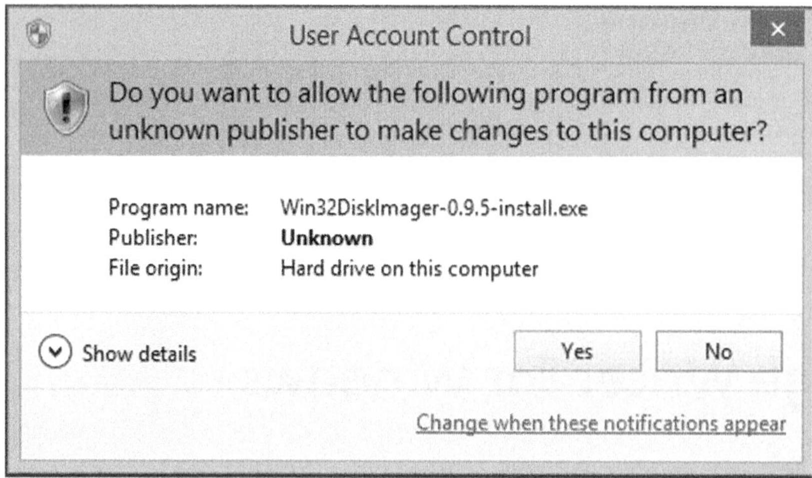

***Figure A-3.** The usual Windows warning*

We didn't notice any problems from installing and using this software, but as always, make sure you're comfortable installing unsigned third party software being using this tool.

So far so good - we have our imaging tool ready. Now we just need to extract the image file. As it's a zip file, just double click it and you'll see the image file inside. You can see that the compression (at least on the version we're looking at) is 69% which is pretty impressive. It's important to extract this file before writing it, otherwise you will end up simply writing out a zip file onto your SD card which wouldn't work well at all. You can either press the "Extract" button or you can drag the image onto your Desktop. Either solution works just as well.

Okay, now you just have to find Image Writer. The easiest way is to press the Start Button and start typing "win32DiskImager" and Windows should auto complete it for you (see Figure A-4).

***Figure A-4.** Finding image writer in the start menu*

Once you get it running it will look like Figure A-5.

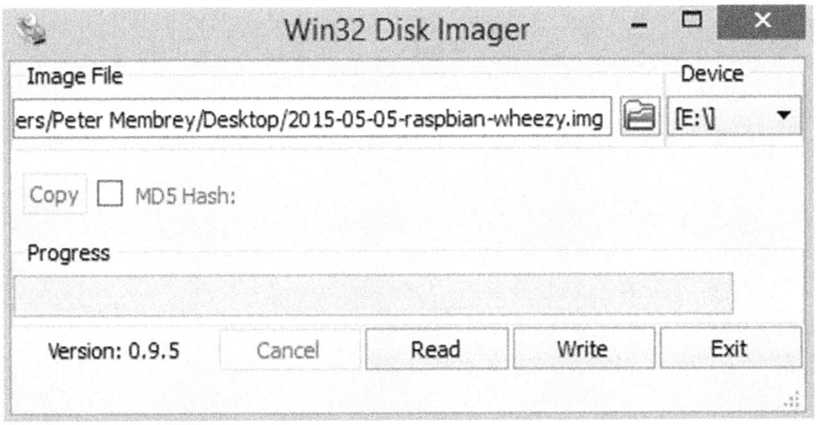

Figure A-5. *Image Writer reader to go*

As you can see in Figure A-5, it already has the relevant details filled in. You can see the path to the image (which I did actually extract to the desktop) and you can see the device that it will be written to (in this case E). This version of Disk Imager seems to be able to detect devices that are added after the application started. Once you've filled in the details, you just need to press the "Write" button. That should give you a warning prompt as per Figure A-6.

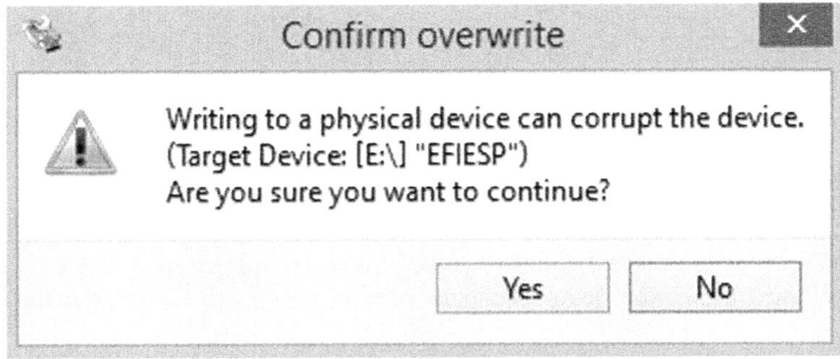

Figure A-6. *Last chance to change your mind*

It is definitely worth checking the device name here and ideally making sure that you don't have any other external devices plugged in. You really don't want to accidentally write the image onto a camera's SD card for example. We've seen it happen before, so it certainly can happen!

Once you start writing, you'll get the screen shown in Figure A-7.

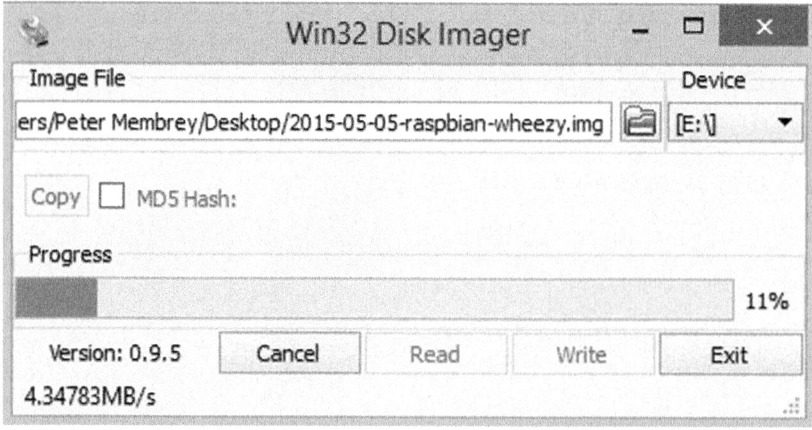

Figure A-7. *Writing in progress*

And ultimately the one shown in Figure A-8.

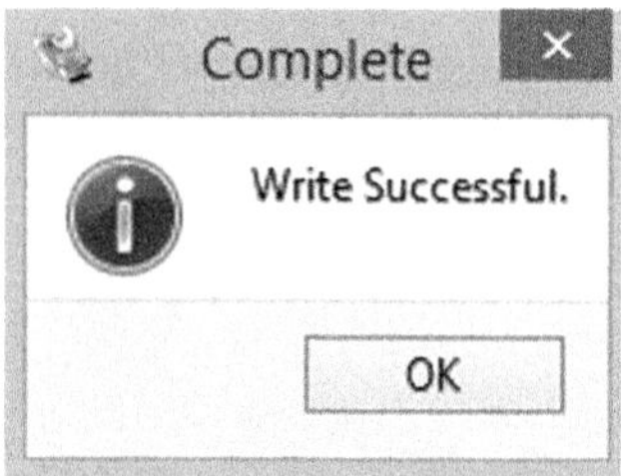

Figure A-8. *Just what it says on the tin*

Once you get the above pop up, you know it's safe to remove the SD card and use it in the Pi. Normally when writing to this sort of media, you need to eject the device to make sure that everything that should have been written has been (so yes there is a good reason why Windows complains when you remove a device "improperly"). When writing a disk image though you're bypassing the file system and writing directly to the device.

Right, that's it, you're done! If you picked Raspbian and are looking for some help setting it up (maybe NOOBS didn't work for you for some reason), you can head back to Chapter 1 and follow on from the first boot.

Using dd on the Mac

If you are using a Mac, we want to show you how simple it is to write an image to your SD card. Alas, we can't do that because there isn't a simple, easy way to do it (although there might be some by the time you read this, so do check with Google if you would rather not use dd). Disk Utility, which excels at so many other things, simply does not know how to handle our standard image files. We tried converting it to a `.dmg` file (the native image format for a Mac), which didn't work, either. We also looked at online tools that you might have been able to download to help with the problem, but we didn't find anything that made the task significantly easier than doing it by hand in the first place.

So we're going to get our hands dirty on the command line a little bit earlier than planned. We're not going to go into too much depth about what it is we're actually doing because most of these commands you'll see a little later in their Linux incarnations. For now, you'll just have to trust us.

Finding the Terminal

First, we need to open the terminal. You can find it in the `Utilities` directory under `Applications`. To put the following into context, we end this section with a complete transcript of all the commands that we used. The process is reasonably straightforward; it just has a fair number of moving parts.

We opened the terminal and now we need to use `sudo` to become the root user, the equivalent of Administrator on a Windows machine.

Now, tinkering with low-level devices is dangerous for security reasons (you don't want a virus being able to write directly to a hard disk, for example), so a normal user is not allowed to issue commands at that level. Because we need to write our Raspbian image directly onto an SD card, we simply have no choice: we need direct access to the card. Fortunately, root has effectively unrestricted access to the machine, so as root we can write the image to the card. The command we need to use is this:

```
sudo -i
```

This command opens an interactive prompt as the root user and gives "super user" privileges. You can use `sudo` to execute commands directly, but because we are going to be executing a few of them, it's more convenient to do it this way. `sudo` will then prompt you for your password (the one you normally use for your user account). Once `sudo` can confirm that it really is you sitting at the keyboard, you will end up at a root prompt.

■ **Caution** We now have permission to do anything we like on the system and although that means we can now make our image, it also means that we could really mess things up if we aren't careful. Under Unix it is assumed that root knows what it is doing and there is very little in the way of safe guards. Be very careful when running any command as root, double check it (and then do it again) and only when you're completely sure should you hit the Enter key. As soon as you're done, you should also close the Terminal window, just in case.

Okay, so what now? Well one of the challenges with writing to the SD Card is knowing which device on the system that card actually is. You don't want to accidentally mistake your main hard disk for it because that would have some rather unpleasant consequences. There are generally some assumptions you can make (for example we know that /dev/disk0 is pretty much always going to be the system disk so you never ever want to write to this) but in order to limit the risk, we're going to do this one by the numbers.

First, make sure your SD Card is not attached to your Mac and then run the mount command like so:

```
mbp:~ root# mount
/dev/disk0s2 on / (hfs, local, journaled)
devfs on /dev (devfs, local, nobrowse)
map -hosts on /net (autofs, nosuid, automounted, nobrowse)
map auto_home on /home (autofs, automounted, nobrowse)
mbp:~ root#
```

Now, you will probably see something similar to this but it might be a little different. We can ignore devfs and the map lines as they're really just parts of the operating system. What we're interested in here is the first line that identifies /dev/disk0s2 on /. This is the system disk and we want to make sure we don't touch this one. You might have additional entries in your list if you have any network drives mapped or disk images attached. That's okay because we're not really looking for anything in particular at this stage, we just want to establish a base line for your system.

Okay, now it's time to slot in your SD Card. SD Cards come preformatted for use in cameras (although these days many cameras will reformat them anyway) and so you should see it show up in Finder under Devices. For our particular card, it looked like Figure A-9.

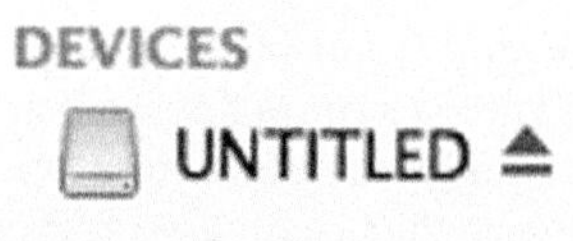

Figure A-9. *What you'll see in Finder after inserting your SD Card*

As the card has been automatically mounted, we can now go back and re-run our mount command to see how things have changed. Here's what we got when we reran it:

```
mbp:~ root# mount
/dev/disk0s2 on / (hfs, local, journaled)
devfs on /dev (devfs, local, nobrowse)
map -hosts on /net (autofs, nosuid, automounted, nobrowse)
map auto_home on /home (autofs, automounted, nobrowse)
/dev/disk2s2 on /Volumes/UNTITLED (msdos, local, nodev, nosuid, noowners)
mbp:~ root#
```

What we care about here is the addition of a new disk, in this case disk2. We can see from where it is mounted (/Volumes/UNTITLED) that this is the disk we are interested in. So now we know where we want to write our image.

■ **Info** BSD systems split disks out in slices. In our example, the mounted file system was on disk2s2. This translates to disk2, slice 2. This allows you to reference a slice directly, but for our purposes here we want to write to the device itself. So in our case we will be writing to /dev/disk2.

There is one little wrinkle though. We can't write to the SD Card directly whilst we have it mounted and usable. If we eject it from within Finder, it will not only unmount the filesystem but it will also eject the device as well. That doesn't help us because we still need the device to be present in order to write to it. To solve this issue, we will unmount the filesystem manually using a Mac specific command called 'diskutil.' The Mac does have the general Unix umount command (which we'll cover in later chapters) but if anything on your Mac happens to be looking at the SD Card, umount will fail and claim that the device is busy. Diskutil on the other hand is aware of this and can usually unmount the device without any problems. For us we ran the following command:

```
mbp:~ root# diskutil unmount /dev/disk2s2
Volume UNTITLED on disk2s2 unmounted
mbp:~ root#
```

So after all that, we've gained super-user privileges, we've isolated the device that we want to write to and we've unmounted the filesystem so that we can write directly to the card itself. All we have to do now is actually go ahead and do the writing!

The tool of choice for this task is called 'dd'. This tool is a bit old school in that it only cares about reading from a device and writing to a device. It has no interest in filesystems nor is it aware of any of the subtle differences between say a hard disk and an SD Card. It just reads and writes without caring where it reads from or writes to. This is a fundamental Unix principle that we will be revisiting in later chapters. For now, we're going to take advantage of this to make an exact copy of our image file on your SD Card.

dd only needs to know two things, where to read from (the if= argument) and where to write to (the of= argument). We've figured out the writing bit (it's going to be /dev/disk2) but what about the source? If you followed the instructions earlier, you should have the image file sitting in the Downloads directory in your home area. The easiest way to get the information we need into Terminal is to type this in:

```
dd if=
```

and then, going to your Downloads directory in Finder (or wherever you extracted the image file to), click and hold on the image file and then drag it on to your Terminal window. This should then paste in the full path for you without you needing to type anything in. This should mean you end up with something pretty similar to this:

```
dd if=/Users/myuser/Downloads/2012-08-16-wheezy-raspbian.img
```

Now we have our input file specified, all we need to do is specify where exactly we want dd to write it. Thanks to our earlier experimentation we know that this will be /dev/disk2. We're also going to add "bs=1M"which lets dd write the image in bigger chunks (meaning you won't have to wait four hours for it to complete). So the full command we need for dd looks like this:

```
dd if=/Users/miggyx/Downloads/2012-08-16-wheezy-raspbian.img of=/dev/disk2 bs=1M
```

Running this command might take some time (i.e. hours not seconds). The image itself is around 2GB in size and your average smart card reader is not particularly fast. With our USB adapter, our recent MacBook Pro took a good 25 minutes. After coming back later, you should find that dd has completed its task and you're back at the command prompt.

Okay, admittedly this wasn't quite as simple or straight forward as writing the image on Windows, but if you look at everything we had to do, using the command line allowed us to express what we wanted in a very compact and precise way. This is something we come back to in Chapter 4 where we look at the various benefits of learning to use the command line.

Here is the full transcript of the commands we entered in order to write the image to the disk. If something in our explanation above didn't quite click or you're not entirely sure what the end result should look like, you can use the transcript below as a reference to compare your version with ours:

```
Last login: Wed Sep 19 13:48:40 on ttys000
mbp:~ pmembrey$ sudo -i
Password:
mbp:~ root# mount
/dev/disk0s2 on / (hfs, local, journaled)
devfs on /dev (devfs, local, nobrowse)
map -hosts on /net (autofs, nosuid, automounted, nobrowse)
map auto_home on /home (autofs, automounted, nobrowse)

<<SD Card inserted>>

mbp:~ root# mount
/dev/disk0s2 on / (hfs, local, journaled)
devfs on /dev (devfs, local, nobrowse)
map -hosts on /net (autofs, nosuid, automounted, nobrowse)
map auto_home on /home (autofs, automounted, nobrowse)
/dev/disk2s1 on /Volumes/UNTITLED (msdos, local, nodev, nosuid, noowners)
mbp:~ root# diskutil unmount /dev/disk2s1
Volume UNTITLED on disk2s1 unmounted
mbp:~ root# dd if=/Users/pmembrey/Downloads/2012-08-16-wheezy-raspbian.img of=/dev/disk2
bs=1M
mbp:~ root#
```

Right, with our (painstakingly) prepared SD Card, we can finally boot the Pi! If you've installed Raspbian and you want to follow along with the initial configuration, you can jump back to Chapter 1 and follow the instructions from the first boot. Good luck!

Index

A

B

C

D, E

F

G

H

I, J, K

L

M

N

O

P, Q

R

W

X

Y, Z

Get the eBook for only $5!

Why limit yourself?

Now you can take the weightless companion with you wherever you go and access your content on your PC, phone, tablet, or reader.

Since you've purchased this print book, we're happy to offer you the eBook in all 3 formats for just $5.

Convenient and fully searchable, the PDF version enables you to easily find and copy code—or perform examples by quickly toggling between instructions and applications. The MOBI format is ideal for your Kindle, while the ePUB can be utilized on a variety of mobile devices.

To learn more, go to www.apress.com/companion or contact support@apress.com.

Printed by Printforce, the Netherlands